THE MIRACLE WORKER

Steal a moment of peace with this extraordinary book and discover the power that has liberated millions from the enemies that enslave and erode our lives—lack of faith, uncontrolled desires, selfishness, fear, anger, anxiety, negativism, guilt and inferiority.

Here are daily meditations and startling insights that will guide you toward new peace, fulfillment and inner strength.

Restore your soul, your sanity, your self with ABUNDANT LIVING.

Abundant Living

E. Stanley Jones

Abingdon
Nashville

Scriptural quotations designated "Moffatt" are from *The Bible: A New Translation*, by James Moffatt, copyright, 1922, 1924, 1926, 1935, by Harper & Brothers, and are used by special permission of the publishers and copyright owners.

ABUNDANT LIVING

A FESTIVAL BOOK

Published by Jove Publications, Inc. for Abingdon

Festival edition published April, 1976
Third Printing May, 1980

ISBN 0-687-00689-9

Printed in the United States of America

PREFACE

Everyone may and can live abundantly. The business of life is to live and to live well and adequately and abundantly. But this age knows almost everything about life except how to live it. It is not enough to know *about* life—we must know *how to live* life. "I have lived through everything except life," said one disillusioned son of this age. We can pick life to pieces and explain its constituent parts and then fail miserably to put it together again in such a way that it becomes a co-ordinated, harmonious whole. We are long on analysis and short on synthesis.

The reason is not hard to find. We have dissected life and desiccated it in the process. We have picked the flower of life to pieces, petal by petal, and have lost its beauty in the procedure. We have handed the body over to the doctor, the mind to the psychiatrist, and the soul to the minister, treating these three parts as separate entities. They are not separate. Life is a whole. You cannot affect one part without affecting all three.

Doctors vary in their estimate of the percentage of people who pass on mental and spiritual sickness to their bodies. In a group of Johns Hopkins doctors, a psychiatrist said that 40 per cent of the cases that came to their clinic were mental and spiritual in origin. But the surgeons present insisted that the percentage was probably 60 per cent. A pastor friend of mine, while being examined by a very able doctor, remarked, "Doctor, I wish I had the equipment for dealing with people that come to me as you have for dealing with those who come to you." The doctor replied, "Forty per cent of the people who come to me should not have gone past you." While he put the percentage at 40 per cent, an outstanding neurologist put it at 80 per cent, and another able doctor put it at 85 per cent, with only 15 per cent physical. The American Medical Association officially approves of the statement of Dr. C. Raimer Smith in *Hygeia*, June, 1931, that the percentage is about 50–50.

Here, then, we have estimates varying from 40 per cent to 85 per cent of people who are passing on their mental and spiritual sicknesses to their bodies. But what of those whose mental and spiritual disharmonies have not yet affected their bodies in any obvious way? The human body is often very tough. It can resist and throw off not only microbes, but noxious mental and spiritual attitudes as well.

But although these mental and spiritual disharmonies may not break the body, they do disrupt the personality and render it ineffective and unhappy.

A successful management engineer, a man who takes hold of sick businesses and puts them on their feet again, said to me that 95 per cent of the difficulties in a sick business are not in the business, but in the persons concerned. They get snarled up in their lives, and pass on their inner snarls to their outer circumstances. They cannot get along with themselves and hence cannot get along with others. The spirit dies out of the business, for there is no real cooperation. The business cannot be straightened out until the persons are straightened out. Hence this man often sits till past midnight talking with executives and heads of departments on how to get oneself unsnarled. As they talk, they are driven to the necessity of religion, the need of some higher Power to believe in and get resources from in order to win release and victory. When I quoted the above to the personnel man of Bethlehem Steel, he thoughtfully replied, "You are absolutely right in saying that 95 per cent of the difficulties in business are in the persons concerned. I've found it so." Dr. Irving Fisher, the economist, claims that of 5,000 failures in business which were investigated as to cause of failure, 2,500 were found to be personality failures. These 2,500 were sufficiently obvious to be traceable, but what of the personality failures so hidden that they could not be traced? They are none the less devastating.

Then what of those who, while not at open war with themselves and not failures outwardly, are nevertheless living under par? Someone has described the sharecroppers as "submarginal people living on submarginal land." But the submarginal people are not all on submarginal land; many of them are in the fashionable suburbs of our great cities—dwarfed souls living in mansions. "I have learned how to make money, but I have not yet learned how to live," said a very successful businessman with a sigh as the organ recital in his home came to an end—a recital that had momentarily lifted him up out of himself. He had accumulated physical resources to meet any outer emergency, only to find that life had reached behind his physical armor and had dealt him a staggering blow on the inside. There he had no resources with which to protect himself—he was unprotected at the vital spot.

But perhaps my readers are about to throw up their hands, saying, "Don't open our wounds any further. We know them too well, and they are now raw and sore. Tell us how they may be healed. Tell us *how*."

That last statement echoes a letter I received: "I don't

know how to find God in the way that He gives me spiritual uplift and strength. How—how do I find that?" Note that she says she wants to find God as something beyond a concept or belief—she wants to find God as a working way to live, as Someone who gives strength to live by.

This book will attempt to put the "How" into abundant living. The "ladders" I shall use have grown out of thousands of personal interviews which I have held with baffled and defeated souls in the West and in the East. The ladders have been corrected and added to by the American Ashrams, where for two weeks groups of 150 selected people entered into a corporate disciplined quest for abundant living.

The arrangement of this book will follow the one used in *Victorious Living*, to which it is a sequel. Since that writing I have been led to see, in a clearer way, the intimate connection between states of mind and soul and physical health, and have tried to expound that connection in my last preceding book, *Is the Kingdom of God Realism?* This book is intended to be the applied side of that book. I take the background of that book and apply it here for daily living.

As in *Victorious Living*, I try to supply a threefold need. First, there is the need for a daily devotional book to be used in the Quiet Hour, a page a day. Second, I have gathered up the discussion into units of a week, one subject having at least a seven-day treatment. This makes it possible for the book to be used in study groups on a weekly basis. Third, I have written it as an ordinary book which can be read straight through. In other words, I have carried one theme, abundant living, right through, beginning at the lowest rung of the ladder and going on to the application of the theme to the social relations of life.

If I begin far down and make my latchstrings low, the mature Christian must be patient with me. For I am persuaded that we, who have lived out our lives in a Christian atmosphere, do not realize how utterly illiterate are many otherwise intelligent people when they are faced with the problem of the meaning of the Christian faith and how to get hold of its power. I start where the "pagans" live—and many of these "pagans" are inside, as well as outside, the Church.

The socially minded must also be patient with me if I begin with and lay a great deal of stress on the personal in the first part of the book, for life begins with the personal. Later I will deal with the social—perhaps too much for some to follow. Not that I would separate the personal and the social, for they are one; but for purposes of treatment I begin with that which comes first. Perhaps my position can be summed up in these words: "Christianity that doesn't begin with the individual doesn't begin; Christianity that ends with the individual, ends."

One word of caution before we start on our quest. This book is dealing with abundant living in its total phases—physical as well as moral and spiritual and social. In dealing with the physical it recognizes the function of the science of medicine and surgery in producing health. The techniques given here for healthful physical living are not intended to supplant, but to supplement the work of the doctors. If it is true that we pass on our mental and spiritual sicknesses to our bodies, it is also true that the body passes on its ailments to the mental and spiritual. They intertwine. If, therefore, some of my readers are in doubt as to whether their ailments are rooted in the mental and spiritual or in the physical, it might be well to have a thorough physical checkup by a competent doctor. They may discover a physical basis for their under-par life and lack of contagion.

We believe that God heals the body in one or more of these ways: (1) by medicine; (2) by surgery; (3) by scientific nutrition; (4) by climate; (5) by mental suggestion; (6) by deliverance from underlying fears, resentments, self-centeredness, and guilts; (7) by the direct action of the Spirit of God upon our bodies; and (8) by the resurrection. Some ailments may have to wait for that final curing, the resurrection, for we live in a mortal world where the body is bound to break down sometime. In that case we can not merely bear the infirmity; we can use it. We can take it up into the purposes of our lives and transmute it into character and achievement. If, therefore, you have a bodily infirmity, you have these alternatives: God will cure you through one or more of the first seven ways; or, if not, He will give you power to use it, and to make it contribute until the final cure in the resurrection.

But this Preface must not end on the physical, for the purpose of this book is abundant living in the total person and in the total society.

E. STANLEY JONES

CONTENTS

Gen. 1:1–3; John 1:1–5; Matt. 28:20

WE BEGIN THE QUEST

Life can never be abundant unless it has abundant resources. It is obvious that no organism can expend more in energy than it takes in from without. Just what does "the without" consist of—physical nature and human society only? Or is there a third dimension in addition to "the within" and "the around"—is there an "Above"? Many have decided that there is no "Above"—at least, there is none they can contact; so they have short-circuited life to "the within" and "the around." But, to their dismay, they find that "the within" and "the around," instead of offering resources to abundant living, offer resistances to it—"the within" is clashing, and "the without" is contradictory. The resources are in reserve, pulling the other way.

Someone has said, "If we haven't that within us which is above us, we will soon yield to that which is around us." We become circumstance-conditioned and circumstance-fed, and grow weak and anemic on the fare. And if we turn within for our resources, we find the well is dry. Professor Hocking, speaking as a philosopher, says: "Man comes up to a certain point and then finds he hasn't resources in himself to complete himself, so he remains incomplete and frustrated." There ensues what an able and earnest man said he had—"a sense of cosmic loneliness." "I am not sure," he continued, "whether my doings have anything cosmic back of them, whether I am working with anything significant, or just working meaninglessly alone with no one to back my work or care." An atheist has been described as "a man who has no invisible means of support."

"A sense of cosmic loneliness"—that is the frigid thought that lays its cold hand on our hopes and our endeavors. Can it be lifted and the sense of a warm, living, cosmic Presence, who is with us and for us, take its place? If so, then that would hit the spot—the central spot. For if the central spot is empty and meaningless, then all life turns empty and meaningless with it. But if that central spot is full and meaningful, then all life turns meaningful with it.

O warm, living, cosmic Presence—if there be such a Presence in this inscrutable universe—help me as I begin this quest for Thee and Thy resources. I shall need Thy help even to inspire me to begin the quest, for I am not sure at all that Thou art there. I am only sure of this—that Something beyond myself ought to be there. So I begin. Help me. Amen.

IS THERE A COSMIC PRESENCE?

We began yesterday with the question of whether a cosmic Presence is in the universe, and we ended by saying that Something ought to be there. If there isn't Anything there, then we have no framework of reference, no star to steer our little boat by, and so we are tossed from wave to wave of inane and meaningless existence—with no star, and hence no harbor. We are beginning to see the result of losing God; if we lose God, then we lose the meaning out of life—the bottom drops out of it. For if there is no God to give worth and meaning and goal to life, then we are only animated bubbles that rise to the cosmic surface, glisten in the sunlight for a brief space, and then burst, leaving a nasty wet spot on the surface of things. And it is all over. Or, to change the figure, "Life is a fretful child that must be played with until it falls asleep." If there is no God, we go through "loud days that have no meaning and no end"—a weary round of nothingness.

We know now that, if we lose our Sky, we shall soon lose our earth. An artist said of his nature paintings, "I can get the picture right if I get my sky right." If you can get hold of God, or God gets hold of you, then the Sky is right and everything falls into its place, the whole thing meaningful.

Someone has said, "Man has never been the same since God died. He has taken it very hard." He has. For life has become hard, since the Sky has turned to brass. "I sometimes wish that God were back," said a wistful soul.

A modern man of insight reported a dream: "I thought," said this friend, "that I saw you standing on a hilltop and we, a great host of us, were crowding around eagerly waiting for what you might say. We could see your lips framing the word, but no sound came. . . . . We tried to help you by calling out the word your lips were shaping; but we also were dumb! And that word was. . . ." Was it God?

O God, if there be a God—I still have to say that—help me to get this matter clear. For my Sky is overcast. In the words of the Brittany sailors: "Our boats are so small and Thy seas are so great." I need a star to steer by. Let the clouds open and let me see—really see. Amen.

Gen. 31:53 (Moffatt); 27:35–36; 32:24–30

GOD FADING OUT

How has God faded out of the mind of this age? Well, the age, like thoughtless children, believed that the toyland of material wealth was a sufficient world; then God faded out, smothered by preoccupation. As a prosperous New Yorker and his wife came to the small town where they had grown up, he said to her complacently, "Well, that's where we came from, dear." And she replied with an unexpected answer: "Yes, and I am just wondering where we got to." She felt the emptiness amid the plenty.

Professor Summer put it this way: "I never consciously gave up a religious belief. It was as if I had put my beliefs into a drawer, and when I came again to look for them the drawer was empty."

The thing has happened to this generation that happened to the three generations of Abraham, Isaac, and Jacob. Jacob could say, "my father's God, the God of Abraham, the Awe of Isaac." (Genesis 31:42, Moffatt.) God was God to Abraham; he had ventured forth with Him, his "Friend"; He was intimate and firsthand and real. But in the next generation God was not "the God of Isaac," but only the "Awe of Isaac." He had faded and become secondhand. Still Isaac stood in "Awe" of his father's God. In the third generation —in Jacob—the result of this gradual fading of God began to be shown in the decaying morals of Jacob; moral rottenness appeared. He stole his brother's birthright. He was ready to take the main chance without regard to God.

The same things have happened with us: Our forefathers had a firsthand experience of God through the Evangelical Revival. The next generation clung to the Church for their fathers' sake, but God was only the "Awe"—the afterglow of a fading faith. The third generation is reaping the result of a fading faith which is producing decaying morals and a decaying civilization. Our loss of God is working out in moral decay. We are going to pieces morally, for we have gone to pieces religiously. We have lost God and have thus lost the basis of morals. Jacob met God on Jabbok's banks in his midnight wrestle and emerged a new man. Unless we, like Jacob, find a moral renewal in finding God, we are done for.

O God, I know that with the loss of Thee some chord has dropped out of my symphony. Life has lost its music; but now I see further. I see that I have no basis for action, no moral world that makes sense without Thee. I must find Thee again, as Jacob did. Amen.

Deut. 32:20; Heb. 10:38–39; Mark 4:40; 11:22

WE CANNOT LIVE BY A "NO"

We saw yesterday that if God goes, then the basis of our moral universe is gone. The "Lie Detector" has shown that only 3 per cent of employees in department stores were honest through character honesty; that only 5 per cent of tellers in banks were dependably honest if there were no outer measures for checking fraud. Suppose we double the percentages of the "Lie Detector"; nevertheless, a nation that is living on this narrow margin of moral reserves is drawing too heavily on its resources, and is nearing moral bankruptcy. Before the war our crime bill could have paid our national debt in two years. Our moral basis is decaying. We must get God back. But can we?

I think we will, for the half-gods which have taken the place of God are letting us down. If reason cannot lead us to Him, then disillusionment may drive us to Him, or sorrow may yet "toss us to His breast." But is there any hope of a reasonable faith? Can we be believers with the consent of our whole beings, including our minds? I think we can, for the situation is clearing for the modern man.

Modern man is beginning to see that he cannot live, as he once thought, on the denial of other people's faith. The generation of people that lived on denials soon found themselves disillusioned even with their disillusionments. They had "three sneers for everything and three cheers for nothing." And they soon found they couldn't live by sneers—to live by sneers is poor fare. If we should walk to the table each day and look over the food and then turn away in high disdain, we could get away with this disdainful attitude for awhile—but only for awhile. In the end, hunger would bite us and drive us to affirm something about food and to act on our affirmation. Both physically and spiritually we are positive beings and cannot live on a negation. We cannot live by a "No"; we must live by a "Yes." And that "Yes" must be God, or it will let us down.

The future of the world is in the hands of believers, for the non-believers cannot act. They are suffering from "the paralysis of analysis." They can only deny.

O God, I come to Thee for clear light. The light is dawning—I see that without Thee my universe tumbles to pieces. With Thee it makes sense; my sums come out right. Help me to find Thee—the Key. Amen.

Job 38:31–33, 36; 42:1–6

COULD THE UNIVERSE HAVE HAPPENED BY CHANCE?

The situation is clearing for the modern man. He sees more and more that he must affirm some "Yes" about the universe, and that "Yes" may be God. For how could this universe come by chance into a cosmic orderliness that stretches from the molecule to the outermost star, and controls everything between? And how could this orderliness just happen to stay by chance through millions of years? That would be a stark materialistic miracle—universal chaos by chance gives birth to universal order! The one who believes that must spell his "chance" with a capital "C" and mean by it—God. How long do you think it would take for you to throw up a font of type into the air and have it come down by chance into a poem of Browning? I asked a printer that question and he replied, "Both you and the type would wear out first."

Someone has figured out how many chances to one it would take for the world to have happened by chance, and the figures go round the world thirty-five times. "A preposterous figure," says Dr. Millikan the scientist. Sir James Jeans has figured out that it would take a hundred million years for a hundred thousand monkeys, pecking at random on a hundred thousand typewriters, to happen by chance upon the plays of Shakespeare. And then, after they had happened upon the arrangement of the letters, they wouldn't know what the letters meant!

When I pick up a book and see that there is intelligence in it—that sometimes does happen!—then I know that behind that intelligence is an intelligent mind expressing itself through that intelligence. When I look at the universe, I find that it responds to intelligence—it can be intelligently studied. Intelligence has gone into it—into its very structure. Then the simple conclusion must be that behind that intelligence, which is built into the structure of things, is an intelligent mind, and since that built-in intelligence seems to be universal, I will have to spell it in capitals—a Universal Mind.

O God—I say the word now with more confidence—I begin to see Thee; help me to act as though Thou art. Thou art beginning to come into my intelligence. Help me this day to take Thee into the rest of my life. Amen.

Ps. 14:1; John 14:8–11; Isa. 8:19–20

THE INTELLIGENT OUT OF
THE NONINTELLIGENT?

Yesterday we began to see how impossible it would be for the nonintelligent to bring forth the intelligent. "Out of nothing, nothing comes," is the universal law. But here is intelligence—you and I have it. Did that intelligence come out of the nonintelligent? If so, that is a materialistic miracle. Nature brought forth something she didn't have. Again, you and I have purpose—we choose. Did that purpose come out of a nonpurposive universe? That too would be a materialistic miracle. As someone puts it: "Do we see the inkpot determine to write a Bible? Do the stones decide to come together to form a Taj Mahal?" If one does not believe in God, he is forced to believe in miracle, the very thing he condemns in the believer.

Suppose in the end I find that there is no God, that belief in God was all a mistake. Then I would not regret having held to a God, for life works better with this hypothesis. My life sums come out better; the results are superior. The universe is meaningful, and my life is happier. Moreover, I would rise up in the end and confront the universe and say: "Well, I thought better of you; I thought there was Intelligence, and now I see that there is none. I thought there was Purpose; now I see that the universe is purposeless. You have let me down; I am superior to you, for I acted on a higher hypothesis than you could sustain. I have thereby been superior. I cannot regret that I was."

A professor of electrical engineering, after passing through agnosticism to faith, put it this way: "If anyone could prove to me scientifically that this thing I have found is not true, I would still have to believe it, for the universe wouldn't make sense without it." He was profoundly right. The universe does not make sense without God. As Rousseau says: "If there is no God we would have to invent one to keep people sane."

O God, I am being hemmed in to a faith in Thee. Life is closing in on me and forcing me to faith. Faith is becoming inescapable. And yet I would not escape, for escape would be escape from sanity, from the Open Door. Help me to enter. Amen.

Isa. 25:9; Mal. 2:10; Isa. 40:28, 31

GOD IN THE UNEXPLAINED GAPS

While the matter of God is clearing, doubts still linger. Has not the doctrine of evolution made God unnecessary? Is not the whole thing being worked out by resident forces? Isn't science filling up more and more the unexplained gaps in nature—gaps into which we used to put God?

We made a mistake in trying to put God into the unexplained gaps, for science has come along and has filled up these gaps. Then God was gone! Instead of putting God into the gaps, we should have put Him into the intelligence, into the order, into the dependability, into the very process, for there He belongs. That intelligence, that order, that dependableness cannot get along without Him! The universe is orderly and dependable, because God is an orderly, dependable God—He works by law and order instead of by whim and notion.

About evolution. When you say that "resident forces" are capable of producing the universe, we ask: How could resident forces move toward intelligent ends without being intelligent? Toward moral ends without being moral? You smuggle God into the process and then say He is not necessary! But God would be as necessary for evolution as for a once-for-all creation. Which takes the more intelligence—to strike a billiard ball straight into the pocket at one stroke, or to strike a ball, which in turn strikes another, and that another, and that another, until the last one goes into the pocket? Obviously, the latter stroke. God seemingly creates something, which creates something, and the whole thing moves on to a moral universe in which you and I stand, not pushed from behind by blind forces, but beckoned to from before by ideals—a universe of moral freedom, where our evolution is in our hands; we can go up or down according to choice. The framework has been created in which the greatest thing in the world can emerge by choice—character.

O God, I begin to see the school, the framework in which I have to win or lose the battle of life. The framework is hard, unbending, exacting, but I am grateful; for while the rules of the school are strict, they are working for one end—my character. Help me to obey and help me to win. Amen.

Isa. 36:6–7; Job 31:24–28; I Pet. 1:24–25

OUR PEGS COME DOWN

We saw last week that if God goes, then everything worth while goes with Him—everything lacks basis, permanence, ultimate meaning. The whole situation is summed up in these words: "And then—so the Lord of hosts declares—the peg driven in so firmly shall be wrenched out and give way, till everything that hung upon it shall come down." (Isaiah 22:25, Moffatt.) When the peg of material civilization upon which we have hung everything is wrenched out by economic dislocation, and gives way, then everything we have hung on it—our plans, our hopes, our futures—gives way with it and goes down in a crash. We have hung everything on the wrong peg—the insecure peg of money. That peg should have been God; for, as He holds amid the stress of things, everything holds.

One of the richest men of a Middle Western city thought of what he could give his daughter as a heritage. He began with financial securities, went on down the list, but rejected all material legacies as too insecure. He finally fastened on religion as the only secure inheritance he could give his child—an interesting conclusion, for he himself was not religious. But there was a difficulty with that decision—the child could not take religion as a heritage. For religion to become really hers, she had to choose it.

But it is not easy to choose a faith now, for the intellectual climate has changed from traditional to scientific. In the traditional climate you simply took what was passed on from generation to generation without question; but in a scientific climate everything has to be verified, for science believes in verified knowledge. Can the knowledge in the schoolrooms be verified knowledge, and the knowledge in the churches be unverified hypothesis? This is an impossible dualism, and it makes religion impossible for the modern man.

The pegs on which we have hung our modern civilization are coming down. We are at the end of what Sorokin calls a "sensate society." It has exhausted itself against the facts of life. It is becoming bankrupt. When we take a new center—God—will that center be capable of verification? Will He verify Himself to us as self-authenticating?

O God, if I find Thee at all, I want to find Thee with my whole being, for I know that a faith which does not hold my intellect will soon not hold my heart. I would have both held by Thee. Help me. Amen.

I Thess. 5:21; Phil. 4:8; John 7:17

SCIENCE AND RELIGION

If possible we must work our way through this scientific climate to God. We now see a little more clearly the relationship between science and religion. Science has reference to that which can be weighed and measured, and religion to that which can be evaluated; the one has reference to the quantitative aspects of life, and the other to the qualitative.

Science comes to a mother's tear and defines it in terms of its physical structure—so much water, so much mucus, so much salt. But is that an adequate definition of a mother's tear? Hardly, says religion, for there are ideas, emotions, values, meanings using the physical structure of the tear. Religion would evaluate those imponderables. Thus it would take the answer of both science and religion to give an adequate definition of a mother's tear.

True. But the snag is this: You can verify that which can be weighed and measured; can you verify values? Why not? You can put values under life to see what life will do with them. You can test them by the test of experiment. If the values are real values, life will approve them, will back them; but if they are not real, they will wither—they will not be able to stand up to life; the universe will not approve them. When you live by them, you will fight a losing battle; they will let you down.

I was about to leave a broadcasting station when an announcer followed me to the elevator, saying to me: "I am supposed to be hardened by hearing speeches all day long, but you got me. And the reason is that my life has broken down at the center. The central thing upon which I have leaned has gone out from under me. I face an inner ruin and a broken home. My life hypothesis hasn't worked. Yours seems to be working. Tell me about it." I could tell him that life to me, since I have committed myself completely to God, is one long verification of my central life hypothesis—everything corroborates it. My world of values holds up under the strain of life. This way works.

O God, I want to test Thy way. If Thou art, Thou will show Thyself to me, for all other ways let me down; all their joys give me a hang-over. I want something that remains permanent amid change, has sweetness amid sorrow, and light amid darkness. Give this to me. Amen.

Gal. 6:7–8; Rom. 1:19–20; 14:10

THE FIVE STEPS OF SCIENCE

Can we take the same steps in verifying our knowledge of God as science takes in verifying its knowledge of things that can be weighed and measured? There are five steps in the scientific method: (1) *the statement of the problem;* (2) *the picking out of the most likely hypothesis that will meet that problem;* (3) *experimentation with that hypothesis;* (4) *verifying the hypothesis on a wide scale;* (5) *a simple and humble sharing of verified results.*

Can we take this fivefold method and apply it to the realm of value? First, *the statement of the problem.* The problem is how to live in a universe of this kind, and to live well. It is a moral universe, and it seems to take sides on moral questions. In this moral universe we are free to choose, but not free to choose the results of our choosing —they are in hands other than ours. This moral universe is not something that we create out of our taboos and rules— it is something we discover; it is a "given." A father was explaining Newton's Law of Gravitation and how it held things together, but his son answered, "Well, Dad, what held things together before they passed this law?" Just as Newton did not pass the Law of Gravitation, but discovered it; so we do not pass the moral laws written in the constitution of things; we discover them. And we must come to terms with these moral laws, just as we must come to terms with the law of gravitation. If not, we shall be broken. We do not break these moral laws; they break us. If we run afoul of them, they will throw us back bleeding, broken, blighted things. These laws are color-blind. If the white man, the black man, the yellow man, or the brown man breaks them, he will be broken. And they are religion-blind. If the Christian or the agnostic breaks them, he will be broken. As Sophocles puts it:

> "The unwritten laws of God that know not change,
> They are not of today nor yesterday,
> But live forever, nor can man assign
> When first they sprang to being."

O God, I see I am free only to obey. I must come to terms with Thy laws written in me and in the constitution of things. Help me this day to begin to find my freedom in obedience to Thee. Show me how to begin. Amen.

Luke 17:20–21; Rom. 14:17; Heb. 8:10

THE KINGDOM OF GOD IS WITHIN YOU

The central theme of my last preceding book, *Is the Kingdom of God Realism?* is the statement of Jesus: "The kingdom of God is within you." He said this not to His disciples, but to the Pharisees, unchanged people. Is the Kingdom of God then in us all, changed and unchanged? Yes. Of course, it is true that those who have been spiritually changed "see," "submit to," "enter," and "inherit" the Kingdom of God in a way the unchanged do not. The changed have related themselves to the laws of the Kingdom and to the God of the Kingdom, and therefore receive the resources of the Kingdom—the sum total of that Kingdom works with them and not against them. Those who are unchanged find the Kingdom is within them, but they are at cross-purposes with it. In the changed person the Kingdom works as self-realization, and in the other as self-frustration. But in both it is there.

The laws of our being are not other than the laws of God —they are the laws of God. These laws are not something imposed on the situation, but are written into the very structure of our being, into our tissues, our nerve cells, our blood stream, into the total organization of our life. They are the way we are made to live. Just as the engineer stamps within an engine which he constructs a way to work, and if it obeys that way it works well and harmoniously; so God has stamped within the structure of our being His Kingdom. The Old Testament calls this stamp "making man in his own image." If we live according to it, we live. If we don't, we don't. A railway engine is made to run on tracks, and if it remains on the tracks it finds its freedom, pulls its loads, and gets to its destination. But if, in order to gain its freedom, it jumps the tracks, the result is not freedom, but ruin to itself and everybody concerned.

There is a trackage to freedom, to efficiency, to full living, built into your being and mine. It is the Kingdom of God—it is within you.

O God, I have looked for Thee to rend the heavens and come down, and here I find Thy footsteps within my own being. Thou hast traced Thy ways in my make-up. Thou hast been so near I have run afoul of Thee and thought I was only running afoul of law. Forgive me. Amen.

Acts 9:5; John 3:13; Rom. 6:20–23

WORKING WITH OR AGAINST THE KINGDOM

We saw yesterday that the laws of our being are the laws of God, the will of God wrought out in terms of nerves, tissues, and total structural being. We must then come to this breathtaking conclusion: *We cannot revolt against God without revolting against ourselves.* I say it reverently: God has us hooked! We cannot run away from God without running away from ourselves. The sum total of the result of the modern revolt against God is this: We who decided we would not live with God, find that we cannot live with ourselves. A sinner is one who is literally a problem to himself. The hell which modern man banished from the universe by politely putting it out at the door, has now come back through the window in the form of neuroses, fears, inhibitions, inner conflicts, guilts. It has moved into the center of his being. So the counterpart of "The kingdom of God is within you" is "The kingdom of hell is within you, too." Obey the Kingdom of God within you and you have heaven; disobey it and you have hell—have it right now as a condition, a state of mind.

Hell and heaven are not something God sovereignly gives you at the end of your earthly life. They are things you choose here and now. When you obey the Kingdom of God you find heaven here and now, for its other name is "the Kingdom of Heaven." If you take out heaven with you at the end of this life, you will get heaven, for you will have brought it with you—in you. On the other hand, if you take hell out with you, you will get it, for you will have brought it with you—in you.

I do not know where heaven and hell are as places, but I know where they begin. Sin is hell begun—it is disruption, disintegration, disease. You take the state out of this life with you, and you get the place suitable to that state. Goodness is heaven begun—it is fellowship, harmony, life. You take that out with you and you get a place suitable to that state.

The Kingdom of God will work with you or against you according to whether you obey it or disobey it.

O my God—I can now say, "My God," for whether I acknowledge Thee or not, Thou art my God—I cannot run away from Thee. Nor do I want to. Can I run away from life? from myself? I fly to Thee. Take me. Amen.

Heb. 1:9, 11, 13; Prov. 29:6; 28:16

THE LAWS OF THE KINGDOM ARE
SELF-ACTING

This fact of the kingdom of God within us is so important that it must be pursued. These laws which are written in us are self-acting. The action and the result are one. The result is not something imposed by God from without. It is something inherent. Sin and its punishment are one and the same thing. Sin literally is "missing the mark," the thing for which we are inwardly made; and to miss the mark is, by that very act, to sin against oneself.

That fact has fooled this age. We have been taught that God will punish us for our sins in some extraneous way. But since no thunderclap of punishment followed our sins we began to think that nothing had happened. A little girl put it this way: "We don't have grace at our table, or pray in any way, but nothing has happened yet." "No, my child, nothing outwardly, but the inner deterioration, the decay that has set in as God has been shut out—that is the punishment." "I preach just as well now as I did before I committed adultery," said a puzzled minister. Perhaps so, but the inner chaos and conflict, the lack of self-respect, the deterioration of character—that was the punishment.

"A grasping nature is its own undoing," says Proverbs 15:27 (Moffatt)—the punishment is inherent in the attitude. Even in ancient times this was seen: "As the old proverb runs, 'Evil men bring evil on themselves.'" (I Samuel 24:13, Moffatt.) The evil they brought on themselves was the evil itself. The Old Testament speaks of the forbidden wedge of gold, symbol of Achan's greed, as that "doomed thing among you." Evil is doomed, not because God pronounces judgment on it, but because of its own nature; it has the seeds of decay in it.

When you do right that act is written in the Book of Life. It has the seeds of permanence in it. When you do wrong that act is written in the Book of Death. It has the seeds of its own ruin and death in itself.

O my God, I begin to see. This moral universe begins to close in on me. I must come to terms with it. Or is it an *It?* Is it a *Thou?* Art Thou in these very laws? And when I come to terms with them, do I come to terms with Thee? I want Thee, for I am not a subject asking for a law, but a son asking for a Father. Help me. Amen.

Prov. 22:8; 20:17; 10:2, 9

WALKING WITH THE LIGHTS

The converse of what we are discussing is also true: If the nature of reality guarantees the instability of evil, it also guarantees the stability of good. Evil, by its very nature, is unstable; good, by its very nature, is stable. Evil could not exist unless there were enough good thrown around it to make it float. Hence every evil that persists has enough good in it to keep it going. Were it pure evil, it would collapse. There is "honor among thieves"; if there weren't, they could not hold together long enough to loot the rest of us. The honor is the cement that temporarily holds them together. The further saying goes, "When thieves fall out"—for they do sooner or later fall out when the honor decays.

Dr. Richard Cabot of Harvard says, "When you speak the truth, the whole universe is behind you; when you lie, the universe is against you." For the universe is not built for the success of a lie. You may try to hold lies together with all the cleverness and scheming possible, but in the end they will break down. Someone put it this way: "You must have a willingness to rely on the moral nature of the universe which guarantees the insecurity of evil."

This discussion may be summed up then in the words of a historian: "There is one fact that history sounds—the moral law is written in everything." It is "the way" stamped into the nature of things—the way it is made to work; and if it tries to work some other way, it works its own ruin.

A friend of mine was about to walk across a street against the lights when a plainly dressed man stepped up to him and said, "My friend, if you want to live long, walk with the lights; if you don't, then walk against them." That is the lesson of life: If you want to live well, walk with the green lights which God has hung in the constitution of things. If you don't, then walk against God's red lights—and be hurt.

O God, my Light, I looked for Thee in the sky. Thou art there, but I see Thou art here too, in the very nature of things. Help me to walk with Thy green lights. Forgive me that I have walked against Thy red lights. I thought I was only hurting Thee. I was hurting myself, too. Amen.

Luke 10:27–37

THE KINGDOM OF GOD IS AMONG YOU

We closed last week on the fact that "the Kingdom of God is within you." But there is another translation which says, "The Kingdom of God is among you." Which is correct? Jesus probably used both, for both are profoundly true. If the Kingdom of God is stamped into the constitution of our own beings, it is also stamped into our relationships with one another. There is a way to get along with ourselves, and there is a way to get along with other people, and that way is God's way. The Kingdom of God is *among* you.

If you try to get along with others on some basis other than God's, you won't. Your relationships will break down. Try to get along with your family on the basis of dominating the rest. Result? There will be seething revolt and your own frustration and unhappiness. In trying to dominate, you break the law written into the constitution of human relationships. No, you do not break the law; you break yourself upon the law.

The central law of human relationships is expounded by Jesus: "Thou shalt love thy neighbor as thyself." Now, you needn't obey that law; you needn't love your neighbor as you love yourself, but if you don't, you can't get along with your neighbor. Your relationships will break down. When you do not love your neighbor, you do not get rid of him; he comes back on your hands as a problem and a pain. Loving your neighbor is a forced option like eating—you do not have to eat, but if you don't eat, you can't live. You do not have to love your neighbor, but if you don't, you can't get along with him. The Kingdom of God is among you—it is the way we get along with others when we get along with them well.

Dr. Alfred Adler, who was the originator of the phrase "inferiority complex," attributed all human failure to inability to grasp the fact that "It is more blessed to give than to receive." Why does life break down if you do not love your neighbor as you love yourself? Because you are made that way.

My Father, I see that Thou art Father to Thy family. Thou hast made me so that I cannot get along with myself without getting along with the rest of the family. I see I must live by love or live by loss. Help me this day to live by love. Amen.

James 3:16–18; 4:1–3; Phil. 3:19

THE KINGDOM WORKS AS SELF-FRUSTRATION

Yesterday we saw that the Kingdom of God is among us —is the way we get along with one another, if we get along at all. Look at the breakdown of human relationships on a world scale. Why have they broken down? For the simple reason that we have tried to get along with other nations on the basis of pure selfishness. That broke the law of the Kingdom which is among us. Hence our relationships with one another broke down. Hence, this war. We cannot violate the law of love any more than we can the law of gravitation and not get hurt. The law of gravitation will hold up our buildings if we build plumb with it, but it will pull them to the dust if we build them out of plumb.

People ask, "Where is the Kingdom of God in this war?" As someone plaintively put it: "I am wondering when God will come into this war and take a hand." Where is the Kingdom of God? It is here in the very frustrations that are taking place—it is working as self-frustration. Since we wouldn't take the Kingdom of God as our collective fulfillment, we must now take it as our collective frustration. We cannot live the way we have been living without having the kind of a world we now have. When we are at war with the Kingdom of God, we are bound to be at war with one another.

Suppose the opposite had taken place. Suppose our collective revolt against God had turned out as prosperity, as peace, as progress, as mutual helpfulness. Then we could have asked, "Where is the Kingdom of God?" since its opposite had turned out so well. The success of our revolt would indeed smite our faith a fatal blow. But this kind of messed-up world corroborates everything the Christian stands for. Revolt against God and a resulting chaos work out as prophecy and fulfillment, as seed and fruit. We cannot live on a collectively selfish basis without having a collective clash. That collective clash is war.

The Christian has then the key to the situation—the Kingdom of God is among us. Live collectively according to it and we live; if not, we collectively perish—as now.

O God, I begin to feel a sense of personal and collective guilt. We have been trying to live against the universe and not with it, and now we are up against it. I'm up against it —we all are. I lift pleading hands to Thee to help me, save me. Amen.

Matt. 6:24; Josh. 24:15; Deut. 30:15–20

PICKING OUT A HYPOTHESIS

We have now come to the end of our discussion of the first of the five steps in the scientific method, "the statement of the problem." The problem is how to live and to live well in a universe of moral law, written in us and written in the constitution of our relationships. We have not lived well in that moral universe. We have run afoul of it and wear great inner bruises—guilts, fears, inhibitions, frustrations, complexes. If not these, then just that sense of incompleteness, of something missing, of emptiness.

We must now come to the second step, "the picking out of a hypothesis to meet that problem." The picking out of a hypothesis involves choice. "Does the whole thing rest back on my choice? Will God not choose for me and make me take His choice? I wish He would." But that would be the most fatal thing He could do. He would thus break down the citadel of personality, the will; and when will is gone, we are gone—we are things instead of persons. "There is nothing good but a good will; there is nothing bad but a bad will."

When God created another person He had to limit Himself—to move back, as it were, to give that will room to act. For the essence of personality is freedom. That was a dangerous move—terribly dangerous—for that free will in acting might make a mess of things, might break its own heart, the hearts of those around it—and God's. True. But God took the risk, just as a parent takes the risk when he brings a child into the world, for the child might break its own heart and the parent's. But God and man create, because, well, they each say, "I'll enter into this and take the consequences—the sins of these created persons shall be mine, their failures mine; but also their joys and developments shall be mine. We'll work it out together." Nothing but love could make God and man take that risk. Had God not seen a glorious end, He would not have dared to create. It took nerve to do it.

O God, I see, I have to choose. I would shrink from that responsibility and lay it over on Thee. But I can't. I must stand up and choose. Help me to make the right choice, take the right way. For the future—Thy future and my future—is in this hour of choice. Help me to choose aright. Amen.

Gal. 2:21; John 4:34; I Cor. 16:13

OUR FREEDOM COMPLICATES GOD'S GAME

In this freedom of ours lie God's problem and possibility. Our freedom is a problem to God. Someone has put it this way: "Here is a chessboard, and all the figures on the board, instead of being made of wood, are flesh and blood with wills of their own, persons. The game for God would be simple if the figures would go where He desires them to go. But suppose, when God would make a move in the game against Evil, that the figures should balk and refuse to move, and instead should move, on their own, to other positions without reference to the Player—God. That would complicate the game and mess it up badly." That has happened. And that is God's problem.

But our freedom is also His possibility. Suppose those figures should learn that failure and mix-up come through moves on their own and refusal to co-operate with the Player, and should thus be chastened into choice of co-operation with the Player. Then, suppose God and man should play the game in co-operation—and win! How much finer that would be than to win against Evil with only wooden pawns to play with!

You and I can co-operate with God, can align our wills with His, can make His wisdom our own, and in the end can make the victory a joint victory. What a possibility for God and us! I would rather be a discontented man than a contented worm, for that discontent would drive me to His feet. "Blessed are the homesick, for they will come home," says a German proverb.

A little boy of five, after seeing a puppet show, expressed his reaction thus to the doctor: "I'm glad I'm not one of those pretending persons. They have to do what they are told." The lad was right—with all the hazards, all the possibilities for breakdown, all the heartaches involved in freedom, we don't want to be one of those "pretending persons." We would rather be real persons, standing up and making our choices with all their possibilities of good and ill.

O God, my Father, I feel I can begin to call Thee that now, for I want to co-operate with Thee. I have been making foolish and disastrous moves on my own and getting into a mess with myself and others and spoiling the game. Help me to play Thy game. Amen.

Ps. 19:1–6; Heb. 1:10–12; 2:6–9

HOW GOD REVEALS HIMSELF

Since you are a free being and can do the most important thing in the world—choose—now you want to choose your highest hypothesis. What shall it be? Let us come straight to the issue: Do you know of any better hypothesis than Christ? Let your mind sweep the horizon of possiblities. After eliminating this thing and the other thing, this person and that person, does it not settle upon Christ as your best bet?

The highest thing in our moral universe is moral character—if God can be found anywhere He ought to be found here. The highest illustration of moral character ever seen on our planet is Christ. If God can be found anywhere He ought to be found in the highest thing in our moral universe—the character of Christ. How could God show us His character except through perfect moral character?

The character of God matters. For what God is like we must be like; His character determines ours. Just what is God like in character? I look up through nature and I come to the conclusion that God is law. I am grateful for that, but I want something beyond law. I am not a subject asking for a law; I am a son asking for a Father. Nature cannot tell me of my Father—not clearly. Nor could the perfect revelation come through prophet or teacher, for the revelation, in going through them, becomes limited, sometimes distorted, because of the faulty human medium. Nor could the revelation come perfectly through a book, for literature cannot rise higher than life—the life that surrounds the literature puts content into the literature. So the book would be pulled to the level of our highest experience. The only complete way of revelation is through a Life—a Character which would show us what God's character is like. That Character is Christ—the human life of God, that part of God we have been able to see. The Bible then is not the revelation of God; it is the inspired record of the revelation. The revelation is seen in the face of Jesus Christ. Is God then Christlike? He is! I can say nothing higher. I can be content with nothing less.

O God, I begin to see that Thou art coming to me in Christ. He seems to be that personal approach from the Unseen to me. I would not block that approach. I want Thee, O God, nothing less than Thee. Art Thou, O Christ, God coming to me, that I may come to Thee? Then receive me, for I receive Thee. Amen.

Heb. 1:1–3; John 1:1–5, 17–18; Heb. 12:1–2

GOD IS MY ADVENTURE

We now see that God could not show us Himself except through another self, a self that would be in human surroundings and would speak the language we speak, a human language. Jesus was God speaking the language of the man in the street, interpreting God in understandable terms. Just as when you take hold of my words you get hold of my thought, so when you take hold of the Word, Jesus, you get hold of the Thought, God. They do not rival nor push out each other. The Word is the Thought become available, near at hand, intimate, human.

"God is in nature, but the nature of God I find in Christ." And what a nature! If I were to try to think out the kind of God I'd like to see in the universe, I could think of nothing higher than that He should be Christlike. For, "Jesus stands erect amid the fallen, clean amid the defiled, living among the dying, the Saviour of men." Said the blind George Matheson: "Son of Man, whenever I doubt of life, I think of Thee. Nothing is so impossible as that Thou shouldst be dead. I can imagine the hills to dissolve into vapor, the stars to melt in smoke, and the rivers to empty themselves in sheer exhaustion, but I feel no limit in Thee."

Surely here in Jesus is one spot in my universe that will not let me down, something that is utterly trustable. Here, if anywhere, I can commit my life, and confess my sins; for this one spot is not only trustable, it is sympathetic—it loves, it cares.

Here, then, is the place of my adventure. My adventure shall be God—and the kind of God I see in Christ.

Just as a planet rushing through space is only a comet on its way to destruction until it is caught by some central sun and begins to revolve around that sun as its center and its life; so my life is an aimless comet burning itself out in its own self-will, till it finds the pull and attraction of Christ's love, halts its deadly way, and forever revolves around Him, its central Sun and its Life.

O Christ, I am so grateful that Thou art God near at hand, God bending to my need. I cannot scale the heavens to find Thee, for I am mired in my own fears and sins. Thou dost come to me. And now there is response within me. I come to Thee! I thank Thee that I come. Amen.

Matt. 27:3–5; Acts 5:1–5

FASTENING ON DEAD BRANCHES

You are on the verge of the great decision. But before you make it I would utter one word of warning. Go clear through; tolerate no halfway measures. The temptation will be to start out to be wholly Christ's and end up in feeling a little more relieved. As some put it, "They want to feel a little less elderly, to experience a slight rejuvenation. They do not want to be born again." Don't try to make a home out of a halfway house.

On the prayer knoll at Sat Tal in the Himalayas I watched a vine stretching across space to fasten itself upon a pine tree. That vine seemed to be Aspiration, a stretching to fasten itself upon the Higher. One morning I came out and found the vine had arrived! It had securely fastened its reaching tentacles around the tree. I rejoiced with it. But the next morning I was saddened to find catastrophe. A storm during the night had swept across the mountains and had torn the vine from its moorings, and there it lay, a pathetic thing, with its face to the earth, still holding in its grasp the broken branch of the tree. The tree had broken and had let it down! But the tree really had not, for what had happened was that the vine had fastened itself upon a dead branch, and that dead branch had broken. Had the vine reached the central trunk, no storm could have torn it away or broken the trunk.

Many start out with high aspiration toward the Tree, God, and then they stop at some dead branch of religion and fasten themselves on that. They stop at a good resolution and fasten themselves to that; but no mere good resolution can hold anyone up amid the storms of life. Others fasten themselves upon an institution—a good thing, but not good enough to fasten one's life upon. Nor will a rite or ceremony do; it will let one down in a crisis. Others fasten themselves upon a favorite minister and pin their faith to him. No man is good enough to be the center of one's faith; he may let one down. Others fasten on ideas about God instead of their acquaintance with God.

Go clear to the central trunk—God. Don't stop short.

O God, the hesitancies within me make me want to fasten upon some compromise, some halfway measure. Save me from this. I want nothing less than Thee. I know that anything less than Thee will ultimately let me down. I come to Thee. Amen.

THE FIRST STEP UPWARD

You are now ready, I trust, to put your feet upon the ladder and climb out to release and victory. I shall make that ladder very, very plain, for the greatest moment in life has come. The moment of the great choice has come—a decision that will decide all other decisions down the line—a master decision. In psychology there is what is called a "major choice"—a choice that doesn't have to be made over again every day. Lesser choices fit into it, not it into them.

The ladder will have seven steps. It will be built around the thought of "turn," for that word is a central word in Scripture.

(1) *Turn over in mind your life, its direction and spirit.* As you turn it over, you will be tempted to get on the defensive, for it is a hard thing not to defend your life patterns. But be relentlessly honest; look at yourself objectively and refuse to defend any wrong thing in your life. The first step toward complete mental and spiritual health is complete honesty. That ugly self of yours, which you perhaps have dressed up in righteous garments, will plead, excuse, and rationalize. It will try to keep the throne amid all marginal changes. But fasten your attentions on yourself as the center of your difficulties. You will be tempted to confess marginal sins and leave untouched the central sins. But nothing permanent has happened until the center of your difficulty, a wrong self, is replaced by another Self—God—as the center of reference, the center from which you get your life commands and orders. A highly cultured and beautiful woman, after reviewing her life, said with a sigh, "We have everything—and nothing." Everything in the way of outer comforts, yet empty of heart.

You remember the blind man sitting by the wayside begging, who, when they told him that Jesus was calling him, "flung away his garments" and ran to Jesus. You must fling away everything that would hinder you from getting to Christ—your inner dishonesties, and your outer ones too, your resentments, your wrong sex relationships, your self-centered attitudes—yes, your very self—and run to Him.

O Christ, where else can I run? If I run away from Thee, I shall run away from life, from release, from the Open Door. Help me, then, to fling away everything—yes, my very self—and come to Thee. For I cannot live any longer with myself until I find Thee, my true Self. So I come. Amen.

John 11:28; Eph. 2:1–8

THE SECOND STEP

Yesterday you began to put your feet upon the seven-runged ladder to release and power. I trust you have taken that first step. Turn over in mind your life, its directions and spirit. As you turn over in mind your life, change your mind. Repentance in the New Testament is *"metanoia,"* a change of mind. There must be a complete reversal of life values, a complete changing of your mind as to what you really want. The Chinese version of the verse, "If any man would come after me, let him deny himself," is, "let him fling away himself." This recalcitrant, ugly, tangled self must be flung away, lost, in order that a new, disentangled, co-operative self may be found.

You must now come to the next step: (2) *Turn to Christ.* You need a Lord and Master. Perhaps you have been like the little dog Bang, who, in search of his master, ran onto a football field. People called to him from every direction; but there was no dominant voice, so he stood confused. You have been listening to many voices, a perfect babel of them, that call to you from all directions—the voice of money, of sex passion, of self-interest, of pride. And you are confused, for there has been no dominant voice. Now above the din you are hearing one. "The Master is come, and calleth for thee." You hear a Voice that grows authoritative. You feel that there is Destiny in that voice. You have one thing that is yours—yourself. You can decide what to do with it, who shall master it. A science student making his way through the mazes of possible choices, went out of my meeting, walked upstairs, and as simply as a child said, "I will say 'Yes' to Jesus." He kept repeating that to himself. It transformed him. Across that simple bridge of "Yes" he walked out of the slough of despond to abundant living. And that choice has worked through the years.

Perhaps you have been trying to be several selves at once, without all your selves being organized around a single mastering Life within you. There was the plaintive cry of a confused and defeated doctor: "I try to nail down one of these selves, so that the rest of them may organize themselves around it." Don't. Turn over all of them to one mastering will—the will of Christ.

O God, I need a Master. Chain me back into freedom; darken me back into light; stab me back into wholeness; quiet me back into singing; and erase me back into fullness. In Jesus' name. Amen.

Rom. 6:2, 5–6, 11–14

THE THIRD STEP

We come now to the third step: (3) *Having come to Christ, turn and look at your life through His eyes and break decisively with everything He cannot approve.*

I have purposely waited for this stage before asking for the decisive break with all hindrances, all barriers, all sins; for you cannot really see yourself until you see yourself through His eyes. Up to this moment you may have been comparing yourself with yourself, or with others, and in the light of these you have not come out badly. But now, having come to Christ, you see things through His eyes—a very different light. Things which, seen in the half-lights of our former standards, were not so bad, now turn out to be intolerable. They must go. Don't trifle.

At our Saugatuck Ashram one woman buried a little box, symbol of the tyranny of a habit, in the sand at the foot of the cross. Another said she buried her fears and sins in the stars, so far out of her reach that she could not get at them again. Whether you bury them in the sand or in the stars—bury them, and over their graves put the inscription, "No resurrection."

In the same Ashram we were all assigned work to do with our hands; mine was picking up paper. I found that people's consciences were developed regarding throwing paper around as the days went on. But not far enough! For many would hide the paper under bushes—they had just enough conscience to hide the paper, but not enough to get rid of it! Do not let this matter of getting rid of sin end in a stalemate, a compromise; don't be content with a conscience that will hide sins, but will not get rid of sins. Go back into the hidden recesses where you have tucked sins away, to the margins of the subconscious, and bring them all out—all. They will plead, will excuse, will procrastinate, but be relentless—bring them all out—not a thing must be left behind.

O God, I have put my hand to this plow, and I do not intend to look back. I am going all out for Christ. This shall be no halfway business. I shall take the whole cross and not ask for a half cross. Help me to cut loose. In Jesus' name. Amen.

Luke 9:23–24; Rom. 12:1; I Thess. 5:23

THE FOURTH STEP

We come now to the most important step of all: (4) *Turn over to Christ yourself and all you have.* This is the crucial point, and if you bungle this you block the process. Between two persons there is no love without an inward self-surrender to each other. If either one withholds the essential self from the other, love is blocked; it will not spring up no matter how hard you try to love around and past that core of an unsurrendered self. So between you and God there can be no love without an inward self-surrender. Not the surrender of this thing or that thing, but the surrender of you, the essential you.

A brilliant woman came to the end of her resources. Her self-centered life had run through its inner assets. She was bankrupt. She saw clearly that the self would have to resign to find itself. But the struggle was great. It always is. One man put it this way: "There were many battles fought on great fields, but there was never a harder one than that between myself and myself in that little room." I told this woman that the initial battle was the hardest, that it takes twice as much power for an airplane to get off the earth as it does for it to fly. We bowed in prayer. At the close of that prayer she opened her eyes and said, "But I'm off!" She had broken with the old life. And there was wonderful release. She gave me her whisky bottle and her gold cigarette case, saying, "I have no more use for them." She gave up her sleeping tablets too. She let go all crutches.

For several days this woman was supremely happy—and then a cloud. "I am like a child adopted into a new family; everything is beautiful, but one thing is lacking—I cannot see my Father's face." And then the reason for it dawned. She had given her whisky bottle and her cigarette case in lieu of herself. She had tried to buy off God with these! When she saw what had happened she hastened to add herself to the bottle and the case; and then did she see her Father's face? Yes, with nothing between! And now she is radiantly happy. She lost a tangled, snarled-up self and found a united, released, and happy self.

O God, I see that I cannot buy Thee off—Thou relentless Lover. Thou dost want the inmost shrine—myself. So I vacate and give it to Thee. For I have no right to the Throne. I am not God—Thou art. So I abdicate and give Thee supreme charge. Thou dost command. I obey. It is done! Amen.

Mark 11:22; 9:23; 11:24

THE FIFTH STEP

Yesterday you decided that God should have first place. Someone wrote to a great Russian writer: "It seems to me that to put ourself into the second place is the whole significance of life." To which Turgenev replied: "It seems to me to discover what one should put in the first place is the whole problem of life." You have decided that problem: God, and no one else, shall have the first place.

Now you are ready for the next step: (5) *Turn to Him in confidence and faith and believe that He receives you and that you receive Him.* Having given the one thing you have, you have the right to accept the one thing God has—Himself. Many fail at this place. They are forever giving but fail to receive. Suppose you should do that in a marriage relation—always give and not allow your partner to reciprocate—would not the relationship be blocked? The alternate heartbeats of your relationship with each other and with God are, "Give, take"; "Give, take." If it's all giving and no taking, the heart will stop beating; it cannot beat in this lopsided fashion. A great surgeon expressed it this way: "Christianity is pure receptivity. As many as *received* Him, to them gave He the right to be called the sons of God." If you are always breathing out and never breathing in, your breathing will stop.

A Roman Catholic girl, a student of sociology, entered this new experience and is alive with God. She puts her resolution this way: "More than ever before I am going to stop searching and let Christ permeate my life. He alone had the answer to life by giving us life itself—life abundant and real and not loaded with unanswerables." "Not loaded with unanswerables—stop mulling around on the inside of yourself, chewing on unanswerables. Go out in positive faith and accept the gift of God. He offers Himself. Take Him. For in that self of God you find all you need—forgiveness, power, fellowship, motive and energy to contribute to others —Life!

Take that step—now!

O God, my Father, this step is taken. You have me. That sums up everything, for I now see the other truth: I have Thee. I have lost myself and have found Thee. Can I ever cease to be eternally grateful? Let my life spell out its gratitude day by day. Amen.

James 1:27; 2:1–4, 14–18

THE SIXTH STEP

You have taken the greatest of all steps. You wonder what will happen. Perhaps you will have your doubts and fears. A young man came to Dr. Poling and said, "I'm ruined. Stanley Jones ruined me in that meeting last night. All my plans I've had to surrender to God." "Thank God," Dr. Poling replied; "now God can do something with you. He can remake your 'ruined' life." That is the point: He shakes your life to the dust to rebuild it—but only with your cooperation. You and God now work it out together.

Take the sixth step: (6) *Turn and look at all your human relationships and go into them with Christ.* Work out to all of these relationships, with your relationship with Christ as the basic fact. This basic relationship must not be fitted into them—they must be fitted into it. You have six major relationships. (1) The Church. Get into it. With all its faults it is the greatest serving institution in the world, filling the earth with schools, hospitals, orphan asylums, leper asylums, and so on. The Church has many critics, but it has no rivals in the work of human redemption. Get into it and become a part of this world fellowship. (2) The home. Take Christ into your home. Set up grace at meals and family prayers. Begin confessing your own sins and not those of your partner. (3) Your business. Make your business an outer expression of your chief business—serving God. You have no business to be in any business that cannot express your chief business—serving God. Change your business, or change to some other. (4) Your class and race relationships. You now enter a new society—the Society of the Kingdom of God. This Society is a classless society, and it is race- and color-blind. Recast all relationships that cannot be fitted into that. (5) Your international relationships. You now have no more enemies because you have no more enmity. You are for everybody, so-called enemies and all. (6) Your relationship with the one next to you, in school, in shop, in office—your neighbor. Witness to him of what has happened to you. Win him.

O God, I begin to see the greatness of my adventure. Nothing lies outside the domain of the Kingdom—not as far as I am concerned. Thou dost demand a total obedience in the total life. And I give it—gladly. Amen.

Mark 1:35–36; Acts 10:9; Eph. 6:18; 1 Thess. 5:17

THE SEVENTH STEP

You come now to the last of the seven steps: (7) *Turn to God each morning—set up the Quiet Hour.* Perhaps you are appalled at the ramifications of your new life. How will you be able to transform all these relationships? You must get resources, and you can get them from the Quiet Hour. Many feel that they can live in a state of prayer, without stated times for prayer. This is a mistake.

Jesus felt the need of three simple habits: (1) He stood up to read, "as his custom was"; (2) He went out into the mountain to pray, "as his custom was"; (3) He taught them again, "as he was wont." These three simple habits: reading and meditating upon the Word of God; exposing oneself to God at the prayer hour; and teaching others—passing on what we have found—are as basic in the spiritual life as two and two make four are in mathematics. If He couldn't get along without them, how do we hope to do so? You and I need "the pure strong hour of the morning, when the soul of the day is at its best." Start the day right, and you will end it right.

Someone asked me how I maintained my spiritual life—what was the secret. I replied that it was by doing two things: first, by keeping up my prayer hours. I established the habit in college. Certain hours do not belong to the day—they're out. They belong to the getting of resources for the day. If I let down those hours, the day lets down with them. I'm better or worse as I pray more or less. Someone described a certain place as "a home in the country where those who have lost spiritual tone and margin through the wear and tear of work may come for rest and reinvigoration." The prayer hour is that "home," where those who have lost spiritual tone and margin can regain them. I repeat, My days sag if the prayer hour sags. The second secret is, I am always up against a task I cannot do—deliberately so. This throws me back on the resources of God. Life then becomes what a youth resolved his would be as he looked up at and listened to Rufus Jones: "I am just going to make my life a miracle." He did.

O God, I need Thy silences just as I need physical food. I dedicate myself to them. May I resolve to cut my physical food each time I cut my spiritual intake. Thus soul and body will go up and down together. For I am resolved to see this through and to pay the price to do it. Amen.

Luke 13:3, Rom. 2:4; Acts 2:38; 3:19

REVIEW YOUR LIFE AND REVERSE

This matter of taking the initial step is so important that if you do not really take it the rest of abundant living will be a sealed book to you. As someone said of another, "He hasn't the combination"; and when you haven't it, you can't get at the locked treasures of God.

At the risk of seeming tedious we will go back again over some of the same ground, this time using a different ladder. For I know that many may have gone through our last week's study of the steps without actually taking them. I would gather in that last hesitant soul before we go on. For what lies ahead is too good to be missed!

You will remember we are working our way through the five steps of the scientific method found on page 10. We have lingered on the second and third steps: picking out the most likely hypothesis and experimenting with it. We have picked out Christ as the most likely hypothesis and are now experimenting with Him as the Answer.

This ladder will be even simpler than the other, using nine R's upon which to step up and out. (1) *Review.* Take an honest look at yourself. Perhaps you will find not so much positive sin as a lack of divine life.

> "Outwardly splendid as of old,
> Inwardly sparkless, void and cold,
> Her force and fire all spent and gone,
> Like the dead moon she still shines on."
> —WILLIAM WATSON

Or life may be at cross-purposes with itself, "sweet bells jangled out of tune." Or you may feel you are not getting anywhere. A Negro redcap said, "No, don't take that coach, for it ain't hitched to nothin' that is goin' somewhere." You may feel your life is hitched to something that isn't getting you anywhere. Then let us take the second step: (2) *Reverse.* Repentance is reversal. You have been going in a wrong direction; now you turn on your heel and reverse. Don't confess other people's sins; confess your own. If you begin with yourself, then like may beget like—they will confess theirs.

O God, I do begin with myself. I've been a coward. I've laid things on others and blamed them for my condition. I am to blame for what I am. But I do not stop with useless regret—I about-face. I honestly, even bitterly, repent. Forgive me. Amen.

Luke 15:11–32

RETURN TO GOD

You have taken two of the nine steps to release. You now take the third: (3) *Return*. Repentance is the negative side. It releases you to return—return to God. But you say: "Will God receive such as I am? Shall I not have to make myself better, so that I shall be worthy?" Worthy? No one ever is. Go back to God with these words on your lips: "Just as I am, without one plea."

A minister was in a train, the only occupant of the coach except a young man who seemed very ill at ease. The young man would sit in one seat and then get up and go to another, take up a book and drop it again. The minister went over to him, sat down beside him, and asked what was the matter. The boy shut up like a clam. But at last the dam broke, and he told his story: "I've run away from home, and I've been away for a long time. I've wanted to go back, and I wrote my father asking if he would take me back. But there has been no reply. So I have written my mother and told her that I am not going to wait for a reply, that I am coming home, and that if they will take me back she must hang a white rag on the crab-apple tree, down near the railroad tracks, so that I can see it when the train goes by. If I do not see the white rag, I shall understand and go on by. We are getting near and I am afraid to look—afraid the white rag won't be there." The minister told the lad that he needn't look, that he would look for him. The boy sat with his eyes closed, the hand of the minister on his knee. As they drew near to where the tree was, the hand of the minister closed tight on the boy's knee, and he said, "My boy, there is a white rag on every limb of that tree!"

Something like that awaits you—you who are returning to God. A welcome so ungrudging, so overflowing that it will break down all your hesitancies, all your fears and doubts. Take one step toward Him, and He will take two steps toward you.

"But when he was yet a great way off, his father saw him . . . . and ran . . . . and kissed him."

O God, how dare I close my heart to Thee? I cannot; I will not. And now I come to Thee, just as I am. If anything can be made of me, then you have me. I am at your disposal. I've come with all I have. In Jesus' name. Amen.

Luke 19:8–10; John 1:12–13; Rom. 5:1

RENOUNCE, RESTORE, AND RECEIVE

Now that you have taken the third step, take the next: (4) *Renounce.* At the heart of this new life there is a "No." It is the hardest word psychologically to say—"Yes" is much easier. But you will have to say "No" to some things in order to say "Yes" to the real things. Among the effects of James Russell Lowell were found these lines:

> "Here lies a part of J. R. L.,
> The things that kept him from doing well."

A man promised a pastor that he would not drink again. After the pledge had been taken the man appeared in late evening and said he must be allowed to drink, or he would die. The pastor told him to go home and die, and went on with his work. The next day the man appeared with a new confidence in his face and said, "I died last night." He had, but a new man was alive.

(5) *Restore.* As you go over your life you will find things which you will have to right. You may have to ask forgiveness for wrongs done to others, for resentments harbored; you may have to make up a quarrel; you may have to restore money. In one of our missions, a young lady hesitated about dropping in the box a letter asking forgiveness for resentments harbored. But the moment the letter hit the bottom of the box a tied-up condition within her broke. She was free. In another mission the hotel management called us up thanking us for the mission—a woman had come and returned an armful of towels she had taken when she had been a guest at the hotel. Make a clean sweep with no compromises or half-performances.

(6) *Receive.* Here is the simple act of faith. To receive is an affirmation that God is as honorable as you are. You have given what you have, now you believe He will not do less—He will give what He has. And the best thing He has to give is *Himself.* He gives that. Keep repeating to yourself: "I take into my inmost being the forgiving love of God," Affirm, affirm, affirm.

O God, I do affirm. I have lived on denials too long. Now I live on the positive affirmation that Thou art love; that I can bank on that love; that that love will not let me down; that I can draw on it for all I need. And now, O God, I am on your hands forever. I am glad to be there. Amen.

Ps. 1:2; 63:6–7; 119:148; 121:1

RELATING THE NEW LIFE

Now that you have taken the step of receptivity you are ready for the last three. (7) *Relate.* Jesus was not a moralist relating you to an imposed moral code. He wasn't saying, "Do this"; "Don't do that." His method was to get people into right relationships, and then everything would follow from that. His first word was, "Follow me." Out of that relationship with Him would flow all other relationships. The most beautiful tribute I ever heard a man pay to his wife was that paid by a Negro bishop when he arose and said, "Fifty years ago I looked into the limpid depths of her eyes, and I've never got over the spell of it." Everything flowed from that central loyalty. Now that you have your central relationship with Christ pegged down, make all your other relationships fit into it. And remember that nothing is more central in the Christian way than bringing all your relationships under the guidance of this central relationship.

The central principle of your relationships with people is: "Do unto others as you would that men should do to you." Give your employees the same treatment you would like if you were an employee. And thus go on down the line with every human relationship. But for the Christian there is something beyond even the Golden Rule: "Treat one another with the same spirit as you experience in Christ Jesus." (Philippians 2:5, Moffatt.) In other words, "Treat others as Christ treats you"—that puts a plus, a beyond-ness, in the whole thing. Surrender yourself to that plus, that beyondness.

To do this you will need resources. Get them in the next step. (8) *Refill, Replenish.* This will be done in the Quiet Hour. A sheep rancher, living all alone on his Idaho ranch, found that his violin was out of tune and that he couldn't tune it without some standard note to go by. So he wrote to the radio station in far-off California asking them to strike that note. They did. They stopped the program, struck the note, the sheep rancher caught it, and the violin was in tune again. Your Quiet Hour will help you hear God's standard notes. Then you can tune up your flattened notes to His. Keep that Hour intact.

O God, I know there is nothing better than what I have found except more of what I have found. Help me to open every pore of my being to the incoming Life that heals, sustains, reinvigorates, empowers. I do so now—come in, Thou Life of my life, Thou Being of my being. Amen.

Rom. 8:1–2; II Cor. 3:16–18; Gal. 5:1

RELEASED AND RELEASING

You come now to the final step of your ladder. (9) *Release*. This release is in two directions. First, there is release within. All your tied-up conditions—your inhibitions, your fears, your guilts—are now gone. You have now entered abundant living.

But, second, there is release in another direction. You are released to serve. You are released *from* and released *to*—from fears to folks; from inhibitions to inspirations; from guilts to guidance. The doors now turn outward. From being an introvert, you become an extrovert—not entirely, of course, for in reality you are now an introvert-extrovert, an ambivert. You turn inward, no longer to mull around in useless regret over failure, but to get quiet in "The Trysting Place," so that communion with Him will recoup the soul and make it adequate for the next step—extroversion. For that communion ends in commission. Life is now outgoing, positive, affirmative, contributive.

A woman who had gone through the ways of the world and had come out zero put her experience this way in a letter: "I've been full of questions and doubts and wonderings; then all of a sudden everything falls into its place like pieces of a jigsaw puzzle. And when this happens, I want to tell someone. I want to say, 'Why, there is no question about the reality of this. It's there; it is; it's a fact.' " This letter has the authentic notes in it: (1) "Full of questions, doubts, wonderings." (2) "Everything falls into its place like a jigsaw puzzle." (3) "I want to tell someone."

Release is the last stage—rightly so. The doors of the unreleased person all turn inward; the doors of the released person turn outward. His goodness now is good for something. And nothing, nothing is more absolutely sound, psychologically, than just that. Relief comes through release.

You are a released person—released to follow the unfolding will of God.

O God, my Father, how can I express the gratitude my happy soul would tell? "O for a thousand tongues to sing my great Redeemer's praise." Now help me to tell my gratitude not merely in ecstatic praise, but in quiet ways of human helpfulness. Help me to help the next person I meet, and so on through this day. Amen.

I Pet. 1:22–23; 2:1–2; Gal. 5:22–23

THE FOUR STAGES OF LIFE

The spiritual life passes through the same four stages as
the physical life: (1) Gestation. (2) Birth. (3) Growth.
(4) Flowering.

Gestation is the period spiritually when this new life is
forming within one. A brilliant doctor, after a period of awful struggle and darkness, described this first stage thus:
"There is a little plant of faith growing in my heart. But I
am almost afraid to look at it, lest it wither."

After this period of incubation, when we alternate between doubt and faith, between hating God and surrendering to Him, between plunging deeper into sin and surrendering it entirely, there comes the birth. That spiritual new
birth may be sudden, or it may be gradual. It may be as
gradual as the opening of a flower to the sun, or it may be
as sudden as a lightning flash. But even in the gradual birth
there is a moment when the decision is made, as when the
hand of the clock, gradually turning round the dial, comes
to a moment when it strikes twelve. Sometimes the new beginning is sudden and over-whelming, as in Masefield's *The
Everlasting Mercy:*

> "I did not think, I did not strive,
> The deep peace burned my me alive;
> The bolted door had broken in,
> I knew that I had done with sin.
> I knew that Christ had given me birth
> To brother all the souls on earth. . . . .
>
> Oh glory of the lighted mind.
> How dead I'd been, how dumb, how blind.
> The station brook, to my new eyes,
> Was babbling out of Paradise,
> The waters rushing from the rain
> Were singing Christ has risen again.
> I thought all earthly creatures knelt
> From rapture of the joy I felt."[1]

O God, these words echo what I feel. And yet I do not
depend upon my fleeting feelings. I depend upon the certain faith that Thou art and that I am, and that we have
come together to be knit together in a common purpose and
a common life. This is the rock beneath my feet. Amen.

[1] Reprinted by permission of The Macmillan Co., publishers.

1 Cor. 6:9–11; 1 Pet. 1:8–9; Rom. 8:15–17

SWALLOWING SUNSHINE

We ended yesterday with the wonder, the miracle, of the new birth. A friend of mine in the South called a Negro on the station platform to the train window and said, "Uncle, is there anybody in this town enjoying religion?" To which the old Negro replied, "Them's that's got it, is." He could have said nothing more profound. He expressed in homely language what an able woman said in these words: "In the first place, the terrible clouds of questioning and of doubting have dispersed. I find I am no longer torturing myself about the 'rightness' and 'wrongness' of things. Victory is mine and I find that praying has taken on a new vitality. . . . . I scarcely know just what has taken place, but I do know that something within me has been released, something that had been throttled."

A college girl put the same truth in her own language: "I felt that I had swallowed sunshine." Quite a contrast to some people who look as though they had swallowed a storm cloud! A woman who had gone through the mazes of psychiatrical analysis and had been left rather picked to pieces without a synthesis, experienced this change and described it this way: "I feel all clean within. All the old hymns about cleansing which I had laid aside as outworn superstition have come back. I find myself singing them again."

Justice Holmes expressed the same fact in stately words when he said, "You have a feeling of intimacy with the inside of the cosmos." You do. You are no longer orphaned, estranged, alone. You have a feeling of belonging—not only to "the inside of the cosmos," but to people. The biggest grouch of a certain city called up a friend over the long-distance telephone and said, "Everybody is changed in —— after that meeting in the high school with Stanley Jones last night. Everybody is different this morning. Of course, it may be that only I am different, but everybody seems different." His world was different, for he was different.

O God, I have come into a new world, for a new world has come into me. Help me to live so that people will seem different to me and I seem different to them. For I am different. And I am so grateful. Thank you, Father. Amen.

1 John 1:7; Col. 2:6–7; Eph. 4:11–16

CULTIVATION, THE SECOND LAW

You have now taken the preliminary steps in beginning the Christian way. Remember it is a *way*, and not merely a decision once made. A Christian is "one who is responding to all the meanings he finds in Christ." Those meanings will unfold as you respond to them, but only as you respond to them. Those meanings will become meaningless unless you respond.

So many start well, but soon the glory fades, and they settle down to respectable mediocrity, without the spark of contagion. This often happens in the minister. In one pulpit I know, there is a fire extinguisher fastened underneath. The probabilities are that the precaution was unnecessary. No fire would break out in that pulpit! The life was non-contagious. One man prayed, "O God, grant that if any spark of divine grace has been kindled in this meeting, water that spark." Many of our sparks have been dampened out of existence, put out by mere neglect.

If conversion is the first law of the spiritual life, then cultivation is the second law. The way to fight disease germs is to raise the tone of health in the total organism, and the fact of health throws off the disease germs as they come— expelled by health. When disease germs do get a footing, then nature sends up the temperature into fever in order to get rid of the germs.

Professor William James speaks of "religion as a dull habit or an acute fever." If religion is going to be an acute fever, burning up disease germs in the process, you will have to cultivate it.

I went into a radio station and noticed that the room was marked off into portions: "Live End"; "Semi-live End"; "Dead End." You and I can live in the live end of the Christian faith, the semi-live end, or the dead end.

If we are going to be a plus sign and not a minus sign, we shall have to face all enemies and down them by taking hold of the resources of God.

O God, I have begun this way. I am all eagerness to continue. This new life has the feel of the real and the eternal upon it. I would therefore cultivate my spiritual health so that it will have enough and to spare. Lead on; I follow— follow with the consent of all my being. Amen.

Gal. 5:19–21; Matt. 15:19–20; II Tim. 3:2–5

SEGREGATING OUR ENEMIES

We come now to the stage where we must examine specifically some of the mental and spiritual disease germs that throw disruption and disease into human living. There is a par life, but many of us are living below par; and when we do, disease germs rush in and gain a footing. We must now try to segregate those disease germs, so that we can deal with them intelligently and effectively.

When I wrote *Is the Kingdom of God Realism?* I segregated four enemies of the human personality: (1) Resentments, anger, and hate. (2) Fear, worry, and anxiety. (3) Self-centeredness. (4) A sense of guilt. In the subsequent discussions it was found that while these four are basic enemies, the list must be added to by other major enemies. In the weeks of study and discussion and spiritual quest in our Ashrams in America we finally fixed upon fifteen major enemies. Under them were grouped lesser enemies, but these fifteen were the seed enemies.

(1) A lack of faith in and loyalty to Something beyond oneself—a Something that gives ultimate meaning, coherence, and goal to life. (2) Self-centeredness. (3) Anger, resentments, hate. (4) Fear, worry, anxiety. (5) A sense of unresolved guilt. (6) Negativism and inferiority attitudes. (7) Insincerity, conscious and unconscious. (8) Uncontrolled desires. (9) Divided loyalties. (10) Unbalanced virtues. (11) Ignorance and lack of judgment. (12) Physical disharmony. (13) An unchristian social order. (14) Lack of a total life discipline. (15) Lack of a positive, outgoing love.

Please do not think that these enemies are merely spiritual, throwing disruption only into the soul; they are enemies of the total life, causing physical disease, mental disruption, and spiritual disharmony and decay. They attack the total person. They may begin in one portion, but in the end they extend their effects to all.

O God, I thank Thee that I see my enemies. I have brought the hidden ones into the light. They are many, and they attack me in subtle, unseen ways. But I am not dismayed. If sin abounds, Thy grace doth much more abound. In that confidence I face them all, expecting Thee to give me nerve and courage and strength to down them one by one—or perhaps all at once. Amen.

Matt. 9:20–22; Mark 10:51–52; Rom. 8:11

YOU ARE MADE FOR LOYALTY TO GOD

We now take up these fifteen enemies and face them one by one. The first is one that we have been dealing with in our preliminary study: *The lack of a faith in and loyalty to Something beyond oneself—a Something that gives ultimate meaning, coherence, and goal to life.* We, of course, believe that Something is a Someone—God.

But whether you believe that "Something beyond oneself" is God, or not, the basic necessity is the same. In order to be well, in order to be the kind of person you ought to be, you must believe in something beyond yourself and be loyal to it. Why? The answer is that you are made that way —structurally made that way. That way is stamped into your being. Is that the statement of a minister and therefore supposed to be prejudiced? All right, then take the statement of Dr. Jung, who certainly was not prejudiced in a religious direction. Dr. Jung (to a patient): "You are suffering from loss of faith in God and in a future life." Patient: "But, Dr. Jung, do you believe these doctrines are true?" Dr. Jung: "That is no business of mine. I am a doctor, not a priest. I can only tell you that if you recover your faith you will get well. If you don't, you won't."

Why did this famous psychiatrist say that? For the simple reason that he had found by experience that life works that way. Life needs something outside oneself to fasten its love and loyalty to, or it will break down. I deal with hundreds of cases myself. The last one was an intelligent woman with a lovely family of four and a faithful husband, who, because her husband would not go to church with her, gave up going herself, gradually lost her faith in God, then lost interest in her family, then nervously broke, and has been in the hands of the doctors for months. There is nothing wrong with her, except that, when God faded out, the meaning dropped out of life, and the whole of life sagged with it, with resultant nerve collapse. She has now found God again and with him the basis of health. After she found God, she slept that very night without a sleeping draught—the first time for months.

O God, can my lungs do without air, my eyes do without light, my heart do without love, my aesthetic nature do without beauty, my conscience do without truth? No more can I do without Thee, Thou Life of my life, Thou Soul of my soul. I belong to Thee as glove to hand. Amen.

Eph. 2:12–22

SUBSTITUTES FOR GOD

If faith in and loyalty to Something beyond oneself—Something that will give ultimate meaning, coherence, and goal to life—is necessary to health, then may it not be that faith in anything beyond oneself may be a substitute for God? Art, music, patriotism, causes of various kinds—will these not take the place of God? Why is God necessary?

There is no doubt whatever that all these interests will help to lift you out of yourself and are thereby real helps, but they do not ultimately hit the spot. For the last portion of the statement is important—"A Something that gives *ultimate* meaning, coherence, and goal to life." Do the things mentioned as substitutes give *ultimate* meaning, coherence, and goal to life? They may give local and temporary "meanings" to portions of life, and may therefore give local and temporary "coherence" to life, but if they lack "total meaning" and "ultimate goal," then the "meaning" and the "coherence" drop to pieces. None of these things give ultimate meaning and goal to life, except God; therefore only God can make life "cohere." Paul says of Christ, "In Him all things cohere." They do, for He is ultimate Being, the human life of God.

Everything less than God will let you down. Coué suggested the method of autosuggestion, of saying to yourself, "Every day in every way I am getting better and better." This is good, but not good enough, for Coué died of a broken heart because the newspapers of the world and people in general made fun of his method. He could not stand that poking of fun. His own method should have made him able to say in spite of the attitude of his detractors, "Every day in every way I am getting better and better." But he couldn't take it on the chin and get up smiling—in spite of. His lifting-himself-with-his-bootstrap-method failed him. It wasn't rooted in eternal reality; hence it let him down in the pinch. As a friend started on a world speaking tour, a very wise old lady said. "Give them nothing less than God." Anything less than God will let you down.

O God, only those rooted in Thee, the Eternal, can stand up under life. They can take it. I, too, would be able to take it. Then let all my being be rooted in Thee—my thoughts rooted in Thy thoughts, my emotions rooted in Thy love, my will rooted in Thy will. Then shall I live. Amen.

Luke 15:1–10; Eph. 2:8; Heb. 11:1

BEGINNING THE PRACTICE OF THE PRESENCE OF GOD

A little girl was dying of meningitis. She asked, "Where is God?" and when told that He was in the room, she replied, "Then where can I find Him?"

The answer to the question, "How do I find Him?" is: (1) You do not have to find Him; you have to allow Him to find you. If the New Testament teaches us anything, it teaches us not merely man's search for God, but God's search for man.

> ". . . . those strong Feet that followed, followed after.
> But with unhurrying chase,
> And unperturbèd pace,
> Deliberate speed, majestic instancy,
> They beat—and a Voice beat
> More instant than the Feet—
> 'All things betray thee, who betrayest Me.' "[1]

You must put yourself in the way of being found by God. That means, stop running away. (2) Turn toward Him in an attitude of expectancy. Faith is expectancy. (3) Act as though God is, and is with you, and with you *now*. (4) Set up little habits which will express that fact. Dr. Frank Laubach suggests several, such as: Walk on the inside of the pavement with the suggestion that your Divine Companion is walking on the curb side. Leave a vacant chair at the table as a symbol of the Invisible Presence in it. (5) Order your day on the basis of a Divine partnership in it. (6) Play the Game of Minutes: See how many times an hour you can think of God. Count the minutes you thought of Him. (7) Take some time off during the day to quiet your heart in His presence: "Be still, and know that I am God." (8) As you take a breath say to yourself: As this physical breath I am taking in is cleansing the blood in my lungs from all impurities, so the breath of God, when I take it within my whole being, purifies my inner life.

O God, I now begin the practice of living in Thee—I am actually practicing the presence of God. Be in all things great and small. And the small things become great, and the great things become possible. How wonderful to live on this co-operative plan! Amen.

[1] Francis Thompson, "The Hound of Heaven." Reprinted by permission of Dodd, Mead & Co., publishers.

Heb. 3:7–15

GET THE CENTER RIGHT

You have to relate yourself to four words: (1) yourself; (2) things; (3) your brother; (4) God. Until you relate yourself to God in fellowship and obedience, none of the other three relationships will come out right. You will be out of sorts with yourself, with things, with your brother, until you get the center right. When you get the center right, the circumference takes care of itself. Said a wife concerning her husband, "He has a brilliant mind, but he will not rest in the Eternal." Hence he was restless with himself, with things, with his fellow men.

The chapel steeple of a great university, where the minister is humanistic, has a weather vane on it instead of a cross, symbolic of the fact that people point in every direction, turned by the winds of circumstance, until they have a faith in and a committal to God. That gives an unchanging steadiness to life.

Then why is it that men do not rest in Him? Because they try to rest in something else. They love God with the top of their minds, but not with the bottom of their souls. Something else holds the bottom of their affections. That deep affection then decides their thinking, for men think more with their emotions than with their minds. The affections draw reasons to themselves as a magnet draws iron filings. Men lose faith in God not so much by honest doubt as by dishonest sin. A brilliant headmaster, on a salary of $25,000, talked beautifully about faith in God—and he had it. Then his faith changed. He gave a commencement address and shocked everybody by saying, "Christianity is outworn; it has lost its hold on the world." At the bottom of that decay of faith was a decay of morals. He had begun to keep a mistress. He was dismissed in disgrace. The mind had tried to find reasons to justify the emotions.

After one of my meetings a banker walked the floor all night and his daughter wept the long night through. Both had sin in their lives, and would not rest in the Eternal. Hence their restlessness.

O God, I cannot rest until I rest in Thee. I am made for Thee, as the eye is made for light; so I cannot find my peace except in Thy will. For Thy will is my peace. Oh, let me settle down in Thee. Let the wandering, restless needle of my affections at last rest in Thee, Thou polestar of my life. I do, I do at last rest in Thee. Amen.

Heb. 4:16; 6:9–12; 10:39

HAVING OUR BEING IN HIM

Life is a restless, disrupted thing until we give ourselves to Something beyond ourselves, until we obey Something ultimate, and obey it supremely. Science corroborates that. A doctor said to me, "If three quarters of my patients found God, they would be well." A psychiatrist in Hollywood, who is paid handsomely by his disrupted patients of filmdom, said to a friend, "Most of my patients do not need me; they need a mourner's bench; they need God."

This being true, then why do not more of us find Him and live by Him? Here is one reason: The harboring of moral wrong makes God unreal. We will know as much of God as we are willing to put into practice, and no more.

Another reason is a lack of appropriating faith. Paul says, "In him we live, and move, and have our being." We do live and move in God, for He is the inescapable. We can only deny Him with the very powers He gives us. We must perforce live and move in Him even when throttling Him in our lives. And yet we do not "have our being" in Him. We live on surface roots—the taproot has not gone down into God. We do not have our very being in Him. We fail to appropriate His amazing resources. And we fail because we do not take. And yet nothing is simpler.

Jesus says, "You believe—believe in God and also in me." (John 14:1, Moffatt.) Note, "You believe." Belief is the habit of your life; you have to believe in order to live. If you should start a day without faith, you wouldn't eat your breakfast in the morning, for you wouldn't be quite sure it wasn't poisoned; the eating would be an act of faith in the cook. You wouldn't go to the university because you wouldn't be quite sure the professor would be there; the going would be an act of faith in him. All day long you are exercising faith. You live by it. Life would be paralyzed without it. Now then, says Jesus, "You believe—believe in God." Since you do believe, then believe in the highest—God. Why expend your faith on lesser things and refuse to give it to the Highest?

O God, I see that faith is not some extraneous thing introduced from without. I must live by it, or not live at all. Then I take this everyday necessity of life and fasten it upon Thee, Thou source of my very life. From this moment I not only live and move in Thee—I have my being in Thee as well. I will draw my very life from Thee. Amen.

Mark 8:34; Rom. 15:1; I Cor. 10:24; II Cor. 5:15

WHEN WE BECOME GOD

We have looked at the first of the fifteen major enemies of healthy, rhythmical human living. We come now to the second—*Self-centeredness*.

This follows from the first, as fruit from root. When God is no longer the center, then we become the center—we become God. Deuteronomy 4:25 (Moffatt) has the phrase, "if you lose your freshness in the land and deprave yourselves by craving an idol." Note that when the freshness of God's presence is gone, and with it the freshness of life itself, then the result is that we "deprave ourselves" by craving an idol; and that idol is usually just ourselves. Aldous Huxley says, "One strange result of scientific progress has been the reversion of monotheism to local idolatries." And when those "local idolatries" are not state and race and class—which are the self writ large—then they are just the personal self. When we lose God, then we become God.

But this centering on ourselves works badly; in fact, it works havoc to the very self upon which we are centering. On the face of it, it would seem that if we turn to ourselves and center on our own selves, we should grow under that cultivation. The very opposite takes place. Every self-centered person is a self-disrupted person, even though he centers upon himself for religious motives. Whether you center upon yourself for artistic, for religious, for financial, or for just purely selfish reasons, the result is the same—the self goes to pieces.

Those who center upon themselves and have their way, don't like their way; they do as they like, and then don't like what they do; they express themselves, and then find the self that is expressed souring on their hands. And this disruption and souring doesn't merely stop with the soul; it extends straight out into the nerves and tissues, and poisons them with disease, functional and structural. Apparently they are running against a fundamental law of life, deeply imbedded in the constitution of things. More people are being broken by that law than by any other one single thing in life. Just what is it?

My Father God, I would find adjustment to life. But when I am adjusted only to myself, I am not adjusted to life. Then teach me—oh, teach me this lesson; for if I miss it, I miss life itself. But I want to live fully, abundantly, overflowingly. Then teach me how. Amen.

James 2:8–9; Rom. 12:3, 10, 16; 13:9–10

THE SELF-CENTERED AND
THE SELF-DISRUPTED

The law upon which individuals and groups and nations break themselves when they become egocentric is this: "Whosoever will save his life shall lose it"—concentrate yourself on yourself, and that self will go to pieces, not only spiritually, but mentally and physically as well.

The reason for this is obvious. The three driving urges or instincts within us are self, sex, and the herd, or social, instinct. The self instinct is obviously self-regarding; the herd instinct is other-regarding; the sex instinct is partly self-regarding and partly other-regarding. So there are just two driving instincts—the egoistic and the altruistic, the self-regarding and the other-regarding. Both of these must be fulfilled—and fulfilled in the proper proportion—or life will be frustrated and unhappy.

There are those who think that Christianity teaches that they must love others, but not themselves. This is a mistake. Christianity teaches self-love. "Thou shalt love thy neighbor *as thyself*." If you did not love yourself, you would not develop yourself. So all attempts to eliminate the self end in hypocrisy and disaster. If you put your self out of the door, it will come back through the window, probably in disguise. Frankly and honestly you must love yourself—not as a master, but as a servant; for the self is a glorious servant, but a gruesome master. Those who love others and not themselves, allowing others to sap the life out of them, end in disaster. On the other hand, if one organizes life around himself and becomes self-centered, then, as sure as fate, disaster overtakes that self. Does God pronounce judgment from heaven upon that life? No; by the very inherent laws within one the judgment takes place. The person is at war with himself. His altruistic instinct is frustrated and undeveloped; hence the person is dissatisfied and unhappy. He probably doesn't know what is the matter with him. The malady is simple—he is a house divided against itself, and hence cannot stand. Every self-centered person is trying the impossible—to live against himself.

O God, my Father, I see that Thou hast wrought Thy laws into the texture of my being. How foolish for me to run against those laws and think I can get away with my folly! For I cannot get away with myself. Forgive me the folly of warring with myself and hence with Thee. Amen.

Matt. 25:24–25; II Tim. 4:10; I Tim. 6:6–10

LIVING IN A STATE OF SELF-REFERENCE

All self-centered persons when self-frustration begins to set in will probably turn towards themselves in self-pity. They will feel that life is hard on them. They will blame everything except themselves. A case in point: A brilliant woman who had a nervous breakdown for no other reason than that she lived in a state of constant self-reference, mulled over herself in self-pity. Those who tried to change her attitudes were persecuting her. Her life was all jammed up, and the one key log in the jam was self-centeredness. Had she pulled that log out—had she changed her center from herself to God—the whole inner clogged-up condition would have broken loose, and she would have been cleansed and released. She could not say the words, "I am sorry." It was all self-defense. The nearest she came to saying, "I am sorry," was when she said, "Yes, I am sorry—sorry that I did not take better care of my health." The repentance still had a self-reference to it. She is clogged up still, and will be till that key log is pulled out. She has tied the hands of both God and man—they are powerless to help her.

Such a self-centered person usually draws disease to himself as a magnet draws iron filings to itself. The underprivileged person has my sympathy and will have my endeavor to gain equality of opportunity. But the overprivileged person in our civilization is in far greater danger than the underprivileged. They are the disrupted souls—and bodies—of our civilization. I know a girl who has had thrown into her lap everything that civilization can offer—money, opportunity, etc. But since she is self-centered, she can enjoy none of them. Every sickness that comes into her neighborhood visits her. She draws sickness and melancholy to herself like a magnet; for that is the end of the egocentric. They start out to draw life to themselves—its joys, its thrills —and all they succeed in drawing to themselves is sadness and disillusionment and sickness—spiritual, mental, and physical.

O God, I see I cannot center on myself without that self going to rack and ruin. I would present this self of mine to Thee. Lift me out of myself into Thyself, that there I may find my freedom and myself. For Thy will is my home. Amen.

Eph. 3:16–20; Luke 1:37; Col. 1:29

PUNISHMENT OF EGOCENTRICITY
IS INHERENT

The egocentric is his own punishment. Budd Schulberg, in *What Makes Sammy Run*, after tracing Sammy's egocentric but apparently successful life, sums up in these words: "Unconsciously, I had been . . . . hoping to be around when Sammy got what was coming to him. And now I realized that *what was coming to him* was not a sudden pay-off but a process, a disease . . . . ; a cancer that was slowly eating him away, the symptoms intensifying: success, loneliness, fear. . . . . I thought . . . . You can't have your brothers and eat them too. You're alone, pal, all alone. That's the way you wanted it, that's the way you learned it. . . . . All alone in sickness and in health, for better or for worse, ... till death parts you from your only friend, your worst enemy, yourself."[1]

In the play *Peer Gynt*, the hero, committed to the faith that he would "be myself," visited the lunatic asylum where, he assumes, people were "outside themselves." The director corrects him: "It's here that men are most themselves—themselves and nothing but themselves—sailing with outspread sails of self. Each shuts himself in a cask of self, the cask stopped with a bung of self and seasoned in a well of self. None has a tear for others' woes or cares what any other thinks."

There is one way out of that hell of egocentricity. Dr. Fritz Künkel says: "It has been shown that all mistakes, weaknesses, and aberrations can be traced back to man's egocentricity. Accordingly, the fundamental problem of self-education may be described as the problem of overcoming one's own egocentricity." (*God Helps Those . . . ,* p. 135.) How then do you overcome your egocentricity? By a deliberate act of self-surrender. A willingness to die to this petty self in order that a larger self might live. An able woman, speaking before club women, wept. She was so chagrined that she could do such a thing that she wrote to each one asking her not to mention it. But that breakdown of herself was the best thing that ever happened. It led to her consciously offering that petty self to God—to her conversion. Tears did it!

Dear Lord and Father, Thou art leading me out of my petty self to Thy ample self. I thank Thee that I have a door out of myself into Thee. I would die into Thee—and thus live now and forever. Amen.

[1] Reprinted by permission of Random House, Inc., publishers.

Isa. 65:6–7; Rev. 22:11; Jas. 4:2–3

OUT OF SORTS WITH OURSELVES—
AND OTHERS

The egocentric cannot get along with himself and hence cannot get along with other people. He shuts himself up within himself and by that very fact shuts himself off from others—except in blame. The egocentric usually lays all his troubles to the other people or to surroundings. If only other people or his surroundings were all right, he would be all right. He will do everything except face the source of his trouble—himself. The source of his bad temper with others is the fact that he is out of sorts with himself.

During the Civil War a young man from the South, visiting a hospital in Washington where his brother lay wounded, came out of his brother's room in a hurry and ran straight into Lincoln. Not knowing who he was, he said bitterly, "Can't you get out of the way of a young gentleman?" To which Lincoln, without disclosing his identity, replied, "Young man, what's troubling you on the inside?" He knew by a swift insight that something was troubling him on the inside or he would not be so out of sorts with everybody else. Someone put it this way: "Do you want to find out a man's weak points? Note the failings he has the quickest eye for in others." Usually he will point out what's wrong in others, or in his surroundings, as mental compensation for what is wrong in himself.

That vicious circle must be broken. How? Either through a deliberate breaking of it by a self-surrender into a larger center of life or by an act of love sweeping one off his center to another. Dr. William Sadler, an outstanding psychiatrist, tells of a child of eight who was incorrigible; nothing was right. She had heard her mother say that she was "an unwanted child." "Nobody loves me," the child said bitterly. And soon nobody did! Dr. Sadler heard her complaint and said: "Why, it isn't true. I love you. I really do like you." The child came over and sat on his knee and kissed him, with tears streaming down her cheeks. She went back to her mother, made up, and was a different girl in school. Someone broke the vicious circle of egocentricity by a love that swept her to a new center.

O God, Thou wilt have to do something like that act of love. Where my deliberate, calculated self-dedication to another Center will not "break the vicious circle of my egocentricity," sweep me to a new Center by Thy invading Love. For I must be loosed, be free. Amen.

John 12:5; Matt. 26:14–16, 23, 25; 27:3, 5

THE STEPS DOWN

The most penetrating story of the results of egocentricity is seen in Judas. Judas began high, a loyal disciple. But—

First: He thought one could give too much to Jesus. (John 12:5.) He objected to the woman's lavish gift. His objection was a sign of an inward holding back. Second: "What will you give me?" (Matthew 26:15, Moffatt.) Note, he was the center—"Give *me*." That request was the first step down for the prodigal son: "Give me." When anyone begins to say, "Give me," he is on the way down. Third: "He sought opportunity to betray him." (Matthew 26:16.) He tried to arrange his world so that it would not fall to pieces. Fourth: But that world did fall to pieces. Said Jesus, "One who has dipped." (Matthew 26:23, Moffatt.) "Surely," said Judas, "it is not I?" And the answer came back, "Is it not?" (Matthew 26:25, Moffatt.) The heart of things began to be revealed—his world collapsed.

Fifth: "Then Judas . . . . saw"—saw his world beginning to tumble to pieces. (Matthew 27:3.) (a) He "repented" (verse 3), but he repented in the wrong direction. He turned in useless regret to the high priest and elders— turned to them, instead of to Jesus. (b) "He brought back." (Verse 3.) He tried to steady his tottering world by a half-way restitution. He brought back the money, but retained himself. (c) "What does that matter to us?" (Verse 4.) He finds his world, built up so securely, not trustable. His companions let him down. Sin has no cohesion in it. Sin doesn't care. (d) "Flung down" (verse 5) the money, the thing that seemed to matter so much in the beginning. The precious thing turned to ashes. (e) "Went off" (verse 5)—off from opportunity, from life, from Christ. Sin is centrifugal. (f) "Hanged himself" (verse 5)—the self that was so demanding and so central in the beginning, saying "Give me," became impossible to live with. So he hanged the self that started him down.

Complete collapse will be the end of an egocentric self.

My Father, I see that this imperious, demanding self, like the camel's nose inside the tent, will soon put me out of this earthly habitation. I shall soon not be able to live with it— unless I give it back to Thee for cleansing, for adjustment, for a new basis of living. I do. Amen.

Matt. 7:1–5; 1 John 3:17–21

EGOCENTRICITY IN RELIGION

Egocentricity may be very religious, may be occupied in an attempt to save one's soul, or the souls of others. But it will still be egocentric, and as such destructive.

A very religious woman was suffering from arthritis. It was discovered that her anxiety to dominate her family, even for their own good, was at the basis of this arthritis. She surrendered this anxiety to God, ceased to desire to dominate the family, even though it was for their supposed good, and both her spiritual life and her physical life cleared up—the arthritis disappeared.

A businessman was in the hands of a psychoanalyst. Over a period of five years he spent sixty thousand dollars in having himself picked to pieces. He submitted to the psychoanalyst over a thousand dreams for deciphering—often five or six a night. He kept a pad and paper handy to note them down when these dreams awakened him. At the end of five years the man was thoroughly disrupted and picked to pieces. The psychoanalyst didn't know how to put him together again on a new basis. Self-knowledge was not healing. It straightened him out here and there, but could not heal the central hurt—a disrupted self. He saw all this self-probing was ending in futility, so he gave up his last prop upon which he leaned—the analyst. As he left the hotel a sense of infinite sadness and loneliness came over him—his last prop gone, and nowhere to turn. Suddenly a Voice seemed to say, "Look this way." It was the Voice of Christ saying, "Look away from yourself, your misery, your fear, and your failures! Look to Me." The Voice came like a breath of health into the fetid atmosphere of self-concentration. He looked away from himself to Christ. That look was followed by a lift that took him out of himself, freed him from himself. Today, with an entirely new lease on life, he is healthy, harmonious, and useful.

Thou Living Christ, I do look to Thee. To whom else can I go? for Thou hast the words of eternal life—of eternal life not only in the hereafter, but in the here and now. And so I look to Thee with eyes of faith, and I take from Thee the power, the release, the victory I so deeply need. And I take it now. Amen.

Mark 9:33–35; Ps. 34:5; Isa. 45:22

THE THIRD ENEMY—ANGER, RESENTMENTS

We have now looked at two of the fifteen enemies of the human personality: lack of a vital faith in God, and consequent self-centeredness. We now come to the third: *Resentments, anger, and hate*. In taking up these three we are entering the realm of the emotions.

This age is afraid of being emotional, and yet it is turning out to be a very emotional age; in fact, emotionalism is rampant. Most of this emotionalism is self-disruptive. An age that is afraid of emotion ends up in following the thing it fears. It has tried to suppress the emotions, and the emotions put out at the door have come back by the window.

For the emotions are a part of us and cannot be eliminated. All attempts at elimination end in complexes. They are pushed into the subconscious, and there they become a festering point. We cannot set aside the emotions; we can only direct them, sometimes redirect them to great aims and purposes. The emotions are the driving forces of the personality. They can drive toward the rocks or toward the open seas of expanding accomplishment.

Take anger, for instance. It is an instinct of self-protection, and for the protection of others. It causes us to stand up and fight against harmful enemies of the human personality. We are angry with evil, and therefore we stiffen ourselves against it and oppose it. Otherwise we would allow it to invade us and others. Nietzsche is right when he says that "virtue is of no use unless it can be lashed into a rage." Otherwise we would be "moral cows in our plump comfortableness." Our capacity to love the good, determines our capacity to hate the evil. But the note that it is our virtue that is to be lashed into a rage—not our pride, our hurt egoism, our fears. There is all the difference in the world between the two: one is harnessed to higher ends, hence constructive; the other is harnessed to the ends of a wounded self, and hence destructive. The one is a righteous anger, and the other is unrighteous.

O God, I do not sail calm seas. I am driven by tempests of emotion. Help me to harness these to the purposes of Thy Kingdom, for unharnassed they drive me to the rocks upon which both I and my relationships are broken. I surrender myself and my emotions to Thee. Amen.

Mark 3:5; Ps. 95:10; Eph. 4:30; Prov. 8:3; Ps. 97:10

A GOOD ANGER

Yesterday you saw that anger is a driving force—it throws adrenalin into the blood stream, and you are then ready for fight or flight. If anger is to be constructive, it must be harnessed to great causes. It must be like the explosions in the engine of your automobile—these explosions are under the control of purpose and will drive you to your destination. But if, instead of harnessing the explosions, you lighted all the gasoline in your tank at once, with one great "blowup" you would blow yourself and the car to pieces. That is what happens to the insides of you when you have a "blowup" of uncontrolled, nonconstructive anger. It leaves you and your situation torn to pieces.

Jesus was an example of controlled anger. When He was about to heal the man with the withered arm, He saw the hard faces of religious men who opposed the act because it was being done on the Sabbath. He "looked round about on them with anger, being grieved for the hardness of their hearts." Here His anger was not personal pique, a wounded egotism—it was grief at the hardness of men's hearts that could block the healing of a poor unfortunate. His anger drove Him to oppose these men on behalf of the underprivileged. It was therefore a righteous anger.

Anger is righteous if it has in it grief on account of what is happening to others, and not a grudge on account of what is happening to oneself. But one must be careful at this point, for the mind plays tricks on itself: it will dress up its personal resentments in garments of righteous and religious indignation so that they will pass muster before our religious self. Many a man fights "for principle," when he is fighting only for personal pique and pride.

But righteous indignation, even when it is simon-pure righteous, should not be kept overnight: "Be ye angry, and sin not"; "Let not the sun go down upon your wrath." Here is an anger that sins not, and yet it must not be kept overnight lest it corrode the soul into bitterness.

O God, give me clear insight and courage to see myself truly, for I may be cloaking my resentments with garments of piety, and I know these resentments are deadly in whatever form they gain a footing in my life. I would harbor no dangerous Trojan-horse enemies within me. Help me then to be completely honest with myself. Amen.

Gen. 49:7; Eccles. 7:9; Col. 3:8

THE DISRUPTIVE EFFECTS OF ANGER

Now that we have seen the possibilities of righteous anger for good, let us look at the possibilities of resentments for evil.

There was a time when men thought that to get angry and hold resentments was just too bad; holding resentments made people difficult to get along with but nothing much happened except just that. We know now the fallacy of that belief, for in the cold white light of science the effects of anger are being revealed.

First, upon the intestinal tract. Some doctors put a tube down through the nostrils of a man into his stomach. They tested the contents of his stomach according to the states of his mind. When he was in good humor, digestion went on normally; but after they had purposely made him angry, digestion completely stopped. Only when they brought him back into good humor would digestion start again. This fact was at the basis of a doctor's advice when he said: "You ought to feel good-minded when you eat. If you don't feel good-minded, you'd better lay off from your eating."

A doctor could not find any physical basis for the constant vomiting of one of his patients. One day she incidentally remarked that her mother-in-law was coming to visit her at Thanksgiving. Taking this chance remark as a clue, he sent for the husband, persuaded him to wire his mother suggesting the postponement of her visit, told the wife that the mother-in-law was not coming, and the vomiting stopped. The resentments had upset her digestion.

The doctors tell us that stomach ulcers are often caused by anger and resentments, and that they will return even after they are cut out by operation, the edges of the wound becoming ulcerated again, if the resentments are not eliminated.

Such scientific revelation makes it quite clear that the stomach in its very constitution is made for good will and not for ill will.

Anger may cause arthritis. A mother-in-law did not like her son-in-law, whom she visited once a year. Every time she went to visit him she developed arthritis, and every time she came home again she was well.

O God, my Father, I see that good will brings harmony and peace and effectiveness, and that ill will makes for disharmony, upset, and ineffectiveness—it lays a paralyzing hand on soul and body. Then save me from any clinging resentments. Help me to pull them up by the roots. Amen.

Ps. 37:8; Eccles. 7:9; Col. 3:8; Prov. 16:32

ANGER IS POISON

In yesterday's study we saw that the stomach is made for good will and not for ill will. Good will "sets up" the stomach and ill will upsets it! What is true of the stomach is true of every other portion of the body. A counselor tells me that he knows of no single thing that causes more havoc in the human body than resentments. For resentment is poison.

A doctor was baffled over the cause of sickness in a baby. One day in visiting the child he came into the home while the parents were quarreling, and saw the mother suckling the baby meanwhile. The doctor threw up his hands and said, "Now I know what is the matter with your baby —you are poisoning it by this ill will." The poison was in the mother's milk, put there by anger. In two days the child was dead.

A missionary in China did not want the wife of the doctor to visit her when she had her baby. The knowledge of this upset the doctor's wife—there were strained relations. The flow of the mother's milk stopped two days after the child was born. The upset with the doctor's wife was responsible for the stoppage.

A doctor in the Mayo Clinic told me that he could see a stomach ulcer healing before his very eyes on the X-ray pictures when a patient surrendered her resentments.

A pastor had his heart set on a certain appointment. When he did not get it, his wife became embittered and ill and died shortly afterward, and he himself became spiritually so upset that he left the ministry. Resentment killed the body of one and the soul of the other. It was poison.

It is becoming more and more clear that qualities of character determine frequently the physical health of the person. We do not mean to say that they determine all diseases, for there are contagious diseases and they are real, and there are structural diseases and they, too, are real. But in all probability 60 per cent of diseases root in the mental and spiritual.

O God, I see that I pass on to my body the health and unhealth of my mind and soul. I want, then, to be healthy in soul and in mind. Therefore I would take into my very being the health of Thy mind. Let me be saturated with Thy ways and Thy thought that I may live in radiant health through and through. Amen.

SUBCONSCIOUS RESENTMENTS

They tell us that if a rattlesnake is cornered it will become so angry that it will bite itself. That is exactly what all harboring of hates and resentments against others is—a biting of oneself. We think we are harming others in holding these spites and hates, but the deepest harm is to ourselves; for many times these resentments are dropped into the unconscious, the lid is shut down on them, and there they work their unconscious havoc. Unconscious resentments are often just as potent for disruption as conscious ones.

A young woman could not raise her arm, which seemed paralyzed. It was found that, when angry, she had a secret desire to strike her mother. When the reason for the paralysis was shown and she gave up her resentments against her mother, the arm was restored to normal health again.

A similar case was that of a man who was constantly falling from his horse. He wondered why he couldn't stay on. It was discovered that he had a secret desire to commit suicide, and this falling was the outer sign of that secret desire. When he gave up the hidden resentment he held against life, then he ceased falling from his horse.

A pastor and his wife had a disagreement over their pastoral appointment—he wanted to move, and she didn't. When the bishop made the appointment and moved them she was very bitter and resentful—especially as the husband, wanting to avoid a crisis, stayed away and let her do most of the packing up! After some weeks of harboring this resentment she became ill—she could not get her breath. She went to the new appointment an invalid and rather resigned herself to a life of invalidism. When she saw that the harbored resentments were at the basis of her illness—had paralyzed the nerve fibers which control breathing and that she literally was choking herself to death by her resentments—she surrendered the whole thing to God, became reconciled to the new place, arose out of her invalidism, and is today a radiant, happy, and useful person.

O Christ, I now begin to see why Thou wert always urging man to get rid of anger and resentments and ill will, for Thou didst see by Thy penetrating eye the havoc wrought within the whole person by his hates. Forgive us that we have not seen. And forgive us that, after seeing, we do not surrender them. Amen.

Acts 13: 10, 11; Ps. 34:21; Gen. 19:9–11

ANGER DIMS THE VISION

We saw yesterday that resentments, though unconscious, may be just as havoc-producing as conscious resentments. Ofttimes we consciously use the illnesses produced by resentments to harm the person against whom we hold resentments. A girl in India was constantly having fits. One was so violent that her mother-in-law was visibly frightened. When the mother-in-law was out of the room, the girl whispered to the doctors, "I'll have these fits as long as I have to live with her."

Someone asked a husband why he got drunk, and he replied, indicating his wife, "It is the only way I have of getting even with her."

Sometimes these resentments are unconsciously used against others. A girl of twenty-one walked in her sleep, a habit which, of course, greatly upset her mother. It was found that she was holding a grudge against her mother and was taking this unconscious method of getting even. When the girl saw the connection between the sleepwalking and her resentments, she confessed the whole matter to her mother, made it right between them, and the sleepwalking stopped.

Resentments and anger not only dim the spiritual vision so that the inner life becomes blurred; but they also literally dim the physical vision. Some doctors experimented with rats and found that after the rats had been kept angry for an extended period of time, opaque films came over their eyes. The report continues: "One realizes the picturesqueness and accuracy of the old expression 'blind with rage,' and the lesson to be learned is to avoid being angry. As the children say, 'One might freeze that way.' " (*Southern Medical Journal,* November, 1940, p. 1237.)

An optometrist tells me that he can never examine the eyes of an angry man—such a man literally cannot see straight. As Dante puts it, "The wrathful travel in a cloud." They do.

Neither spiritually, mentally, nor physically can those who hold resentments and angers see straight. Their outlook on life is distorted because their inner condition is out-of-joint through hate.

O God, we see that Thou hast made us, in the inner constitution of our being, for love. Forgive us for having introduced into the delicate fabric of our inner being the havoc of hate. We are made for Thee, and Thy way is love. Help us to live Thy way. Amen.

Luke 23:28; Acts 21:13; Jer. 31:15–16

RESENTMENTS RESULTING IN SELF-PITY

A woman, involved in an automobile accident, suffered a broken neck and a severed nerve at the base of her spine which left her lower limbs useless. She is doomed to a wheel chair the balance of her days after terrible initial suffering. But she has met the whole tragedy in a spirit of faith, confidence, and good will. Hence she is radiant—in spite of! At the table in the institution where she stays she presides as a queen—and does so from a wheel chair. Depressed patients are assigned to her table so that her very presence may cheer them up. She is on top of her circumstances. But her husband reacted differently. He was unhurt by the accident, except in soul. He became embittered, held resentments against the man who was driving. The resentments have spoiled his lifework. One tragedy occurred to both—they reacted differently. One emerged with a broken neck, but with her spirit intact; the other with his body intact, but with a broken soul. Resentments broke him.

A well-educated woman with every opportunity before her is frustrated and defeated, because she resented her sister's getting married and leaving her unmarried. The manifestation of the resentment was self-pity, resentment that she was left alone in the world. Her life has been rendered impossible to herself and to others by that basic resentment.

It is obvious that to hold hate and resentments is to throw a monkey wrench into the machinery of life. Structurally you are made for positive good will, in other words, for the Christian way of love. When you try the other way, then the machinery of life breaks down, or at least works so badly that it leaves you exhausted and ineffective. Hate is sand in the machinery of life; love is oil—and life works better with oil than with sand. The lovers love others—and themselves; the haters hate others—and themselves.

O God, my Father, I have now come point-blank to the necessity of getting rid of all resentments, all hates. If I live with my hates, I shall not be able to live with myself. So now I ask for help. I shall need Thy help to get rid of these things which have become rooted in me, which have become me. I offer them all to Thee. Amen.

Col. 3:8; Eph. 4:31–32; 1 Tim. 2:8

HOW NOT TO DEAL WITH RESENTMENTS

We have seen how disruptive resentments and hate are to the total person. If we are to live abundantly, we must get rid of them at all costs. But how?

First of all, we must look at some of the ways we are *not* to use in getting rid of our hates and resentments. (1) *We must not suppress them into forgetfulness and try to act as though we no longer have them.* This treatment drives them only into the subconscious mind where they work as unconscious resentments. There they will produce conflict and disturbance, the person scarcely knowing what is causing the upset. He will be under nervous strain and will probably lay his upset to all sorts of causes—everything except the real cause. To suppress the resentments does not get rid of them, for then they simply work their havoc at deeper and more dangerous levels. No one can play tricks on life and escape the consequences. He must bring the resentments to the surface and face them honestly, with no subterfuges, no evasions, no suppressions. He must not push his resentments down into the subconscious mind.

(2) *If we avoid suppression, we must not try the contrary method—that of expressing our hatreds and resentments.* Some psychiatrists prescribe this way, lest suppression set up a complex in the subconscious; and there is no doubt that we can get temporary relief by giving the other person "a piece of our mind."

A young lady who had been tense and frustrated came away from the telephone quite relieved and elated after having told someone just what she thought of him. Her outburst did relieve dammed-up resentments. A woman who had pains, first at the base of her spine, was asked by her doctor what it was that was bothering her inwardly. To which question she blurted out, "Well, I think I'd be well if I could tell my husband just once to go to——" Perhaps she would have been relieved momentarily, but the resentments would fill up again and be ready for another spillover. No; expression is not the remedy—it is merely dealing with a symptom instead of with the disease.

O God, my heavenly Father, I am dealing with something too devastating to try to heal it lightly or to temporize. Help me to go to the roots and find release there. But I will need more than Thy help—I will need Thy grace. Help me to take Thy grace for this task. Amen.

Titus 3:3; 1 Pet. 4:8–9; 3:8–9

FURTHER SUGGESTIONS OF HOW NOT TO DEAL WITH RESENTMENTS

Yesterday we considered two ways we are *not* to use in dealing with resentments and hates, namely, suppression and expression. To suppress them means to create a sore boil at the center of our subconscious being. To express them makes us sore boils on the body of our social relationships. Moreover, if we give people "a piece of our mind," we shall probably lose our own peace of mind!

(3) *Nor is there much use in trying to run away from circumstances which give rise to resentments.* A doctor found a patient nervous, unable to sleep, collapsed. He asked if his home relations were adjusted and happy, and was told that they were. Then, as an afterthought, the patient replied that he and his mother-in-law didn't get on. That was the point of conflict. The doctor sent him and his wife off for a vacation, away from the mother-in-law. Good, but not good enough; for while there would be temporary respite and a letting down of tensions, yet they would tighten up again as the prospect loomed up of having to meet the same situation. The remedy was a mere temporizing, for the relief was only temporary.

(4) *To try to do as one woman said she did is good, but also not good enough*: "When filled with resentments I would go to the piano and bang out my resentments through Mozart's Sonatas, with apologies to Mozart." That would give temporary relief and act as a feeling drainer, but it did not tackle the causes.

(5) *Nor will it do to nurse our resentments in our minds.* That only makes them worse. They will carry over into the whole of life and spoil it. One woman said that when she entered the quiet time for prayer, the only thing she could do when she became quiet was "to chew on my resentments." The quiet time simply brought to the surface what was a continuous face—a nursed grievance.

All of these methods are attempts to heal over a boil. And to heal over a boil is a dangerous act—it may drive the poison in. The poison must be drawn up and out.

O my Father, I am tempted to do everything about these resentments—everything except the one thing I must do: get them up and out. But I shall resist that temptation and be inexorable with myself. I shall need Thy help, for I cannot get them up alone. The roots have gone deep. Help me. Amen.

Luke 6:37; 23:34; Eph. 4:31–32; Matt. 18:21–35

FORGIVING FOR CHRIST'S SAKE

Perhaps you are saying, "If the methods just discussed are not the way to overcome resentments and hates, then what is the way?" A young Chinese student looked into my face at the close of an address and said, "Please teach me how to love the Japanese." The iron had gone deep; so it was a real problem with him. An Armenian said the same thing to me: "How can I forgive the Turks?"

I could tell him only how one Armenian girl had been enabled to forgive a Turk. She and her brother had been attacked by Turks in a lane, and while she had escaped by climbing over a wall, her brother had been brutally killed before her eyes. She was a nurse, and later on while nursing in the hospital recognized one of her patients as the very Turkish soldier who had murdered her brother. Her first feeling was: Revenge! He was very ill, just hovering between life and death. The slightest neglect, and he would die. And no one would know. His life was absolutely in her hands. But instead of revenge she decided for Christ's sake to forgive him. She fought for his life and won, nursing him back to health.

When he was convalescent, she told him who she was. The Turkish soldier looked at her in astonishment and said, "Then why didn't you let me die, when you had me in your power?" "I couldn't," answered the girl. "I just couldn't, for I am a Christian, and my own Master forgave His enemies who crucified Him. I must do the same, for His sake." "Well," said the hardened Turk in astonishment, "if that is what it means to be a Christian, I want to be one."

You can do what that Armenian girl did: You can forgive for Christ's sake. No matter how bitterly wronged you may have been, nevertheless, for His sake you can forgive the wrong and have only positive good will toward those who have wronged you. It isn't easy, but it can be done—by His help.

O God, the wrong has entered deep into my spirit. In my own strength I cannot forgive. But I am willing to be made willing. Take my willingness and add Thy power, and then I shall be able to forgive. For through Thee I can do anything—yes, anything; even this. Amen.

Acts 7:59–60; Matt. 14:3–12

THE BASIS OF RESENTMENTS:
AN UNSURRENDERED SELF

While the central and fundamental motive for forgiving injuries against us is that God forgives us, and we therefore copy God as His children, nevertheless there are minor motives and techniques which we can use in dealing with resentments.

(1) *Remember that at the basis of most resentments is a touchy, unsurrendered self*. The fact that we have been able to hold the resentment shows that there is a self that is oversensitive because unsurrendered to the will of God. When surrendered to the will of God we throw off resentments as a healthy skin throws off disease germs. Unless there is inner disease or an abrasion of the skin, the disease germs can get no foothold. So, when resentments have gained a footing, it shows that there is a raw, sensitive self underneath that has become a culture soil for the rooting and growth of resentments. Suspect a self that can grow resentments—it is probably diseased with self-centeredness.

(2) *Raise the question with yourself as to whether your resentments aren't rooted in imaginary slights, insults, and wrongs*. A self-centered person can imagine a group is talkng about him when that group is talking about everything else but; he can read into actions and statements meanings never intended; he can go around with a suspicious, looking-for-slights attitude, and will find imaginary ones aplenty. A sensitive person can by his very mental attitude throw people around him into unnatural, closed-in attitudes which he interprets as intentional hurts and slights; but all the time he is oblivious of the fact that his own attitudes of self-centered sensitiveness created the very things in others against which he reacts.

Remember that "when you go around with a chip on your shoulder, the chip is probably from the block above."

O God, my Father, help me to see myself clearly, for I defend myself; I gather self-defensive arguments around myself as a magnet. Let me then lay this resentment-gathering self at Thy feet for cleansing and release. In Jesus' name. Amen.

Rom. 12:17–21; Matt. 5:38–48

DISSOLVE RESENTMENTS THROUGH PRAYER AND APPRECIATION

We continue our steps to get rid of resentments and hates. (3) *Every time the name of the person against whom you are tempted to hold a resentment is presented to your mind, breathe a prayer for him.* Meet every invading resentment with a barrage of prayer. It was said of John Forman, a saintly missionary, that all his thoughts of his friends turned to prayer. Make the rule in your mind that, invariably, all your thoughts of your enemies, real or imaginary, are to become prayers for them. Make the mind understand that and admit no exceptions. Soon you will have no enemies, for you will have no enmity. Prayer dissolves enmity as certain bacteria dissolve filth and turn it into clear water.

(4) *Say everything good you can about the person or persons with whom you are unfriendly.* The probabilities are there are many fine things in them. Fasten your mind on those fine points instead of on the resentment points. The outcome will be, in all probability, that the good will so overbalance the bad that you will find yourself thinking more and more of the overwhelming good and less and less of the insignificant bad.

(5) *When you do have to sepak of the faults of a person, don't say, "I don't like that person."* Rather, say, "I don't like certain things in that person, and they are these." After stating those faults, proceed to say, "But I do like these things in him," and name them. End on the positive note. Negative thinking makes a negative person; positive thinking makes a positive person. If I have mentioned mothers-in-law in a derogatory way in many of my instances, let me end my thought of them as mothers-in-love, as one couple does.

(6) *Remember that fastening upon other people's faults is usually a defense-mechanism.* By doing so you are probably attempting to lift yourself up by pushing them down. It won't succeed. In mentally picking flaws in others you create a worse flaw in yourself—you become a sensitive, critical person, like the thing you habitually center upon.

God, my Father, I would be rid of all that corrodes my soul. I know that my attitudes of resentment and criticism eat like acid into my moral nature. I would ask Thee to deliver me completely from the last tiny root of resentment. Root it out. Amen.

Luke 22:32; Matt. 5:25–26; Gal. 6:1–2; II Cor. 2:7

LOVING PEOPLE FOR WHAT THEY MAY BECOME

We continue climbing the ladder out of the pit of resentments and hate. (7) *If, in going over the things in the person against whom you hold resentments, you find little to love or admire, then love and admire him for what he may be.* You do not have to be dishonest in your thinking and like the things a person does. But you are now committed as a Christian, and you love people as Christ does—He loves them not for what they have been, or are, but for what they can be. Your love then becomes real and redemptive.

(8) *If there is a sudden flare-up and a consequent breakdown in relationships, get into the habit of settling disagreements at once.* Don't let them get cold and become fixed in thought and attitude. Jesus said, "Agree with thine adversary quickly." This is sound, psychologically and morally. I know of one couple who have a beautiful wedded life. Perhaps one of the secrets of their happiness is that they decided, when they married, never to leave a room in which any disagreement should take place until they had settled the matter. Their difficulties, therefore, always ended in laughs, because neither of them could go until an agreement was reached—they were prisoners of their own agreement, and there was no open door except into good will.

(9) *See if there isn't a reason in the other person for the things you resent in him.* A very outstanding surgeon would see red every time he saw W.P.A. workers. Their slowness, their dawdling got on his nerves; and he was fast developing a complex, for every time he saw them his face would flush and his ears go red. Then one day he noticed them at quitting time, putting away their tools with the same slowness. "Why," he said, "these men are sick from undernourishment, from lack of vitamins, and from parasites." He set himself to rehabilitate them, and in doing so helped himself—he lost his own complex.

O God, I come to Thee to gain understanding sympathy. I am resentful because I don't understand. Give me clear insight and sympathy that I may read in the lives of others the things that make them unattractive to me. And when I understand, help me to forgive. For Jesus' sake. Amen.

Matt. 11:25–26; Luke 6:37; 17:3–4; Eph. 4:32

FINAL STEPS FOR OVERCOMING RESENTMENTS

(10) *Go out each day to do some positive good to the person against whom you hold resentments.* Wear down his hate and opposition with your own good will. A Japanese student and a Chinese student were in the same university, and the Japanese disliked the Chinese intensely. But when the Japanese was ill, the Chinese brought food to him every day. This kind attention broke down the enmity, and they became fast friends.

A man and his wife were constantly quarreling. The quarrel usually began over the radio—she wanted music, and he wanted the news. Then one day he was changed and let God into his little soul. When he returned home, and the tension point came, he walked to the radio and turned on the music. His wife looked at him in surprise and said, "But this is the news hour." "Yes," he replied, "I know, but I thought you would enjoy the music." She could scarcely believe her ears, but responded by getting up and turning on the news! From that moment they solved their problems by thinking of the other person first.

(11) *Be inwardly "too glad and too great to be the enemy of any man."* Be so preoccupied with good will that you haven't room for ill will. Dr. George Carver, the great Negro scientist and saint, has risen to fame through his chemical discoveries and service to the farmers of the South. Someone asked him to reveal the name of the university which had accepted him as a student and then, on discovering he was a Negro, had refused him admittance. Dr. Carver consistently refused to tell, passing the incident off as nothing. He had what somebody called "the peace that passeth not only all understanding, but all misunderstanding." Someone said to me, "I don't think you know when you are insulted." I replied, "I am not looking for insults and so don't see them." When Jesus announced His program at Nazareth, He read from Isaiah until He came to the words, "the day of vengeance of our God." Then He closed the book. You do the same. Leave vengeance to God—use only redemptive good will.

O God, my Father, nothing that anyone can do against me compares with what I have done against Thee. Thou hast forgiven me—help me to forgive others. And help me to forgive graciously, not grudgingly, for Thou hast forgiven me so graciously. For Jesus' sake. Amen.

Prov. 29:25; Matt. 8:26; Ps. 27:1–5

THE FOURTH ENEMY: FEAR

We have looked at three of the fifteen enemies of the human personality. We now come to the fourth: *Worry, anxiety, fear.*

Almost every evil is some perverted good. Worry, anxiety, and fear are perverted good. There is an instinct within us to look ahead, to plan, to think about meeting possible situations before they come. This capacity of foresight is probably one of the basic reasons for man's rise beyond the animal. The animal has only a limited capacity to foresee; man has a very great capacity to foresee. So the animal stops at a dead end, and man marches on to infinite goals.

That capacity to foresee and foreplan and forestall is the power that lifts us out of the "is" into the "can be"—it is the secret of progress. And as such it must be cultivated. Without it we sink back to the animal. The will to live must be projected not only into the "now," but also into the "to be." We must master today, and we must master tomorrow. Jesus commended this: "Well, the master praised the dishonest factor for looking ahead; for the children of this world look further ahead, in dealing with their own generation, than the children of Light." (Luke 16:8, Moffatt.) A lack of intelligent planning makes us the prisoners of today, instead of the pioneers of tomorrow.

Christians, above all others, are people of the long view, the long purpose, and the long plan. They plan how to live today, how to live tomorrow, how to live forever. And they plan this for all people, for they have not only the long view; they have also the wide view. They think in terms of the world as a whole. The idea that the Christian is a lackadaisical simpleton looking at the moment because he is afraid to look at the morrow, a human ostrich with his fearful head in the sand of today because he is afraid to look at the morrow, is false. We are to love God "with all thy mind," and a part of the mind is foresight. Therefore, the Christian must cultivate this quality of intelligent planning.

O God, Thou hast taken long views, for the millions of years of history tell us Thou art working out Thy long-range purposes. Help us to catch the sweep of Thy mind and the glory of Thy purposes and become a part of them. Amen.

Prov. 14:27; 19:23; Luke 21:26; Heb. 2:15

ANXIETY AS ASSET AND LIABILITY

We saw yesterday that the Christian is one who cares about the past, the present, and the future—he is not a lotus-eater. The fact is that he cares more than anyone else, for he is in the process of being sensitized on a world scale. This is his greatest asset. It gives him drive, direction, and determination. It makes him a progressive person. All other things being equal, the Christian should be the most progressive person on earth. He is awakened in every fiber of his being, and he is a man of the open road.

But if this awareness is his greatest asset, it may also become his greatest liability. The fact that he is sensitive and aware to himself and to all men may make him worry. If so, then his light has turned to darkness. For worry and anxiety and fear can block the whole process of progress and paralyze and disrupt the personality. Up to a certain point, fear on the part of a surgeon may make him more skillful and careful lest he cut in wrong places, but fear pushed beyond a certain point could paralyze him. There is a healthy fear that gives us skill and drive. There is an unhealthy fear that takes away both skill and drive—it inhibits us. "The fear of the Lord is the beginning of wisdom," but, "I was afraid, and went and hid thy talent." Both are profoundly true—there is a fear that is wisdom, and a fear that makes one bury his life talents.

Fear, like any other drive, has to be brought under control and used for constructive purposes. Out of control, it turns into worry and anxiety and becomes destructive to itself and others. "Fret not—it only leads to evil." (Psalm 37:8, Moffatt.) Or, as another version puts it, "it tendeth only to evil-doing"—its whole tendency is destructive rather than constructive. Jesus says this new life is often "choked with worries." (Luke 8:14, Moffatt.) The probabilities are that fear, worry, and anxiety are the greatest single trinity of evils a man can take into his life. He must root them out at all costs.

O God, I fear the fear that gets rootage in my life. I am anxious about the anxiety that infects me. I am worried about the worry. Give me deliverance from them. Help me to complete freedom from any cramping inhibition and fear. Amen.

Ps. 37:1, 7–8; Job 3:25; John 14:1, 27

FEAR AND DISEASE

A doctor said to me, "Fears are the most disruptive thing we can have." And all life bears this out. I know a lady who is in a mortal dread of germs. She stays inside her house, the prisoner of her own fear, lest she meet one. She doesn't realize that the fear itself is ten times more deadly than the germ. Besides, if she had a confident attitude toward life, germs would probably not get a foothold in her life—her very confidence and faith would act as an antiseptic. Her fears become a culture ground for the germs she fears. "The thing which I greatly feared is come upon me," said Job; and that was not chance, but cause and effect.

A teacher had a basic fear which brought on a stomach ulcer. When she got rid of the fear, she got rid of the ulcer. Doctors wanted to operate on a friend of mine for cancer or ulcer of the stomach. The facts were these: After he had failed in business, worry had stopped the gastric juices. When he saw the cause and surrendered his worries to God, he gained 30 pounds in two months. A Y.M.C.A. secretary came up to me at the close of an address and said, "I am an illustration of what you have said. I'm tense and worried and bear on my mind all the troubles of the world. Hence I am fighting stomach ulcers all the time." He will never be well until he relaxes and surrenders all those strained worries to God.

Dr. Felix Cunha says that "the incidence of stomach ulcers goes up and down with the stock market." Investigation showed that when the Dow-Jones averages on the stock market skidded down, the number of businessmen with upset stomachs went up. Worry would bring an over-acidity of the stomach, and that in turn would upset the digestive tract.

Men of old saw the connection between worry and disease: "Banish all worries from your mind, and keep your body free from pain." (Ecclesiastes 11:10, Moffatt.)

O God, my Father, I see that in my inmost being I am made for confidence and trust and not for worry and anxiety. Thou hast fashioned me for faith and not for fear. Help me then to surrender to what I am made for—faith. Let me this day walk forth in confident faith, afraid of nothing. In Jesus' name. Amen.

Rom. 8:15; John 7:13; 9:22; 20:19

FEAR IS COSTLY

Sometimes fears are not basic, but marginal. Even so, they can upset the rest of the life. A woman went through surgical operations, a fire, even chased out a burglar from her house with a gun, and yet her life was tormented with the fear of what her neighbors might say of her. Here was a marginal fear which pushed out a basic courage.

A woman had a fear of having a cancer. Her mother had had one, and she kept saying, "I am just the image of my mother. I'm so like her that I am going to get a cancer as she did." As a result of this brooding fear she was afflicted with constipation. There was this difference between her and her mother: the mother had had ten children. She had none! Said the doctor, "She will never get rid of that constipation unless she gets rid of her useless fears." Her useless fears had tied her up not merely physically, but mentally and spiritually as well—a tied-up personality, of which the constipation was a symbol.

A young minister began to complain of tightness of the chest, and developed a hacking cough. The doctors found no physical reason. Then he began to complain of severe pain in the lower bowel, saying he had a cancer there. Examinations by several doctors found nothing physically wrong. He resigned the ministry, and sits around moping and groaning most of the time. His mentality is giving away under the strain, and yet he is basically sound. It is the fear that is upsetting him. The fear itself is the disease. For fear is sand in the machinery of life.

A woman sent a friend of mine to buy gladiolas, but being tight-fisted she repented of the impulse to buy this beauty. When my friend returned, the woman was in an agitated state of mind. She went to bed ill and was in the hands of doctors for weeks, spending a hundred times as much on doctors and medicine as she had on the gladiolas. Fear is costly.

My Father, I see that fear is indeed costly. It is so costly I cannot keep it. But I cannot easily get rid of it, for it has put its roots within me. Help me tear it up root and branch. Or hast Thou a better way? I follow. In Jesus' name. Amen.

Luke 8:26–31; Ps. 31:13; 53:5

HOME-GROWN FEARS

Fear attacks the digestive system in a great number of subtle ways. A mother had a daughter who was shy. Wanting her to "come out," she arranged a party for her, against the daughter's will. The daughter was afraid of people, and before the party she became violently ill and went to bed. Never again did the mother try to get rid of fears in this frontal-attack method. She built up confidence in other ways.

Some friends brought a man into one of my meetings. He was afraid of crowds, suffering from ochlophobia. When he got to the door, he tried to run away. But they insisted and took him in. During the whole service he sat full of fear, with perspiration rolling down his pale and clammy face. At the close he said, "I'm glad to get out of here." The fear of crowds was an obsession. But there was nothing to fear except his fear. That fear was a disease.

At one of the maneuvers of the West Point cadets some of the students for a prank put some chestnut burrs under the saddle of a horse. The cadet riding the horse was thrown twenty-five times on a twenty-five-mile ride. The experience filled him with fears and shock, so that he became a wreck. The gland secretion was so upset by the shock and fears that he could not move when placed in a certain position. If he was stood up and his arm raised, he could not put it down. Only by a course of mental training which helped him past the fears and shock did the youth return to normal health.

In the last World War one of the amazing discoveries made by the doctors during the draft examinations was that so many perfectly healthy young men had all their lives been convinced that they had heart or kidney trouble or some other malady and had feared to undertake arduous occupations for that reason. With very few exceptions, says Dr. Albert Wiggam, their fears had been started by hearing symptoms discussed at home. They were home-grown fears.

To implant fears in the minds of children is a crime against the child. Parents try to rule the child by fear, and then fear rules the child.

O God, our Father, we have filled Thy world and our hearts with fears—needless, devastating fears. Help us, we pray Thee, to find release from these fears and power over them, for they are not our real selves—they are an importation. In Jesus' name. Amen.

Prov. 29:25; Eccles. 12:5; Luke 21:26; II Cor. 7:5

PHYSICAL EFFECTS OF FEAR

The physiological effects of fear and worry have been scientifically studied. Doctors have put a tube down the nostrils of a patient into his stomach and have measured the effects of states of mind on the stomach secretions. The secretion of hydrochloric acid often doubled during states of worrying. One man was found worrying because a fellow worker had died unexpectedly, and he had an obsession that he would share the same fate. His stomach trouble had started after this worry began, and after he had tried to conceal it from everyone—even his wife. The stomach of another sufferer showed rushes of acid when he was telling how his wife dominated him. One sufferer even had a flow of the extra acid when sound asleep but dreaming of his troubles.

A young man had been jilted while church bells were ringing. Ever after whenever anything was mentioned connected with the church, such as the name "bishop," he would be upset.

Another young man was afraid of crowds, and so did not want a public wedding. Three times he fainted before the wedding could take place; the fourth time he fainted after it had taken place. Two things emerged as the basis of his fainting: fear of crowds, and fear of being dominated by his fiancée, who was very insistent on going through with the public ceremony. The fainting after the ceremony came as the result of fear of domination.

A man who had worked faithfully and long to get promotion in his office was so upset when the turning point came, which would decide whether he was to be office superintendent or not, that when he actually got the promotion he was unable to take it, for worry had so upset his heart that he had to go to the hospital instead of to the superintendency. Worry and anxiety snatched the prize from his hand and left him a broken man.

A doctor who suffered from stomach ulcers told me that worry and fear produced more stomach ulcers than any other cause.

O God, I see that I, too, have lost much of life's fullness and power on account of worry and fear. I see that I cannot rise to my full powers until I have shed all fears and forebodings and march forth to meet life in triumphant faith. Help me to do this. In Jesus' name. Amen.

Isa. 8:12; 11:6–9; 35:4

THE EFFECT OF FEAR ON ANIMALS AND CHILDREN

Fears and anxieties upset the animal kingdom as well as the human kingdom. When bad dogs are around cows, the cows will often refuse to give their milk; and even when they do give it, that milk, fed to calves, will cause colic. So "milk from contented cows" is no mere slogan—it is a necessity. One pastor, who treated his Jersey cow well and had a real affection for her, found that the babies of the neighborhood brought up on the milk of this cow thrived in a way in which other babies did not. Treating the cow in a Christian way had produced a better quality of milk.

A chicken fancier told me that after the Fourth of July with its explosion of firecrackers, many eggs had to be thrown out, for candling showed blood spots on them which had been produced by fear. The same thing happened when an airplane flew very low over the chickens. The father of a friend of mine was a chicken fancier; and when he died the hens would not lay for a long time until they got used to the new keeper. They were frightened and worried. Experiments show that superior turkeys cannot be raised unless they are treated kindly and are in charge of one person, who always dresses in a certain way. A stranger frightens and worries them, and they become stunted.

If worry and anxiety can stunt chickens and turkeys, they can stunt children as well. A schoolteacher told me that when she is worried and upset the children do not study well, and they quarrel with one another. The scholastic level is lower on those days, and it goes up when she is inwardly harmonious.

We have spent a week on the effects of worry, fear, and anxiety; and perhaps some of you have had a growing fear that I would continue too long with the discussion of the effects of anxiety, instead of going on to think about the remedy. I have no apology, for the first step in the remedy of fear is to see fear as the fearsome thing it is.

O God, now that I see, and see clearly, the devastation that worry and fear can bring, I would turn with eager heart and mind from the devastation to the deliverance. Oh, give me an expectant soul—a soul that believes that deliverance is at hand; I have but to take it. In Jesus' name. Amen.

Acts 5:1–11

FIRST STEP IN DELIVERANCE: COMPLETE HONESTY

We now turn to the more joyous task of setting up a ladder so that the defeated and harassed may climb to peace and poise and power.

(1) *Let us clearly understand that any step we may suggest is to be an honest step and real.* There will be no attempt to deceive the mind, no effort to entice it into entering a fool's paradise of make-believe. No one can play tricks on the universe—least of all on the universe of mind. There can be no waving of a wand over fears, no telling the mind that they are no more. That is the way of opium. It has an inevitable letdown. The Christian way is the way of complete honesty. The verse that most clearly expresses the spirit of this way is: "See and do *not* be alarmed." (Matthew 24:6, Moffatt.) Jesus did not try to teach men to win release from alarms by refusing to see them. He told them to "see"—to look fears straight in the face and yet not to be alarmed. His way is the way of open-eyed honesty.

(2) *Be sure you want to give up the thing you are afraid of.* Very often your fears produce bodily ills which in turn determine your life strategy. Some people use their illnesses to gain attention or to gain power over others. A cockney girl had a large purple lump on her forehead. This lump had come as the result of a great fear. When couseled by Dr. Fox she surrendered the fear, and the lump disappeared. On seeing her again Dr. Fox remarked about the lump being gone. "But," said the girl, grabbing her middle, "I've got terrible pains in my stomach." She was afraid to let go of her fears, for she lived by the attention which these illnesses brought her. So she invented the stomachache. She was afraid she would be without attention and without sympathy if she should let go all her maladies. She "enjoyed" bad health!

I know a family that lived by recounting to one another their various ailments, each bidding for sympathy from the others. They nearly all died before their time. The one member that survived found interests outside that circle of self-commiseration.

O God, I want to be completely delivered from fear and from the results of fear. I know how fears mark my soul and body. Help me then to be perfectly whole. My subconscious mind plays tricks on me. Save me to complete honesty. Amen.

Luke 8:50; 18:4; 18:41–42; John 5:6; 4:49–53

THE WILL TO BE WELL

Yesterday we saw that the first step toward deliverance from fears and anxieties was to desire to be free. We may subconsciously desire the attention and sympathy which our maladies bring. If some people couldn't talk about their ills, just what would they talk about? You remember, the definition of a bore as "a man who talks about his rheumatism when you want to talk about yours." Talking about one's maladies focuses attention on one's self, even though that self is a shabby, shattered self. Still, the center of interest is the self; and when one is self-centered, he will use any means to gain attention.

So Jesus went straight to the heart of self-centeredness when He confronted the sick with this question: "Wilt thou be made whole?" "Do you really want to be well? If not, I cannot do a thing for you." The will to be well had to be there. Dr. Everett C. Drash of the University Virginia told me that he operated on a schoolteacher for tuberculosis, and she died. But there was no apparent reason for her death until her relatives found among her papers a statement to a friend that she was convinced she would die. Her lack of faith had killed in her the will to live.

That brings us to the third step: (3) *Will to be well.* Throw your will on the side of deliverance. Just as there is a will to believe, so there is a will to be well. In contrast to the schoolteacher who died for lack of will to be well, there is the case of a mother who died of tuberculosis and left six small children. Her sister stepped in to take care of the children, and she, too, caught the infection. She, too, was slated to die, for this happened in the days before modern science had begun to cope successfully with this plague. Instead, she willed to live and raise that family. It was her life task, and she would perform it. She had one of the children stand in the corner of her room each day, so that she could see the child and say to herself, "I must live to raise this family." She did live, and she raised the family, and today is one of the most radiant and useful persons I know. Whether you seek deliverance from illness or from fear, will to be well.

My Father, I cannot will to be well unless I am reinforced at the center of my being. For I am inwardly flabby. Help me, then, to take the strength of Thy will into the weakness of my own. In Jesus' name. Amen.

John 16:33; I John 5:4–5; Isa. 41:10; 43:5

EVERY FOE YOU FACE IS
A DEFEATED FOE

When you will to be well the whole of the universe of reality is then behind your will. And the whole of the universe of reality wills your release, and provides for that release. This fact is summed up in the words of Jesus: "In the world ye shall have tribulation: but be of good cheer; I have overcome the world." Here is an open-eyed frankness that does not deny the fact of a world of tribulation in which we must live—this world of tribulation which lies around us and in us. And yet, after looking at it, with all its brutality and its power to hurt, He says: "Be of good cheer; I have overcome the world." In other words: every foe you face is a defeated foe.

That brings us to the fourth step: (4) *Remember that every fear, every trouble, every sickness, every sin you may face has been and is defeated and overcome by the One you follow—Christ.* When fears and sicknesses and sins come upon you to overwhelm you and to beat you into submission by their very overbearing presence, just calmly look each one in the eye and say: "I am not afraid of you. You have been and are decisively beaten by my Lord. Will you bend your neck? There, I knew it! The footprint of the Son of God is upon your neck." This confidence is your starting point: nothing can touch you that hasn't touched Him, and that hasn't been defeated by Him; and if you open your life to His power every ill can be defeated again by you through His grace. You need not be defeated by anything unless you consent to be. If you throw your will on the side of victory, then the whole of the Universe of Reality throws itself behind your will, releases it, reinforces it, redeems it —and you! You are caught up in a tide of victory, and nothing can stop it except your refusal to co-operate. Paul could say, "I do not frustrate the grace of God"—I do not block its redemption, nor frustrate its healing purposes. Therefore an Almighty Will worked within his will, and he arose a rhythmical, harmonious, adequate person. You can be the same.

O God, my Father, I have closed my heart to Thy healing and to Thy deliverance. I have wrapped myself within myself—afraid of salvation! I have protected my lungs— from air! My heart—from love! My aesthetic nature—from beauty! Myself—from Thee! Forgive me. Amen.

Matt. 10:28; Luke 9:34; II Tim. 1:7; Heb. 13:6

WORRY IS ATHEISM

When I say to you that you can live without fear and worry, I mean that. This is not an academic statement, but a fact. I think I shall pause in my theology and give a testimony. By all outer signs the week during which I was writing these pages should have been a week of worry and defeat, for everything had gone wrong! All my intensive efforts for months at Washington to find a basis for peace between Japan and America had come to naught. Agreement had seemed so near and so possible—and then the crash. A long war stared us in the face. I was cut off from my work in India. My wife and family were there—cut off for the duration of the war—and worse—the war was slowly moving in upon them. By the time this is printed they may be in the conflict—or they may not. At any rate, that week should have brought me anxiety and fear. But it did not. There hadn't been a moment's worry. There had been peace. When a woman said to me one evening, "You have had a quiet day; you've had time to worry," I felt inwardly startled. "Time to worry"—as if a Christian ever has "time to worry"! The Christian has expunged worry from his vocabulary.

That leads us to the fifth step: (5) *Remember that worry or fear is a kind of atheism.* A person who worries says, "I cannot trust God; I'll take things in my own hands." Result? Worry, frustration, incapacity to meet the dreaded thing when it does come. With God, you can meet it, overcome it, assimilate it into the purpose of your life. Alone, you fuss and fume and are frustrated. Worry says, "God doesn't care, and so He won't do anything—I'll have to worry it through." Faith says, "God does care, and He and I will work it out together. I'll supply the willingness, and He will supply the power—with that combination we can do anything." You remember the story of Luther? One morning, when he was blue and discouraged, his wife appeared in black. At Luther's inquiry as to what the mourning meant, she replied, "Haven't you heard? God is dead." Luther saw the absurdity—and so should you. God lives—so will you!

O God, as long as Thou dost live, I too shall live. Nothing can shake the rock of Thy existence on which I stand; and as long as that fact continues, I shall not worry nor be afraid. That means, then, that forever and ever I need not worry nor be afraid. I thank Thee. Amen.

1 John 4:18; 3:20–22; 1 Pet. 3:12–14

FEAR IS THE FIFTH COLUMNIST

Now we come to the sixth step: (6) *Hold in mind that nothing that you fear is as bad as the fear itself.* I mean that seriously: nothing that can happen to you is, or can be, as disastrous and disruptive as the entrance of fear and worry into your life; for if you keep the center of life intact, then you can come back from anything. Healed at the heart, you can say, "Let the world come on"; but, hurt at the heart by fear and worry, you are knocked down by happenings—real and imaginary. The man who fights life's battles without fear fights one enemy—the real thing confronting him. But the man who fights with fears within him fights three enemies—the real thing to fight, plus the imaginary things built up by fear, plus the fear itself. And the greatest of these is fear. Fear is the Fifth Columnist within the soul, the Trojan horse that looses from within itself the enemies that capture us within before the real fight with the outward enemy begins.

> Then take your fear
> By the ear,
> And say, "See here,
> If the thing I fear
> Were already here,
> It could not cause a tear
> So scalding, nor could it sear
> My soul as much as you, the fear,
> So, now and forever, out of here!"

So, boiled down to its essence, the conclusion is that there is nothing to fear save fear, nothing to worry about except worry.

But to leave the matter there with that trite saying is to leave us with fear feeding on fear and worry feeding on worry. That would be just as bad as fearing and worrying about something objective. Even the fear of the fear must go. How? By fastening our attention not on the thing to be feared, or on the fear of this fear, but on Christ, the Saviour from fear.

O Christ, my Saviour, Thou dost know everything that causes me fear—Thou hast gone through it all. And yet no fears or worries rooted themselves in Thee. I would know Thy secret; unfold it to me. I obey completely and fully. Amen.

Ps. 55:6; 16:9; Isa. 11:10; Zeph. 3:17

RELAX IN HIS PRESENCE

We ended yesterday by saying that the attention must be
fastened on Christ—the Man who met everything we meet
and more, and didn't worry. Fasten your attention on Him;
for it is a law of the mind that whatever gets your attention,
gets you. If your worries get your attention, they will get
you. If Christ gets your attention, He will get you. But how
can you fasten your attention on Him? You're pulled off
from Him to worries. Then take the next step: (7) *Relax in
His presence.* His power cannot get across to you unless
you learn to relax. Fear and worry tighten you up. Faith relaxes you. Often fear and worry keep the motor running
even after you are parked. You are worn out even when sitting still. In one of my meetings recently, it was announced
that someone had left his motor running in a parked car. A
lot of people there in front of me still had their motors running, using up energy and power. They were tense with
anxieties and fears. In that condition nothing can get
across; for it is a fact that you cannot engrave anything on
a tense conscious mind. Therefore a tense conscious mind
cannot take in energy; it can only expend it. The end of
tension is bankruptcy. In quietness and confidence you absorb; you are in a state of receptivity, and hence life energies are taken in and stored up.

A Negro maid said to her mistress: "I notice that when
you sit, you sit tight. You are all screwed up and tight on
the inside. Now look at me. When I work, I work hard; but
when I sit, I sit loose." There was a real philosophy of life
in that statement: When you work, work hard; but when
you stop working, then stop working—relax. You cannot
repeat to yourself too frequently the oft-repeated, and yet
always healing, statement: "Let go; let God." Let go your
inward fears and worries, and let God absorb them in His
grace and love. Let God replace the false energy of fear
and worry with the true energy of faith working through
love.

My Father God, I've burned up my soul and body and
mind energy in the false energy of fear and worry. Such
tenseness has taken me nowhere, except deeper into the
mire. Help me this day to link all my energies to the calm
of Thy purposes and to the peace of Thy power. Then I
shall know harmony and accomplishment. Amen.

Matt. 6:25–34

ONE DAY AT A TIME

In our meditation yesterday we saw that worry is a useless expenditure of energy. In India we have a bird called "Pity-to-do-it." It goes around all day saying, "Pity-to-do-it." And they say that at night it sleeps with its feet in the air to keep the sky from falling! It is a champion pessimist and worrier. It doesn't relax night or day, according to the story; hence it is thin and scrawny and fussy. Some of us are like that bird. But we do not have to be like it. We may contemplate instead the artist's picture of rest, depicting a bird on a nest overhanging a mighty waterfall. Amid the roar and confusion that bird is the symbol of quiet, rest, and calm. We must learn that. How?

(8) *Meet today, today.* Jesus showed very penetrating insight when he said: "So do not be troubled about tomorrow; tomorrow will take care of itself. The day's own trouble is quite enough for the day." (Matthew 6:34, Moffatt.) He was not saying there were no troubles to be met. There are. Life is bound to bring trouble. It is made that way. But don't telescope the troubles of tomorrow and of the next day into today. Meet today, today; for if you put the troubles of next week into today by anticipation through worry, then you spoil today. You are meeting two sets of troubles at once—one set that is actually here, and the set that you bring in by worrying about tomorrow's troubles. You are therefore meeting your troubles twice—once before they come, and once when they are actually here. Such a telescoping of trouble is a double expenditure of energy and needless. Worry is the advance interest you pay on troubles that never come. Some of them do come, and you can meet and conquer them separately. But tomorrow's troubles plus today's break you.

The theory of "divide and conquer" is applicable here. Divide your worries, and meet one day's worries at a time, and conquer them. But don't let worries gang up on you and come piling all at once into one day. Divide and conquer. Meet today, today.

O God, I see that I have been needlessly burdening myself. Thou dost give me a sufficient load for today, and Thou dost help me bear it. But I add to my burden, and thus diminish my strength for legitimate tasks. Forgive me, for I see that this is sin—sin against myself and Thee. Amen.

Prov. 1:33; 3:23–26; Isa. 30:15; 33:24

IN QUIETNESS AND CONFIDENCE

Last week we finished on the note of meeting today, today. This is sound psychology, for it gives us inward freedom from distraction. This is important, for all distraction is destruction. All the energies can be gathered up into constructive achievement and not frittered away with senseless worry.

Now step off and look at the situation in a detached way: "Today is the tomorrow you worried about yesterday." Today isn't so bad; is it? It has its troubles, but they are bearable. Even at its worst today is bearable. Said a youth who had lost both legs and both arms in the war, "Thank God, I've still my health and strength left!" And more, he had an unconquerable soul left. With such a soul left, you can meet anything that belongs to today.

If even the whole day seems too difficult—then divide it up into hours. You are meeting this hour now with your full resources. Pack it with God and His resources. Throw all your energies into meeting the enemies as they come one by one. Keep them segregated and fight them one at a time. And fight them, not by strained endeavor, but by quiet faith. That leads to the next step: (9) *Say over and over: "In quietness and confidence shall be my strength."* Note two things there—quietness and confidence. You must quiet everything in the presence of God. Still your being before Him and drink in His quiet strength. Let His healing quiet get into every pore of your being, bathing the tired and restless nerve cells with His healing. But quietness alone will not be enough—confidence is necessary. Quietness is passive, and we must be passive to God; but confidence is active, and we must be active to God. And note the kind of activity, for confidence is *con*—"with," *fideo*—"faith." In other words, it is not an alone faith; it is a faith "with"—a faith with God's faith. Your faith and God's faith flow together, and hence can do anything.

My Father, I begin to see that my poor faith alone is not all that is left to battle with life's sorrows and troubles. I have a faith, plus Thine. And that "plus" is enough and more than enough. I will work life no longer on the unit principle, but on the co-operative plan. I am no longer afraid—not with Thee. Amen.

Ps. 23

FAITH IN HIS FAITH

We did not quite finish the step of the inward repetition of the words, "In quietness and confidence shall be my strength." If "confidence" is having faith with God, then the Christian life is not lifting oneself by the bootstraps. It is linking our littleness with His greatness, our incompleteness with His completeness. It is doing what the little boy did when he offered his five loaves and two fishes to Christ. That multitude could not be fed without his co-operation, and the feeding couldn't be done with his five loaves and fishes alone. He and Christ together did everything necessary.

Very often when I haven't faith in my faith, I have to have faith in His faith. He makes me believe in myself and my possibilities, when I simply can't. I have to rise to His faith in me. A woman who was inwardly collapsed said to me, "Well, I have no faith of my own, but I do have faith in your faith." "Good," I replied; "take faith in my faith as a first step, and then you will go on to something infinitely better—faith in His faith." With faith in His faith you can do anything—anything that ought to be done.

There is a passage which touches your need. "For the Eternal . . . . will not let you go." (Deuteronomy 4:31, Moffatt.) Faith is not merely your holding on to God—it is God holding on to you. He will not let you go! As Walt Whitman puts it, "Not until the sun refuses to shine, do I refuse you." Then keep saying to your soul, "Your strength is quiet faith." (Isaiah 30:15, Moffatt.) Then repeat to your soul these words: "To say what ought to be cannot be is a brief and a complete statement of atheism." It is. Say to yourself, "What ought to be can be, and I will make it so." And you will. You will go beyond yourself.

One saint keeps repeating, "God is. God is here with me." That creates confidence and faith."

O living Christ, I see that life is communion—a union with Thee. Not merely in the quiet segregated moments, but in the moments of stress and strain and toil. I now see I can be the happy warrior, for I am drawing heavily on Thy power and going forth in Thy confidence. I can actually do what I can't. I thank Thee, I thank Thee. Amen.

SURRENDERING OUR FEARS

We come now to the next step: (10) *Surrender the thing you fear into the hands of God.* Turn it right over to God and ask Him to solve it with you. Fear is keeping things in your own hands; faith is turning them over into the hands of God—and leaving them there.

There was the case of Mrs. ———— (but how I dislike the word "case," for she was a *person* suffering deeply). Sorrow and pain left her with an upset heart. She was on her bed for a year, and had various treatments. She came to a gathering some distance away and told me she was afraid she would die on the way, as her heart began behaving very badly indeed. Her uppermost thought was, "How expensive it will be to ship back my body to my home." After a talk with her I saw that anxiety and worry were causing the functional disturbance of the heart. The disturbance was not imaginary; it was very real, but caused by worry and fear. I got her to surrender the whole matter to God. She did. The strained lines on her face relaxed, and she began to act like a normal person. But let her tell the story: "Let me say that my body was not shipped home, but that I was very much alive, and scarcely tired, when I reached home after a 550-mile drive in one day! And there has been no relapse since coming home. This recovery is so real; it is not neurotic, for my nerves are becoming steady, and my heart is beginning to act like a normal heart should. It is wonderful. . . . . When the doctor saw me yesterday he said: 'Something has happened to you since you were here before. There is a transformation in you which is almost unbelievable. What is it?' When I told him, he said, 'I know what you say is true, for you yourself are the proof of it.' And then he added, 'What you have found is what 75 per cent of our patients need more than medicine, for a great many of them would get well physically if they were well mentally and spiritually.' "

My Father, forgive me that I hold my worries, my troubles, my fears in my own incompetent hands and do not turn them over into Thy competent Hands. Just now I do turn them over to Thee. They are Thine, not for an hour, but forever. And I accept my own release. I am grateful— so grateful. Amen.

1 Cor. 15:57–58; Phil. 2:12–13; Rom. 15:1–3

GETTING RID OF FEARS BY TASKS

Now that you have turned over your fears and anxieties to God and have left them there, take the next step. (11) *Deliberately take on yourself some task to help others.* You have turned over your fears and anxieties to God, not to become a vacuum, but to have a heart that now has room and inward leisure for other people's troubles. Dr. Woodall tells of a woman who was an invalid with high blood pressure and other ailments. She was always thinking about herself and rarely ever talked of any subject other than her disease; she lay in bed and performed no household duties. Her husband was suddenly taken very ill and seemed to be on the point of death. Aroused by this danger, she got out of bed and helped to nurse her husband back to health. When she forgot her own ailments in her endeavor to help him, she herself got well. Health will come only in healthy activity.

John Wesley speaks of living "with a slack rein." That was true of him—he knew how to relax; but when he worked, how he did work! The slack rein was in order to have a tighter rein.

A watchmaker told a friend, in reply to his question as to why he kept his watches and clocks always running: "In order that they may be kept in better condition." You and I are made for constructive activity, and health will come to us as a by-product. Don't sit and talk about your ailments, or you'll have more and more to talk about. We are told that frogs will not croak in running water—only in stagnant water. You will become a croaker if your life is stagnant. Get into the stream of helpful activity and you'll cease croaking, and in the end you'll not "croak" before your time!

You must learn to be passive before God and active before men. Take in from God as you live in the passive voice; then give out to others as you live in the active voice. These are the two heartbeats of your life: passive, active. You submit to God, but you don't submit to anything else. Then you are creative and masterful.

O God, Thou art healing me in order to make me a center of healing. This precious gift I hold within my hand, not to gaze at in joyful reverence, but to pass it on. Freely I have received; help me freely to give. In Jesus' name. Amen.

Isa. 55

THE FEAR OF FAILURE

With all our fears and anxieties surrendered to God and our energies committed to constructive helpfulness to others, we are now in a position to look these particular fears and worries in the face and render them innocuous by a straight gaze. (12) *Look at your worst fears one by one.* You now dare look at them, for you have already looked at Christ, and you know that all these fears have the footprint of the Son of God on the back of their necks. They are half defeated in Him and are wholly defeated when you accept and act on the fact of their defeat.

(a) *The fear of failure.* A great many people go through life in bondage to success. They are in mortal dread of failure. Why should they be? Jesus cared little about success or failure. The story of Jesus is a story of apparent failure— rejected by His nation and crucified by the Romans, He ended on a cross. A faith that has a cross at its center cannot be a faith that worships success. I do not have to succeed; I have only to be true to the highest I know—success and failure are in the hands of God. On my way to India, I once said in England: "The romance of missions has gone for me. I know what I'm up against. If you should say to me that I go back to India to see nothing but frustration and failure and that I would see no more fruit whatever, I would reply: 'That is an incident. I have the call of God to India, and to be true to that call is my one business; success and failure are not my business—to be true is.' " I made that statement one day in a meeting, and a minister came up and said: "All my life I've been in bondage to success; I've looked at everything from the success standpoint. You have released within me the greatest tension of my life. I have only to be true, thank God."

"There is a lion in the way," says fear. But when you walk straight up to the lion of fear, he turns out to be a mouse of fact. Suppose you should fail. Is that so terrible? Not to have tried is a worse failure.

My Father, I've been afraid of failure. In fear of failure the self still lurks, afraid of what others will say. Forgive me that I've looked at the verdict of others, instead of at the verdict of Thy "Well done," as through failure and success I've been true to Thee. O help me to be true—I care for naught else. Amen.

Isa. 46:4; Acts 2:17; Ps. 91

FURTHER FEARS TO BE CONQUERED

We have been looking at specific fears and anxieties. We take another: (b) *the fear of losing the affections of a friend or loved one.* To become anxious and worried about this is the quickest way to lose the affections of those we love; for it becomes difficult or impossible to love a person all inwardly tight with anxiety. That very anxiety blocks the passage of love. An anxious, worried person is unlovable. Some love may exist in spite of anxious tension, but anxiety is a strain on love. Therefore, when you become strained and anxious about the love of a loved one, you defeat your very purpose. So surrender that anxiety.

(c) *Fear of being dependent on others in old age.* Why should you fear this? Your children were dependent on you; why would you fear being dependent on them? Life is so made that we grow by accepting responsibilities for which there is no return. Don't deny your children that privilege of growth. Be the kind of person they would love to have to take care of. If it is fear of being taken care of by the state, then again, why should you be afraid? If you have been a good citizen and a useful member of society during your active life, in that way contributing to the up-building of the state, then why shouldn't the state take care of you when you are no longer able to work? There is no shame whatever in either being supported by your family or by the state if you have been a useful member of society.

(d) *Fear of the unknown future.* Many live in dread of what is coming. Why should we? The unknown puts adventure into life. It gives us something to sharpen our souls on. The unexpected around the corner gives a sense of anticipation and surprise. Thank God for the unknown future. If we saw all the good things which are coming to us, we would sit down and degenerate. If we saw all the evil things, we would be paralyzed. How merciful God is to lift the curtain on today; and as we get strength today to meet tomorrow, then to lift the curtain on the morrow. He is a considerate God.

O God, I know if I fear to lose the love of those who love me, I shall lose confidence—and confidence is conquest; so I shall lose the conquest. I am dependent on Thee, and Thou art dependent on us—help me not to be ashamed to be dependent on others. And as to the future—I meet it with a salutation and a song. Amen.

Heb. 2:14–15; II Tim. 4:6–8; II Cor. 5:1–6

THE FEAR OF DEATH

We come now to the greatest of all fears: (e) *the fear of death.* Many go through life spoiling life through fear of death. But why should we be afraid of death? Some time ago I was being taken out to be hanged. On the way to the hanging my brother said to me, "It looks as though you're not going to get out of this, doesn't it?" To which I agreed. But on the way we met the woman I was supposed to have murdered. "There," I said, "I told you so—here is the woman." We took her along. A large crowd had gathered, and I said, "I told you I was innocent; there is the woman." But the crowd replied, "We've come here to see the minister hanged, and we're going to go through with it." To which I replied, "You are doing an injustice, but I am not afraid to die." They were adamant; and I was taken to the scaffold, the blackcap put over my head, and the rope around my neck, and I stood on the trapdoor. But just as the trap was about to be sprung—I woke up! Of course, I was glad to find myself in bed rather than on a scaffold, but there was a sense of inner exultation, even of joy. I said to myself, "Why, that wasn't so bad, even at its worst!" It couldn't be much worse than that!

Why should a Christian be afraid of death? To be afraid of that larger life is a species of atheism. Doubt of the future means doubt of the present. It means that the Master, who went down through death and came up and said, "I am the resurrection, and the life: he that believeth in me . . . . shall never die," is not dependable for the ultimate things, and therefore not for the immediate things. As the little bird on a twig of the tree, when the storm is about to twist it off its perch, might say, "All right; twist me off —I have another alternative—I have wings," so we can say to Death, "Twist me off my earthly perch—I have another alternative—I have immortality, God." Nothing can shake that.

Real Christians live well and they die well.

O God, when I have Thee, I have all—and more than all. No death can touch that fact, for Thou dost live amid earthly changes. So I too shall live on amid earthly changes —deathless. I am invulnerable—in Thee. Amen.

Matt. 9:29; 17:20; Mark 11:22; Acts 3:16

FASHIONED FOR FAITH AND NOT FOR FEAR

It had been my original intention to close the meditations on the conquest of fear last week, but the more we have faced this matter the more fundamental has it become. As I wrote the above, a letter came from a highly gifted woman with this sentence in it: "Oh, Dr. Jones, everything is wrong, and I am so afraid I am going to crack up completely." She says that "everything is wrong." She blames her circumstances; but there is nothing wrong whatever except her fear, which in turn is rooted in her self-centered attitudes. Her universe continually falls to pieces because of her self-centered attitudes giving birth to fears. If she would change the center of her life all her sums would come out right; but with the center wrong nothing comes out right.

This week, then, we shall gather up our inward resolves and register them. These resolves will not be a screwed-up, clenched-jaw type of resolves, but a calm, relaxed registration of life committed to certain attitudes.

(1) *I see that I am inwardly fashioned for faith and not for fear.* Fear is not my native land; faith is. I am so made that worry and anxiety are sand in the machinery of life; faith is oil. I live better by faith and confidence than by fear and doubt and anxiety. In anxiety and worry my being is gasping for breath—these are not my native air. But in faith and confidence I breathe freely—these are my native air. A Johns Hopkins' doctor says that "we do not know why it is that the worriers die sooner than the nonworriers, but that is a fact." But I, who am simple of mind, think I know: we are inwardly constructed, in nerve and tissue and brain cell and soul, for faith and not for fear. God made us that way. Therefore, the need of faith is not something imposed on us dogmatically, but it is written in us intrinsically. We cannot live without it.

To live by worry is to live against Reality.

O God, since the need of confidence and faith is written in me, and they are therefore inescapable, I will not try to escape from them. I surrender myself to the healing and the renewing of faith and confidence. Their healing goes now into every fiber of my being. I am grateful. Amen.

Matt. 6:30; 9:2; Rom. 14:23; Gal. 2:20

WITHOUT FAITH YOU CANNOT MEET LIFE'S EMERGENCIES

To gather up the meditation of yesterday: we are inwardly fashioned for faith—faith is healing; doubt and fear are destroying. Insurance statistics say that people who have annuities live on an average five or six years longer than those who do not have any. The annuity relieves them from anxiety regarding security in old age, and the very fact of having that relief prolongs life.

(2) *I see that I cannot meet life's emergencies unless I have confidence and faith.* A doctor told me of this procedure in the Mayo Clinic: "A patient who was being prepared for one of the wonderful new operations for reducing high blood pressure had passed every preliminary examination successfully and thought no more were to follow. She was mistaken. Before the surgeon would operate, the patient must pass the test which would make sure that no spiritual or mental trouble was bringing on the chronic headaches and hypertension. The doctor, who was firm and would not be sidetracked, questioned the patient closely as to her home life, her married happiness, her religious state. Was she happy? Worried over money? Was she satisfied with her home conditions? Her religion? Until she could pass that test she was not ready to stand the operation, for the doctors knew she could collapse from within in spite of all scientific efforts if there were conflict and worry at the citadel of her life." A schoolteacher was suffering from heart trouble, her heart beating so loud and rapidly that at the least effort it "seemed to jump out of her body." The doctors could find no physical reason for her heart condition, but they discovered that she was worried over a lump in her breast; she was sure cancer was developing there. When she was assured that there was no lump and no cancer, she went home happy and relieved. The heart became normal, and she is happy and efficient in her work. The fear and worry had caused functional disturbance. The disturbance was real, but it had been caused by an unreal fear.

O God, I see that I am the enemy of my possibilities if I admit inward fear and anxiety. I throw disturbance into my organs, upset my brain cells, tire out my faithful heart, and paralyze my constructive energies. I am the enemy of myself. Forgive me. In Jesus' name. Amen.

1 Tim. 6:11–12; Heb. 4:2; 10:22; 13:6

FEAR AND ANXIETIES KEEP US FROM BEING AT OUR BEST

We saw yesterday that fear and anxiety keep us from being at our best. They paralyze the center of life. A Mexican saw a snake and was nipped by a barbed wire at that moment. He thought he was bitten, foamed at the mouth and was about to die. The doctor arrived, saw that there was no swelling at the abrasion, assured him that he had not been bitten, and the man got well almost immediately. The fear produced the symptoms. So fear will often produce the very symptoms you fear. Why is it that people with "poker faces" play a better game of tennis than those who go up and down emotionally according to the score? The simple reason is that the "poker face" is an outer expression of unperturbed confidence. Victory flows from that.

Ty Cobb, of Detroit, and "Shoeless Joe" Jackson were running neck and neck in baseball batting averages—each wanted the championship. When the two teams met in an important series, Cobb refused to speak to Jackson. As they had been good friends, Jackson was worried, afraid that he had offended Cobb. He worried so much that he went into a batting slump; worry and fear took away his "batting eye." Cobb won—his morally doubtful strategy had succeeded.

It is a fact that the worrier has a small chest, made that way by the fact of worry. The person of faith takes in deep breaths of God's air, God's power, God's hope. The worrier is afraid to breathe deeply, afraid of the healing of fresh air, of the healing of God's hope, of God's power. He therefore smothers himself—sometimes to death. "I was afraid, and went and hid thy talent," said the man in the Scripture. And that happens everywhere—those who fear bury their talents, and often bury themselves prematurely. Worry makes an eight-cylinder person into a four-cylinder person.

Worry is a species of myopia—nearsightedness.

My God and Father, I would be at my best—at Thy best. But Thy best cannot get across to me if I am fearful, for I block Thy redemptive power. I now resolve to be a person without blocks anywhere in my life. For how dare I block Thee?—my Lord and my God. Amen.

John 16:22–24; 14:27

RESOLVE TO ACT ON NO FEAR

(3) *So I resolve not to act on any fear, but to wait till I can act on faith.* Never act on a fear, for fears are usually false. "See that thou make all things according to the pattern shewed to thee in the mount." Note that the pattern was seen *"in the mount."* Don't build your life according to any pattern shown to you in the valley of fear. Wait till you get to the mount of faith and then build your life plans. A strong healthy wife was afraid to have a baby, and so allowed an abortion. There was no physical reason why she shouldn't have had that baby, but fear paralyzed her creative instinct. And now her arms are forever childless. Fear left that emptiness. Nothing that could have happened in childbirth would have been as hard as the lifelong pain of empty arms, the mother instinct frustrated. She loved herself; and hence had nothing to love except herself. And the self she had to love was a bitter self.

One of the greatest souls of this age says, "Whenever I get down, I shut off my mind from decisions—no decisions until I am on top of things."

All my decision moments, then, will be faith moments, not fear moments. I will instruct my mind that no decisions are to be made except in faith. And there are to be no exceptions. I therefore use a mind purged of all acting on fear. It is marvelous what the mind will do when it is single-pointed and decisive. In college I decided I would act on no fear. It happened one night that I was in a shower of stones which were raining all around me in the dark. My first impulse was to get behind a tree; but I remembered my resolve and stood there in the open, letting them fall all around me, with my face turned toward the falling stones. I was surprised at my own boldness, for I'm not naturally courageous. My resolve, made beforehand, never to act on fear had held me in that crisis. Make a life choice of faith as a permanent life attitude.

O Thou living Christ, Thou didst never act on any fear; so Thy course was always forward. I, too, would do the same, for with Thee life has no retreats and no regrets. Give me the simple impulse of faith in every circumstance and help me to act on nothing else. In Jesus' name. Amen.

Heb. 6:12; 12:2; 13:7; Jude 20

CREATING FAITH IN OTHER PEOPLE

(4) *I resolve to create faith in other people. I shall think faith, talk faith, live faith, impart faith.* That means that I will turn over all my nonfaith attitudes to God and help others to do the same. A pastor told me he was unable to eat, was getting thinner every day, had pains in his stomach. He went on his knees and said, "O God, you delivered one man, Stanley Jones, from physical and nervous exhaustion; you can deliver another; you can deliver me." He turned the whole thing over to God, went to bed, relaxed and received —just received, breathed in the healing of God as the lungs breathe in the purifying air. Today he is the picture of health and is contagious—he radiates health.

A father was about to be operated on, and the mother and son could not sleep through worry and anxiety. They sent word to a Christian layman: "Please come down and stay with us at night; we are afraid. Can't you come and talk to us? for we have nothing to hold on to in the dark." The layman came, and mother and son both surrendered themselves to God and were changed. The son spoke to the father, who for a long time lay there uncomprehending; but he finally recognized the son's voice, responded to his testimony, opened his heart to the love of God and was himself converted and died happy. The spark of faith in that son, a convert of two days, kindled something in the father's heart and changed him.

You, too, belong to the great contagion—the contagion of faith. A friend working in a college had a period of worry which brought on high blood pressure. She dropped a letter in the box, telling me she had turned the whole problem over to God. That was an act of faith. But the moment her letter dropped, so did her blood pressure! She is now poised and calm and effective. Up to the dropping of that letter in the box she had been an introvert; she is now an extrovert, turning out upon others in contagious faith.

O God, break down within me the last barrier of fear that would check the flow of faith. I would have the doors of my spirit turn out and not in, for I am made for creative activity by Thee, the Creator. Help me to create hope and faith in others. In Jesus' name. Amen.

James 1:3; Heb. 11:6; 1 Thess. 5:8; Eph. 5:20

CULTIVATING FAITH

(5) *In order to have that faith and confidence which I am to impart to others I must deliberately cultivate faith.* But cultivation of faith does not mean that I will *try* to cultivate it. I will let go, relax, become a channel of a power not my own, and then God will do the rest. The pious statement of a minister? Then listen to Dr. Fritz Künkel, an outstanding psychiatrist: "As long as I am confident, have faith, good humor, as long as I allow my body—my organs, my brain—to function as they want to function, I trust my nature, and all goes well. But when I distrust, become afraid, begin to control my nature, don't trust my nature, try to replace the unconscious function of my organs by will power, then I find that will power is powerless. I try to replace my natural functions by conscious controls. That is, I try to replace God by myself. I cannot replace nature. I cannot make my muscles, nerves, knees function. When I try this replacement I find the new government is worse than the previous one. Therefore my fear increases; therefore conscious strain increases; therefore the danger increases; therefore I strain the harder. The way out would be trust, faith, calmness, relaxation." (Notes from a lecture.)

A businessman said to me: "I am physically and mentally well, but emotionally I am sick. I have hold of a 110-volt wire, and cannot let go." He had begun by trying to add a cubit to his stature by being anxious, and having taken hold, he did not know how to let go. To let go means that you have more faith in God and His processes than you have in yourself and your processes. The essence of cultivation is relaxation. You will never be a good musician if you try too hard; you must let go and let the music get into your finger tips, so that you do not play the music—the music plays you. So with God—don't use God; let Him use you.

Then you will be able to say with Walter Rauschenbusch: "My fear is gone in the great quiet of God."

O God, I have not been fighting the good fight of faith; I have been fighting the fight of fear. I have been strained. Now help me to go limp in Thy presence, that Thou mayst impress on me Thy ways, Thy poise, Thy power. In Jesus' name. Amen.

Rom. 12:8; Prov. 15:13–15; 17:22

FACING LIFE CHEERFULLY
AND WITH ANTICIPATION

(6) *I shall face life cheerfully and with anticipation. I shall learn to laugh, even at myself.* The Scripture says, "A merry heart doeth good like a medicine: but a broken spirit drieth the bones." It also says, "Your strength is quiet faith." (Isaiah 30:15, Moffatt.) And again, "Let all your anxieties fall upon him, for his interest is in you." (I Peter 5:7, Moffatt.)

I know that Elsie Robinson is right when she says: "Unpleasantness can be a disease. It provides an escape for our cowardice, an excuse for our laziness, an alibi for cussedness, and a spotlight for our conceit." I shall therefore do as Muriel Lester suggests: "Hunt for self-pity as you would hunt for lice"—and loathe it with the same loathing. I shall keep my capacity to laugh, even at myself. When I get tense and take myself too seriously, I shall deliberately walk to the looking-glass and burst out laughing. Even if I do not feel like laughing when I go, I feel more like it when I see the man in the glass laughing. "You will never break down," said a doctor to a friend of mine, "for you have a hair-trigger laugh."

Here is what Dr. Emily T. Wilson says about the recuperative power of laughter and cheer: "Those who are cheerful and confident, who are free from anxieties and fear, make far more satisfactory progress than those who keep themselves in a turmoil of distress and worry. Once we remove the conflicting emotions and maintain our patients in a peaceful, hopeful, fearless attitude we have won more than half the battle. We do not know why worry causes an increase of pain in angina, a recurrence of ulcers in a harassed businessman, an elevation of blood pressure in the diabetic. The sincere Christian has no time for nerves. The religious man faces life confident and unafraid, and saves himself from countless ills, the creation of a purposeless and disintegrating personality." "No time for nerves"—just too busy with faith and confidence to let them get a toe hold, let alone a foothold.

Thou confident God, going steadily on amid the deflections and betrayals of men, help me to have Thy patience and Thy confidence. For from now on I'm eternally linked with Thee. When Thou dost fall, I shall fall—until then, I stand. Glory be! Amen.

Ps. 51:1–17

A SENSE OF UNRESOLVED GUILT

We have looked at four of the fifteen enemies of the personality: (1) A lack of faith in and loyalty to something beyond one's self that gives ultimate meaning, coherence, and goal to life; (2) Self-centeredness; (3) Anger, resentments, and hates; (4) Fear, worry, and anxieties. We now continue: (5) *A sense of unresolved guilt.* A sense of unresolved guilt is destructive to harmonious personality.

The older evangelism threw a great deal of emphasis on "guilt," but it was in large measure connected with what would happen to you after death—how would you be able to stand before God's judgment?—you, a guilty soul! That emphasis ceased to appeal to the modern mind, and was thrown into the discard. But it is now coming back through psychology. Ernest Renan said, "The twentieth century will spend a good deal of its time picking out of the wastebasket things which the nineteenth century threw into it." One of the things now being picked out is just this necessity—that the inner nature be absolved from guilt. We cannot live with guilt, that is, truly live.

It must be acknowledged that a good many ideas in reference to guilt did have to be thrown into the wastebasket. They were false guilts which needlessly tormented many sincere people. A lot of false guilts were fastened on people —these needed to be shed. For example, we know now that sex feelings are not sin; they are a part of our normal, healthy life—everybody has them, saint and sinner. We also know that a normal self-love is right and natural; to act as if you had none is to end in hypocrisy. Every normal person has self-love, and ought to have it. Many false guilts that tormented humanity have been shed, and should be shed. The fear of having committed the "unpardonable sin" is usually a false fear, for the unpardonable sin of which Jesus spoke was saying that Jesus had "an unclean spirit," that the Spirit within Him—the Holy Spirit—was unclean. Seldom is that sin committed. Therefore, do not fear that you have committed the unpardonable sin.

O God, if I have built up within me false guilts which hide my real guilt, forgive me, for I want to be inwardly absolved from all haunting guilts that rob me of my confidence and power. Cleanse the depths, for I cannot live with guilt. I can live only with fellowship and reconciliation. Amen.

1 Cor. 8:1; Rom. 11:33; John 1:17; 8:32

PAGAN PSYCHIATRY OFTEN DISRUPTIVE

We saw yesterday that many false guilts had to be discarded. The conscience can be taught to approve diametrically opposite things. I said to a Hindu one day, "Suppose you broke caste, and no one would know it?" "But I would know it, for my conscience would trouble me if I broke caste," he replied. His conscience would trouble him if he broke caste, and mine would trouble me if I kept caste. Conscience will stand guard over the values you put into your moral nature. It is important what value you put there. The conscience should be trained at the feet of Christ; only then is it a safe guide.

A word of warning must be uttered against pagan psychiatrists, who, finding persons at conflict with themselves, suffering from split personality—with ideals high and conduct low—try to unify the persons on the level of conduct, dismissing the whole world of moral ideals. This usually results in greater disruption—disunity—for a new conflict is introduced at the level of conduct. The moral world cannot be dismissed by a wave of the hand, or by a slick phrase of a pagan psychiatrist. Put out at the door, it will come back at the window. One such psychiatrist, a very outstanding man, urges women who are nervous and upset to find "a boy friend." Some of these women who had been given advice by this psychiatrist to practice adultery came in great distress to a ministerial friend of mine. Through him they found God, and are released and happy. The wife of this psychiatrist, divorced from him, because he naturally had acted on the advice he gave to others, came to this same friend, and she too found God and is radiant. The false advice given by this psychiatrist produced disunity in the personality, and broke up homes—his own included. The only possible level on which to be unified permanently is the level of your ideals. Everything else will let you down.

If you go to a psychiatrist go to one who has a Christian background and outlook. Such psychiatrists are the salt of the earth and help many to release.

O God, my Father, I see that amid all the ways of men Thou hast a way—the way that is written into the nature of reality. Help me to find that way that I may live, for I cannot fumble this business of living. Time is too short, and living too serious. In Jesus' name. Amen.

John 2:23–25; Heb. 2:6–9; Titus 2:12–14

WHAT ARE YOU, MY BROTHER?

No, the human heart will not be put off with subterfuges; it needs reconciliation, forgiveness, assurance.

"Is this the place where they heal broken hearts?" asked a Korean girl of a mission station. Whether that broken heart comes from outer sorrow or inner guilt, the need is the same. Dr. Howard Kelly, the great surgeon, said to a patient, "What you need is a New Testament." And the healing in that New Testament which the patient needed was the certainty of forgiveness, of grace, of reconciliation. We need a forgiving God.

As one modern writer puts it: "For what are we, my brother? We are a phantom flare of grieved desire, the ghostling and phosphoric flicker of immortal time, a brevity of days haunted by the eternity of the earth. We are an unspeakable utterance, an unsatiable hunger, an unquenchable thirst; a lust that bursts our sinews, explodes our brains, sickens and rots our guts, and rips our hearts asunder. We are a twist of passion, a moment's flame of love and ecstasy, a sinew of bright blood and agony, a lost cry, a music of pain and joy, a haunting of brief, sharp hours, an almost captured beauty, a demon's whisper of unbodied memory. We are the dupes of time.

"For what are we, my brother? We are the sons of our Father, whose face we have never seen, we are the sons of our Father, whose voice we have never heard, we are the sons of our Father, to whom we have cried for strength and comfort in our agony, we are the sons of our Father, whose life like ours was lived . . . . , we are the sons of our Father, to whom only we can speak out the strange, dark burden of our heart and spirit, we are the sons of our Father, and we shall follow the print of his feet forever." (Thomas Wolfe, *Of Time and the River*, pp. 869–870.)[1] Yes, we are sons of the Father, and our spirits will never rest until they see His Face; but when we see it, we must read in that Face reconciliation and forgiveness.

O God, my Father, I would follow Thy footprints forever, did I not know that Thy footprints have been turned in my direction—Thou art seeking me. It is I who have been fleeing from Thee. I flee no more—I come, I come. Amen.

[1] Reprinted by permission of Chas. Scribner's Sons, publishers.

Ps. 4:4–5; 34:8; 36:7; 91:1–2

RELAXING IN THE PRESENCE OF GOD

We found yesterday that man is his own worst enemy—
he allows into his life alien things for which he is not made,
and crowds out God, for whom he is made.

> "And here at last we find
> Strict diagnosis of our malady,
> Which is, in short, that man is heaven-starved—
> Men are born thirsting for infinity."

But man is not only "Thirsting for infinity"; he is thirsting for something at the center of infinity that has a heart,
that cares, that tells him the universe is friendly, that there
is a Being that is infinite and good and redemptive. Give
man that assurance, and man can stand up against anything.

How can man be assured? A girl of German extraction,
used to being told just what to do and what to believe,
wrote to me and said, "Please tell me that I am forgiven. If
you say I am forgiven, I can be assured." I could assure her
that she was forgiven, but the assurance of one person to
another is slender assurance. The whole of life must assure.
How can we get that life assurance? Let us take the steps
which the psychoanalyst uses. We will use his analysis to
arrive at our synthesis.

(1) Recline in some semidarkened room, put a towel
over your eyes, and relax. Talk about yourself, letting your
mind free to roam across your life as it will. Do not debate
with yourself, but in a calm, detached way bring to the surface anything to which the mind returns again and again.
You will probably touch this alien thing buried within you
in a frightened, startled way. It is a sore point, a buried
fear, a hidden guilt. At first you may not even want to
acknowledge that there is any sore point in your life, for
you have argued with yourself that everything is all right;
you have built up defenses against raising any questions
about anything—"Let sleeping dogs lie," has been your attitude. But now you are resolved to be perfectly honest and
perfectly frank, even with yourself.

O God, I enter now a life of complete frankness and
open honesty. I live with no hidden, closed caverns in the
depths of me. I am from now on "a child of light," and
know no secrets withheld, no sore points suppressed. I am
to be simple and unaffected—and Thine. Amen.

1 John 1:5–10; 2:1–2

BRINGING UP ANYTHING TOUCHY

Since you have begun to bring up everything to the light you are ready for the second step: (2) *Anything that appears touchy bring up gently, but decisively.* Perhaps this sensitive spot is your difficulty. If so, segregate it, and see what is to be done about it. Don't push it down out of sight and try to forget it. That makes it work havoc at a deeper depth—in the subconscious mind. Perhaps your difficulty is a hidden resentment, something you had pushed down into the subconscious mind and put the lid on. Now it is up, and you are looking at it frankly.

A farmer allowed one of his neighbor's calves to be merged into his own herd and sold with the rest. But every time he looked to God he could see nothing but that calf! Only when he confessed and restored did he find peace with himself and fellowship with God.

A young lady suspected that a hidden resentment against a minister for whom she had worked was the cause of her sense of a spiritual blank wall. She wrote a letter saying she was sorry for the resentments and kept it several days, hoping the mere writing of it would suffice. But the mind is a relentless thing—it won't say peace when there is no peace. Only when she had dropped the letter into the mailbox did peace and release come.

Don't do as a high-school girl of fourteen recently did. She was intelligent and beautiful. She came to me and said, "I'm like that girl you spoke about—all inwardly empty; worse, I'm in a tangle. I've been kicked out of four high schools and am about to be kicked out of the present one. Isn't it too late to do anything now?" Too late at fourteen! She had concocted new lies to cover up old ones, and life had gone on from tangle to worse tangle, until now the law was closing in on her for forgery of checks. She started to be frank and have me help her, then suddenly decided to run away literally—and did. She ran away from her surroundings, but not from herself.

Bring up everything that appears touchy.

O God, when I begin to untangle my life, help me to go clear through with it. Help me to come clean; for compromise will only compromise my happiness, and any pulling back will only pull me back from release and from Thee. I'm going all the way through. Amen.

Mark 5:5; Eph. 5:8–17; 1 John 5:11–12, 20

BACK TO NORMAL WITH THE HELP OF GOD

You perhaps are tempted to look to your surroundings, or to others—to everything except to yourself and God—as the way out. Don't—there is no other way out. Listen to the doctor's story of this once-desperate soul. Mrs. ———, twenty-five years old, was suffering from arthritis. She had gone from place to place in the United States seeking health, and had no faith in doctors as she had consulted over fifty. She was in a hopeless state of mind and was filled with fears: afraid of getting well; afraid of losing her home; afraid of losing her husband's love; afraid of never being able to walk again. She was convinced that life was a "total loss," and was filled with a definite sense of guilt. Many times nurses would come out of her room in tears because they could not do anything right—she was so hard to please.

Her first step toward God was to trust Him with some of her simple fears. She began to co-operate, so that nurses no longer dreaded taking care of her. Then she began to walk. Suddenly she developed all the symptoms of a gastric ulcer when a malicious friend wrote telling her that her husband was unfaithful. She surrendered this sorrow to God and the symptoms of the ulcer left. Then her husband came and the matter was straightened out. Twice she had a return of pain —once when she lost her temper with her father-in-law; but after she had straightened out the difficulty with him, her pain left.

This patient confesses that two years prior to the arthritis she had been running away from life because of an affectional conflict, and that during the two years when her husband was studying she had been living a double life, staying out late at night, drinking in order not to think, and smoking incessantly. She saw that her way of life was what had broken down her health and had given her arthritis—that the cause of her ill-health was not physical but spiritual. She concludes, "I'm back to normal with the help of God." Sin is the abnormal; it is a trying to live against life, and that cannot be done.

O my Father and my God, I face, as this woman did, the tangled strands of life—tangled by my own sins and follies. Here and now I promise Thee that no stone will be left unturned, no pledge unfulfilled until I am free in Thee. Amen.

Heb. 12:1–2; Isa. 45:22; John 3:14–16

TURN FROM YOURSELF TO CHRIST

We now come to the third simple step. (3) *Since you
have brought to the surface all conflicts, all guilts, now turn
your attention and your loyalty from yourself to Christ.*
The bringing up of all these conflicts and fears and guilt
will leave a vacuum which only Christ can fill. When He
comes in and takes possession, then, as you turn your attention within, you are not turning your attention to yourself,
but to the Christ who is within you. Now you can be an introvert, for at that very moment you are an extrovert!

A very intelligent woman, of excellent character and
ability, loved her father devotedly. When he died she had
no one she really loved, so her frustrated love turned upon
herself. This upset her nerves and ended in further frustration. That frustrated love could be released and satisfied
only as it centered on Christ, the Eternal and the Unfolding. Our love, fastened supremely on Christ, will give all
lesser, legitimate loves their meaning and their place. They
are hallowed by that supreme love. You dare love yourself
if you love Christ supremely.

Dr. Paul Scherer told me of a brilliant woman, the brains
of a dope ring, who listened-in over the radio to find arguments against God; for she didn't merely disbelieve in God
—she hated Him. At that time she was taking three times
the legal dose in order to sleep. Something in the words she
heard broke her antagonism. She was converted. And then
the fight of disentanglement began. Again and again she
would faint for want of the drug, but she refused to take it.
She went among her gang and told what had happened to
her. Her testimony broke up the ring. Five of them were
killed in action after they went to England to help the
wounded in order "to make atonement for what they had
done to destroy others." She herself is now a radiant Christian, in social-service work in a great city. A new loyalty
and love broke the power of the old. Love Christ, and then
do what you like, for you will like the right. You will be
free!

O my Lord and Master, I see that I can be free only
when I am in love with Thee, for love of Thee is love of myself. What bondage—what freedom! I know now what the
promise means when it says, "If the Son shall make you
free, ye shall be free indeed." I am free indeed. I thank
Thee, Father. Amen.

II Cor. 8:11–12; I Cor. 1:26–29; 3:21–23

NEGATIVISM AND INFERIORITY ATTITUDES

We come now to the sixth outstanding enemy of human living: *Negativism and inferiority attitudes*. One is almost tempted to put this down as Enemy Number One. The probabilities are that Fear is Enemy Number One. But as negativism and inferiority attitudes are closely allied to fear, we may put this down as Enemy Number Two.

This enemy is all the more dangerous because it is often manifested as its opposite—superiority attitudes. One who is not sure of himself talks loud, boasts, swaggers, to impress others, and tries to bolster up himself with outward show. "I am coming to see you in a Cadillac," phoned a friend of long ago. He had wasted his great possibilities, and so tried to make himself big by talking "Cadillac" instead of "Ford." Jesus saw small men trying to be big; so He said, "Which of you by taking thought can add one cubit unto his stature?" We try to add cubits to our stature by taking thought of outer decorations to make up for inner inferiorities. A sign on a livestock market appealed to this underlying psychology by saying, "Call Attention Through Cattle." Small men, who could not call the attention of others to themselves because of what they are inherently or because of what they have accomplished, could gather the attention of people through being associated with fine cattle. Standing on a steer's back to appear taller! A feat which, to say the least, is precarious, for the steer might pull out from under you and let you down—perhaps with a ridiculous bump! That is what usually happens, for those who try to appear great end in being ridiculous. A psychologist says that "there are a million chances to one that those who claim superiority are unpopular." They defeat their own purpose. "He that saveth his life" by concentrating on it, dressing it up to appear bigger than it is, is bound to defeat his own purpose—in the words of Jesus, he "loses it." Superiority attitudes and delusions of grandeur are the reverse side of an inferiority complex. Shun superficial superiorities as you would shun the devil, for they are much the same.

O God, I want to be what I am without any sham. But I want to be more: I want to be the man Thou dost intend me to be. Then I shall stand with simplicity and dignity in Thy will and purpose. For everything in Thy will is great —perhaps I shall be great, too, if I stay in Thy will. In Jesus' name. Amen.

Rom. 12:3, 16; 141, 4, 10, 13, 15

TOUCHY PEOPLE AND UNSURE PEOPLE

Yesterday we began our meditations on negativisms and inferiority attitudes, and we saw that some assert themselves most when they are least sure of themselves. I know of a man who, feeling inferior to his wife, asserts his superiority by insisting on buying her clothes and telling her what to wear—to his wife's dismay! He insists on bossing her outer life, for he feels inferior before her mental and spiritual life.

Sometimes there is an alternation between aggressive attitudes and periods of discouragement and self-depreciation. This cycloid behavior results in moodiness. Such a person ranges in temperament from very high mountains to very low valleys. But often the attitudes of retreat and defeat result not in mood depression, but in the "tic." Professor David Eitzen says, "Slamming the door, walking rapidly, stamping the floor, arguing with one's associates, spanking the children—these are manifestations of a difficulty not faced and intelligently approached." Whether manifested as moodiness and sulkiness or as an outburst of temper with surroundings or with others, the difficulty is the same sense of inward inferiority. The man is out of sorts with himself; so he vents his ill-humor on his surroundings. He creates outer earthquakes usually in order to hide his own inner soul-quakes. Just as bodily shivers are an attempt of nature to bring up one's temperature when it has fallen below par, so these shakes of temper are a psychological attempt to bring up the temperature of the inner self! The man is inwardly slipping; so he takes to outer shouting. This is the law of overcompensation at work. Touchy people are unsure people. They are looking for slights, for they have a subconscious feeling that they deserve them. You can tell the size of a man by the size of the things that upset him. Not long ago I received a special-delivery letter from a woman asking me to come a rather long journey to see her, for she was afraid she was going to have a total breakdown. Cause? Her plans for Christmas had been upset!

O God, I come to Thee to find power to be really strong. Save me from these make-believe strengths that leave me weak. I want to be the kind of person nothing without can upset, for I am so sure within. But only as I am inwardly fortified by Thy strength can this happen. I expose myself to Thy true strength. In Jesus' name. Amen.

Heb. 10:38–39; Acts 13:13; Gal. 2:11–13

MADE FOR POSITIVE ACHIEVEMENT

You and I are made in our inmost being for positive achievement—to be outgoing, to master our circumstances, to create. If we are not positively creating and producing, the machinery of life will get out of gear; for we are geared to creation. Negativism, therefore, not only keeps us from achieving; it also keeps us from being. The personality breaks down under negative attitudes. We are not made for them.

I know a person whose first attitude toward everything new that is presented is "No!" She lives in the objective mood. And hence her life is frustrated, when, with her powers, it might be fruitful. A more dramatic illustration is that of a woman of intellectual ability who became afraid of life, pulled in, and made retreat her life strategy. When she pulled in on herself, and refused to be outgoing, Nature began to take her toll—her knees began to stiffen. She became a confirmed invalid. But not only did her knees stiffen; her brain cells also began to decay through worry and anxiety and fear. As the doctors put it, "Her brain cells are rotten with fear." She became impossible—for herself and others. The life forces were breaking down under this retreatism. So the doctors decided to cut off that part of the brain which presides over foresight, now corrupted through fear and worry, and let it atrophy, so that the rest of the brain would function, but without the fear and worry. That fear and worry had to be got rid of either by operation or by the cleansing power of faith. She refused the faith: "I have run away too long. If you had got hold of me years ago, you might have headed this off—there is nothing now but the operation."

Retreatism and negativism are infections that corrupt the brain cells, make flabby the tissues, and poison the spirit. You must decide that they will have no part nor lot within you, since you want to live abundantly.

My God and Father, I belong to Thee, Thou Creator God. I would link myself with Thy Creative Spirit and become creative and positive and victorious. For I belong to today and tomorrow and forever. I do not belong to a wistful sighing over a dead past, nor to a fear of today—I belong to victory! Help me take it. Amen.

Gal. 5:1; II Tim. 1:7; John 6:66–68

DO NOT DRESS UP NEGATIVISM AS A FRIEND

If we are to get out of negativism and inferiority attitudes, we must take certain positive steps. Our getting out will not just happen. No startling miracle of deliverance will happen unless we co-operate. The miracle of deliverance will work as we work, but only as we work. Don't sit helplessly and expect either God or man, to perform a miracle *on* you. But both God and man can perform a miracle *through* you if you co-operate. Then take these steps: (1) *Recognize negativism and inferiority attitudes as enemies —do not try to dress them up as friends.* You will be tempted to look upon negativism as prudence, and inferiorities as humility. Strip off these false cloaks, and see these attitudes in their nakedness—as enemies of you and of your possibilities.

When a hard thing comes before you, you will take one of four methods in dealing with it, according to Dr. M. S. Congdon, a psychologist: "(1) Flee it! (2) Fight it! (3) Forget it! (4) Face it!" The first three ways will end in failure—only the fourth opens a door. Your first step is a facing of the facts—the whole of the facts. Don't be like the Scotch minister who began by saying, "This is a difficult text; having looked it in the face we will pass on." Don't pass on until you have really looked your difficulty in the face and have seen it for what it is—not something that must be excused, or defended, or explained away or rationalized, but something that must be ousted.

A minister took the first step to victory when he arose and said in a meeting: "'I can't' and 'tomorrow' are the twin evils of my life, crippling me and my ministry. 'I can't do things,' or 'I can't do them today'—these are the paralyzing hands laid on me." He was on his way to victory in the honest segregation of these enemies and in the recognizing of them as such. After segregation comes elimination—but first segregation.

Thou frank and openhearted Christ, help me to be frank and openhearted, for I want to be adequate and contributive. Take from my life all negative thinking, all refusal to accept responsibility, all fearful attitudes, and let me face life with a confidence and a with a song. In Jesus' name. Amen.

Gal. 2:21; II Tim. 3:16–17; 4:10–11; Phil. 4:13

FRUSTRATING MYSELF

Now take the second step to release: (2) *Let this idea grip you: I am made in the inner structure of my being for creative achievement; when I draw back from that I frustrate myself.*

One of the outstanding ministers of this country is Dr. Shirkey of San Antonio, Texas, a radiant soul and contagious. But he came near living up to his name—or down to it! For he told me that as a lad he had supersensitive finger tips, and at last his mother consented to let him grow long fingernails to protect them. But one day his schoolteacher called him up before the class and made him cut his nails publicly. This humiliation turned him against school: so he had to invent sicknesses to keep away. One of these make-believe ills was a pain in the hip. The pain became a real pain and grew so serious that a surgeon decided to put him in a cast, for which measurements were taken. Then the lad saw what was happening; he broke down and told his mother the cause. He never went back to the doctor. He is an Apollo in health today, but he came near being a cripple all his days. The negative retreatism was arrested in time by an honest facing of the facts.

A doctor was dealing with a patient whose life was running on half of its cylinders. "You were brought up by women," said the doctor. "How do you know?" the man asked, rather startled. The doctor replied, "I can see all the 'don'ts' you got before five years of age coming out in you now." It was true—he had been brought up by unreasonable maiden aunts. Those "don'ts" had got down in his subconscious mind and were controlling his conduct, inhibiting him from being a creative person, and filling him with fears. In the account of Pharaoh's refusal to let Israel go there is this passage according to Moffatt: "The whole land was ruined with gnats." (Exodus 8:24.) Many a life is ruined by tiny things like gnats; and the worst gnat is a fearful "don't."

O God, Thou who willest that I will, help this will of mine to will Thy will. Help me to link my littleness to Thy greatness, my faintheartedness to Thy loving aggression, my holding back to Thy ongoingness, my fear to Thy faith— then nothing can stop me. Amen.

II Cor. 9:8; Eph. 2:19–22; Rev. 19:10; Jer. 1:6–10

SHUT YOUR MIND AGAINST ALL
NEGATIVE THOUGHTS

We saw yesterday that the second thing to do was to realize that all negativism and inferiorities are unnatural—are
a sin against ourselves and our possibilities as well as a sin
against others and against God. A country girl who had
moved to a city fainted every time she saw a cow, even in
the city. That cow was connected with something unpleasant back on the farm; so the girl's mind went into reverse
at sight of the animal and she fainted away to escape the
cow and what it stood for. It was necessary for her to recognize that such a retreat was unnatural, something imported, something for which she was not made—a mind infection.

(3) *Shut your mind against all negative thoughts the moment they come.* Do not entertain those thoughts and give
them a seat; for if they get your attention they will get you.
Meet them at the door and slam it in their faces; lock the
door and throw the key under a red-hot stove, so you cannot get at it. Paul literally says that: "Shut your mind." A
nurse disliked a patient exceedingly. On the threshold of
going in to see this repulsive patient, she paused for prayer.
The words came, "Inasmuch as ye have done it unto one of
the least of these, my brethren, ye have done it unto me."
Love came. No patient was ever repulsive again. It was well
she did not act on the negative thought.

Don't admit, even to yourself, let alone to anyone else,
that you are inferior or afraid. Above all, don't talk about it
as a virtue—it isn't; it's a sin. "Why don't you admit your
inferiority?" said someone to a Negro. To which the reply
came: "I am a child of God, and out of loyalty to my Father I cannot accept that I am inferior. " As a child of God
he was not inferior—he was capable of infinite possibilities.
So our faith in ourselves is not a lifting-ourselves-with-our-
bootstraps faith. It is a faith rooted in the fact of our
relationship with God. That mystic, Rufus Moseley, puts
it in these quaint and beautiful words: "The Holy Ghost
makes me put back my shoulders."

My Father, in Thee how can I be a worm of the dust?
I'm not. I'm Thy child, made in Thine image, enforced by
Thy mind, empowered by Thy purposes, rekindled by Thy
love, and remade by Thy redemption. I cannot be inferior
since Thou art not, for I am in Thee. Amen.

Rom. 12:3–8; I Cor. 3:18–23; 6:19–20

NO ILLUSIONS OF GRANDEUR!

If you are to shut your mind against all negative think-ing, you must also (4) *shut your mind against all illusions of grandeur.* The temptation will be for you to swing back from one attitude to its opposite, and, as mental compensa-tion, to indulge in extravagant notions about yourself. You are neither a worm nor a wonder—you are just a bundle of fine possibilities, if developed.

A father said to his daughter who had been slipping in her achievements: "You are not the least bit inferior." To which the girl replied: "No; the fact is, I'm superior in many things." That reply was revealing, for it showed the secret of her ineffectiveness. She had rebounded from thoughts of inferiority to illusions of grandeur, nursing the idea that she was not like the common herd, and filling her mind with phantasies and daydreaming. From being in the dust, she had gone to living in fairy castles in the air. She had to get back to earth. You don't belong either to grovel-ing in the dust or to soaring in the clouds; but you belong to the earth, with your feet on it, and walking straight into tasks that you can do.

That leads to the next step. (5) *Discipline your aspira-tions to possibilities.* If you set up too high standards of achievement, beyond the reach of your powers even when they are used by God, then you may become discouraged and give up and do nothing. I know a youth who, because he had such high aspirations of achievement that he couldn't reach those high goals, would lie on his bed and read. Since he couldn't do everything, he would do nothing. He should have disciplined his goals to the possible.

A minister felt that he should do the work of Moody. He prayed hard and worked hard, but no spectacular Moody results came. And then he came to the conclusion that when God got hold of Moody He got hold of a bigger man, and that God expected him to do his own work, not Moody's.

O God, stretch me to my utmost—and that utmost means all I can be in and through Thee; but don't let me cry for the moon. Help me to evaluate what I can be in Thee, and then let me go out for that goal with all I have and with all Thou canst give to me. In Jesus' name. Amen.

Matt. 9:29; 17:20; Mark 11:22; Rom. 14:23; Mark 11:24

YOUR POSSIBILITIES IN GOD

We left off last week by suggesting that we are to discipline our expectations to our possibilities. To "hitch your wagon to a star" is good, provided in following that star you keep to the roads of open possibilities; otherwise you may find yourself in a swamp of discouragement and disillusionment. But having said the above, we come now to the next step. (6) *You are to gage your possibilities not in yourself, but according to what you can be in God.* That leaves you with a disciplined, but an ever-expanding, possibility; for possibilities in God are infinite. All this is not you, but you plus God.

Hannah sang this prayer: "My heart thrills to the Eternal, my powers are heightened by my God." (I Samuel 2:1, Moffatt.) Our powers are heightened by our God. True, they are *our* powers, still subject to limitations and not supposed to do the work of someone else, but they are heightened—provided they are surrendered to God and to His purposes. And then anything may happen—yes, anything.

Dr. Ray Allen translates into rigorous but true language the passage where the father of the epileptic boy pleads for Jesus' help. He says, "But if you can do anything, help us." To which Jesus replied, " 'If you can'—everything is 'can' to those who believe." Men of faith have thrown out "can't" and put in "can." Across the hall from where I am writing once lay a cripple—a hopeless cripple, living in a darkened room. "The Little Sister"—for so they affectionately called her—set up a home for cripples in China on the site of the pond into which people used to throw crippled children. In that darkened room faith worked through love. Her faith inspired others, and money came in and was sent through her loving hands on its healing mission. A cripple sets up a home for cripples! Everything is "can" to those who believe.

"My religion," said Lao-tse, "is to think the unthinkable thought, to speak the ineffable word, to do the impossible deed and to walk the impossible way."

O God, in Thee I cannot be defeated nor fail, for I am now under a living mind and a living will, and the future is open. I haven't much to offer, but what I have is Thine. Heighten these powers, so that I shall be a continuous surprise, even to myself. Amen.

Heb. 11:8–12, 33–40; 12:1–3

DOING WHAT YOU CAN'T!

Yesterday we saw how a darkened room, filled with physical agony, brought light to hundreds across the seas. That is the meaning of "everything is 'can' to those who believe." And it was all so human and so divine. Dr. W. V. Kelley spoke at her funeral of "the miracle of her healthy mind." It was a healthy mind because a harnessed mind; it was disciplined to the possible, and yet how utterly impossible! Her faith had its feet upon the ground; but sometimes faith walked so fast that those feet seemed to leave the earth. No wonder Dr. Kelley could dedicate his book, "To one who through years of suffering bears an illumined face." A crippled body, a healthy mind, an illumined face, a home for cripples—why? In and through it all God worked as she worked.

Someone has put it this way: "It is good to work; it is better still that our work should lead us to let God work." My work then will be—to let Him work! That is what Jesus meant when He said in answer to the question, "What must we do to perform the works of God?" "This is the work of God, to believe." (John 6:29, Moffatt.) When I am believing then I am really working, for I become a channel of the Infinite.

One day in Washington as we waited on God in a small group to see what next step we could take to help bring peace between Japan and America, I told them that I had a very difficult assignment that day—I was to see someone I didn't really want to see and yet it had to be done. A layman quoted this inscription on a tombstone: "She hath done what she couldn't." I went forth with those words ringing in my heart. I kept saying to myself, "I'll do what I can't." And did! When we are completely surrendered to God we can do what we can't—we find ourselves miracles to ourselves. "I like my poems best," said Emerson, "because I did not write them." He felt that he had surrendered to a Power that wrote through him. So he was a surprise to himself.

O God, now I begin to see that the way of open possibilities lies before me. I adventure with Thee. For then nothing is too small, beneath our dignity to do; and nothing too large, beyond our powers to do. I am following—lead on! Amen.

John 1:42, 47–51; Luke 19:1–9

THE MAN JESUS SAW

See yourself not in what you are, but in what you are and can be in God. There were three persons in Matthew the publican: (1) the publican whom his associates saw; (2) the Matthew whom Matthew saw; (3) the Matthew whom Jesus saw. Each thought he saw the true Matthew. Who was right? The Matthew whom Jesus saw was the true Matthew, and so he turned out to be—the Matthew of infinite possibilities. There are three people in you: the one your associates see—the outer you; the one you see—the present you; the one whom Jesus sees—the future you.

Everything depends on which "you" you center upon. If you are centering on the "you" your associates see, you will be in bondage to what others think about you; you will look around before you act to see what effect your action will have on others—you won't act; you will react. You will become an echo and not a voice—a thing and not a person. If you center upon the "you" you know, then you will be discouraged. For who has not had some skeleton in his closet —things in his life that make his cheeks burn with shame and humiliation? If you are centered on this "you," you will be caught in the bondage of inhibitions, by what you have been and are. But there is this third "you" that Jesus sees —what a "you" that is! It is a "you" surrendered to God, co-operating with Him, taking His resources, working out life together—a "you" loosed from what you've been and done, reinforced with divine energy and insight; a "you" that does things beyond your capacity, amazing both yourself and others—a "you" poised, progressive, and productive. That is the real "you." Center on Christ's "you," and you will become it.

Jesus always looks not on what a man has been or is, but on what he is going to be. And that is right. The artist looks not on what a stone has been or is, but on what he is going to bring out of it—the living figure. A group of radiant Christians have as their motto, "My adventure is God." Good; and under your breath you can add, "My adventure is God, and the self I'm going to be in God."

God—I'm adventuring in Thee! I'm pushing back my small horizons as I see Thine. I'm sloughing off my littleness as I see Thy greatness. I'm leaving my outgrown self by life's unresting sea. I'm exchanging my "you" for Thy "you." My bonds are bursting—and I come. Amen.

Gal. 5:16, 24–25; Rom. 13:14; Eph. 3:14–21

LOOK BEYOND SELF TO GOD

You must linger upon this thought of seeing yourself in God, for it needs correction. (7) *Don't look too long at this self in God—look at God.* A great many cults center upon self-cultivation and leave behind a multitude of wistful, but frustrated people, lifted for a moment, and limping for a lifetime. Why? You dare not center on yourself, for, if you do, as sure as fate you will lose yourself. "Whosoever will save his life"—centering on his life, loving it even for purposes of cultivating it—will lose it.

As long as Peter looked at himself or the waves around him, he started sinking. Only as he looked at Jesus, did he walk firmly on the waters. Look at yourself, or at others, and you will sink; look at Christ, and you can walk on anything. As someone has suggested: "Say to yourself, 'Salivate,' and the probabilities are that no water will come into your mouth; on the contrary, it will probably dry up. But think of a savory dish, and without your saying anything the water will flow." You must think, not of yourself even to cultivate yourself; but think of Christ, and the self will be cultivated. Glance at yourself in God, but gaze at God.

This law of losing one's life to find it runs through everything. Jesus said, "Consider the lilies, *how they grow.*" How do they grow? By being self-conscious, and fussily trying to grow and to look beautiful? No; they look at the sun, and in their sun-centeredness they themselves grow beautiful. Beauty cults and classes to teach one charm lose themselves, for they break themselves upon this law of saving one's life and losing it. The beauty cults end in painted dolls, and the charm classes lose their charm. The only beautiful people are people who lose themselves in a great Cause; and they grow beautiful as they continually gaze at Beauty. The only charming people are people who charm you to great ends; and they themselves become charming as they lose themselves in you and in others: "The Little Sister of the illumined face," and Pennefather to whom as he walked the streets a beggar cried, "Oh, you with Heaven in your face!"

O God, I dare not gaze on myself, even in Thee. But I do gaze on Thee and find myself. In Thee I gaze and grow—in myself I cultivate and deteriorate. So now my eye is getting in focus. I begin to understand what Thou didst mean: "If thine eye be single, thy whole body shall be full of light." My whole body is full of light. Thank Thee, Father. Amen.

Eph. 1:17–23; Phil. 4:8–9

A PROBLEM-CENTERED GAZE IS UNHEALTHY

Just a word before we leave the point of looking at yourself even in God. Whatever gets your attention gets you, and you must not be the center of attention even when you are in God. Our faith is God-centered, not you-centered. So look away from your sins and diseases; look away from yourself—look away to God.

Look away from your sins and diseases. If your gaze is on sin and disease—is sin-centered and disease-centered—you'll never get well. I asked some people in a sanitarium to sew and knit for China, that "continent of pain." As they had countless hours upon their hands, I thought they would crowd the lady whom I designated to take their names. Not a person gave a name. Then I saw what had happened: these people weren't self-centered because they were sick; they were sick because they were self-centered. And they would never get well until they turned their attention from themselves to God and others.

In airplanes in France there is a cup in front of each passenger with a sign, "For airsickness." In English planes the notice reads, "In case you feel indisposed, the steward will help you." In the English planes scarcely anyone gets sick, but in the French planes almost everyone does! Passengers look at the word "sickness" and the cup—enough! But when they read the sign in the English planes they think of a "steward"; the attention is called off from self; the sickness is pushed to the margin. In an airplane in America we were riding a gale of 80 miles an hour, and over mountains —the air was churned up terribly. A lady opposite me reading a book on "Health" yelled when the plane seemingly dropped out from under us, and she forthwith got sick. But I pictured myself as riding a bucking bronco, felt the exhilaration of the experience, and rode the bronco and the storm unscathed. A prominent minister preached ten consecutive Sundays on "How to avoid a nervous breakdown," and ended up with one. His psychology was bad—it was centered on a breakdown. It should have been centered on the Resources.

My Father, God, I see where I should be centered— Thou art my center and my circumference. In Thee I am safe and steady and growing. In sickness and sin and myself, I wither. For I am fashioned in my inmost being for Thee—Thou Homeland of my soul. I thank Thee. Amen.

Matt. 5:1–10; Luke 18:16–17

THE KINGDOM BELONGS TO YOU!

We turn again from considering the problem-centered gaze to the Resources. (8) *Remember that you do not merely belong to the Kngdom of God—the Kingdom of God belongs to you.* Here is a fact which you must lay hold of, for in grasping it you turn the whole tide from defeat to victory. Possess this, and it will possess you.

Jesus said three classes possess the Kingdom: "Blessed are the poor in spirit: for theirs is the kingdom of heaven"; "Suffer the little children to come unto me, ... for of such is the kingdom of God"; "Blessed are they which are persecuted for righteousness' sake: for theirs is the kingdom of heaven." Here the "poor in spirit," "the little children," and those who are sufficiently positive to be "persecuted" —they all possess the Kingdom, the Kingdom belongs to them; its powers are theirs.

The first two classes are alike: "the poor in spirit," literally "the renounced in spirit," and those who have the spirit of a little child—simple, unaffected, teachable. Here we find the key that unlocks the resources of the storehouse of the universe—the Kingdom of God. The wealth of it is all "theirs." This truth is applicable everywhere. Huxley once wrote to Kingsley: "Science seems to me to teach in most unmistakable terms the Christian conception of entire surrender to the will of God. Science says, 'Sit down before the facts as a little child, be prepared to give up every preconceived notion, be willing to follow to whatever end nature will lead you, or you will know nothing.' " How does the scientist gain mastery over nature? By surrendering to it! If the scientist is proud, unteachable, he will learn nothing, master nothing. Every great scientist is a humble man —has to be, or he could not be a great scientist. He advances, as it were, upon his knees—then he stands straight and masterful; all the powers of nature are at his disposal. "The meek inherit the earth." So you, too, as you surrender to the Kingdom of God, inherit its powers—they are all yours.

O God, it seems too good to be true—that all these powers are mine! Mine? I, who have been defeated and negative and afraid; can I dare take all these powers of victory and release and usefulness? Then I do take them, for I keep nothing back—absolutely nothing. And, giving all, I take all. In Jesus' name. Amen.

II Cor. 5:20; Eph. 6:20; Acts 4:13–20

THE KINGDOM SPEAKS WHEN YOU SPEAK

We must continue to pursue the thought that we do not merely belong to the Kingdom—the Kingdom belongs to us. This is so important, that once you get hold of it all argument and hesitation and fear are at an end. You enter abundant living.

An ambassador represents his country—all the powers and privileges of his country center in him. When he speaks, the country speaks; when he decides, the country decides—provided he is not speaking on his own, provided he is surrendered to the will of his country, provided he has merged his interests in the interests of his country. When entirely surrendered, he is entirely masterful—up to the limit of the resources of the country he represents.

If you have merged your interests in the Kingdom of God, if you are entirely surrendered to it, if you speak representing not yourself, but the Kingdom, then all the powers of the Kingdom center in you—a Universe speaks when you speak; a Universe acts when you act; a Universe lives when you live. The resources of earthly kingdoms are so limited—the resources of the Kingdom of God are so unlimited. That Government which stretches from the lowest cell to the farthest star comes to focus in you—it is all yours! Some high-school boys were discussing a certain Christian, and one of them said, "He's got what it takes!" Yes, for he takes what he's got! Had he been standing alone, he would not have what "it takes." But taking from the Kingdom, he could "take it" from life. He was invulnerable.

A little boy of five, son of a minister, said to me, "We preach down in Troy." I loved that: when the father preached, he preached, and when the little boy preached by his life, the father preached. He accepted the corporate responsibility—he merged his interests in the father's, and felt the corporate accomplishment.

You work with the Spirit of God, and the Holy Spirit is the Comforter, the Strengthener, or, to use a colloquial translation, "the Stand-by."

O God, I merge my interests in the Kingdom; I accept its responsibilities; and, and—dare I say it?—I inherit its powers! Help me to be unafraid of being great—of being great in surrender, great in responsibility, great in resources, great in myself, because great in Thee. Amen.

John 1:12–13; 15:1–18

RECEPTIVITY—THE FIRST LAW OF LIFE

We carry over from last week our ladder out of negativism and inferiority. Since the Kingdom belongs to you, (9) *remember the two conditions for receiving and transmitting the resources of the Kingdom: receptivity and response.*

These two words are not only the alternate heartbeats of the Kingdom; they are also the alternate beats of the whole of life. Everything grows and develops by those two things: receptivity and response. John sums up this thought in these words: "As many as received him, to them gave he power to become." How did he get power—power to become? First, by receptivity—"as many as received him."

A universal principle is here laid bare. Take a plant—how does it get power to become? By being proud, self-sufficient, unrelated, and unresponsive? No; by surrendering, adjusting, receiving, giving. Suppose a plant tried to get power by asserting itself, by trying to "lord it" over the other plants—result? It would lose its power over other plants and its power to become. It gains power by surrender and by response to its environment. When it is adjusted it takes in from air and soil and sun, and gains power to become. Plant sin is anything that hinders that receptivity and response.

Someone has defined life as response to environment. You and I live physically when we respond to our physical environment: we can take in food and light and air. When response is shut off, we die physically. Our spiritual environment is the Kingdom of God. When we respond to it, surrender to it, adjust ourselves to it, receive our very life from it, then we live—and live abundantly. We are in a state of receptivity, which is a state of faith, confidence, appropriation. We absorb Kingdom life as the body absorbs food; we breathe in its purifying breath as the lungs breathe in air; we take up its vitality as the skin takes in vitamins from the light of the sun.

To believe is to receive and to receive is to replenish.

O God, Thou who dost wrap me round as the atmosphere wraps my body round, let me respond to Thee as my physical body responds to its environment and lives. Let me breathe Thee now—deep breaths of Thee; let me receive Thee into every pore and fiber of my being. Help me to live by Thee—then I shall live. Amen.

II Cor. 6:1–10; Rom. 8:13–14

RESPONSE—THE SECOND LAW OF LIFE

If receptivity is the first law of life, response is the second law. Perhaps we can say that they are two sides of one law. Jesus revealed the two sides in His summing up of the whole meaning of religion: "Thou shalt love the Lord thy God"—receptivity; "Thou shalt love thy neighbor as thyself"—response. Love makes you receptive to God and responsive to man. Or better still: love makes you receptive to God and responsive, too—a two-way traffic. You receive from God, and you give back to God. In receiving from God you are completed and perfected, and in your responding to God—shall we say it?—God is completed and perfected. For, having created another personality, God is not complete till He gains the love and loyalty of that personality. Our response is as necessary to God as it is to us. For a Love that loves, but is not responded to, is thwarted. God is all-important to us; we are important to God.

If receptivity and response are the two heartbeats of our relationship to God, they are also the two heartbeats of our human relationships. Love lets you receive from the other person; but, just as truly, it makes you respond in self-giving to the other person. Without this clear two-way traffic the relation will break down. One who is always receiving from another and not giving will break down a relationship, and one who is always giving and not receiving will just as truly destroy the relationship. Moreover, the receptivity and the response must be about equal. If one overbalances the other, if you are more of a receiver than a responder, or more of a responder than you are a receiver, you cripple the relationship.

Impractical mysticism is strong on the receiving side, but weak on the responding side, and hence results in a lopsided religion, weak in positive contribution to human welfare. Activism is strong on the responding side, but weak on the receiving side, and hence ends in a religion lacking resources, depth, and permanence. A heart that tries to beat in one direction and not in the other ends in not beating at all.

O God, am I—I, who thought myself inferior—necessary not only to others, but to Thee? Then help me never to let Thee down. Help me humbly to receive from Thee and humbly to give back to Thee—a two-way traffic with Thee! I shall grow as I get and give. I thank Thee. Amen.

John 16:32; Matt. 28:19–20; 14:16–21

NEVER ALONE!

As you turn away from all negativism and inferiority attitudes to positive, abundant living, now take the next step. (10) *Remember that you are not alone—never alone.* At the time of seemingly greatest aloneness He is closest, watching every move on the checkerboard of life.

The American Indians trained their boys in courage by making them spend a night in the forest amid the wild animals. How dreadfully alone each boy would feel on the night of his testing; but when the day began to dawn he would see his father behind a nearby tree with drawn bow. Without the son's knowledge, the father had been watching all night to see that no harm should befall the son. So is God with us. John Wilhelm Rowntree tells how, when he left a great physician's office where he had been told that his advancing blindness could not be stayed, he stood by some railings for a few moments to collect himself. "Suddenly he felt the love of God wrap him about as though an invisible presence enfolded him, and a joy filled him such as he had never known before." That Presence will manifest Himself when most needed.

Say to yourself, "I live and move and have my being, in all inner thoughts and outer expression, in the wealth of God every moment." And say this when you least feel the truth of it and keep saying it.

And to the above statement add these words as you go forth to meet life: "With the peace of God in my heart and with good will toward my fellow men I am ready for the work of the day." And you will be ready for the work of the day!

Then when you lie down to sleep say to yourself again: "Today I have lived and moved and have had my being in God, and while I sleep I still live and have my being in Him. He will guide and purify my dreams and in the morning I shall be further along." "Those who have the gales of the Spirit are carried forward even in sleep," says Brother Lawrence.

O God, You and I will work this out together. I am yet weak and can take only a small part of the load—You'll have to take the heavy end. But You have my will and, when it develops, You'll have my strength, too. I thank Thee. Amen.

II Cor. 10:10; 11:6; 12:7–12

YOUR HANDICAPS YOUR HANDLES!

In your going on to victory remember this fact: (11)
Your very handicaps may be new points of departure. Perhaps you may have had a bad start in life—your heredity
may be against you. But that need not be other than a spur
to you to pass on to others a better heredity. If you look
back into the human heredity of Jesus, you will find some
ugly spots: "David was the father of Solomon by Uriah's
wife." "By Uriah's wife"—what a tragedy to have such a
label stuck on one's life! But what a glory it is that both
David and Solomon survived that tragedy and contributed,
in spite of it! And think of the honest courage it took to put
that statement into the genealogy of Jesus Christ. He who
was going to begin a new humanity had the blood of the
old humanity in His veins. But the divine inheritance so
overcame the human inheritance that He passed on a new
inheritance to humanity. Through His divine inheritance
you can begin a new heredity.

Or suppose you are handicapped by a lack of beauty;
then you can make up in accomplishment what you lack in
endowment. Almost all great beauties have nothing but
physical beauty. And the reason is plain: they get tangled
up in their beauty and cannot free themselves from it to
pass on to constructive achievement. But a person who is
plain in features looks in the looking glass and says to himself, "There is nothing in my looks for me to bank on," and
so he goes out and does something worthwhile. With rare
exceptions, the women who have achieved great things in
the world were women of ordinary looks. As I have gone
about the world, I have found that missionary women on
the whole are not noted for beauty of face—but, oh, the
beauty of their accomplishments and their characters!

As you look at your handicaps and make up your mind
to use them as handles, it is well to remember that a secondary failure may make you a primary success; whereas a
secondary success like beauty may make you a primary
failure.

My Father, what I lack by nature I shall make up by
grace. I cannot draw heavily on many things, but I can
draw heavily on Thee. Make my very weaknesses into Thy
strength. Help me to take hold of my handicaps and convert them into handiwork. In Jesus' name. Amen.

Acts 5:40–42; Phil. 1:12–19; I Pet. 4:14

FLEE FORWARD!

Yesterday we saw the possibility of using our handicaps. Today we are going to see them as spurs that drive us forward. Jesus told His disciples that when the people turned them out of one village, they were to "flee to the next." In other words, if you have to flee, flee forward—to the next opportunity on your list. Some flee backward; but the Christian, when he flees, always flees forward. (12) *If you have the impulse to flee, then flee forward.* All of us sometimes feel like running away. We differ only in our manner of running—some flee forward, and some flee backward.

Not having a college education made Rabindranath Tagore, India's great poet, the greatest literary figure of India. He fled from the lack of a college education—forward! He could have drawn back and bemoaned his inferior education; instead he turned that lack into a spur, became superior in himself, and founded a new type of educational institution.

Once I was sitting in the back seat of a car—the kind of car that has a sliding seat in front. The man who was driving called to his wife in the back seat and said, "Please kick me forward, dear." Life is bound to kick you, for all get knocks—some more, some less; the important thing is the direction in which you are kicked. Make life kick you forward!

A young woman told me that when I was talking to an audience about mental states of fear and resentments producing stomach disorders, she blushed, for she felt that I was talking personally to her! She had not accomplished as much as she was capable of doing in her teaching of voice, and so lost her own voice to give her an excuse for her failure. The trouble was not in her vocal cords, but in her defeatist mentality. She encountered this difficulty in accomplishment, and fled backward—backward into subterfuges and excuses. She should have taken the obstacle and turned it into opportunity—her failure into fruitfulness.

My Father and my God, I see that my life will be made or broken at the place where I meet and deal with my obstacles. Help me not to run away from them, but to run toward them, to tackle and overcome them. Help me to take the impulse to flee and compel it to make me flee forward. In His name. Amen.

I Cor. 1:27–28; 6:9–11; Philem. 10–16

NOBODIES BECOME SOMEBODIES!

(13) *Remember it is never too late to be a creative personality.* No matter what happens to you, or when it happens to you, it is never too late to become creative. I know a woman, wife of a professor, who did not touch a paintbrush until she was fifty. Then she awakened, began to paint, and her paintings are being exhibited in this and other countries. She has gathered around her a group of women who before fifty had done nothing contributive, but after fifty began to be creative. One took up sculpturing, and though she had never tried that branch of art until she was fifty, became a teacher of sculpture in a great college and exhibited her own products in America and Europe.

Some artists gathered on a farm to paint the landscape. The farmer, becoming interested, painted the landscape on his own. The teacher, seeing the painting, asked who had done it. The farmer was "discovered" and became a famous landscape artist. His awakening had come at sixty-eight.

Jesus is the great Awakener. Paul speaks of "all the stimulus of Christ." He stimulates the creative center in each one of us, making it first aware of God, and then aware of the infinite possibilities in God. I was at the bottom of my class until I met Christ, and then I said to myself, "This is no place for a Christian," and left it.

Someone said of a certain great city, "I never live a week in ———— when, bang, there goes another horizon!" That is the thing that happens when we are in company with Jesus —"bang, there goes another horizon!" In His company we begin to see farther, feel for people on a wider scale, and act more decisively. Jesus takes the nobodies and turns them into the somebodies. He was the maker of men and still is. No one can be in His company long without feeling an irresistible impulse to roll up his sleeves and say, "Where do I begin?" For the creative impulse comes from contact with the creative God.

O Christ, Thou creator of living thoughts in dead brains; Thou stimulator of living love in petrified hearts; Thou arouser of living action in decayed wills; Thou giver of life, I ask Thee to enter into me and to stimulate and quicken every fiber and nerve cell that I may too become creative. Amen.

Acts 9:19–20; I Pet. 4:2–11

PLAN FOR CREATIVE ACHIEVEMENT

We come now to the last step in our ladder, (14) *Plan for creative achievement and put your plan into operation by however small a beginning.*

Say with Jesus, " 'Weep not for me'—I'm through with asking for pity, for compassion—I don't want sympathy—I want a task, an open door—I'm through with living on a No; I'm going to live on a Yes—I'm not inferior since I have hold of a superior God, and He has hold of me. I no longer belong to those who look back, for those who look back cannot fit into the Kingdom of God, and I belong to the Kingdom of God—the Kingdom of the forward-looking."

Say to yourself: "What God suffers for He means to have, and what He takes hold of He never lets go. He has taken hold of me, and He will never let me go even though I stumble. Is not the Chinese word for Jesus, 'the One who saves again and again'? He will save me again and again even though I fail."

Pray as one man did who had gone insane: "O Jesus, come into my soul, my mind, my body, into every brain cell." Jesus did come into every brain cell, and the man is well and contributing today.

Write down all your negative thoughts, and then tear them up as a symbol that they no longer exist. Then write down your positive thoughts about what you can do, and begin at once to express these thoughts in however small a beginning. If you cannot do one thing, flee forward and do the next thing. Then decide to do what you have decided to do, and do it now.

"The Spirit entered into me and made me stand upon my feet." The spirit of God has entered into you; now you are to stand upon your feet and do a man's work in the world.

Say as you go out each day, "I can do all things through Christ which strengtheneth me." Repeat it the last thing before you fall asleep at night and the first thing in opening your eyes in the morning. The subconscious mind is very susceptible at those two periods. It will get into the subconscious and work with you, making you positive and creative.

O Christ, at last the doors of my life are turning outward instead of inward. At last I have lifted my feet out of the quicksand of self-pity. At last I have love in my heart, courage in my will, and faith in my inmost being. So let life come on. I thank Thee. Amen.

1 Tim. 1:5; 1 Cor. 9:19–27

UNDISCIPLINED DESIRES

We have led you to the top of our fourteen-runged ladder and trust you now find yourself victorious over all negativism and inferiority attitudes—a positive, outgoing soul. For two weeks we have been meditating on the negative side of the picture—on people who are inwardly collapsed, afraid, negative. We now turn to the other side of the picture—to those whose desires are very positive, but uncontrolled, undisciplined. If there is danger from life being negative and afraid, there is just as much danger from life being desire-assertive. You may be ruled and ruined by undisciplined desire. Therefore, the next outstanding enemy you must face is number seven, *Undisciplined desires.*

There is a way of living which may be likened to the horse that lies down in harness and won't move; and there is the other way which may be likened to the horse that runs away and breaks the harness and smashes everything. Abundant living has to find the poise between the two—has to find something between lying down and running away; it must find the constructive, but disciplined, life.

Desires are the God-given forces of the personality and as such are right. Without desire life would turn back to the vegetable and vegetate. Buddha tried to make man victorious over the desires of life by cutting the root of desire itself, so that man would go out into desirelessness, into Nirvana. But you cannot cure the ills of life by reducing life; you cannot get rid of your headaches by getting rid of your head. The remedy of life is not less life, but more life. You must have enough inward life to master outer environment and circumstance.

But if life is to be raised, it can only be raised through disciplined desire. The only way to get rid of a desire is to replace it by a higher desire, or to fasten the already existing desire upon higher ends and higher goals. Desires are the driving forces, and driving forces cannot be taken out of life—they must be redirected through discipline. There are three great elemental desires which have to be converted and controlled and disciplined to great ends: self, sex, and the herd.

O God, we are now at grips with the raw materials of human living; out of them we must fashion a person—Thy person. This raw material is recalcitrant and needs a master: be Thou the Master of my desires. I give the reins into Thy hands. Control them for me; I consent. Amen.

1 Cor. 6:12–20

THE URGES REDEEMED

We saw yesterday that the three driving urges of the personality are self, sex, and the herd. We saw that they cannot be eradicated or replaced—they must be redirected through discipline.

Take the frst—self. It is the primary urge and the first to be developed. When the developing child is crossed, it expresses its displeasure in various unpleasant ways. The same thing happens in the grownup. Adler says that the will to power, which is the assertion of the self, is the organizing primary urge—everything is organized around it.

Now what does Christianity do with this primary urge of self? Does it try to wipe it out and make one selfless? Try to crucify it and make it impotent? The answer to both questions is "No!" Christianity believes in the self, for the self is God-given and is not given to be cancelled out. "Thou shalt love Thy neighbor *as theyself.*" The self is to be loved, even as the neighbor is to be loved. The self is affirmed, and is worthy of love. It is your right and your duty to be the best possible self you can be.

Christianity therefore accepts the struggle for life that goes on in nature, expressed in the survival of the fittest: in lower nature the unfit are eliminated. If they do not excel they are exterminated. This is a hard and ruthless law; and Christians have drawn back from accepting such a process, questioning whether such a merciless manner of survival can have anything to do with God. It seems utterly at variance with the plan of redemption. But I am coming more and more to feel that this ruthless process is redemption—it redeems those that fit into the physical environment and eliminates those that will not. In a physical environment the physically best survive and pass on their fine physical qualities to the next generation. This is right. For if the law were otherwise, the survival of the unfit would end in physical degeneration. One generation would pass on its unfitness to the next generation, and so on to extinction.

My Father, I see that Thy school is strict, but the end is redemption. Thy laws, however uncompromising, are our salvation. They are made for us, and they mean to make us. Help us then not to chafe at them as enemies, but to embrace them as friends. For all Thy laws are Thy loves. I thank Thee. Amen.

Acts 17:28; Rom. 11:36; Eph. 4:6; Luke 17:21

THE KINGDOM OUR REAL ENVIRONMENT

Yesterday we saw that we must accept the struggle in nature that produces a superior physical self. The end of this struggle is redemption from weakness and from unfitness. While we must accept this fact, nevertheless the danger lies in taking the laws of adaptation to a moral and spiritual environment. The laws of struggle and adaptation to a purely physical environment do not fit a moral and spiritual environment, and when applied to this higher environment they break down and cause confusion. For the moral and spiritual world in which man lives has its own laws of adaptation and survival. When a man acts in accordance with these laws, he survives and develops; when he doesn't, he decays and is utterly destroyed.

Christianity, founded on the laws of the Kingdom of God, believes in the survival of the fittest: in a moral and spiritual universe, the morally and spiritually fit survive, and pass on their spiritual and physical qualities to the next generation. This law of the survival of the fittest and the elimination of the unfit operates before our very eyes.

The environment into which man must fit, and to which he must adapt himself, is therefore the Kingdom of God. When we fit into this Kingdom, we live; and when we don't, we are self-frustrated—the structure of our beings breaks down. In the words of Jesus, we "Perish." Here and now the process of perishing takes place, and the life forces break down through what we call evil. A suicide in England left this note: "Many explanations will be given of this act, but I think it is this: I see that it is the result of a private war going on inside myself, and which cannot be solved." The war that was going on inside him was his war with the Kingdom, the laws of which were written into the constitution of his being; and when he was at war with the Kingdom, he was at war with himself. That war could not be solved—on his basis; hence, suicide.

My Father and my God, Thy Kingdom is written into my flesh and blood and bone and nerve cell. How can I escape it? For if I do, I escape from life itself. Help me therefore to come to terms with that Kingdom, and hence with life. For I would live and live fully. In Jesus' name. Amen.

John 3:16; Ps. 1:6; 37:7–9

THE CHRISTIAN'S SURVIVAL VALUE

If we accept the law of the survival of the fittest in regard to the moral and spiritual life, we then redeem and make usable the parables of the talents and the pounds. Otherwise they have no meaning—they are extraneous to the Christian system. But if we accept this law, then they become an integral part of a consistent system. Those parables are terrible—those who do not develop the talent or the pound have them taken away. However, they are no more terrible than life itself, for that is what life does. If we do not develop any faculty or organ it will degenerate—it is taken away.

The acceptance of the law of the survival of the morally and spiritually fit also redeems and makes possible the ideas of heaven and hell—ideas which have been lost to this generation, for heaven and hell have usually been taught as something extraneously given by God. No wonder this generation lost these ideas! They were morally indefensible. But teach heaven and hell as inherent results and they come back as natural corollaries. Good, by its very nature, is self-sustaining and self-perpetuating; evil, by its very nature, is self-disintegrating and self-destroying. A judge sentenced a man to go and look in the looking glass. After the man took one look at his face, he immediately sat down and took the pledge. The signs of disintegration were obvious and compelling. But the signs of disintegration on the face were only the outer signs of a total disintegration—the outer registration of an inner fact.

On the other hand, goodness within registers that fact in the face. An unruly young artist, noting the change in his mother's face, asked her the reason. She said, "Your mother has prayed much for you." To which he replied, "Well, it makes fine lines."

Response to the Kingdom of God does make fine lines, for it makes fine lives. It is the way to live. Not to respond to the Kingdom makes bad lines—lines that turn down—for it makes bad lives—lives that turn down toward disintegration and, if persisted in, final destruction.

O my Father, I have taken discipline from too many things. I have obeyed this and that. Result, I have become this and that—and nothing. But now the needle of my life, oscillating in many wrong directions, comes at last to rest in Thee and Thy Kingdom. It shall be first and always. Amen.

Rom. 15:1–2; 1:24; II Cor. 5:15; Phil. 2:4

THE UNDISCIPLINED SELF

Now we see that the three urges within us—self, sex, and the herd—must be disciplined, and must be disciplined to one thing—the Kingdom of God. Otherwise life will be like a brush heap instead of a tree. A brush heap has no central organizing principle, and hence is a decaying mass destined to the dust. A tree has an organizing principle, and its branches fit into that principle. Hence a tree is a growing organism, destined to the skies.

The self, then, must know its Master. The self as a servant to the Kingdom of God is rhythmical and harmonious and adequate; the self as a servant to itself is halting and inharmonious and incompetent—its own slave. A woman who is entirely egocentric, and who has therefore had a nervous breakdown, and is entirely miserable, said to me recently, "I spent all afternoon going from room to room before I got one to suit me, and now that I have selected one I don't like it." I gently replied, "The disorder is within you—you don't like anything, because you don't like yourself." Her self was out of place on the throne, and the kingdom of her personality was in disorder.

Dr. Fritz Künkel says: "Life does not allow egocentricity to put its own order, which life regards as disorder, in place of the natural rhythm. That is why every natural capacity for accomplishment, no matter how skillfully developed, is restricted sooner or later by egocentricity. Only the objectively oriented individual is unrestricted in accomplishment because he does not come into conflict with life's demands." (Let's Be Normal! pp. 97, 98.)

The self, then, must be disciplined to die. It must die as first, in order to live as second. That is why at the center of the Kingdom is a cross. You must go through spiritually what Jesus went through physically—you must die and be buried in order to experience a resurrection into freedom and fullness of life.

O Christ—I understand. The whole meaning of life is made plain. I am to follow Thee to no trifling cross, but to this decisive cross on which I shall die—die to my own futile self-will in order to live to Thy will; die to my own petty self in order to live to Thy free and strong self. Help me then from this moment to discipline my life to Thy will. Amen.

Il Tim. 2:15; I Tim. 1:15, 16; 6:11–14

ATTENTION, MEEKNESS, POWER

One of the most radiant persons I know, whose life story I shall tell later, has overcome an invalidism stretching back for forty-four years, and has made of her bed a throne. Her room is the confessional of the city. She told me that the three words she is living by this year are: *"Attention, meekness, power."* She could not have fastened upon three more important words. So vital are these words that we are going to use them as three steps to a disciplined self. (1) *Attention.* What gets your attention is all-important, for whatever gets your attention gets you. If you give self your primary attention, self will be drawn to the center of your consciousness, and everything else will be arranged around self. "Arranged" around it? Disarranged around it! For to have self at the center is to have a cancer at the center, because cancer cells are cells that make other cells contribute to them, instead of making themselves contribute to other cells. A self-attentive person lives in a state of self-referece. "How will this affect me? What do I get out of this?" Such a person is disliked by others and is disliked by himself.

Decide, then, what shall have your primary attention. Decide, as you go into the shrine of your heart, to what you are going to bend the knee. If the Kingdom of God has your allegiance, then make your loyalty absolute. Don't say "Yes" and "No." Don't be what my friend calls a "Yes, but-ter," "I'll do it, but—." Let there be no "buts" anywhere. Put Christ once and for all at the center of your attention. Then you live in a state of Christ-reference instead of a state of self-reference. To shift the very basis of your life in this way will not be easy; the self will wriggle and twist and beg off and compromise—will do everything except abdicate. A pastor arose in our Ashram and said, "I see what I need, and I see that I don't want what I need." He still loved himself first, even amid the wreckage caused by that fact of self-love. But this resolve to center Christ in your life is a decisive decision. It is a decision that decides all decisions—a seed decision.

O my God, I have been out of focus, and all life's pictures have been blurred and distorted. But now I am getting into focus, and my pictures are becoming clearer—life looks different, for I am looking upon it differently. My eye is now single, and my whole body is now full of light. I am grateful—grateful. Amen.

Ps. 22:26; 25:9; 37:11; Matt. 11:29

THE MEEK INHERIT THE EARTH!

We saw yesterday that the first step in self-discipline is "attention." We come now to (2) *Meekness*. How we have shied away from that word! We have thought of meekness as weakness. We have purposelessly misunderstood the word, for we have been afraid of what it would demand of the self, namely, surrender. For meekness is just that—surrender.

The scientist is meek, and therefore gains power over nature. The scholar is meek, and therefore gains power over knowledge. The Christian is meek, and therefore gains power over the universe. Jesus stated this truth thus: "Blessed are the meek, for they shall inherit the earth." His words seem absurd—"inherit heaven," yes; but not the earth, here and now. But the meek do. They are the only ones who do inherit the earth. To whom do the stars belong? To the Siseras who aspire to conquer the earth and heaven? "The stars in their courses fought against Sisera." The stars belong to the astronomer who meekly surrenders to them, and enters the Kingdom of the Stars through that surrender—the stars belong to him. Who owns the mountains? The man who has enough money to bring the mountains under his control? No; the mountains belong to the geologist who loves them, surrenders to them, gains their secrets, and is at home with them. Who inherits the world of the mind? Those who say they are free to do as they like with their minds? No; such people literally lose their minds! The mind belongs to the psychologist who meekly surrenders to the laws of the mind, who learns of the mind's ways —he inherits the world of the mind.

Jesus was right—as always—the meek do inherit the earth. Literally, the word is, "the disciplined shall inherit the earth." Those who bring themselves under the great Discipline, the Discipline of the Kingdom, inherit the earth. Browning expresses the same thought: "Who keeps one end in view makes all things serve." The one end is the Kingdom—all things serve those who serve the Kingdom.

O God, I now begin to feel the meaning of being disciplined. It is getting into my blood and brain cells—into me. When I shall have become a disciplined soul, I shall be free. Help me to emerge as a disciplined spirit—disciplined for the highest by the Highest. Amen.

Rom. 12:1; Deut. 28:1–6; 30:11–14

A DISCIPLINED SELF IS A SELF OF POWER

Last week we were concentrating our attention on the three steps to disciplined power: (1) Attention, (2) Meekness, (3) Power. We gain this third step only as we master the first two—there is no gaining of power by tricks, by mental legerdemain. Power comes by discipline, and by discipline alone.

An aviator told me that every moment while he is in the air he has to obey the laws of aviation—one moment's disobedience or carelessness and the machine would be wrecked. There can be no "moral holidays" while in the air; the obedience must be complete, or the mastery will not be complete. Only by attention, by meekness, does he gain power.

Begin to be hard with yourself. Paul says, "The soft shall not inherit the Kingdom of God." (I Corinthians 6:9, 10 —"effeminate" is literally "soft.") Jesus stressed the same thought when He said, "He who puts his hand to the plow and looks back is not fit [literally, cannot fit into] the Kingdom of God." Those who are undisciplined, soft, looking back toward things given up, cannot fit into the Kingdom of God, which is a Kingdom of the disciplined.

> "Severe with self,
> Gentle with others,
> Honest with all."

If all this discipline seems like a diminution of life instead of an augmentation of life, let me say that the control which discipline exerts on the self is the same kind of thwarting which is applied when a dam is thrown across a river—the even flow of the river is interrupted and restrained, but only in order that a powerhouse might be installed to create power and light. The disciplined you is not free to do as others do, but free to do what others cannot do—to be a contributive soul, full of light and power. Some will say, "I am free to do as I like," but you will say, "I am free to do as I ought." You are dammed up on one level, but only in order to raise the level of life, so that you can function on a higher level.

My Lord and my God, I am putting my head into Thy yoke—putting myself in bondage to Thee. But Thy yoke is easy, for I am made for it—Thy yoke is my yearning, for Thy laws are my life. I take Thy weights upon my shoulders only to find they are wings. Amen.

II Tim. 2:22; I Tim. 5:6; Gal. 5:24; I Pet. 2:11

A DISCIPLINED SEX LIFE

We have talked about disciplining the first of the three driving urges, the self. We come to the second—sex.

Life seems very heavily loaded on the side of sex. Some would think there is far too much sex for purposes of procreation. The human race, they think, could have procreated itself without the sex urge being so strong and imperious. It is quite probable that in normal human nature the sex urge is not so strong or so continuous as it is in abnormal modern life, but is occasional as in animals and birds —active during mating seasons, dormant the rest of the time. This is true among primitive peoples. But modern life has become strongly sexed. Everywhere the sex appeal meets one. Even advertisements carry it to attract attention. A cartoon shows a man hitting a golf ball, and a picture of a woman is drawn near the ball to make sure that he will "keep his eye on the ball." Can we not keep our eye on the ball of human living without sex being used to focus our attention? Life has been tending more and more in the direction of sex. Sex has been occupying the center of the stage, the center of literature, the center of dress, the center of our thinking. Freud explains this modern absorption in sex by saying that all life must be interpreted in terms of sex.

With all this emphasis upon sex, one would have expected this age to have found itself sexually. On the contrary, no age seems to have become more sexually dissatisfied and thwarted than this. The fact of one divorce in every six marriages tells the story of breakdown within marriage relationships. A young man committed suicide and left a note saying, "Died of old age at 21." This tells the tragic story of breakdown in sex outside marriage relationships. He had run through his sex experiences at twenty-one, and they had turned to ashes in his hands. Evidently in the matter of sex man is up against something that cannot be set down to taboos and restraints. Can it be that the nature of reality is working against modern sex attitudes and causing them to break down?

O my Creator God, Thou wilt have to take me by the hand lest I be lost in the jungle of sex desire. For if I get off the track here, I find myself in a jungle which grows more tangled every moment. Help me to see things clearly and to see them whole. Amen.

Jude 16, 18–21; Eph. 2:1–3; Rom. 8:4–9

THE LAW OF DECREASING RETURNS IN SEX

They tell us that the word "Bedlam" used to be "Bethlehem"—the place of the birth of Christ has changed to the name of a place of confusion. Is this not what has happened sexually in our day? Bethlehem, symbol of the birth of a Child—the epitome of sex in its most beautiful and tender phase—now degenerates into a veritable "Bedlam" of sex frustration and defeat. Why?

The nature of reality is working against our sex attitudes. We are working under "the law of decreasing returns"—we have to put in more to get out a corresponding result. No age ever emphasized sex more than this age has done, or enjoyed sex less. Restraints are gone; Puritanism has been banished. But now that the age is free to do as it likes, it finds it doesn't like what it does. We have gone in for thrills, only to find that ills are in thrills. We grow sick of our sex liberties. Why? The nature of reality, which is Christian, is working against our unchristian sex attitudes.

Sex in itself is neither moral nor immoral; it is amoral. The way it is used makes sex moral or immoral. Sex is like fire—you can use it wisely and be blessed by it, or you can use it unwisely and be burned by it. A great historian said, "There is one fact that history sounds—the moral law is written in everything." And that moral law is written in sex. This thing which in itself is amoral has a moral law written within it—there is an immoral way to use sex, and there is a moral way. And that way of moral use is written into the constitution of sex.

Men thought that, if they could only get rid of puritanical taboos and of moral codes written in the Scriptures, they could be free to do as they liked with sex. But they now find that the moral law is written in sex itself. Keep that moral law, and there is heaven; break it, and there is hell—here and now.

O God, as I come to Thee, I would find the moral way written into the essence of things, for I would offer my sex powers to Thee that Thou mayest use them for their best and highest purpose. I shall need wisdom, and I shall need power, for sex is very clamorous and often drowns out Thy still small voice. Help me. Amen.

I Cor. 6:12, 15–20; I Tim. 5:14; I Cor. 7:9

STEPS TO SEX VICTORY

If we are to use the powers of sex aright, then we should take the following steps: (1) *We should recognize sex for what it is—a God-given power, neither moral nor immoral in itself, but moral or immoral according to its use.*

This should take the shame out of our consideration of sex itself and put it where it belongs—on our use of sex. There is no shame in sex; there is shame in the wrong use of sex. If people would be ashamed of what they do with sex and not of sex itself, then there would be more normal, healthy attitudes toward it. Sex has brought more heaven and more hell into life than has any other thing. And we make the heaven or the hell according to what we do with sex.

Every normal person has sex desire—to act as if we have no sex desire is to produce hypocrisy and probably complexes. Bring the fact of sex up into the open in your thinking—look at it, but not too long, and then decide what you are going to do with it. Note: What you are going to do with it, and not what it is going to do with you. For sex is a wonderful servant, but a terrible master. It can serve all the interests of life, or it can ruin all the interests of life. The battle of life as a whole will probably not rise above the sex battle. Lose the sex battle and defeat spreads into every portion of your being; win the sex battle and all life is uplifted by that victory.

(2) *The place of sex is not the first place, and sex is not an end in itself.* If you put sex first, it will corrupt your whole life. Those who most ardently give sex the first place and make it an end in itself get the least out of it—little except kickbacks in the form of disgust and self-loathing. The law of sex life is this: He that saveth his sex life—makes it first, an end in itself—loseth it. And the law works with mathematical precision; there are no exceptions and no exemptions.

Seek first the Kingdom of God—make sex serve the Kingdom, and every legitimate joy connected with sex will be added.

O God, I see, if sex takes Thy place and rules me, that I shall be the servant of a desire. And that desire will ride me to the hell of self-loathing. I would therefore bring my sex life to the altar of Thy love and there ask Thee to make it the servant of my love to Thee. May these lesser loves fit into my love to Thee. Amen.

Ps. 68:6; Matt. 19:3–15

THE PRIMARY END OF SEX

If the place of sex is not the first place and if sex is not an end in itself, then what is the place of sex? (3) *The primary end of sex is the procreation of children and their nurture in an atmosphere of love.* Sex is primarily intended for the creation of persons, not of pleasures. There is a pleasure principle surrounding the procreation of children, but if this pleasure principle is detached and becomes an end in itself, it will cease to become pleasure and become the very opposite. The pleasure must be the by-product of the will to create, or it will cease to be. The sex urge is first of all a creative urge, and not a pleasure principle.

But another use of the sex urge is to produce an atmosphere of love surrounding the young life that has been created. If the occasional use of sex ministers to this love life, fosters it in the parents, lifts the whole tone of married life, then this use is justified apart from the procreative intention. But if it lowers the tone of married life, becomes a point of conflict in the individuals or between them; if it leaves life weakened mentally, morally, spiritually, or physically, then this use is not justified. It should be renounced entirely. As a sacrament of love—yes. As a sordid sexuality —no.

(4) *The sex urge not only tones up the corporate life of the parents, but tones up the individual life, too.* It gives it sparkle, life, fire. It bathes every cell in the body with new energy, new radiancy. But only as sex has found its place. Those who have an adjusted sex life, within or without the marriage relationship, sparkle. Those who have not, are dull and lusterless. Sex becomes not food, but poison. When I say sex tones up the individual, I mean not only in its proper use, but in its proper restraints. A restrained sex life turns back and bathes the entire person with health.

Alexis Carrel: "In order to reach its highest intelligence seems to require both the presence of well-developed sex glands and the temporary repression of the sex appetite."

O God, our Father, I thank Thee for this fire of sex within me. Let it burn within me as a sacred fire upon Thine altar, lighting up my entire being. For if it is not this, it will be a fire to consume my mind, my tissues, my bones, my possibilities, me. Then help me this day to dedicate this sacred fire to Thee. Amen.

I Cor. 6:18; Gal. 5:16, 22–25; 4:19

SEX CAN BE SUBLIMATED

(5) *Both within the marriage relationships and outside them the sex urge can be sublimated.* This leaves an open door to those who are denied the ordinary outlets of sex expression. The sex urge is the creative urge. But physical creation is not its only creative area. It can function as creation on other levels of life. It can become creative in the realm of the mind—creating new thoughts, new systems of thought, new mental attitudes both in ourselves and others. It can be creative in the realm of the social—it can give birth to new movements for social justice, for social betterment. It can be creative in the realm of the moral and spiritual—it can create newborn lives, new hopes, new moral and spiritual movements.

Some of the greatest work in the world is done by those who, when denied, voluntarily or otherwise, the normal outlets for sex, turn the tides of this strange power into creative activity in other ways. Their sex life is not suppressed, but expressed in other channels. Abstinence then can be health, provided the abstinence of sex on one level is practiced in order to loose it on another level. If sex is just dammed up with no outlet on any level, then it may prove a source of conflict and frustration. The way is always open in some direction for sex expression; so conflict is not necessary.

(6) *But beware of suggested short-circuiting of this power.* There are only two ways of legitimately and helpfully using sex power—within the marriage relationship as creation, or outside the marriage relationship as sublimation. All other roads are roads with dead ends. Beware therefore of the advice of pagan friends, or pagan medical men or psychiatrists, who advise promiscuity or self-abuse as a way of release from tense passions. This way out is the way out to self-loathing, to a deeper conflict in the moral nature—to an inner hell. If anyone is fool enough to advise it, don't you be fool enough to take it.

The right thing is always the healthy thing.

God, my Father, here I come to offer Thee the turbulence of my urges. Still them with Thy quiet, direct them by Thy will, make them fruitful by Thy creative love, and lift them by Thy redemption. We must work this problem out together. For, apart from Thee, I can do nothing. Amen.

Jas. 1:14–15; Prov. 23:7; I Cor. 7:1–2; II Cor. 5:14

FURTHER STEPS IN SEX VICTORY

In order not to be tempted to follow promiscuity or self-indulgence—these enticing near cuts to sex victory—(7) *make up your mind that none of them will work, except to work ruin.* When the suggestion is made, "Now is your opportunity," reply, as I often do, "Yes, I know it is my opportunity—to go to hell, and I don't intend to go." And then turn to the Tempter and say, "If I did this, I would be as big a fool as you are, and I don't intend to be."

(8) *Watch the place of your thinking.* As Emerson says, "The ancestor of every action is a thought." Then stop the action at the place of the thought. Don't dally with the thought, saying, "I'll keep the thought, but I'll stop this side of the act." You won't, "for in any battle between the imagination and the will, the imagination always wins"—so say the psychologists. Mind adultery issues in body adultery.

(9) *If you are to keep the mind away from sex thinking, then keep the body away from sex propinquity.* For the bodily desires are aroused almost mechanically by propinquity. If "propinquity is the soul of love," it is also the soul of lust. Don't put yourself close to the fire and then wonder why you are burnt. This makes all necking and petting dangerous preludes.

(10) *These suggested barriers are only the fences along the sides of an open road—that open road is love to Christ.* You can expel one desire only by a higher desire. Let the love of Christ be the fire that eats up these lesser loves. All the prohibitions against the wrong use of the sex urge will not save you unless the love of Christ be at the center—then the sex urge becomes marginal and right. There are 32,000,000 statutes on the statute books of America to make people good. The Christian has only one: "Thou shalt love." And love becomes the fulfilling of the law. For when you love Christ, you are free—"love Christ and do what you like." For you will like the right.

O Christ, I would so fall in love with Thee and Thy ways that all lesser loves may become a part of that central controlling love. They shall lose themselves in Thee and find themselves in right expression. For Thou are the key to life —all life. I thank Thee. Amen.

Phil. 3:19; 1 Tim. 6:8; Jas. 5:1–6

DISCIPLINED BODILY DESIRES

We have been studying our seventh enemy, undisciplined desires, and we have taken up sex as one. We now turn to another: *A lack of discipline of other bodily desires.*

(1) *Discipline your natural desires.* Some of these bodily desires are natural, as the desire for food. If you are to live abundantly, then you must be disciplined at the place of your eating. Every meal should be a sacrament offered on the altar of fitter living and finer possibilities. We must eat just enough to keep us fit, and a little less than will keep us fat. Rubber tires around our waistlines are not lifesavers, but life drags. Why carry around excess baggage, overburdening the heart?

Doctors tell us that excess of food, as well as too little food, destroys brain power. The wisest thinkers are the wisest tankers. What is in the stomach often determines what is in the head. "The kingdom of God is not meat and drink," and yet our meat and drink often determine our fitness for the Kingdom of God. "Whether you eat or drink, do all for the glory of God"—and the glory of God dwells in a physically fit person.

The Scripture says, "He let you hear his voice out of heaven, for discipline." (Deuteronomy 4:36, Moffatt.) The voice from heaven for discipline is turning out to be the same voice that is speaking out of the constitution of your physical make-up. The doctors and the interpreters of Christianity are now saying the same thing: discipline yourself or perish.

Everyone has a natural desire for security. So man provides against insecurity through possessions. But this outer security may make inner security insecure, by making outer securities the goal and aim of life. John Woolman refused to enlarge his business beyond his actual needs in order to have time for the real business of life. Discipline your desire for security to the place of actual need; beyond that is luxury and decay.

My Lord and my God, help me to harness all my desires and to drive them in Thy purposes lest they drive me. For I become servant or master. Let nothing master me, save Thee. For in Thy mastery I find my liberty, and in the mastery of my desires I find my tyranny. Thou hast me—entirely, desires and all. Amen.

Prov. 20:1; Hab. 2:15; Rom. 14:19–21; Eph. 5:18

THE TAKING OF NARCOTICS IS A FAILURE OF NERVE

(2) *Discipline your unnatural desires.* The outstanding unnatural desire which we must discipline is a desire for intoxicants. It is a personal and collective menace, increasingly so. In the last decade insurance rejections for heavy alcoholic indulgence have increased from 12 per cent to 34 per cent; one out of three otherwise insurable men and women were declined as unsafe risks because of drinking. (Robert S. Carroll, *What Price Alcohol?* Cook County Hospital, Chicago, made an eight-year study of 3,422 cases of pneumonia, ages between thirty and thirty-nine. Eighteen and four-tenths per cent of abstainers, 29.1 per cent of moderate users, and 42.5 per cent of heavy users died. Judge Harry H. Porter, Chief Justice Municipal Court, Evanston, Illinois, offers his personal opinion that alcohol is involved in 60 per cent of our highway accidents. Forel's record in studying the relationship between alcohol and syphilis showed 76 per cent of the men and 66 per cent of the women were infected while under the influence of alcohol. Dr. C. C. Weeks, the English authority on alcohol, cites four medical writers who name alcoholism one of the four great health scourges in modern civilization—cancer, tuberculosis, venereal diseases being the other three.

Teach moderation? It is foolish to counsel moderation in the use of a substance, the first effect of which is to weaken the power to stop. Alcohol affects the functions of the nervous system in the inverse order of their development in the individual and the race. The functions highest and last to be developed are the first to be affected by the narcotic action of alcohol. Alcohol affects first those functions which make man different from and superior to the animal.

It is not smart to drink—it is weak. It is an escape mentality, a failure of nerve. You have no resources on the inside, so you try to take them from a bottle. Only weak people drink. It is crutches for lame ducks. An Englishman, after hearing me say that, went to a bar and said, "He's right; nevertheless, give me a crutch." Remember the name —a crutch. And who it is for—a lame duck.

O God, I need nothing but Thee—the wine of Thy love, the exhilaration that comes from abiding in Thee, the sheer exuberance of spirits that results from being fully attuned to Thee, the rhythm and harmony that are mine in Thee— what need I to add to this fullness to make it fuller? Amen.

Hab. 2:5-7; Eph. 2:3; Gal. 4:9; 5:1

UNDISCIPLINED DESIRE—TOBACCO

Yesterday we were meditating upon undisciplined desires and talked about the desire for unnatural stimulants. I once saw an electric sign which displayed an American eagle standing on a keg of ale flapping its wings. If the flapping of your wings is based on narcotics, you will soon be a drooping bird. And if the American eagle soars only as it is "soaked," then its days of high soaring are over.

We must now turn to another unnatural desire and ask whether it has any place in the life of a disciplined Christian—the use of tobacco. We are about due for a reaction against tobacco. The time is ripe, for we had been propagandized until we were thinking that to use tobacco was the only thing to do, for everybody was using it. Now the reaction is beginning to set in, for we are finding out that chain-smoking, chain-drinking, and chain-living are undermining the health of America. "Ah," you say, with a sigh of relief, "that lets me out, for I go in for moderation; I am not yet in the chain gaing." But wait a moment. The doctors are telling us of the effect of all smoking, and the mounting evidence is startling.

A heart specialist said to me: "Of all the poisons that man takes into his system for his supposed pleasure, the worst poison is tobacco. One puff of a cigarette, and you can register the effect upon the arteries; they tighten up and cause the heart to work faster." And then he added: "When I tell a man that smoking is affecting his heart and that he must cut it out, he usually goes and does it. But when I tell a woman the same thing, she promises and then goes away and continues." Woman is the latest convert to the god of the yellow stains, and is fast becoming its most ardent devotee. Disillusionment hasn't set in—yet.

Why is it that insurance statistics tell us that the mortality from pneumonia among smokers is double that of the nonsmokers?

O God, I come to Thee for freedom. I do not want to be in bondage to a self-imposed craving, a slave to a thing. I want to depend for comfort, not on smoke, but on a Saviour. I want my joy to depend, not on the most boosted brand, but on a quality—of life. Help me to shift my values. In Jesus' name. Amen.

1 Cor. 6:12; 10:23–24, 31–33

UNDISCIPLINED DESIRE—TOBACCO, Continued

We continue our study. Dr. Raymond Pearl of Johns Hopkins, perhaps the leading authority on medical statistics, after examining thousands of heavy smokers (those who smoke over ten cigarettes a day), light smokers, and nonsmokers, found that between the ages of thirty and forty-five the deaths per 1,000 among the heavy smokers were double those of nonsmokers; the light smokers were half way between. After forty-five the lines of the charts converge until at seventy they meet. If you can stand smoking till seventy, then it makes no difference—you are a tough customer and immune. But those who survive until seventy are the especially physically fit. Dr. Pearl sums up: "Smoking is associated with definite impairment of longevity. The impairment is proportional to the habitual amount of tobacco used."

Gene Tunney, the ex-heavyweight champion, says in a stinging article on this subject: "No one has ever denied that nicotine is poison. Taken clear, it is as quick-acting and fatal as prussic acid. A drop of it on a shaved rabbit causes immediate convulsions and death. The nicotine dissolved out of a few cigarettes and placed on the tongue of a grown man would kill him in 15 minutes. Luckily the bulk of the nicotine in tobacco is volatilized in smoke; you do not get the poison straight. But if you smoke a pack a day, you inhale 400 milligrams of it a week. That much in a single dose would kill you as quickly as a bullet."

Tunney continues: "Under the flogging of the nicotine whip, the body burns up sugar faster; heart action, respiration and blood pressure are kept at a ding-dong pitch. At the end of a two-pack day, the smoker's system has received an unmerciful beating. Impoverished nerves and body cells cry out with fatigue and irritation. The chain-smoker suffers from a chronic 'tired feeling.' He is an energy bankrupt and must borrow new energy at the outrageous interest rate of still heavier smoking." ("Nicotine Knock-out, or the Slow Count," *Readers' Digest*, December, 1941.) [1]

My Father and my God, help me to be at my very best for Thee. This business of being a Christian is serious business and needs all my powers at their best. Help me then to offer them to Thee. Help me cut out all parasites that sap my strength and energy. For I have a race to run. Amen.

[1] Reprinted by permission of The Reader's Digest Association.

Isa. 58:6, 8–9, 11; 61:1; Rom. 6:16

UNDISCIPLINED DESIRES—EXPERT OPINION

It would have been easier for me to have left out this section on the use of tobacco, for many of my friends smoke, and they are Christians, too. I do not doubt for a moment their sincerity and their piety; so it would have been easier to skip around this subject and let it alone—easier and more deadly. For the future of the world is in the hands of disciplined people. The user of tobacco is undisciplined.

If you don't believe this, let the top men speak. Edison said: "Cigarette smoke has a violent reaction on the nerve centers, producing a degeneration of the cells of the brain. This degeneration is permanent. No one who smokes can work in my laboratories." Dr. W. J. Mayo said at a dinner party: "Gentlemen, it is customary to pass around cigars after dinner, but I shall not do it. I do not smoke, and I do not approve of smoking. If you will notice, the practice is going out among the ablest surgeons, the men at the top. No surgeon can afford to smoke." Coach Alonzo Stagg: "From personal observation with athletes who have been addicted to the use of tobacco, I can say with confidence that they do not possess the endurance of athletes who have grown up free from the use of it." The late Knute Rockne, coach of Notre Dame, said: "Tobacco slows up reflexes, lowers morale; any advertising that says smoking helps an athlete is a falsehood and a fraud." Ty Cobb, the famous Georgia Peach of baseball, says: "Cigarette smoking stupefies the brain, saps vitality, undermines health and weakens moral fiber. No one who hopes to be successful in any line can afford so detrimental a habit." A throat specialist said to me: "In all my practice I have never known a nonsmoker to have cancer of the throat." No wonder Tolstoy cries out in wonder: "Why do men stupefy themselves with tobacco?"

Jesus refused narcotics even when hanging in torture on the cross. He would face life matching His inner courage against outer circumstances. He refused to deaden Himself with drugs. Only the weak turn to narcotics.

Gracious Father, forgive the wrongs we inflict upon ourselves by trying to live in ways other than Thy ways. Thy ways produce rhythm; our ways produce ruin. Thy ways produce freedom and fitness; our ways produce folly and unfitness. Help me to take Thy ways unreservedly. Amen.

Eph. 5:16; Col. 4:5; John 9:4; Prov. 6:6

DISCIPLINING OUR TIME

We now turn to the discipline of our time. A lawyer who was in one of our meetings said to a friend at the close, "I've had my insides sandpapered today." All of us need our insides sandpapered by the sandpaper of discipline to make us burnished and fit. We must be reminded that this is an undisciplined generation. It would translate the first line of the twenty-third psalm into, "The Lord is my chauffeur; I shall not walk." As someone put it, "The Church faces a generation which is trying to drink its way to prosperity, war its way to peace, spend its way to wealth, and enjoy its way to heaven." It can't be done. We must discipline everything about our lives, especially our time.

In the words of Wesley, that master user of time, "Never be unemployed and never be triflingly employed." As Paul expressed it, "redeeming the time, because the days are evil." In photography we are told that the picture depends not only upon what you put into it, but also on what you leave out. Your capacity to say "No" determines your capacity to say "Yes." You have to say "No" to lesser things in order to say "Yes" to greater things. Life depends upon elimination as well as upon assimilation. Someone asked a successful college president what was the first qualification of a college president, and he replied, "A wastebasket." I go into many homes and hotels, and the first thing I look for is a wastebasket! Throw away things that do not contribute.

I believe in recreations when they re-create. But when they kill time and exhaust you—let them go. Someone has defined "bridge" as "an assault on time with intent to kill." If you kill time, you kill yourself, for you are a part of time. Dr. William Osler, the great surgeon, used to tie knots in a string while riding in a street car, to prepare himself for quick tying in the crisis of an operation.

My Father and my God, I want to be ready for the moment of my highest use, some great moment that shall call for my best. Help me every moment to get ready for that supreme moment. Help me to be prepared, by getting ready every moment. In Jesus' name. Amen.

Luke 12:31; 9:55–62; Matt. 5:29, 30

A LADDER FOR DISCIPLINE

Before we leave these thoughts on discipline we must give a ladder on disciplined living:

(1) *Decide what you are going to be disciplined to— your absolute.* That absolute is Christ. You are going then to be a Christ-ian. To be a Christlike person is the aim of your discipline. (2) *Discipline the center, the self, before disciplining the circumference, things around that self.* Bring that self to the discipline of a complete surrender to Christ. With that center unsurrendered, all disciplining of this, that, and the other is tinkering. (3) *Now that the center has been disciplined by self-surrender, begin with the most difficult thing you have to discipline.* I am afraid I cannot agree with those who advise picking out the easiest things first and then working out to harder things. For in so doing we seldom go on to the harder—we stay caught in the easier. Jesus said, "If thy right hand offend thee, cut it off." He didn't say, "If thy right hand offend thee, begin by paring your fingernails." Someone has said: "In tackling any problem, raise it in its most difficult phase, solve it there, and then you solve it all down the line." I have made it a practice to pick out the worst-looking letter in the pile and open it first.

(4) *In tackling the most difficult thing first, don't taper off in regard to it.* Don't try to give up unnatural habits by reducing them little by little—let them go all at once, bag and baggage. The tapering-off method seldom works. (5) *Since habits become power, make them work with you and not against you.* Make habits the friends and stabilizers of the new life. (6) *Remember that certain things are soils in which the new life grows.* Cultivate those soils which contribute. (7) *Don't admit any exception to your discipline.* The small victories count. "By lighting small successive candles of will power, we generate a beam that becomes a light to the whole of life."

Any exception you tolerate makes it easier to make the next exception and so on down to undisciplined living.

O Thou disciplined Christ, we would be like Thee. Thy disciplines are so hidden, so a part of Thee, we can scarcely discern them. We would be that way, too. May our very disciplines become so naturalized within us that they become unconscious, and, therefore, effective. Amen.

Matt. 7:3–5; 6:24; Jas. 3:10–12; 4:8

INSINCERITIES—CONSCIOUS AND UNCONSCIOUS

I thought we were through with discipline, but I now see we shall have to keep it as an undertone as well as an over-tone of abundant living. Especially will we need it in dealing with the eighth of our fifteen major enemies: *Insincerity conscious and unconscious.* We discovered in our study of the major enemies already dealt with that this enemy, insincerity, while implicit in many of the others, is sufficiently important to stand out explicit. For insincerity is a quality that can undermine the whole of the Christian structure we build, and undermine it in a very hidden way. Insincerity is the termite of the personality.

Since we are all "only Christians in the making," we can find in the best of us insincerities and unconscious hypocrisies. These insincerities and unconscious hypocrisies are the tribute we pay to truth and goodness. Even when we are not good, and not true, we simulate truth and goodness, thus acknowledging that we ought to be true and good.

From top to bottom life is filled with hypocrisies and insincerities. South Africa makes the springbok, a deer, its national symbol—and yet South Africans have exterminated it.

Our cities are decorated for the birth of Christ—but underneath our Christmas celebrations lies the covetous commercial motive which Jesus condemned. A big star hangs in the sky at Bethlehem, Pennsylvania, ostensibly to lead our minds to Christ; but underneath the star is a sign which says, "Hotel Bethlehem." The star is to lead us to this hotel, instead of to the Inn of long ago. A lady indignantly dismissed her maid: "I had to dismiss her. I found that she was stealing those lovely Waldorf-Astoria towels I had." Her moral indignation at someone else's dishonesty made righteous her own!

O Christ, we do not see ourselves, for we look at the sins of others with open eyes and then turn a blind eye upon our own sins and weaknesses. Help us to be as honest with ourselves as we are with others—and more, help us to be honest with ourselves with Thy honesty. In Thy name. Amen.

Phil. 1:10; Jas. 1:8; Acts 5:1–11

INSINCERITIES—ARE YOUR EARS RED?

These insincerities creep into our Christian lives. I have just been looking at a marvelous mosaic of the Last Supper where Jesus is saying that one of the disciples will betray Him. And they are all asking, "Lord, is it I?" On the mosaic all the ears of the disciples are red, but those of Judas are a little redder! When Jesus raises the question of betrayal, we point to Judas with indignation. Our indignation covers up our own betrayals.

If you want to find out a man's weak points, note the failings in others for which he has the quickest eye. We can defend our own inconsistencies because we compartmentalize life—our religion functions in one part, but doesn't go over into the other parts. The workers in a woolen mill struck to get a washroom so that they could wash off the grime and dirt before going home. When the matter was put up to the proprietor, his reply was, "What they need is a revival of religion." And one was started!

A Y.W.C.A. secretary urged upon an employer the necessity of giving sufficient pay to his girl employees so that they could pay even the low rates of board of the Y.W.C.A. hostel. "No," said the proprietor, "but we will increase our gifts to the Y.W.C.A." He was willing to be charitable, but unwilling to be just. He would allow his religion to function as charity, but was utterly unwilling to have it function as justice.

A South India proberb says: "I will love you as my own child, provided you do not ask me for food and clothing." Again, an Indian proverb speaks of *"Hathi ke dant,"* the elephant's teeth—one set for show, the tusks; the other set for chewing—the hidden motives we keep in the rear. The motto of Cortez, the Spanish freebooter, was, "For God and gold." God was first on the motto, but gold was first in the freebooter's affections. The thing that is important and decisive is not what is in our affectations, but what is in our affections.

O Thou Crystal Christ, probe deep within my heart and find there the hidden infections of insincerity. Drain them to the last poisonous drop, lest they poison my whole system. Make me clean within of every hidden contradiction, for I want to be harmonious and effective. In Thy name. Amen.

Matt. 26:34, 35, 69–75

INSINCERITIES—DUALISMS IN OURSELVES?

We must continue ferreting out these insincerities, for they are like lice that must be exterminated to the last one. We who preach the Gospel—why do we do it? For self-display? For purposes of dominating others—their minds and souls, if not their bodies? Do we wait for the approving word at the close of the sermon, rather than the approval of God in the Quiet? Do those who pay the piper really call our tunes? Do we proclaim truth that is palatable to others, with an eye to our own palates and stomachs? Are we afraid to offend a rich contributor, but not afraid to offend our own moral nature?

A Negro preacher was preaching a trial sermon, and at the close one of the members came up and said, "Pastor, it was a wonderful sermon, but we is wondering whether you walks as you talks." Blessed is the man who does, for then his talk and his walk are with power; otherwise they cancel each other. A pastor said to the writer, "I'm like a train caller, calling out stations down the line to which I myself do not go."

Some recognize this dualism in themselves: "I am opinionated, and I call it conviction," said an honest soul. Another put his dualism this way: "I didn't sin, because I was so proud that I didn't want to have to apologize afterward." One sin, pride, kept him from other sins!

I was talking to a leading general of a certain country. He was bitter and critical of other Christians. I suspected that under the bitterness lay the motive of masking his own decaying spiritual life; so I stopped his outpouring with the words of Jesus to Peter when he inquired, "Lord, and what shall this man do?" "What is that to thee? follow thou me." No matter what the other man does, that doesn't excuse you—"follow me." The general went on worse than before. Again I stopped him with the same quotation. Then he pounded his knee and said, "Good; you've got me."

That last sentence of the general was honest and opened the door to his eventual release from insincerities.

O Christ, Thou relentless Lover and Redeemer, corner my soul. Don't let me wriggle and apologize and slip past Thy redemptions. Help me to take my medicine, however bitter to the taste of self it may be. For I would be whole, with no part sick. In Thy name. Amen.

John 6:70–71; Matt. 26:14–16, 47–49

INSINCERITIES—THE MASK

We fool ourselves if we think we can hide behind masks and remain a double person. Either the mask becomes us, or we become the mask. In the Greek drama the actors wore masks. When the Romans took over the drama they called both the mask and the actor—"persona." At first "persona" referred only to the mask; then it was shifted to the person behind the mask. That is true—you become what your mask is. "You don't put a mask on; you put it in," says Gerald Heard.

If it is true to say that the mask becomes you, it is just as true to say that you become the mask.

"Always a mask
Held in the slim hand,
    whitely,
Always she had a mask
    before her face—
Smiling and sprightly,
The mask.

"Truly the wrist
Holding it lightly
Fitted the task:
Sometimes however
Was there a shiver,
Fingertip quiver,
Ever so slightly—
Holding the mask?

"For years and years and
    years I wondered
But dared not ask.

"And then—
I blundered,
I looked behind,
Behind the mask,
To find
Nothing—
She had no face.

"She had become
Merely a hand
Holding a mask
With grace."[1]

It was said of a certain university that it got hold of some wine (some new progressive ideas), but when the wine began to expand and was in danger of breaking the bottles, the authorities decided to save the bottles. They did, and all they had left was empty forms—their education became outer forms veiling emptiness. That is what happens to us, too.

Gracious Master, I do not want to be just an empty person behind a mask. I want to be real—completely real. But there are many things to be faced and brought up. Help me to bring them up until nothing is left behind. Merge my life into a living whole—like Thine! Amen.

[1] Helen Haiman Joseph, "The Mask," from *Saturday Review of Literature*, August 13, 1932.

Matt. 6:1–5, 16–18; 23:2–7

INSINCERITIES—RATIONALIZATIONS

All insincerities kick back. Jesus said, "There is nothing hidden. What you do in secret shall be proclaimed from the housetops"—the secret motives will write themselves into the lines of your face for the world to see. What you are behind comes out into your eyes, creeps into your words, into your looks, your attitudes, your very walk. "There is nothing hidden."

Rebekah persuaded Jacob to cheat Isaac and Esau—the result? Jacob had a feud on his hands and became a fugitive. His inner shiftiness got into his feet and made him run. The effect on Rebekah? She became unhappy: "These Hittite women tire me to death." (Gen. 27:46, Moffatt.) She was tired to death of these women, because she was out of sorts with herself. The cheating she engineered only succeeded in cheating herself of inward peace, so that she couldn't get along with herself or others.

A pastor allowed a love affair with another woman to develop. This illicit relationship kicked back—in fact, kicked him straight in the stomach. He developed stomach trouble as a result of this conflict in his life.

It may be said in passing that all such love affairs, where one or both parties are married, almost invariably result in frustration and unhappiness. No matter how the affairs may be rationalized and excused and dressed in cloaks of self-pity, because, for instance, of unhappiness in each individual's own married relationship, the results are the same—frustration and unhappiness. No matter how you may argue that the affair is of God, since it seems "so sacred," the results are the same. You run against that law written not merely in sacred Scripture, but in the constitution of things: "Therefore shall a man . . . . cleave unto his wife; and they shall be one flesh." You must choose between cleaving to your own wife or husband, or cleaving your own moral nature, introducing a disastrous conflict within. The law kicks back—invariably.

O God, I come to Thee with myself. I have tried to rationalize my insincerities and explain them away. I am through with explaining them away—I want them to be taken away. I want a self I can live with, and I cannot live with a self that is warring with itself. Then help me—and help me now. Amen.

Matt. 23:13–26

A LADDER TO OVERCOME INSINCERITIES

We now come to our ladder on which we may step up out of the pits of insincerities into the open light of frank and crystal living.

(1) *Relax in the presence of God with all defenses down.* In this relaxed condition allow anything to come to the surface of your thinking that will come. Say to yourself, "Here, in the presence of God, with barriers all down, I want every inconsistency to be brought to the surface, however disagreeable." Then let your mind wander at liberty across your life. Let it fasten on any place of insincerity it will.

(2) *Recognize insincerities for what they are—don't rationalize them and try to make them into something else.* The mind is a part of the ego, whose pride is wounded by the discovered insincerity, and it will immediately leap to the defense. It will push its tentacles in all directions to find reasons, clumsy or clever, to explain why. Reasoning is usually finding reasons to justify our own emotions. We think with our emotions. The mind will gather flowers from everywhere, and sometimes from nowhere, and place them on the sore spot to prove that the sore spot is a garden and not what it is—a dung heap.

(3) *If you are not to rationalize insincerities, neither are you to religionize them.* On the bottom of an art object given to an institution, I saw an inscription written so that everyone could see: "Thine, O Lord, be the glory forever. Presented by ———." It was obvious that the first phrase was a pious religious frontage to justify the obvious intention of the donor—to get a good share of the "glory" for himself.

(4) *Don't confess marginal insincerities and sins and leave the central ones untouched.* This is a very definite tendency. I have seen people confess to impatience when they ought to confess to an egocentric life; to unkindness to someone when they should confess to wholesale exploitation and greed; to an unkind deed when the whole life is filled with unkind attitudes. Someone defended Hitler because he did not drink or smoke.

O God, I am boring deep—help me to be relentless. When my drill strikes hard resistances, help me to go on through. For I want to strike the clear living water of Thy presence and power. Save me from stopping this side of that. In Jesus' name. Amen.

Luke 9:55–62; Jas. 5:16; Acts 2:46–47

THE LADDER ON INSINCERITIES, Continued

We continue our ladder: (5) *After throwing out these insincerities, don't smuggle them back.* Phillip Lee, a Chinese minister, tells how his father had a passion for collecting magazines and papers. Every New Year he would clean them out of his house, and then bring them back again! You, too, will be tempted to bring back your dismissed insincerities, perhaps under different names and guises. If you allow them back, you will add to your insincerities the insincerity of allowing them back under assumed names and forms.

(6) *Don't take up the cross and then cancel it.* Perhaps the insincerity is connected with positive purpose to do something at any cost. The tendency will be to take up the cross for a while, soften it, and then finally cancel it. The Russian cross has two crossbars, one rather oblique. The reason is said to be this: A priest said to his flock, "You will not obey the cross, you will not live right; so I will take the cross out of the church." He did. But there was such an outcry that he brought back the cross, "canceled." "I bring it back to you, but I bring it back with a line drawn through it, for you have canceled the cross." This "canceled cross" was taken up and copied as the original. Look for "canceled crosses" in your life—for toned-down resolutions, for softened determinations, slowed-up purposes. H. G. Wells speaks of "a muffled Christianity"—much of our Christianity is muffled.

(7) *Deliberately go out and confess to someone your insincerities.* That act will teach the self that all insincerities will have to be confessed. The self will be loath to harbor insincerities, since they must be confessed in the end. (8) *Be a part of a group disciplined to crystal honesty and frankness.* Your sense of loyalty to that group will keep you from private dishonesties and insincerities. (9) *Every day with "open face" behold as in a glass the glory of the Lord and be changed into the same image from "clarity to clarity."* (Luther—II Corinthians 3:18.)

O God, help me this day to stand before Thee with open face and open mind and open being. For I, too, would be changed into the same image—Thine image. For day by day I want to go from clarity to clarity, a transparent soul. Amen.

Matt. 12:25–26, 33–34; 7:15–20

DIVIDED LOYALTIES

We come now to the ninth major enemy of the fifteen, *Divided Loyalties*. This major enemy is akin to the one we have just been discussing—insincerities—and yet it is different. One may be truly sincere and at the same time find within himself divided loyalties. He may not be covering anything—even from himself—and yet he may face the fact that he is trying to divide his loyalties between mutually exclusive things. Whether the enemy be covered insincerity or frank divided loyalties, in either case the result is the same: the abilities, the effectiveness, and the happiness of the individual are canceled out. There can be no abundant living with inward division.

And yet how prevalent are divided souls. We believe in God with the top of our minds, but down deep at the bottom we obey something else as the way of life. We live by what Dr. Thomas Kelly called "straddle arrangements and compromises between our allegiance to the surface level and the Divine Creator." Again, he says: "We are trying to live several selves at once, without all our selves being organized by a single mastering life within us."

> "I sometimes think there are two of me,
>   A living soul, and a Ph.D."

A supreme Court justice said to me as I was about to leave him: "We should discuss this subject for six hours. I am in a dilemma. For three days of the week I am a conscientious objector, and four days of the week I'm not." And since he believed in majority rule he was an ardent militarist, smothering the conscientious objector, but not quite happy over the murder! There are many of us living on a bare majority—four to three—and with little or no power left over to put into operation the decisions of the majority. How much stronger we would be if we were living unanimously—all our life energies devoted to one great end.

O God, my Father, I am tired of being worn out by inward conflicts before I get to my problems. I expend so much energy on myself that there is no plus to use in my real problems. I have become the problem. I must be unanimous for Thee. If Thou didst ever help me, help me here. In Jesus' name. Amen.

Matt. 7:21–29

DIVIDED LOYALTIES—MAN OR MENAGERIE?

We continue our study of divided loyalties. A poet says: "I'm not a man; I'm a menagerie, I'm a zoo." And he expressed what many vaguely feel. To have a menagerie inside one is, to say the least, not a comfortable feeling. And it keeps one worse than busy to have to throw chunks of meat to opposing temperaments to keep them pacified. And yet that is some people's lifework.

One can see the outer fortunes of Israel go up and down with the inner divided loyalties. "Aaron erected an altar in front of the calf and proclaimed a festival next day for the Eternal." (Exodus 32:5, Moffatt.) Worshiped a calf today and the Eternal tomorrow! Note which was the *now,* and which was the "next day"!

The reason for this turning to the near-at-hand, immediate thing is that God becomes vague—"if you lose your freshness in the land and deprave yourselves by carving an idol." (Deuteronomy 4:25, Moffatt.) We make local idols, because God is not fresh to us. God fades out, and idols barge in. Then we try to put the two together and reconcile them—"silver . . . . you solemnly devoted to the Eternal as your own gift, to make a carved metal idol." (Judges 17:3, Moffatt.) Devoted to the Eternal to make an idol! That sentence is a transcript of a muddled soul expressing itself in a muddled purpose.

A minister expressed this division when he said, "I'm working in too many directions." Another put it this way: "I need to be at one with myself."

On the notice board of a church I saw an announcement of the morning and evening subjects, which ran together:

The Church at Work
Playing Second Fiddle.

Not only is the church at work playing second fiddle to something else that is first fiddle and leading the tune, but in our own lives our Christianity is playing second fiddle to something else. Christianity is subordinate, not supreme.

O Christ, in whose life only the authentic notes of eternity could be heard leading the music of Thy daily living, help me to play second fiddle to Thee and to Thee alone. For otherwise I shall be out of harmony with the eternal realities. Amen.

Rom. 7:15–24

CONSCIOUS AND SUBCONSCIOUS MINDS AT WAR

What I have been talking about concerning divided loyalties most Christians feel, even after being converted. That this experience called conversion brings a great amount of unity into life is obvious. The life forces are gathered up around a single loyalty to Christ. Life has a new center around which to revolve. But all the life forces and affections are not gathered up around Christ. There are some that do not bend the knee and accept this new allegiance.

This residue of recalcitrancy is variously named. Some call it "original sin," others "remains of depravity," "the old man," "another law working in my members." Psychology would probably explain it as "the driving urges in the subconscious mind." These three driving urges—self, sex, and the herd—have a long racial history and are strong and clamorous. They are used to having their way—they have had their way for a long time. And now into the conscious mind is introduced and built up through conversion a new loyalty—loyalty to Christ and His Kingdom. Intelligence, feeling, and will bend the knee to Him. But down underneath in the subconscious mind are subjects which are subdued, but not surrendered. They drive for their fulfillment apart from these new loyalties. They obey, but moodily. They now and then go on a rampage to break into freedom from this new Overlord. Sometimes they are just sullen, but more often there is a definite tension. There is a sense of inner strain. The soul is not relaxed and at ease with itself. Religion is not the natural expression of the whole being, but the forced will of a portion of it. Duty, rather than spontaneity, is the key word. The soul, instead of being poised, is pursued—so pursued, sometimes, that, like the wild duck in the hunting season, it cannot rest to feed. Religion is not release; it is tension, a dingdong, seesaw battle.

The subconscious mind has not been converted. It is at war with the conscious mind.

O God, my gracious Father, is this the best that Thou canst do? Is religion to bring me no more than tensions and conflicts? Can I not be released and poised and spontaneous? I cannot bear within my bosom this constant conflict. Bid it cease and bid me be free. In Jesus' name. Amen.

Rom. 7:24—8:4; 6:22; 8:6–10

CAN THE SUBCONSCIOUS BE REDEEMED?

The new life is introduced in conversion, but is not fully regnant. Someone said, "Being a Presbyterian may not save you from sinning, but it will take the joy out of it." That is just the difficulty in many partly changed lives—the joy of sinning is gone, but the fact of sinning is not. To indulge in joyless sinning is no joy! We have just enough religion to make us miserable by our sinning, and not enough to make us masterful by our Saviour.

Where is the snag? Is this the best that Christianity can bring? Some modern theologians frankly say, "Yes." And, moreover, this sense of guilt burden and consequent penitence is held up as the ideal. One theologian quoted the story of a monk, one hundred years of age, in a monastery in Palestine muttering with every breath, "Lord, have mercy upon us"; and the theologian added, "I hope with my last breath I'll say that." I hope I won't! I hope I'll say, "My Lord and my God." I don't want the emphasis to be upon my guilt, but upon His goodness—not upon me at all, but upon Him. Suppose a child should go around continually in the home muttering to itself, "Father, mother, have mercy upon me." That attitude would just as effectively block the relationships between parents and child as sin would. The attitude of penitence has to come, and come decisively; but it should lead us out of penitence into pardon, and that pardon lead us to fellowship, and that fellowship into joy. The gift of God has been accepted!

But even after that pardon and fellowship have come, there remain the unchanged instincts in the subconscious. Can they be redeemed? Can salvation extend to the subconscious mind? Or is sitting on the lid the best we can do? We know that Christianity unites men; can it unite man? Can the conscious mind and the subconscious both come under one sway and redemption and work unitedly for common ends? That is one of the most important questions we can ask regarding human redemption.

O God, hast Thou been balked in Thy processes of redemption? At the threshold of the subconscious art Thou turned back, baffled and defeated? Is there no cleansing for these depths? Must I go through life with this ghastly contradiction at the center of my being? How can I believe that and still believe in Thee? I cannot. Help me. Amen.

John 14:25–26; 15:26; 16:7–14

THE HOLY SPIRIT WORKS IN THE SUBCONSCIOUS

We come now to the question: Can the *whole* nature be changed—conscious and subconscious? If so, how? The answer is that Christianity provides for this deeper cleansing in its teaching and provision for receiving of the Holy Spirit. The area of the work of the Holy Spirit is largely, though not entirely, in the realm of the subconscious. There the Holy Spirit works—purifying, redirecting, and dedicating age-long driving instincts. The wild horses of nature roaming in all directions are tamed and harnessed to the purposes of the Kingdom. The Holy Spirit is tamer and redeemer, for only He can work at those depths. "For the Spirit fathoms everything, even the depths of God" (I Corinthians 2:10, Moffatt)—and man. But the Holy Spirit not only fathoms the depths of man; He refashions the depths of man and unifies man at the center, so that the conscious and the subconscious speak the same language, understand each other, drive for the same goals, and own a common Lord.

But here is where the Christian Church is weakest. It believes in and teaches the Holy Spirit—partly. The disciples were at this stage when Jesus said to them: "He [the Holy Spirit] remains with you and will be within you." (John 14:17, Moffatt.) The Holy Spirit was with them, but not within them. The same is true today. Most Christians know the Holy Spirit is with them—He disturbs them by momentary touches, by flashes of nearness, by illuminations and insights, by saving here and saving there. But all this is "with," and not "within." He goads us rather than guides us, illuminates rather than invigorates, prods us into activity rather than penetrates all activities—it is from without in, instead of from within out. The capital and government is on the outside, rather than on the inside. This sense of outsideness will persist in religion until we enter into what the disciples entered into at Pentecost. There they passed over from the "with" stage to the "within" stage. Their religion was no longer a prodding, but a penetration; no longer a restriction, but a release.

O Spirit of God, I, too, long for this withinness—I would be every whit whole. I would have the seat of Thy authority within me. For I cannot conceive that Thou hast come so far in Thy redemption and wilt not come the full way. Thou wilt not stop on the threshold—Thou wilt move within. Come, Spirit, come—within, within, entirely within. Amen.

John 19:38–44; 20:19–23

"FOR THEY WERE AFRAID OF"

Suppose the Gospel had ended where the Gospel of Mark was broken off, the rest of the narrative being lost: "They said nothing to anyone, for they were afraid of—" (Mark 16:8, Moffatt, who gives two attempts at supplying endings from various ancient versions.) The Resurrection had taken place, the whole of the redemptive process was complete, the gladdest news that ever burst upon human ear was in the possession of the disciples, but "they said nothing to anyone, for they were afraid of—" Suppose the Gospel had ended there? The disciples with good news but gripped by fears—the whole movement frozen by fear. Suppose they had not gone on to Pentecost where these fears were dissolved by a new invigoration of divine resources within them? How crippled, how unsatisfactory, how far short of human need would our Christianity have remained, if the Gospel had stopped at the pre-Pentecost stage! And yet that is where most of our Christianity has stopped. With glad good news entrusted to it, it has stopped in its tracks, "afraid of—" what? Everything—its inadequate resources, its power to grapple with the complete need of man; in short, afraid of itself and others.

A discerning layman explains the inadequacy of Christianity this way: "The present level of Christianity has exhausted itself against the problems of the present day. It will have to be renewed on a higher level to become functionally adequate." That higher level is nothing less than the powers of Pentecost becoming our working capital.

The neo-orthodoxy of our time illustrates this vividly. It has no doctrine of, or emphasis upon, the Holy Spirit, hence it ends in pessimism and despair—"for they were afraid of." The Christianity produced is a sad, despairing type of the interim days between the Crucifixion and the Resurrection—of the first and second day, but not of the third day. It is a broken-off Gospel—a before-Pentecost message instead of an after-Pentecost—frustrated instead of fruitful.

Holy Spirit, I see what I need; I need Thee. I need Thee, not as an occasional visitor with me, but as my constant Guest within me. This three-storied house of my body, mind, and soul is Thine. Take over charge. Put light and heat in every room, and let the light shine from every window—with no part dark. In Jesus' name. Amen.

Gal. 5:17; Eph. 1:13; Luke 24:49; Acts 2:38–39

STRIKING DEEPER LEVELS

A young minister had a nervous run-down condition which the doctor diagnosed as follows: "You are trying to build a $2,000 house with $1,000 resources. You are strained and worried over the inadequate resources. Cost of diagnosis $50." That diagnosis could be given to the Christian Church as a whole. We are trying to do things beyond our spiritual resources—hence strain. We must tap new resources.

In Texas surface oil was used for a long time, and the supply became meager. Finally someone dared to go down 5,000 feet and struck new levels of oil, which brought forth gushers. Now almost all the oil is tapped at those low levels. When we as Christians go down to the deeper levels and tap resources, "laid up" for us in the Divine Providence, then we shall be artesian and overflowing. Then we shall be ready for anything. Melva Livermore, who knew so well the deeper levels of living, stood up in our Ashram and said with a shining face, "I just go around swishing love about." And then she added as she stretched out her arms, "Come on, life, I'm ready." She was ready for anything that life could bring.

Melva Livermore's life had been transformed from a thermometer to a thermostat—the thermometer merely registers the temperature of its surroundings; the thermostat changes the temperature. Our Christianity is often only registering its surroundings, instead of remedying them. The early disciples did not go around registering the current pessimisms; they changed them. They didn't go around saying, "Look at the problems," but "Look at the Saviour." Their emphasis was not on sin abounding, but on grace much more abounding. And they spoke with transforming force. For the "Acts of the Apostles" were the Acts of the Holy Spirit working through the apostles. And what they began we can continue. "To be continued," is written at the end of the "Acts of the Apostles."

O Thou Living Spirit—Thou bringer of Life into death, of Victory into defeat, of Purity into impurity, of Plus into minus—come within me and capitalize all my nouns and substantives, make life sparkle that has been dull and dead and ineffective. Put Thyself into myself. In Jesus' name. Amen.

Luke 11:9–13; Acts 19:1–7

RECHARGING RUNDOWN BATTERIES

We have been meditating upon our resources for abundant living, and have found that the chief resource is the Holy Spirit. When Jesus said, "How much more shall your Father which is in heaven give good things to them that ask him?" Luke translated His words as, "the Holy Spirit to them that ask him"—"the Holy Spirit" is the "good things." Seek then, not "good things," but go beyond the good things to their Source, the Holy Spirit.

A little boy, when asked what the Holy Spirit means, replied, "I suppose it is what puts the 'umph' in Christianity." He is, but very much more. For He puts everything—everything which a Christian needs for abundant living—into Christianity.

A minister said in one of our meetings: "I have a rundown battery that needs recharging. Can the Holy Spirit recharge rundown batteries?"

A policeman went over to an oil well and deliberately oiled it, for it was squeaking badly, and visitors would not believe that it was an oil well when it itself was not oiled. Can the Holy Spirit put oil into the machinery of the Christian worker's own life while he is trying to pump oil for others? Unless our own machinery is well-oiled and smooth-running, people will not believe that we have oil for others. How can we lift others to a par life if we are living under par? A girl came home from college saying, "I just needed the inspiration of the family life." She was inspirationally run down—needed recharging. That is what we need spiritually. We are not bad, but empty.

> "Lord, I would share,
>   But first possess,
>   That inner gift, serenity.
>   Then, comforted, blessed, free from unrest,
>   Serve Thee none the less,
>   But with Tranquility."

I come now, O Spirit of God, to have my inmost being renewed and recharged. Teach me how to gear in with Thy power, how to lay hold of Thy resources, how to align myself with Thy purposes, how to surrender to Thee. For I cannot go on running a stalling car, working on half its cylinders. I would be adequate for any hill, for any load, for any distance. Help me. Amen.

John 14:16–17, 26; 16:7, 13; Acts 1:8

STEPS IN RECEIVING THE HOLY SPIRIT

We come now to the ladder for receiving the Holy Spirit. Before we begin to take these steps, will you not breathe a prayer, an inward one at least, that you may not stumble on these steps; for bungling or skillfulness in climbing will make all the difference between a life of defeat and one of victory. The steps are simple.

(1) *Believe it is in the divine intention for you to receive the Holy Spirit.* Fix it in your mind that the gift of the Spirit is not an exceptional gift for exceptional people who are in exceptional work, but a gift which is the birthright of every Christian. "But this spake he of the Spirit, which they that believe on him were to receive." (John 7:39.) Note: "were to receive"—receiving was in the divine intention and program for them. For whom? "They that believed on him." Here then is no exception. You, the ordinary Christian, are to receive the Holy Spirit, for you are counted among those who believe on Him. "Ye shall receive the gift of the Holy Ghost. For the promise is unto you, and to your children, and to all that are afar off." (Acts 2:38–39.) You belong to those "afar off." You are in the stream of the divine intention.

(2) *Make sure that to receive the Holy Spirit is your intention.* When I use the word intention, I mean will—not wishes, or passing emotions, or mental concepts, but will. Do you will to receive the Holy Spirit, not as a passing influence that may get you out of spiritual difficulties, give you momentary satisfaction in the thought that you have preached well, lift and inspire you in a crisis moment—not that, but as an abiding Power that will take over the citadel of yourself and reign there as a lifelong, an eternity-long, proposition?

(3) *Bring the matter to a crisis.* The soul grows by a series of crises. There is usually a crisis in conversion; there is usually a crisis here in receiving the Holy Spirit. Wall yourself in on both sides, so that there is no way around—you have to go forward or backward. The crisis moment has arrived.

O Spirit of God, I have come to the crisis hour. I do hedge myself about, so that I shall not sidestep into lame futilities and halfway compromises. I want nothing less than Thee—Thee—Thee. I cannot be satisfied with gifts; I want the gift of Thyself. For the marginal doesn't satisfy me any more—the Center calls. I come. Amen.

Rom. 12:1; John 17:17, 19; Heb. 7:25

STEPS IN RECEIVING THE HOLY SPIRIT—
Continued

(4) *Remember the price you are to pay—yourself.* If you ask for the gift of the Spirit Himself, then it is obvious that this cannot be unless you offer yourself. You can ask for His gifts and in return give your gifts, but you cannot ask for the Gift of Himself and not involve the gift of yourself. Let us repeat what we said before: There is no love between persons unless there is mutual self-surrender. If either withholds the inmost self, love is blocked. So here.

(5) *Then pay the price of a complete surrender.* I mean surrender and not dedication. In dedication you still have your hands on the gift—in surrender you let go. The gift doesn't belong to you any more—it totally and wholly belongs to Another. You now lead a Spirit-led life, instead of a self-led life. You substitute One Will for two wills. You say to yourself, "Let go, let God."

Just as the canvas surrenders itself to the painter, the violin to the musician, the wire to the electricity, so you put yourself at the disposal of the Divine. You surrender for better or for worse, for riches or for poverty, in sickness and in health, in life and in death—you will keep yourself only unto Him. He *has* you.

Are you thereby lost, or thereby found? You are lost just as the musician is, when he takes his violin, surrenders himself to the music, lets go, becomes a part of the music, and is thereby lost. He is lost only to find himself a part of the universal harmony. You lose your petty, isolated, defeated self in the universal Self of God and are harmonized with the heart of reality. As Rufus Moseley says: "I died and I died ungraciously, but I died to nothing but that which caused me to die." You die, just as an engine dies to the thought and purpose of wandering free anywhere and surrenders itself to the bondage of the rails—only to find its freedom there.

Complete surrender means complete Security, for God's will is our way—the way we are made to live.

O Spirit of God, bring this wandering, wavering will of mine to the bondage of Thy freedom, to the narrowness of Thy universality, to the yoke that is easy, and to the burden that is light. I bend my neck—not easily, but I bend it—to the yoke of Thy complete will. I am glad I do. Amen.

Acts 15:8, 9; Heb. 10:22, 35–36; 1 Cor. 15:57

FINAL STEPS IN RECEIVING THE SPIRIT

You are now ready for the next step. (6) *The acceptance of the gift of the Spirit.* Remember: an acceptance of the gift of the Spirit—the Spirit Himself and not one of His blessings. Don't be put off with blessings—you want the Source of all blessing. Blessings come and go—"He shall abide with you forever." Your choice is a permanent choice in solving a permanent transaction with a permanent Companion and Master.

Remember: The Spirit is a *gift*. "Ye shall receive the *gift* of the Holy Spirit." "Thanks be to God, which *giveth* us the victory." "How much more shall your heavenly Father *give* the Holy Spirit to them that ask him." You cannot be worthy of His presence, nor earn the right to it. You can do one thing and one thing alone—empty your hands and humbly take the Gift. Having given yourself, you now have a right to take Himself. Then repeat to yourself: "He comes—He comes. I let Him come. I welcome with open heart His coming. I am grateful for His coming. It is done. We belong to each other, forever." Close the eternal bargain.

His coming may be as gentle as the dew upon the new-mown hay—a new sense that you are not alone; but it may also be like the storm. Welcome His coming and do not dictate the manner. There is a reason for the particular manner.

(7) *If you feel the inner urge, be free to tell others about His coming—share it.* You are not boasting; you are simply telling of the unspeakable Gift. The sharing of it fixes it. Nothing is really yours until you share it.

(8) *Make the surrender and the acceptance something once and for all and yet continuous.* Surrender in marriage is once and for all, and yet it is daily. Paul could say, "I have been crucified with Christ," and yet, "I die daily." "Whosoever drinketh of the water that I shall give him shall never thirst"—"drinketh" is, according to the Greek, "once and for all," and yet, "keeps on drinking." This surrender is *done*, and yet never done—it is final, yet unfolding.

O Spirit of God, I have said a Yes that covers everything, and yet I know how many smaller Yeses are in that central and final Yes. Help me to live in a state of Yes-ness to Thy unfolding will. And help me to live in a perpetual state of No-ness to every little seduction. In Jesus' name. Amen.

Il Pet. 1:5–9; Gal. 5:22–23; Eph. 6:13–17

UNBALANCED VIRTUES

We come now to the tenth of the fifteen enemies of the abundant life, *Unbalanced Virtues*. It is not enough to have freedom from divided loyalties; we must have freedom from unbalanced virtues. One may have only virtues in one's life, and yet those virtues may be out of proportion, unbalanced by opposite virtues; hence those very virtues cease to be virtues and come dangerously near to being vices.

Dr. Frank Sladen says: "There is a rhythm of the body. If this rhythm is disturbed, there is functional disturbance which may run into structural." As there is a rhythm of the body, so there is a rhythm in the virtues. If this rhythm is upset by some virtues being overemphasized and others being underemphasized, then there is functional disturbance in the spiritual life, which may turn into actual structural spiritual disease.

When a philosopher said, "No man is strong unless he bears within his character antitheses strongly marked," he meant that each virtue must be held in tension by its opposite virtue. In that very tension between virtues there is strength. The balanced virtues may be classed as follows: passive–militant; self-effort–God-dependence; world-renouncing–world-participating; introversive–extroversive; mystical–practical; being–doing; love–law; personal–social; freedom–law; artistic–artisan; self-renouncing–self-assertive; meekness–mastery; loving yourself–loving your neighbor. Many others could be added; for instance, the feminine virtues and the masculine.

Suppose you have only one side of those virtues developed; you are weak. If you are only passive, or only militant, you are weak. The truly strong man is militantly passive and passively militant; not now and again passive, and now and again militant, but both in a living blend at one and the same time. You see the blending of the passive and militant in Jesus.

"It is easy for enthusiasm to become fanaticism, for zeal to become hysteria, for integrity to become hard and unforgiving, for thrift to pass over into stinginess."

O Jesus, so perfectly poised and harmonious, help my lopsided virtues to be corrected by Thy amazing balance and sanity. Where my virtues have become out of proportion and have come to the verge of vices, give me grace to correct them—and the power. For my virtues must be redeemed, too. Amen.

Phil. 4:5, 8–9; Jas. 1:3–4, 19, 22; 2:20

VIRTUES MAY BECOME VICES

Ephesians 2:10 could be translated, "We are God's poem." If so, then the poem must be rhythmical, each part balanced against the other, the virtues harmonized by right emphasis. For instance, if there is nothing but self-effort you are weak, and if there is nothing but God-dependence you are weak. But where the two are blended in a higher synthesis, producing a person who works as if the whole thing depended on himself and who trusts as if the whole thing depended on God, then you have a person who has caught the rhythm of "receptivity and response," "receptivity and response"—the alternate beats of a single heart.

One's firmness, a virtue, can become stubbornness, a vice. A minister said, "I am opinionated, and I call it conviction." Over to the United States Senate Chamber goes a one-track subway, going and coming. I remarked to a friend, "Now I see why so many of these senators have a one-track mind; nothing that is said ever changes them—they come and they go on one track." Seriously, many of us are like that—we get an idea and hang on to it as a dog hangs on to a root. Strong convictions may degenerate into stubborn opinions. A Scotch theologian remarked, "God grant that I may always be right, for I never change." The person who is always right and never changes is always wrong.

Sensitivity rooted in selfishness is touchiness, but sensitivity rooted in thought for others is life.

One may emphasize the material or the spiritual and make it into a vice—a materialist or a spiritualist is a part-person. But one who puts his spirituality into material relationships is really strong. One can be so righteous that he is unapproachable, or so loving that he is sentimental. To be righteously loving or lovingly righteous is true strength.

When a man's right leg is too long—longer than the other—he is lame. When one good quality is long in proportion to his other good qualities, a man is morally deformed.

O Jesus, we see in Thee the perfect Man, all Thy virtues so blended that we cannot tell where one ends and the other begins. Thou art everything we want to be and are not. But Thou hast us—chip us here, mold us there; eliminate here, add to there, until one day we wake in Thy likeness. Amen.

I Cor. 13

STEPS TO RIGHT UNBALANCED VIRTUES

If our virtues can topple over into vices, and our strengths degenerate into weaknesses, how can we correct them?

(1) *Step off from your life and see it as a whole.* Just what kind of total life is emerging? Am I an unbalanced person? Have I grown lopsided? What is the total impression I make on people? When people think of me, what do they think of?

(2) *After looking at your life in the large, now go over it in the minute.* Go over your virtues one by one and see if they are virtues still. Has your meekness become weakness? Has your strength become stubbornness? Has your outer doing got out of proportion to your inner being? Have the outer activities become more than your sustaining prayer life? Have you become more of a go-getter than a go-giver? Has your righteousness become rigid and rutted?

(3) *Quiet yourself; let down the bars; let Christ go over your life and point out what needs to be corrected.* The tendency will be to defend yourself and your virtues. Don't. Relax and let Him render the verdict on each one. Accept that verdict. Don't try to amend it.

(4) *Surrender your virtues into His hands for correction.* It is necessary to surrender our goodnesses to Him as well as our evils. He will make all our evils into goods, and all our goods into betters, and all our betters into bests.

(5) *Sit down with some honest, sympathetic friend and go over things in your life with him.* He can see things you cannot. For each one is prejudiced in his own favor. You may come out far better than you suspected.

(6) *Having looked at yourself, now look away from yourself to Christ.* Don't end up by fussily trying to arrange your virtues. Fix your eyes on Christ, for you become like that upon which you habitually gaze. He has all your virtues perfectly blended—plus. Become Christ-centered, not self-centered, even in balancing virtues.

O Christ, I have seen the perfect Man, and I would be like Him. But I cannot be like Thee through my own futile efforts. Together we can be and do anything. Thou hast me —my lopsided virtues included. Remold me until I stand forth—Thy workmanship of which Thou shalt not be ashamed. Amen.

Jas. 1:5, 19; 3:17; Col. 1:9; Acts 6:10

IGNORANCE AND LACK OF JUDGMENT

We pass on now to the eleventh of the fifteen major enemies, *Ignorance and lack of judgment.*

Goodness not guided by intelligence is almost as dangerous as intelligence not guided by goodness. Ignorance has produced as much confusion and suffering in the world as wrong intentions. It is true that it is easier to act yourself into right thinking than it is to think yourself into right acting. The universe is a moral universe, and the greatest organ of knowledge is moral response. You know as much as you are willing to put into practice, and no more. While this is true, nevertheless, whether you learn right thinking through intellectual processes alone, or through moral response, it is necessary to learn right thinking. "For the ancestor of every act is a thought." If the thinking goes wrong, then life goes wrong with it.

Therefore, in nature and in grace, ignorance is not excused. It must be paid for in suffering. Sincerity amid the ignorance won't atone for the ignorance—the results are the same. The Hindus sincerely believe that smallpox is caused by the goddess of smallpox, Sitla. That sincere ignorance blocks scientific remedies, and people die, sincerity or no sincerity.

For a long time people believed that malaria was caused by bad air—hence its name: *mal* = "bad," *aria* = "air." That ignorance let people die by the millions. The same thing is happening spiritually. We are ignorant of the laws of mental and spiritual health, and as a consequence humanity is tearing and lacerating itself like the man among the Gadarenes. Neuroses and the jitters are the weapons with which we flay ourselves.

Since Jesus was the revealer of the nature of Reality, He was always saying, "Don't you understand?" The stupidities of men astonished Him more than their wickedness. He saw that men were trying to live against the nature of Reality —attempting the impossible, and getting hurt in the process.

O God, we hurt ourselves because we do not know Thy laws; and when we know them, do not obey them. Give us minds that know and wills that obey, and then we shall know how to live. We would know the truth and do it, and then we shall be free. Give us light and give us life, to walk in that light. Amen.

Heb. 5:14; Eph. 4:18; Rom. 10:2–3, 14–17

A WELL-TRAINED CONSCIENCE

The Christian is a foe to ignorance; he fights it on every front. To get in touch with Christ is to have a mental awakening. It was no mere chance that 95 per cent of the higher educational institutions of America came out of the Christian Church. Jesus said, "Thou shalt love the Lord thy God with all thy mind." That phrase "with all thy mind" was not in the original Old Testament command; Jesus put it in. Scientists tell us that most of us use only about half of our brains. Jesus would awaken that other dormant half and help us to love God with "all" our minds.

"Where ignorace is bliss, 'tis folly to be wise," does not fit into the Christian outlook which says, "Ye shall know the truth, and the truth shall make you free." Jesus would encourage men to think for themselves: "Why even of yourselves judge ye not what is right?" An upstanding, thinking, free personality is the end of the Christian discipline.

An ignorantly trained conscience is a danger to the world. The conscience is not an infallible guide unless properly trained. It is a capacity within us which decides when a thing is right or wrong, but what it decides as right or wrong is determined by the training we give it. Paul killed people in all good conscience until his conscience began to be trained under the tutelage of Christ. Then and then only was it a safe guide. We make our consciences, and then our consciences make us. Many people have their consciences trained to be sensitive to very marginal sins and shortcomings, and not to be at all acute to central and fundamental sins. They have picayunish consciences which load them with a sense of guilt over trivialities. A truly Christian conscience is a great achievement, as well as a great gift of God.

Not only does conscience approve or disapprove within the framework of what it is taught, but guidance also is within the framework of our intellectual conceptions. To give the safest and highest guidance, our minds must be Christianly informed and trained.

O God, I begin to see that I must love Thee with an intellectual love as well as with an emotional love. Awaken my brain cells to activity and to acuteness, so that I may be the sharpest instrument I can be. Save me from intellectual laziness and help me think Thy thoughts after Thee. Amen.

1 Cor. 2

STEPS IN BECOMING INFORMED AND BALANCED

We said yesterday that both our consciences and our guidance work within the framework of our information and knowledge. One of Wesley's preachers said, "I get my text and my sermons from God without studying." Wesley asked, "Does God ever give you a text you have not read?" "No," replied the preacher. Wesley added, "Then you would better read more."

An uninformed Christian is an uninspiring Christian. That which does not hold the mind will soon not hold the heart.

But the Christian must not only be well-informed; he must also be well-balanced. A lack of judgment is as disastrous as a lack of information. You must know what to do with your knowledge after you acquire it. A judge said to an oratorical young lawyer: "Young man, if you will pluck some feathers from the wings of your imagination and stick them in the tail of your judgment, you will fly better."

Perhaps if we take the following steps we shall become better-informed and better-balanced Christians:

(1) *Go over your life and see where you are illiterate.* You will probably find vital areas of life where you are uninformed. (2) *See if your conscience isn't badly trained, especially on the great social issues.* Your knowledge of these issues being neglected, your conscience will have little or nothing to work on. (3) *Determine to become educated in areas where now you are not.* Break up your mental habits by a mighty effort and a strict discipline. (4) *Set aside a certain amount of time each day to inform yourself in the areas where you are falling down.* Count that time out of the day—a standing engagement with Knowledge. (5) *Review your judgments and don't be afraid to reverse them.* Let the mind know that its judgments will be reviewed. This will make the mind more careful.

Be an informed and balanced Christian—the most beautiful handiwork of God.

O God, I would have an informed and disciplined mind. Help me this day to begin a regime of strict discipline with myself. Help me to admit of no exceptions. For I am in the serious business of being at my best for Thee. Help me to be "a workman that needeth not to be ashamed." Amen.

Heb. 10:9, 5; John 1:14; Gal. 6:17; Rom. 12:1

BODILY DISHARMONY AND DISEASE

We pass on to the twelfth of the fifteen major enemies of the personality, *Bodily disharmony and disease*. We have been a long time getting to the physical basis of abundant living. Some would have started with it as the all-important factor. We have reserved it for this place, for while we consider the physical basis important, it is not all-important. Many are compelled to live abundantly, if at all, in spite of physical conditions—and they do. I know a man left a cripple by the first world war and entirely bedridden. Yet he runs his business from his bedroom. And that bedroom is the center of a wholesome gaiety. He is one of the most magnetic persons in his town. He lives abundantly—in spite of.

While this is true, nevertheless, there is a very definite physical basis of abundant living. Body and mind are intertwined until one can scarcely say body and mind, but body-mind. If the soul and mind pass on their sickness to the body, then just as definitely does the body pass on its sickness to the mind and soul. The whole person becomes sick. Hawthorne says, "A bodily disease which we look upon as whole and entire itself may, after all, be but a symptom of some ailment in the spiritual part." True. And just as truly a soul disease which we look upon as whole and entire may, after all, be a symptom of some ailment in the physical part. There are many people who are castigating their souls and loading them with guilt when they should attend to their nutrition, or have out an infected tonsil. If the nerves are starved on account of the lack of vitamins, they will kick back in spiritual depression in exactly the same way that a starved soul will kick back in bodily depression. Therefore Christianity shows its absolute sanity by taking the body seriously. It is the only one of the great faiths that does so. It is founded on an Incarnation.

O God of my body, I would have it at Thy best. Thou hast made me for health and rhythm; help me to present this body of mine for Thee to make out of it the very finest instrument for Thy purposes. Help every brain cell and every tissue and every nerve to be the strings upon which Thy creative fingers shall play and bring out undreamed-of harmony and effectiveness. Amen.

l Thess. 5:23; I Cor. 6:19–20; II Cor. 4:10–11; 6:16

THE PHYSICAL AND SPIRITUAL BASES OF HEALTH

There are those who say that all disease has a physical origin—they are the materialists. There are others who say that all disease has a spiritual or mental origin—they are the mentalists. To hold either position is to fly in the face of the facts. To hold that all disease is mental in origin is to alienate the whole scientific movement for health. To hold that all disease is physical in origin is to alienate the whole mental and spiritual movement for health. Both positions have filled graveyards as a result of their half-truths. Many people have died repeating the slogan that disease was all in their minds, when a surgeon could have applied a physical remedy and healed them. But, as Dr. Joseph Hersey Pratt says, bushels of tonsils and teeth have been taken out of people who needed to be delivered from fears and self-centeredness and resentments in orders to be well. Both positions have made for hypocrisy and unnecessary martyrdoms.

The time has now come to bring these two positions together. The truth in each has been established; it is now time that the error in each should be eliminated, and the two positions—the thesis and the antithesis—be brought together in a higher synthesis. The fact is that the balance will probably work out as about fifty-fifty—about half the diseases are mental and spiritual, and half physical in origin. A young man once became ill after eating shrimp. Ten years later he became physically ill at the sight of the word shrimp on a menucard. The first time the illness was purely physical in origin—he was allergic to shrimp; the second time it was purely mental. Four times I have eaten shrimp —same result. The last time I ate them I did so unconsciously, as they were camouflaged. This was at noon, and I should have been ill a couple of hours later, but I had an important mass meeting and was absorbed in it until nine o'clock at night, when I returned home. Then I remarked that this time I had conquered my usual reaction to shrimp. I had, until I came near the table for supper—and then I hadn't! The mind held the illness off for eight hours, but at last the physical fact conquered.

O God of my mind and of my body, I come to Thee to have both under the control of Thy redemption and guidance. May I pass on the health of my mind to my body, and the health of my body to my mind. But in order to do this, wilt Thou pass on Thy health to both my mind and my body. Amen.

II Cor. 5:10; Rom. 8:11, 21–23, 26; Ps. 63:1

DOES CHARACTER AFFECT THE GLANDS?

When the effects of glands were first discovered in any real way, many people felt they had found the basis of morality and character—the glands decided everything. One could change a man's moral character by changing the secretion of his glands. So character and morality must be purely physical in origin. This seemed a terrific blow at Christianity, which says that morality has its origin in a spiritual being, God. But now the further truth is emerging: If the secretions of glands determine character, then character determines the secretions of glands. A man's mental and spiritual state determines in what proportion his glands flow.

Moreover, this important fact is being realized: Unchristian mental and spiritual attitudes upset the proper secretion of the glands. I asked an able medical man this question: "If we live in a truly Christian way, will not the glands, provided that they are healthy, function perfectly?" The answer was an unqualified "Yes." Then we have Christian glands! Unchristian fear, hate, selfishness, and guilt upset them, throw them out of proportion. Christian confidence, love, unselfishness, and reconciliation make the glands function naturally and in the right proportion. If our glands make us, then it is equally true that we make our glands. Perhaps the truth could be better stated this way: God made our glands and into their structure He wrote the Christian law, and when we obey that law our glands are harmonious and rightly proportioned for health.

"Three weeks after I lost my boy I went to the hospital with stomach ulcer. Worry and anxiety—grief—had brought the ulcer on," said a pastor. He surrendered his grief to God and found release from the ulcer. "You restored me to health and newness of life," said a radiant young woman. And the two were connected—her newness of life brought health. Said a doctor to me: "If three quarters of my patients found God, they would be well. My wife had a peptic ulcer, but it was functional—when she became straightened out spiritually, she was well."

O God of harmony and peace and health, I bring to Thee my disharmonies, my unrest, my unhealth. Take them all into Thy hands and reshape them into harmony. Where they have missed the way bring them back, and where they are out of balance, balance them. I would be harmonized like Thee. Amen.

Isa. 1:4–6; Ps. 31:9–10; 32:1–5

THE MORAL AND SPIRITUAL BASES
OF DISEASE

The physical basis of disease is so obvious and insistent that we need not emphasize it—it emphasizes itself. Nor need we emphasize its effect upon the spiritual condition. The idea that you can be more spiritual if your body is mortified is false. If that is tried, the body kicks back and clouds the soul; so mortified bodies produce morbid saints, and they are usually more morbid than saintly. The surgeon with his scalpel who lacerates the flesh in order to restore health, helps to produce more saintliness than the would-be saint who lacerates the body in order to produce saintliness.

To the effect of the physical upon the spiritual we increasingly agree. But the other truth—the effect of the mental and spiritual upon the physical—is insufficiently emphasized. One lady put her case this way: "I was informed that there was very little organically wrong with me and that my mental state was causing my trouble. I had lost weight steadily in spite of medication. My mind had become so bad I was afraid to go out by myself, and I avoided meeting people. But a remarkable change has taken place in my life, and my health has steadily improved. My husband's love for me is growing stronger each day. The Lord is truly transforming our home from a morgue to a sanctuary."

"From a morgue to a sanctuary!" Not only are many homes morgues; many bodies are—they harbor death cells of anger, fear, self-centeredness, and guilt. Many a person, instead of having a living vibrant body, awake in every cell and harmonious in every relationship, has a body of death. That body of death can become a sanctuary. "The first concept I had that God could heal a body, wrung dry of all ability to resist disease, came from your book, *The Christ of the Indian Road*," a reader confesses. "The leaven of your ideas was responsible for the metamorphosis of a lump of clay to a seeker after truth." "A body wrung dry of all ability to resist disease"—a Christian has no business with that kind of body.

O God, if my mind and my body are wrung dry of the ability to resist disease, then give to me what Paul meant when he said that our mortal bodies would be quickened by the Spirit that dwells within us. Let me be quickened, quickened. Amen.

Ps. 6:2–3, 6–7; 19:7; Matt. 9:1–7

DISEASE IS NOT THE WILL OF GOD

We carry over from last week our consideration of the twelfth enemy of the fifteen major enemies: physical disharmony and disease. If disease and physical disharmony are ours it is probable that they are from one or more of four causes: (1) actual structural disease, brought about by heredity, accident, contagion, ignorance, or willful abuse; (2) functional disease, which may pass into structural disease, brought about by wrong mental, moral, and spiritual attitudes; (3) lack of, or unbalanced, nutrition, brought about by poverty, ignorance, or willful neglect; (4) environmental factors which directly produce disease, or wrong mental and spiritual attitudes, which in turn produce disease.

Note that in the four sources of disease and disharmony I do not mention the will of God. God does not will disease. God wills health. Disease is an enemy which Jesus fought against and healed whenever He could get co-operation. He never once told people to bear disease as the will of God. "I am come that they might have life, and that they might have it more abundantly." That is the Christian note. It is true that disease comes from breaking the laws of God which He has written into the constitution of things, but God does not send it; we break His law and they break us. But that makes us, not God, the author of that disease. God has provided for health, not disease. A friend once said to Dr. W. B. Cannon, the great Harvard physiologist: "When you know all the diseases it is possible to have (something over a hundred and twenty-five), you wonder how anyone is ever well." To which Dr. Cannon replied: "When you know a great deal about the human body, you wonder why anyone is sick." (Quoted by Dr. Russell L. Dicks, *Religion in Life*, 1941, Vol. X, No. 4, p. 515.) The human frame is organized for health and, if the way is cleared by right co-operation with nature, will produce health.

Gracious Father, Thou hast wrought possibilities for health and rhythm into the structure of my being. Help me to cooperate with Thee so that no crippling disease shall mar the efficiency of my work for the Kingdom. Help me to keep fit for Thee. Amen.

John 10:10; II Cor. 12:7; Luke 13:11–17

SALVATION IS WHOLENESS

Yesterday we ended by suggesting that God had provided for health and not for disease. The fact is that health is stronger than disease. A cancer expert tells me that cancer cells are more susceptible to being killed by radium than healthy cells—the differential susceptibility is lower in healthy tissue. That difference makes it possible, by the proper use of radium, to kill the cancer cells, but not injure the healthy tissues.

Health then is written into the constitution of things. God wills it. If we do not have health, then some law has been broken somewhere, either by our ancestors, or by ourselves, or by society, or by environmental factors. We cannot be responsible for the body we begin life with, but we are responsible for the one we die with. For the body can be improved no matter how handicapped it may have been in the beginning. I have lived for thirty-five years in one of the worst climates of the world—India, a land poverty-stricken and disease-ridden, "the white man's grave." And yet I have come out of it at the end of these years with a better body than I had when I went in. I have missed only about two single engagements in twenty-five years: one from a flu germ—the gift of America—and one by a war regulation in Ceylon. Someone said recently, "You look ten years younger than you did five years ago—that is real religion." I was interested in the linking of real religion with health and vitality. They are linked and they are going to be increasingly linked. Jesus defined salvation as health. Wherever He used the word, "be saved," in the margin it is translated, "Be whole." Salvation is wholeness, health—health in total personality, body, mind, and soul. The time is coming when we shall be ashamed of a lack of health in any part of our being, knowing that some law has been broken by somebody. If through ignorance or carelessness we are unhealthy, still the condition is not hopeless, for both nature and God are redemptive.

My gracious, healing Father, I come to Thee with this body of mine. Forgive me for the sins I have committed against it and thus against Thee, its Creator. Help me to work with Thee to make it the perfect expression of Thy will. Give me insight into the laws of my body and help me to obey them when I see them. Amen.

1 Cor. 12:25–26; II Cor. 9:8, 10; Matt. 6:32

SOME STEPS TOWARD PHYSICAL HEALTH

If we are not at our best physically, if the physical basis of our abundant living is poor, we can improve it, perhaps perfect it. The following steps may help.

(1) *Get a thorough physical examination by a competent doctor,* preferably by one who is not a materialist, but one who sees the interlocking of body and spirit. The mere materialist, the one who sees disease as only physical in origin, is as out-of-date in advancing medicine as the Chinese medicine man puncturing the patients to let the devils out. On the other hand, don't go to one who says that disease is only of mental or spiritual origin. He is equally dangerous and equally liable to write you a pass to a graveyard, or if not as far as that, then to an infirmary.

(2) *If there are physical weaknesses, take the next step and ask whether they are of physical or spiritual origin.* Some may turn out to be of physical origin, and an operation or medication may correct them. Don't hesitate to let God heal you through the surgeon or physician. The real surgeon or physician recognizes that he does not heal. As one doctor says: "I only clear the way; Nature of God does the healing." Jesus did not hesitate to use physical remedies; for instance, He made clay and anointed the eyes of the blind man. Don't be more spiritual than God, who has planted in nature physical remedies for physical disease.

(3) *There is a third important origin of disease or health which is the newest and yet the oldest branch of science— nutrition.* This is the oldest branch in that man has been compelled to deal with it; and the newest, in that we are just now beginning to treat nutrition scientifically. Dr. James S. McLester says: "In the past, science has conferred on those people who have availed themselves of the newer knowledge of infectious diseases better health and a greater average length of life. In the future, it promises to those races who will take advantage of the new knowledge of nutrition a larger stature, greater vigor, increased longevity, and a higher level of cultural development."

God, my gracious Father, I want to live frankly and fully. Help me to face my physical man with complete honesty and a willingness to know the truth which alone can make me free. Save me from all self-deception and subterfuges, for I would be Thy fit instrument. Amen.

Matt. 6:22–23; 7:9–11; 1 Cor. 10:31

LACK OF VITAMINS AND NERVOUS RESULTS

We are now discussing nutrition as the basis of health. Seneca said: "Man does not die; he kills himself." And Hinede adds: "The two chief causes of death are food and drink." Dr. R. L. Greene, a professor of chemistry, specializing in nutrition, says: "The deadly weapons used by man in committing suicide are the knife, fork, and spoon." That suicide may come from wrong food, or the wrong eating of food. I was once in a restaurant, absorbed in thought and paying no attention to my eating, when a waitress came up to me and said, "Sir do you know that you are just gulping your food down?" I've always been grateful for that motherly soul, and while I've not always obeyed her, I often feel her shadow over my shoulder in gentle rebuke when I am wolfing it. Everyone needs a guardian angel to keep him from suicide with the weapons of the knife, fork, and spoon.

(4) *When eating start by thinking on your food.* While thinking on appetizing food you are performing a ritual similar to that used by the Hindu who bids the gods attend his feast, except that you are saying, "Come, Gastric Juices, and attend this feast." For if they don't come, then the Hindu god, Yama, the god of death, will prematurely attend your funeral.

(5) *See that you are getting a minimum vitamin requirement.* Dr. Greene says: "Life's chemical reactions are disturbed more frequently by a deficiency of vitamins than by any other cause." For instance, "a deficiency of Vitamin A gives rise to kidney, skin, and gastrointestinal disorders, diarrhea, poor appetite, bad teeth, chronic colitis, bronchitis, malnutrition followed by a greatly lowered state of general health and a high death rate from infectious diseases, especially tuberculosis and pneumonia." Were there space we could show a table of other diseases caused by a deficiency in Vitamins B, C, and D. For instance, on a diet deficient in Vitamin C the teeth of guinea pigs or monkeys suffer a progressive mineral loss and soon become soft like rubber. Vitamins are necessary to vitality. A third of all rejections in the draft can be traced to nutritional deficiencies.

Divine Chemist, Thou hast hidden in the heart of food the germs of vitality and health—we thank Thee for this. Help us now to hunt them out and utilize them to the full. For they are Thy gift. Amen.

Prov. 30:7–9; Jas. 2:15–16; Matt. 14:14–21

GRACE, GRASS, AND GUMPTION!

The main facts about vitamins are becoming generally known. What is not so generally known is the relation of lack of vitamins to nervous diseases. Dr. J. S. Hughes, a vitamin authority, shows charts of a pig going into severe nervous breakdown, with extreme irritability, as a result of taking away vitamins from the food. A photo of a pig with a nervous breakdown is a pathetic sight. That same pathetic pig is shown on other photos, after adequate vitamins have been fed to it, and now it is a sedate and poised pig!

This same professor said to me at the beginning of the National Christian Mission, in which I was to be speaking from three to five times daily for six solid months: "If you take some grass tablets I will give to you—the compressed blades of wheat when it is only about four inches high, at which stage it contains all the vitamins in a concentrated form—I will guarantee that you will come out of this Mission at the end of the six months without nervous exhaustion." I replied that I was his guinea pig and would try it. It may have been the fallacy in logic of "With, and therefore on account of," but there is no doubt that I came out at the end of that Mission without any nervous exhaustion; in fact, I was far better than when I began. The grass gave me a minimum vitamin requirement. Someone asked me how I was able to come through such a grind of exhausting engagements, fresh and full of vitality. I replied, "I think my vitality can be accounted for by three things: grace, grass, and gumption." I seemed half-serious, but in fact I was in dead earnest. That combination will produce health and vitality: grace for the soul to keep it from inner conflict, so that it will be rhythmical and harmonious; grass for the body to provide the physical basis of abundant living with adequate vitamin supply; and gumption for the mind to use the gifts of God intelligently and not overdo.

When I mention these three things in public people invariably ask me more about the grass than the grace and the gumption!

Gracious Father, I come to Thee to be made into a vital person. I shall need grace to keep me from wearing conflicts within. I shall need Thy stored vitality hidden in nature's storehouse, and then I shall need a quickened intelligence to save me from foolish mistakes. Help me to use all three. Amen.

Exod. 15:26; Ps. 103:3; Matt. 8:7; Acts 5:16

GO OVER YOUR MENTAL AND SPIRITUAL ATTITUDES

Some of our lack of physical victory may result from actual structural disease; some of it may result from inadequate vitamin supply—but some of it may result from wrong mental and spiritual attitudes. (6) *Go over your mental and spiritual attitudes and ask for the answer to the password: "Do you contribute to physical health?"* If they do not, then in all probability they contribute to disease and disruption. For, according to high British medical authority, "there is not a tissue or organ in the body not influenced by the attitude of mind and spirit."

One doctor told a patient that he would remit her fee if she would come and listen to what I was saying on the relationship between mental and spiritual states and health, for the doctor couldn't find a physical basis for the pains she described. The pains were real; she was not malingering; but their origin was in her mental and spiritual condition. She passed on her mental and spiritual sickness to her body.

One doctor commented on my address on this subject: "You are absolutely right, but you didn't tell half." Another comment from a doctor's wife: "My husband says he would die if he harbored resentments." Many people do! Or they live on at a half-dying rate. Another doctor said, "You could have added heart disease as caused by worry and anxiety." Heart disease has increased alarmingly in American life, the death rate rising from one in thirteen during 1900 to one in five in 1926; and this disease now ranks first among the causes of death. The increased worry and anxiety has been responsible for much of this increase. One able doctor said to me, "Fears are the most disruptive thing we can have." Stomach ulcers go up and down with the anxieties of the war. Worry is a frequent cause of constipation. The mind does create or destroy disease.

O God, I see I must be healthy-minded if I am to be healthy-bodied. Give me a mind-purge from all fears and worries and resentments, so that my body will be purged from all crippling disease and weakness. For I would be strong—strong for Thee. Make me the best that I can be. Amen.

Matt. 4:23; Prov. 4:20–22; 16:24; III John 2

THE WHOLE PERSON BECOMES SICK

Dr. Frank Hutchins, a nerve specialist, said, "Seventy per cent of the medical cases need new mental and spiritual attitudes for health." The powerful influence of mind over body is illustrated by Dr. Adelaide Woodard, a medical missionary to India, who had a finger amputated after a painful infection. She still has the pain in her finger though the finger is amputated. "How are you today, Marian?" someone asked a girl. "I'm all right," she replied, "except that I have a pain in my sister's shoulder!" The probabilities are that the pain was very real to Marian!

An elderly woman had vomiting spells, and the cause was found to be worry, brought on by financial insecurity. The worry threw functional disturbance into her digestive tract.

A doctor told me that his brother, a rather wealthy man, had refused to give a special portion of the family estate to a sister who had taken care of the parents during their old age. The portion would be about six hundred dollars. He grew selfish and resentful and refused to consent that this be given to the sister. Stomach ulcer resulted. The doctor called up his brother by long-distance telephone and spent five dollars on the call to tell his brother that the stomach ulcer was the result of his resentments and selfishness. The brother was so impressed with the fact that the doctor would spend that amount of money to give him advice that he gave up his resentments, and the stomach ulcer was healed.

Man is a unit, and he cannot be sick in one part without passing on the sickness to the other parts. The entire man must be redeemed. And the Gospel provides for that total redemption. It provides healing for the body, cleansing for the mind from all conflicts and divisions, forgiveness and fellowship for the soul—the whole person unified and co-ordinated and made effective.

This is full salvation!

O God, my God, I thank Thee that, "body and soul, I long for Thee," and that, body and soul, I need Thee. Give me radiant health in every part of my being so that I will have "no part dark." I yield every part to Thee for Thy healing. Amen.

Ps. 1:1; Hab. 2:12–14; Mic. 2:1–2

AN UNCHRISTIAN SOCIAL ORDER

We come now to the thirteenth major enemy of abundant living: *An unchristian social order*. We have space in this review of the enemies only to touch on the effect of an unchristian social order on the individual—we shall expound it at length later. We must mention it here to get clearly before us the disruptive effects of what many would consider *the* major enemy.

We are now beginning to see the effect of the social order upon the individual. We will not debate the question of whether heredity or environment has the determinative influence in the life of the individual. Perhaps we shall see in the end that the determinative influence in the life of the individual is the individual's own reaction to what he receives from heredity or environment. For only what you respond to influences you. But the fact must be faced that the individual usually responds to his social heredity, and that social heredity then proceeds to change him into its own image. The social heredity has an amazing power to convert the individual for good or ill. Not mechanically, mind you, for we repeat that only that part of your social heredity to which you respond changes you.

The psychoanalysts stress the fact that the cause of maladjustment to life is within the individual, and the Meyer school of psychologists stress the environmental factors as responsible for maladjustment of the individual. Both assumptions are true, for the individual and his environment act and react upon each other. But if I had to choose between them, I think I should have to conclude that an unchristian social order produces more thwarted and disrupted lives than any other single cause. A dean of girls in a public school told me that the three major factors in producing problem children are "poverty, broken homes, and a lack of attendance upon Sunday school or church"—all social factors.

The social conscience is being made more acute and sensitive as the facts are coming to the surface.

O Christ, we are beginning to see more clearly Thy rightness in presenting a new order on earth, the Kingdom of God. We would submit ourselves to that new order and be made into its image. We would yield to its every impulse and thus be responsive to the highest. Amen.

Amos 8:4–7; Hos. 4:1–3

THE SOCIAL ORDER CONVERTS THE INDIVIDUAL

We must continue our discussion of the effect of an unchristian social order upon the individual. Many things which we think are born within the individual are imposed on the child through the social heredity at a very early age. The social heredity in China converts into its image 400,000,000 people every thirty years. A Chinese child transferred at birth to America and put into a purely American home would grow up in the image of the American social heredity, with the outlook, the mentality, and the spirit of the American.

If a dyer's hands are colored by the colors amid which he works, so the soul of the individual is colored by the colors of the social heredity amid which it lives and moves and has its being. A man makes a machine, and then the machine makes him. Someone has expressed it this way: "Some machines lift us up, help us to make the most of ourselves. Some tear us apart, grind us down. A machine geared to a man is one thing, but a man geared to a machine is another thing. One is human, gives you a chance to be at your best self. The other is mechanical, works on you like a gear cutter, whittling you down, chiseling at you, cutting grooves in you, making you like all the small gears on the line."

As the machine cuts into your inner being, so the social surroundings cut into your being, chisel you, and make you after their own pattern. In the interest of individual conversion I am committed to the necessity of social conversion. If anyone shows no interest in converting an unchristian social order, then by that very fact he has little interest in individual conversion, for, apart from the Holy Spirit, the greatest single power to change the individual is the social order.

Jesus sees this clearly and would replace this unworkable, rotten social order with God's Order, the Kingdom of God. He would change individuals; He would change the total order—He would convert the total life.

O God, forgive us that we have made Thee a half-god, ruling over a half-realm. Thou art God, and all life, individual and social, must bend the knee to Thy will and find itself in that will. For Thy will is life to all life. Amen.

Matt. 6:22–24; 7:13–23

A LACK OF A TOTAL DISCIPLINE

We now take up briefly, awaiting a fuller development, the fourteenth of the major enemies of abundant living: *Lack of a total discipline.*

The future of the world is in the hands of disciplined people. "The meek [literally, the trained] shall inherit the earth." But this statement that the future of the world is in the hands of disciplined people must be modified—the future of the world is in the hands of people who are disciplined to the highest total discipline. Very often our disciplines are too small; we are geared to concepts and purposes which are too small; so we remain small with the smallness of our concepts and purposes. Many are geared to the discipline of the family, which may be very good; but it is very inadequate unless the family is geared to something beyond itself—an absolute. The discipline of a lodge, a club, a union, a church, a country, may be good, but they are not good enough. We must be disciplined to something that gives total meaning to the total life.

It is just this total discipline that is lacking in modern life. Modern life is so compartmentalized, specialized, picked to pieces, that it lacks total meaning. Science is abstracted knowledge—it abstracts knowledge about specific things, but fails to deal with the sum total of reality and its meaning; hence science can never exert a total discipline. Psychoanalysis picks people to pieces, but often cannot put them together again on a higher level. It uses psychoanalysis and not psychosynthesis, hence it cannot exert a total discipline. "They picked me to pieces and couldn't get me together again," said a brilliant but disrupted woman. Just as the spokes of a wheel hang loose without a hub, so the powers of life are at loose ends unless fastened into the central hub—God and His Kingdom. There is simply nothing to which we can be totally disciplined, except one thing—God's absolute order, the Kingdom of God. That and that alone gives total meaning to life.

Gracious Father, until I bring every thought to the obedience of Thy Kingdom, and every relationship under its sway, I am hanging at loose ends, and life lacks total meaning and hence lacks purpose and power. Help me to a complete discipline to Thy Kingdom. Amen.

Matt. 13:52; I Cor. 9:23–27

DISCIPLINED TO THE KINGDOM

We have thought that man is made for freedom. He is. But freedom can come only through obedience. I am free from the policeman if I obey the laws he represents—within the framework of the laws he represents I am free. The larger the unit I obey, the larger the freedom I enjoy. If I obey the laws of the United States, I am free within the boundaries of that country.

When I am disciplined to the Kingdom of God and obey its laws, then I am free within the limits of its area. But its area is universal; therefore I am universally free. The Christian, disciplined to the Kingdom of God, is the only universal person, universally free. He is a cosmic person.

The thing works the other way. If you are disciplined to yourself and your own desires, then you are free within the area of yourself and your desires. You have chosen a small unit of allegiance, hence you become small. Moreover, you become disliked by others to whom you have no loyalty or love. In the end, you dislike yourself for being so small, and for being disliked by others. This is a vicious circle, a descending spiral. But if you are disciplined to the Kingdom, you will like yourself for the greatness and nobility of your loyalties and allegiances, and other people will respond to you, for you respond to them; and, best of all, the universe will take sides with you, will back you, and will make you feel at home and free. This is an ascending spiral.

A woman who had been all tied up with fears, a physical and nervous wreck, writes after her release: "The sense of freedom and release, the new understanding, and the something that seems almost like finding a sixth sense is wonderful." That "sixth sense" is the cosmic sense, a sense of being universalized, of a cosmic at-homeness, of being in tune with the sum total of reality. Being disciplined to the total Order, in a total way, with every part moving toward a single goal, you become a *narrow* person with a *narrow* purpose. But at the very moment you are narrowed you are broadened into the purposes and the life of the Kingdom. You are totally free.

O God, I want every area of my life to own one allegiance, and one alone. For I cannot be an undisciplined person, or disciplined to too small an allegiance. I cannot rest till I am under the sway of the Ultimate, nor until the Ultimate has the ultimate sway. In Jesus' name. Amen.

1 John 3:2–3, 11, 14, 16–17, 22–24; 4:21; 5:2–4

LACK OF A CREATIVE, OUTGOING LOVE

We come to the last of the fifteen major enemies: *Lack of a creative, outgoing love.* I have saved this enemy for the last, for it is the *sine qua non* of abundant living. If you were able to conquer the whole of the fourteen major enemies, you would still lack the one thing needful if you lacked an outgoing love. For life is not built for negative achievement—it is made for positive contribution, for outgoing love. He who loves not, lives not; and he who loves most, lives most.

I have purposely put the word "creative" in the title and definition, for there is a kind of love which goes out to get for itself. It goes out to bring in. That kind of outgoing love is just as bad as a turned-in love, for it still says, "Give me." But the "creative" love is the love that stimulates, helps, and awakens others. And as it stimulates, it is itself stimulated; as it awakens, it is awakened.

> "Love ever gives,
> Forgives, outlives,
> And ever stands with open hands;
> And while it lives, it gives,
> For this is love's prerogative:
> To give and give and give."

And the writer of these lines might have added,

> And while it gives it lives,
> For this is love's reward:
> To live and live and live.

You can never get rid of your own troubles unless you take upon yourself the troubles of others. The saintly Keble said: "When you find yourself oppressed by melancholy, the best way is to go out and find something kind to do to somebody else." Or as someone else has put it: "When I dig a man out of trouble, the hole which is left behind is the grave where I bury my own sorrow." Then go out each day and do something that nobody but a Christian would do.

O God, I see, Thou hast fashioned me in my inmost being for creative love. Thou Creator God, Thou hast made me to be a creator, too. I share Thy power to make and to remake. I am so glad I am no more a negative being—I am positive and outgoing and creative. I thank Thee. Amen.

Matt. 12:34–35; 15:19–20; Col. 3:8–15

THE MIRACLE STARTS FROM WITHIN

We pursue today the necessity of a creative, outgoing love. It is, in the words of Professor W. E. Hocking, "the most radically creative attitude yet known to men—the determination to do what the Everlasting Mercy does." The Everlasting Mercy is creative and outgoing in love. As someone has said: "If you want to survive, get faith and make it infectious. . . . . The chances are on the side of that audacity which we call friendliness."

Leslie B. Salter says: "Every normal man or woman longs more keenly for love, for warm friendship, admiration and human responsiveness from his fellows than for anything else in life. . . . . Wouldst thou love life? Then start giving those about you the feeling they long for. Start passing out good cheer and brotherly love, and you will receive in return a personal friendliness and genuine happiness you never dreamed possible, and which will revolutionize your whole life."

Don't wait for some miracle to be performed on you from without, lifting you above your fears and doubts and self-centeredness. You help God from within by turning in outgoing love to others, and miraculously your fears and doubts and self-centeredness will vanish. The miracle starts from within, not from without. Throw your will on the side of outgoing love, and all the healing resources of the universe will be behind you

But neither God nor man can help you if you remain bottled up in yourself. You are not made to live that way, and all the medicine you can take, all the advice you can receive, all the praying you can do, will do you no good unless you throw your will on the side of outgoing love. Get out of yourself, or perish!

Allan Hunter says: "We may discover, as a contemporary philosopher suggests, that loving our enemies because we first love God is better treatment for nervous indigestion than an operation or an analysis." It is a better treatment not only for nervous indigestion, but also for almost anything that ails us.

O Thou Who art always reaching out after me in love and awakening me, help me this day to do the same. Help me to quicken and awaken some life by the touch of my friendliness and love. Here is something I need not be afraid of—I cannot be too loving. Help me. Amen.

Ps. 26:1–2; Col. 3:5–7; Ps. 19:12–14

A FINAL EXAMINATION

We have now reached the halfway point in our year, and with it have reached the end of our study of the fifteen major enemies. Today must be spent in review, asking ourselves straight questions about these major enemies. As we ask our questions let there be no blind spots, no allowing of any enemy to remain. Life or death depends on a full riddance. Ask these questions slowly and give considered answers.

Have I a faith in, and loyalty to, Something beyond myself that gives ultimate meaning, coherence, and goal to life? And is that Something, God? Or are there still areas of self-centeredness? And do these uncleansed areas breed the offspring of self-centeredness—dishonesty? greed and avarice? prejudice and intolerance? pride? refusal of responsibility and co-operation? Have I really shifted the center of my life from myself to God?

What about anger, resentments, hate—any roots left? Am I still harboring worries, anxieties, and fears? Or are they turned over to Him?

Is there any sense of unresolved guilt still lurking in me? Am I now forever turned away from negativism and inferiority attitudes? Is there any insincerity left anywhere in me —conscious or unconscious? Are my desires controlled? Does impure sex thinking have any part in my thoughts? And are my other appetites all under His control? Are there any divided loyalties still left within me?

Am I balancing my virtues with their opposite virtues? Do ignorance and lack of judgment still hamper me? Are there physical disharmonies rooted in wrong mental and spiritual attitudes? Is lack of proper nutrition weakening me? Am I doing my best to change the unchristian social order which so deeply affects us? Am I now under a total discipline in my total life? Am I released and outgoing in creative love to others?

If, on the whole, we can answer these questions on the right side of things, we are on the way to abundant living.

O God, I have faced my enemies, and in Thy name I have downed them. I thank Thee. Now help me to enter into no alliance with any enemy that pleads to stay. Help me to make a clean sweep. In Jesus' name. Amen.

Rom. 5:20–21; Col. 2:6–10; Phil. 4:13

WE TURN TO OUR RESOURCES

We have now completed the first half of our quest for abundant living, in which we looked at the fifteen major enemies of human living. Now and again we paused to glance at our resources to meet and destroy those enemies. This was necessary to keep up our confidence and faith that they could be overcome, for often in dealing with problems we become so obsessed with them that they get on the inside of us and we become a problem to ourselves and others. We must gaze at our resources full-faced until they get us—get us down to every nerve cell and to every fiber of our being. We must gaze at them until we are possessed by them; until we no longer possess them, but they possess us.

Someone has said, "The early Christians did not say in dismay: 'Look what the world has come to,' but in delight, 'Look what has come to the world.' " They saw not merely the ruin, but the Resources for the reconstruction of that ruin. They saw not merely that sin did abound, but that grace did much more abound. On that assurance the pivot of history swung from blank despair, loss of moral nerve, and fatalism, to faith and confidence that at last sin had met its match, that something new had come into the world, that not only here and there, but on a wide scale, men could attain to that hitherto impossible thing—goodness. And not only goodness, but health of mind and body —rhythm and harmony in their total being.

That same sense of confidence must possess you if you are to pass from an anemic, noncreative, nay-saying type of person to one who is master of himself and his circumstances and his destiny.

But this confidence and faith must not be based on a self-hypnosis, a mental and spiritual fool's paradise; it must be based on the solid confidence that your life is related to the sum total of Reality, and that that Reality is working with you and not against you.

The whole secret of abundant living can be summed up in this sentence: "Not your responsibility, but your response to God's ability."

O Gracious God and Father, my heart beats a little faster, my pulses throb in expectation at the prospect of being the person that, now and again, in my highest moments, I have felt I might be. And now I am to be that very person. I follow. Amen.

John 14:1–12; I John 1:7; 2:8–13

IS THE CHRISTIAN WAY UNREALISTIC

We finished yesterday by saying that there can be no permanent or thoroughgoing victory unless we feel that the sum total of Reality is with us, and that we are with and not against that Reality—that we are working with the grain of the universe and not against it. If a doubt creeps in at this point, it is a fatal doubt, and lays its cold, dead hand on all our highest hopes and possibilities.

But this doubt is just the crux—how can we be sure that in following the Christian way we are following the way of Reality? May the Christian way not be a beautiful, but unrealistic, dream that overlies a basis of hideous, but solid, reality? In trying to be Christian, aren't we endeavoring to be something for which we are not made; striving for goals to which we cannot, by the very fact of our human nature, attain? Doesn't the Christian way of idealism break its delicate wings upon the hard facts of reality? It may work in some other world, but in this world we must not waste our time with the impossible—the impossible that only excites us with much ado about nothing; that only gives us an itch that cannot be scratched; that only leaves us fretted and dissatisfied because of failure, inwardly condemned because we cannot be what we long to be, but what by our very nature we are incapable of being.

That is the haunting doubt of the modern man, and we cannot get an inch into the soul of this defeated age until that doubt is faced and laid.

But this doubt can be faced and laid only when we see that inherently we are made for the Christian way, and that to try to live some other way will not only be wrong, but also impossible. You cannot live against the nature of Reality—and *get away with it.* You will get hurt. Jesus was surprised not so much at men's wickedness, but at their stupidity. "Don't you see?" he kept saying. "You are living against life, and that is impossible—you'll be hurt—you are hurt."

Sin is an attempt to act against God, and not against ourselves. That is impossible.

My Father, Thou hast fashioned my being for Thyself, and when I try to fashion it for something else it becomes all tangled up. My life sums won't add up correctly. Help me to take Thy way, for I am discovering it is *my* way. In Jesus' name. Amen.

II Cor. 5:10; John 6:39; Gal. 6:7–8; I Pet. 1:23

THE JUDGMENT OF GOD AND
THE JUDGMENT OF LIFE

Yesterday we ended with the statement that the verdict of life and the verdict of Christ are the same. He is life—"I am the Life"—and to live against Him is to live against life. If that simple statement is true, then it is the most momentous truth ever presented to man. J. Middleton Murry says: "And if men do not care about the Kingdom they will find the same lesson taught by life itself. Life cannot be abused. To the judgment seat of God man must take with him only a life that was lived: and the judgment of God and the judgment of life are the same." (*Heroes of Thought,* p. 24.)

Two lines of human experimentation, conducted for the most part independently, are now converging: the Christian way and the scientific way. Life is bringing them both out at the same place. Someday science is going to lay everything on the table and say: "This is the way to live, and not this." And when we see it all we will be astonished and exclaim, "But the way you assert is the way to live is the Christian way, and the way you assert is not the way to live is an unchristian way." The scientist will reply: "Of that we cannot speak, but we can affirm that life comes out in this way." The Christian way is written into the constitution of things. It is the natural way to live. I heard two thoughtful people render the same verdict. One was an outstanding nerve specialist who had dealt with jagged and frayed nerves all his life, and this was his life conclusion: "Christianity is just plain common sense." The other was a brilliant youth who, beginning to experiment with life, said, "The Christian way is just sense." The youth by a swift intuition and the doctor by a life-time of experimentation came out at the same place: the Christian way is the natural way.

If you try to live against nature you get all tangled up— life goes from snarl to snarl.

Thou God of my inmost being, of my nerves and of my tissues and of my blood, how can I sin against Thee without sinning against myself? Thy judgments are swift and sure, for they are inherent. I cannot escape them. I want to escape into Thyself. Amen.

Heb. 2:6–9; Acts 19:9; John 14:6–7

THE CHRISTIAN WAY IS THE NATURAL WAY

The Christian way is wrought into the texture of life. It is life. There is a striking passage in John 1:3: "And without him was not any thing made that was made." In other words: there is a way stamped into everything—it is the way life is made to work; and that way is the Christian way —"without him was not any thing made that was made." The stamp of Christ is in everything—it is the way life is made to work. It is the divine intention written into flesh and blood and the total organization of life.

Dr. H. F. Rall says that one does not say to a crocodile, "Now be a crocodile," for it will never be anything else *but*. But one does say to a man, "Now be a man." Why? For man can and often does live against, or below, the way he is made to live as a man. He can be unnatural. And to be unnatural is to be frustrated. Sin is "trying to live unnaturally"—it is literally "missing the mark"—the mark for which we are inherently made. That "mark" is fashioned into our blood cells, into our tissues, and into our nerve cells—it is the will of God. The laws of our being are not other than the laws of God—they *are* the laws of God wrought into the constitution of our being. To be true to them is to be true to God, and to be true to God is to be true to them.

The early Christians sensed this when they used the phrase, "those belonging to the Way." (Acts 9:2, Moffatt.) Not merely "the Way of salvation," but "the Way"—the Way that life works, the Way for which it is made—the Way!

In the older presentation of the Gospel we have spoken of that blessed word "whosoever" (John 3:16), and rightly so. It was the "whosoever" of an unlimited, redemptive offer. But there is another "whosoever" (Matt: 7:24) which speaks of an unlimited fact; if you build on my words, said Jesus, your house will stand up under life; if you don't, then it will go down in a crash. There are no exceptions— "whosoever."

O Christ, how can I ever cease to thank Thee that amid the stumblings of life I happened on *this*—the Way! It fills me with constant surprise that I, even I, have found the Way. My doubts are at rest. Now forward—forever! Amen.

John 3:20; Ps. 1:1–6; I Pet. 3:9–13

EVIL IS SELF-DESTRUCTIVE

We have been discussing the Christian way as "the Way" —not *a* way, but *the Way*. In every possible situation it is the way to act. I can admit of no exceptions whatever. If one tries to act in some other way his sums won't come out right; life becomes tangled up.

Evil entangles every situation, for evil is against the nature of reality. Therefore, to try to straighten out a situation by an evil is only to entangle it the more. Therefore, evil is not only evil; it is stupid. Somebody has suggested that the word "evil" is the word "live" spelled backward. It is—evil is the will to live put into reverse; it is life turning against itself. Man's nature is allergic to evil. Evil is the way man's nature is not made to work. In evil, life desires to gain freedom, but gains only the freedom to destroy itself. It runs away—from salvation! It revolts—against life!

Some schoolboys were allowed to take a slot machine apart to study its inner workings. They found that the machine in its inner constitution was made to yield up only one dime in ten to the player. The players might fuss and fume and call on Lady Luck, but in the end there would be one result, and only one result—one dime in ten was the average. Luck was not against them—the machine was against them. So every morning the machine would be empty, and every night it would be full. Men had figured it out scientifically by the law of averages and had built that knowledge into the machine. Anyone who tries to beat that machine is not merely bad; he's a fool!

Every sinner therefore turns out to be one thing and one thing alone—a problem to himself and others. God has us hooked—we cannot revolt against God without revolting against ourselves. If you clash with God, you clash with yourself. The attempt to disprove this statement has filled the world with human wreckage.

Every man who tries it, thinks that he will be an exception, but there are no exceptions.

My Father, Thou hast made it impossible for me to hurt or harm myself without Thy protest. The penalties attached to evil are not the signs of Thy wrath, but of Thy love— Thy redeeming love. Help me to work with that love—not against it. Amen.

JESUS, THE STANDARD NOTE

Yesterday we saw that sin is not only bad; it is also foolish. The opposite is true—goodness is not only good; it is also wisdom. That is the reason Jesus identified Himself with Wisdom: "Nevertheless, Wisdom is vindicated by all that she does." He had just been talking about Himself. He asserted Himself to be Wisdom, and added, "Life approves of that statement, for it approves, vindicates all I do." The emphasis is upon that word "all"—not here and there was He hitting right notes, but never did He miss the right note. When He and His teaching are put under life to see what the verdict will be, there is but one verdict—He is vindicated by *all* that He does.

Paul takes up the same note and says, "Christ the power of God, and the wisdom of God." Note that he connects the two—power and wisdom. They are bound to be connected. For the sum total of Reality is behind wisdom—the whole moral universe backs it. Sooner or later wisdom is bound to win. The opposite is true: sin and weakness are inseparably connected, for the sum total of Reality is against evil. Sooner or later it is bound to fail. Evil has the seeds of its own decay within itself. In evil I cannot win; in good I cannot lose. The stars in their courses work against sin. The stars in their courses work on behalf of good. There is a saying that "only the stars are neutral." But the stars are not neutral—nature is on the side of good and will not respond to evil. Goodness is wisdom, and goodness is power.

In Washington there is struck over the radio each day the note A 440 as the standard note by which the nation is to tune its instruments. Everything that departs from that note is discord, and hence torture. This standard note is not arbitrary; it is inherent. In Jesus the standard note of human living is struck. Everything that tunes to that note catches the music of the spheres; everything that departs from it is discord and torture. God does not inflict any torture. The departure itself produces the torture. It is inherent.

O Christ, Thou standard Note of all human living, forgive me that I have tried to live against that Note. The result has inevitably and invariably been discord and inner torture. I tune my life fully and wholly to Thee from this hour. Amen.

Col. 1:17; Eph. 2:21; Rev. 1:17–18

LET'S BE NORMAL!

We ended yesterday by saying that Jesus is the standard Note which God has struck for us and which He bids all men tune their lives and institutions by, or be a part of chaos. One man said of himself, "The trouble with me is that I am in harmony with chaos." Everything not in harmony with Christ is in harmony with chaos. The choice is literally: Christ or chaos.

Dr. Fritz Künkel, a noted psychologist, has a book entitled *Let's Be Normal!* His psychiatry and his Christianity bring him out at the same place: Christ is the Norm—to depart from Him is to be abnormal, hence frustrated. Let's be normal—let's be Christian. The scientific conclusion of this great psychologist and the intuitive conclusion of a huge laborer are the same. At the close of an address the laborer blurted out, "Well, we can't have too much of Christianity." Is there anything—literally anything else—of which it can be said that we cannot have too much of it? Nothing!

David Seabury says: "Disease is a loss of balance in part or in all of the organism. It may begin in the spirit and in bodily disintegration. It may start from physical causes and react upon the psyche. But always it is a loss of balance in one's basic being. Too little or too much emotion at once records itself on the endocrine system. Neither inhibition nor wild release of feeling tends to health. . . . . Too much or too little food, exercise, sleep, indeed too much or too little of anything . . . . destroys health. Only by achieving a psychical and physical equilibrium on and between each plane of life is a man's vigor maintained." (*How Jesus Heals Our Minds Today*, p. 310.)[1]

We can have too much of everything except one thing—Christ, for He is equilibrium; He is the norm; He is Life itself.

Was it mere chance that the early Christian writers spoke of Christ as "Life," or was it a deduction from the facts? They found He was Life with a capital "L."

O Christ, now at long last I have something I cannot have too much of. I cannot be too like Thee, have too much of Thy spirit. Help me to drink deep draughts of Thy mind and way. Amen.

[1] Reprinted by permission of Little, Brown & Co., publishers.

Luke 8:27–37; Acts 26:22–25; 1 Pet. 4:3–4, 14

AFRAID OF SANITY!

A Church of England clergyman uttered a profound thing in one of our Round Table conferences: "I am trying to live the natural way of life—the Christian way." In II Peter 2:19 we read, "promising them freedom, when they are themselves enslaved to corruption." Note that phrase— "enslaved to corruption," given over to something that is decaying. Evil is just that—it is life under the doom of decay. The Christian way is life under the bloom of development. Hence, the Christian way is the natural way.

It is true there is a false nature built up by our false living, but that false nature is not the real nature that God stamped in us at creation. That false nature which a man attempts to build up is at war with the real nature. Hence, the man who sins is at war with himself as well as with God.

The new birth comes through the surrender and abandonment of this false world of evil and the acceptance of this true world of good. The man becomes "a little child" —he is realigned to God's original purpose. When he becomes God's man, he really becomes a man.

We have become so naturalized in evil that we think the Christian way is the unnatural way. The people came and saw the demoniac, out of whom Jesus had cast the evil spirits, "clothed, and in his right mind: and they were afraid." Afraid of what?

They were afraid of sanity! We have become so accustomed to our insane ways of life that we are afraid of the real sanity of the Christian way. A man told me that he had ridden a bicycle with crooked handle bars for so long that when someone straightened them he fell off. He had become naturalized in crookedness! To us who are naturalized in this crooked and impossible order the realism of Jesus seems idealism; but it is realism so far ahead of us that to us it is idealism. In fact, it *is* realism.

Evil is the great illusion—it is the illusion that you can live against the design of the universe and get away with it!

O Christ, we have been afraid of the splendid sanity of Thy mind, the amazing balance of Thy life—we have been afraid of Life. And now I ask that Thou wilt help me become naturalized in the homeland of my soul—the Kingdom of God. Amen.

Luke 17:20–21; Rom. 8:9–11; Micah 6:8

THE HOMELAND OF THE SOUL—
THE KINGDOM OF GOD

In our prayer yesterday we spoke of "the homeland of my soul—the Kingdom of God." Is that true? Is the Kingdom of God the homeland of my soul? Is it the soul's native air? When we find it, do we find ourselves?

A recent letter from a brilliant but disrupted person said, "I am easy to please, but difficult to satisfy." Why is it that a person's surface sentiments are easily pleased, but in the depths he is difficult to satisfy? Is the reason that the soul knows its homeland and will not be put off with substitutes?

When Jesus said, "The kingdom of God is within you," He voiced one of the most important things ever uttered. The seeds of a new humanity are in that statement. It has seldom been taken seriously by orthodox Christianity; only the cults have taken it up and have used it. It must now be reclaimed and used. It must be put back into the stream of orthodox Christianity and become potent there. For this great truth is potent. I know the fear that has kept that verse from becoming current coin: If the Kingdom of God is within us, in everybody, even the unchanged (for this verse was spoken to Pharisees who were unconverted), then the necessity of a new birth is gone; a merely optimistic view of human nature takes the place of the tragic view of human nature as sinful and in need of redemption—therefore salvation comes by insight, instead of by repentance and surrender and faith. I appreciate that fear, but do not share it.

If the Kingdom of God is within us, written into the constitution of our beings, the way we are made to live, then sin is not less tragic, but more so. For then we sin not only against a God afar off, but also against a God who is in that Kingdom within us—it is intimate rejection, intimate slaying. Moreover, we sin not only against God; we sin also against ourselves. Sin, therefore, is not the nature of our being; it is against nature—our nature—and against the God who made it.

O God, I see that sin grows not less tragic, but more so. If I sin against the Kingdom within, then when I sin, I sin indeed. I disrupt myself, my possibilities, my future, my all. And I sin against Thee—intimate Lover and King of that Kingdom. Forgive me. Amen.

Rom. 7:24–25; 8:1–2; John 7:9; Luke 10:9

WITHIN YOU—AT YOUR DOORS!

There are two great streams of religious thought in the world today. One stream maintains, "Everything is within you; all you need to do is to awaken your latent powers; you have the spark of the Divine within you—kindle it." Or in the extreme form, as in the Vedanta in India, "You not only have the Divine within you; you are Divine, you are God—realize it." The capital of this realm of thought is Benares, India.

The other stream maintains, "You are a sinful creature; there is nothing good within you; you need the invading grace of God from without to awaken you, to redeem you." The capital of this realm of thought is Berne, Switzerland, the home of Karl Barth.

Do we have to vote with our lives on one side or the other of these viewpoints? No. Each has a truth, but it is only a half-truth—the truth is beyond each. The truth is in the Kingdom of God. The Kingdom of God is fulfillment: "until it be fulfilled in the kingdom of God." The half-truth in each is fulfilled in the whole truth of the Kingdom. The Kingdom fulfills the truth in immanence—"the kingdom of God is within you." It fulfills the truth in transcedence—"the kingdom of God cometh," the Kingdom of God is at your doors. The Kingdom is both pervasive in immanence and invasive in transcedence; it is within us and beyond us.

Man is sinful in that he is sinning not only against the God who made him, but also against the Kingdom written into the texture of his being—he is sinning against himself. This view makes sin worse than if man is looked on as naturally sinful; for if he is naturally sinful, then is sin so bad, if it is natural? Why should I be punished for doing what is natural, for fulfilling my own nature? But if sin is not only sinful, but also unnatural, then sin is doubly bad—it is revolt against God and myself. But sin is not natural; it is an attempt to live against my real nature.

So sin is anti-life.

O God, Thou hast not fashioned us in our inmost being and then abandoned us, turning us over to forces too strong for us. Thou art protesting at every step our self-ruin. Help us not to consent to our own ruin. In Jesus' name. Amen.

I John 4:4; Rom. 6:2, 11–23

THE KINGDOM OF GOD AND MORAL TENSION

If the Kingdom of God is within us, then where is the necessity for the tensions that should be set up between the Kingdom and ourselves, leading to crisis and repentance and the new birth? Doesn't this Kingdom-within-you emphasis flatten out those tensions, and do away with the crisis?

On the contrary, this Kingdom-within-you emphasis heightens those tensions and leads more definitely to crisis, for now we see that we are in revolt against God and ourselves. I find I obtain twice the response for repentance and conversion from this appeal that I do under the appeal that man is naturally sinful, and cannot do a thing about it unless God sovereignly rescue him. The emphasis that man is naturally sinful not only flattens out tensions—it flattens out the self. For if man is naturally sinful, why fight against nature? It will be a losing battle anyway. That paralyzes hope, and, consequently, the will. Often in India I have seen a man excuse his sin by saying, "I am a man." Well, if he is a man, that is one of the most potent reasons for his not sinning; for when a man sins he feels less than a man, out of harmony with himself, with God, with his fellow man—even Nature drapes herself in mourning. But when a man does right, does he fell less than a man? He feels his personality heightened; he is at home in the universe; he is universalized; he walks the earth a conqueror. Therefore goodness is native to us, and sin is unnatural, an aberration, a deflection, a defeat, a degradation. It is the accustomed, but not the natural. It is no more natural than a cancer is natural, than sand in the eye is natural.

The view that man is naturally sinful led to these lines:

> "When ———— at Swanick had quit it,
> A young man said, 'Now I have hit it.
>   Since Icannot do right,
>   I must find out tonight
> What sin to commit, and commit it!' "

O God, I do set up a tension between myself and my sin. In Thy name I revolt against it, repudiate it, break with it forever. I accept my native land—Thyself, Thy Kingdom. Here I am at home, free and at my best. I thank Thee. Amen.

Deut. 32:5; Prov. 2:12–15; Isa. 59:8

THE KINGDOM OF GOD AND ORIGINAL SIN

The Kingdom of God is within you! If so, then what of "original sin"? Is it all a mistake and are we to talk about original goodness instead of original sin? Yes, for our origin is in God, and therefore goodness is original, for God is good. He has stamped His ways within us. But there is a truth in original sin, which we should call racially acquired sin. The race has sinned generation after generation and has passed on to posterity unnatural bents to evil. The natural urges—self, sex, and the herd—have been twisted by unnatural use to unnatural bents. The self becomes an end in itself instead of being a means to the ends of the Kingdom of God. Sex also becomes an end in itself instead of being dedicated to the ends of procreation for which it was intended. The herd, or social instinct, becomes fastened on lesser social entities like class, race, or state instead of on the Kingdom of God. All of these become perverted and therefore need to be converted—to be converted to the ends for which they were originally intended.

If we are made in the image of God, then sin is not natural; it is the acquired—it is an attempt to live against nature, to live against life and escape the consequences. We pay tribute to this fact when we say of a bad man, "He is crooked," implying that he is departing from goodness, the straight. But if sin is the natural, then it is the straight, the standard, and goodness is the unnatural crookedness. When we say of a man, "He is impure," we thereby suggest he has departed from the pure, the original intention. Impurity is therefore unnatural; purity is natural. "My strength is as the strength of ten, because my heart is pure." Why? Because the sum total of reality is behind the pure man—he is aligned to the nature of things; therefore he is strong with the strength of ten. Impurity is lined up against the nature of things; hence, any impure person is weak in personality. The eyes are shifty; the face grows dull and lusterless; and the personality sags.

O God, Thou art teaching me Thy ways, written in Thy Word, and also written in me. My flesh, my nerves, my very being begin to be vocal with Thy purposes and vibrant with Thy vitality. I am the vehicle of Thy victory—help me to surrender to Thy purposes that I may live abundantly. Amen.

1 Cor. 2:15–16; Phil. 4:8–9; Col. 1:12–18

THE KINGDOM OF GOD IS THE NORM

When we say, "The Kingdom of God is within you," are we talking theological fiction or teleological fact? In other words, are we imposing our views on nature, or are those views written within the purposes of nature? I have mentioned Dr. Fritz Künkel's book, entitled *Let's Be Normal!* Did he as a psychologist, studying the human personality in the cold white light of science, find that there is a norm written within us, and that to depart from that norm is to end in disruption and self-frustration? Yes! The psychologist would spell that "norm" with a small "n," but we who believe that our origin is in God would spell it "Norm." The Kingdom of God within us is that Norm. To depart from it is to lose ourselves, to frustrate ourselves. To this Dr. Künkel would agree, for his Christian faith and his psychological studies bring him out at the same place: there is a Norm written within us, and to depart from that Norm is to be abnormal, hence unhealthy and frustrated.

The Christian is the normal person; everyone else is abnormal. Everyone else is a little "off"—sometimes very much "off." He is not merely bad, but foolish, trying to live against the Norm—an impossible attempt. It is bound to end in only one way—in self-defeat and self-frustration. Self-defeat and self-frustration are inescapable, for the nature of things works that way. Sin and its punishment are one and the same thing, for sin is "missing the mark"—*amartia,* a departure from the Norm. A cancer is abnormal tissue; hence it is a cancer. One does not have to impose punishment on a cancer for being a cancer, because being a cancer is its own punishment—it is bound to destroy itself and the other tissue in the body by its very nature. The end is death. "The wages of sin is death"—"the wages," the natural outcome, the pay-off, is bound to be death, for the sin itself is death—a departure from Normal; it is "on its own," has no roots in Reality, hence will perish from lack of sustenance.

O my Father God, I stand in awe of Thy goodness. I see Thy footprints everywhere. They are within me. When I turn within, I am on holy ground, for Thy presence is in every flaming bush of emotion, in every call that comes from the deeps of my being. I am Thy Temple. "May everything within Thy temple say, Glory." Amen.

Eph. 5:8–18; Isa. 11:2; Ezek. 2:1–2

THE KINGDOM OF GOD AND THE
NATURAL MAN

The Kingdom of God is within you! If the Kingdom of God is our real nature, then what shall we do with the statement of Paul: "The natural man receiveth not the things of the Spirit of God"? Moffatt recaptures the original in his translation: "The unspiritual man rejects these truths of the Spirit of God." (I Corinthians 2:14.) The context shows that the discussion is not between the natural and the unnatural, but between the "spiritual" (vss. 13, 15) and the unspiritual. The spiritual man is a man controlled by the Kingdom of God; hence he is the truly natural man. The unspiritual man is a man living against that Kingdom within; hence he is the unnatural man.

Again, we ask, "Is psychology, when it becomes truly biological—that is, when it is accoring to the facts of life —coming out at the same place as the Christian?" Let Dr. Henry Link, a psychologist, answer: "I define personality as the extent to which the individual has developed habits and skills which interest and serve other people . . . . Its emphasis is on doing things with and for other people. Its essence is self-sacrifice, not self-gratification. Indeed, the pursuit of personality just to win friends and position is quite likely to result in self-consciousness." (*The Rediscovery of Man*, pp. 60-61.)

Note that Dr. Link defines "personality" in Christian terms—self-losing service to others—and this with unmixed motives. But a person losing himself in service to others with unselfish motives is the picture of a Christian. Dr. Link says that this is "personality." Are the Christian and personality one and the same? Yes! When you discover the Christian way, you discover your own way as a person. To adopt the Christian way is to have your personality heightened. For it is unified, adjusted to the nature of Reality, and is therefore no longer under the law of self-frustration, but of self-fulfillment. "The Spirit enabled them to express themselves." (Acts 2:4, Moffatt.) True self-expression began when they were filled with the Spirit. Now they could let nature caper!

O God, I tave been afraid to surrender myself to Thy will, lest my own will be lost. How foolish I have been. I now see that Thy will is my own deepest will, and that to find Thy purposes is to find my person. Oh, let me express myself in Thee! Amen.

Matt. 25:34; 13:44–45; 16:24–28

THE KINGDOM OF GOD IS THE CAUSE!

Last week we studied the statement, "The Kingdom of God is within you," and tried to recover the thought underlying it for the main stream of Christendom. We must pursue this thought until it becomes not an argument, but an axiom—something which we no longer hold, but something that holds us.

We saw that the psychologists, by the very pressure of facts, are defining personality in Christian terms—the Christian is the norm. The educationalists are coming out at the same place. Someone asked Professor W. H. Kilpatrick, the great educationalist, what was the greatest discovery of modern education, and he replied: "The greatest discovery of modern education is: He that saveth his life shall lose it, and he that loseth his life for some great Cause shall find it again." No, Professor Kilpatrick, that was not a discovery of modern education—it was a rediscovery, for Jesus used that phrase five times, except that for the "Cause" He substituted "the Kingdom"—"the Kingdom" is the Cause. Modern education, in its experiments with human nature and the way it works, comes to the conclusion that if a man centers himself on himself his self will go to pieces; only as he loses it in some great Cause beyond himself does he find his self coming back to him integrated and heightened. That is a law of human living as deeply imbedded in our moral and spiritual universe as the force of gravity is embedded in our material universe. A Roman Catholic businessman said to me at the close of an address to a service club: "You didn't preach to us; you just told us things." He saw that I was lifting up laws of the moral and spiritual world written into the constitution of things, and that they are self-authenticating—one doesn't have to argue them; he simply states them and they argue themselves. One doesn't argue an axiom in geometry: "Things equal to the same thing are equal to each other." One states it and it argues itself.

The people who heard Jesus wondered at His "authority" —it was the authority of the facts.

O God, we have been feverishly trying to support Thy universe with our puny arguments. We are like those who organize a society for the protection of the sun, when someone slings mud at the sun. Forgive us and help us to trust implicitly in Thy self-authenticating truth. In Jesus' name. Amen.

Matt. 22:36–40; 25:34

THE KINGDOM OF GOD AND BUSINESS

The Kingdom of God is within you! Psychology, education, and even business are stumbling upon the laws of the Kingdom in their search for a workable way to live. I say "stumbling upon," for that expresses the chance discoveries that are being made. Someday our prejudices will drop away, as all other ways become manifestly unworkable, and we shall methodically and with abandon give ourselves to the discovery of the laws of the Kingdom. Then in a decade humanity will leap further forward in progressive abundant living than it is now doing in a century.

When someone asked Daniel Willard, the great head of the Baltimore and Ohio Railway, what was the outstanding qualification for a successful executive, he replied: "The ability and the willingness to put yourself in the other man's place." But that is distinctly Christian—it is loving your neighbor as you love yourself, doing unto others as you would be done by, projecting yourself in understanding sympathy and making the other man's difficulties and troubles your own. This great executive came to that conviction not through dogmatic assertion from a pulpit, but through the method of trial and error—nothing else would work; life approved of this attitude and would approve of no other. In a business journal there is this blocked-off statement: "More and more companies are finding it pays to treat callers with friendly courtesy." Why? Because good will is written into the constitution of things; ill will is sand in the machinery. Life will work with good will, but not with ill will. You may try with infinite cleverness to make your universe hold together by ill will, but sooner or later it will topple and fall to pieces. Ill will is against the nature of reality.

"*Anima naturalis Christiana*"—"the soul is naturally Christian," said Tertullian. It is unnaturally something else, working against itself and ending in futility and frustration.

O God, how can I thank Thee enough for constituting me within so I can take Thee as naturally as the lungs take air? Thou and my soul have been estranged, but they are not strangers; we have been separated, but are not separate. Thou art my life, my breath, my being, my all. I thank Thee. Amen.

Luke 17:21; Prov. 3:29; Luke 10:29–37

THE KINGDOM OF GOD IS AMONG YOU!

The Kingdom of God is within you! But a further doubt arises: Is not another translation, "The Kingdom of God is among you"? The answer is that "among you" and "within you" are so profoundly true that Jesus may have used either or both. We have seen that the Kingdom of God is written into the constitution of your physical, mental, and spiritual make-up, so that you have a Christian brain, a Christian nervous system, a Christian stomach, Christian glands, and a Christian organism in its total make-up. One who said that he went about "awakening that of Christ in every man" was expressing this. So also was St. Francis when he sympathized with wicked men because they could not express the suppressed holiness within them. The Kingdom of God is within you! But the Kingdom of God is among you!

If there is a way to get along with yourself, there is a way to get along with other people—in both cases it is God's way. If the Kingdom of God is stamped into the constitution of your personal beings, it is also stamped into your social relationships with one another. Unless your relationships with one another proceed along the lines of certain inherent laws, they break down. You do not make or pass those laws—you only discover them; and if you break them you break yourself and the relationship. You may try with infinite patience and skill to build on some other than God's way, but in the end you won't get along with yourself or others. For instance, you needn't love your neighbor as you love yourself; but if you don't you cannot get along with him. You do not get rid of your neighbor by not loving him; you transform him into a problem and a pain. He is back on your hands, not as a neighbor but as a problem. You broke the law of human relationships and so those relationships broke down.

Sociology does not construct the laws of human relationships—it discovers them. They are a "given"—something written into human relationships by a pen other than our own.

Gracious Father, Thou hast written the family spirit into our relationships with the rest of the Family. When we break those laws we turn the Family into a feud, snarling up our relationships—and ourselves. Forgive us and help us to catch Thy mind in our relationship with other minds, Thy spirit in relation to other spirits. In Jesus' name. Amen.

Gal. 6:7–8; I John 4:7; Col. 2:19

THE KINGDOM OF GOD AND HUMAN RELATIONSHIPS

The Kingdom of God is among you! Note the ways men try to get along with one another: (1) Some try to dominate others; (2) some are aloof from others; (3) some are indifferent to others; (4) some work with others; (5) some work with and for others.

Which one of these attitudes will life approve? Suppose you take the first and try to dominate others in one way or another—what happens? The relationships break down and get snarled up. One man summed this up rather sadly when he said: "In the home I tried to be *it,* and I found my wife oppo*si*te." The type of action determined the reaction. A dictator tries to conquer the world and finds an initial success; then he inevitably has to meet a combination of the world against him—he goes down. Like produces like. "They that take the sword shall perish with the sword." "Be not deceived; God is not mocked: for whatsoever a man soweth, that shall he also reap." "Be not deceived" over initial success in domination, for "God is not mocked"—the nature of reality is against you and in the end will break you. "He that soweth to his flesh," the flesh of domination, "shall of the flesh reap corruption"—the situation and you will be corrupted, will deteriorate, will go to pieces and will collapse. The nature of reality foredooms the collapse.

But "he that soweth to the Spirit," aligns himself with the eternal realities, "shall of the Spirit reap life everlasting" —the sum total of reality will back you; you will have the power of survival, for you are living with and not against the grain of the universe. You reap an everlasting way to live—eternal life.

Assistant Secretary of State A. A. Berle, Jr., says, "No group of human beings, however implemented, has been able to challenge the great Design." The great design is the Great Design—the Kingdom of God. Live according to it, and you live; go against it, and you perish.

Thou Designer of the Great Design, we thank Thee that our hearts are set upon the Great Design, to fit into it, to mold our lives by it, to be fully surrendered to its purposes, and thus to live and live abundantly. Amen.

I John 4:20; II John 5–6; I Cor. 12:12–27

THE KINGDOM OF GOD IS MUTUAL AID

The Kingdom of God is among you! It is stamped into our relationships with one another—it is the way we are made to live corporately. A college president tells of how as a boy he and another boy were on a seesaw and were playing nicely until the idea struck him of jumping off when his end was down, letting the other boy down with a crash. The other boy then refused to play with him. Finally he persuaded him to play again, and then the other boy let him down in the same way, with the same crash. Then neither one would trust the other; so the play ended permanently. The one boy broke the law of friendship, and in the end lost the friendship of the other boy—and the game. "You can't eat your friends and have them."

You cannot violate the law of love any more than you can violate the law of gravity and not get hurt. Suppose the law of mutual aid, which is the law of life among the organs and members of our bodies, should be violated by the members—the stomach falling out with the heart and refusing to give it nourishment; the heart retaliating and refusing to give the stomach any blood; the feet refusing to co-operate with each other, one going in one direction and the other in the other; the arteries and the veins refusing to co-operate, the arteries withholding pure blood and the veins holding up the elimination of impurities—in short, if the organs of the body became selfish and competitive instead of unselfish and co-operative, the whole system would collapse, and with it the parts. If the parts should save their life in self-centeredness, they would lose it. Only as they lose themselves in the interest of the whole, do they find themselves again.

This law of mutual aid is not something imposed on the body from without as a decree; it is written into the very constitution of its being. As no one has imposed the law, so no one imposes the penalties—they are inherent and self-acting. Break the law of mutual aid, and the results come automatically—breakdown and disaster.

Our Father God, we come to Thee as foolish children—children who try to live against Thy ways and end only in hurting ourselves. Forgive us. And give us sense—just plain sense—so we may see that Thy laws are Thy love, and that Thy laws are our life. In Jesus' name. Amen.

I John 4:21; Gal. 2:11–13; I Cor. 1:10

THE RETREAT AWAY FROM PEOPLE

The Kingdom of God is among you! We saw that there were five ways in which men try to get along with others. We have considered the first—the method of trying to dominate others. That breaks down the relationships. The second: Some try to live aloof from others. This is the opposite swing of the pendulum—if we cannot dominate others, then we will live aloof from others.

What happens to one who tries this attitude? Can he cut human relationships, retreat into his own shell, without affecting his own being? Not at all. Such a person deteriorates. If he cannot have a world of real human relationships he builds up a world of false relationships—he fills his mind with phantasies and day-dreaming of superior personal grandeur; he is a superior type, hence remains aloof from the common herd. Or he looks on himself as inferior and justifies his retreat, on the grounds that he is not worthy to get into relationships with others. In either case the recessive individual hurts his own mental and moral nature. Man is made inherently for relationships with others, and any attempt to live apart brings inherent penalties.

You break the law of love just as much by receding from people as you do by trying to dominate them. You can no more cut yourself off from people and live fully than a brain can cut off relationships with the heart and live. All life is bound up in a bundle of life, and one person cannot be separate without disruption. That is why a lonely recluse is queer, off balance. He is trying to live against the Kingdom of God, which is a Kingdom of loving relationships.

To try to recede from people in order to protect oneself morally and spiritually from temptation is also false strategy. I find more temptations when I am alone than when I am with people. People can help us to be at our best by their expectancy.

If receding from people will not work, neither will the third attitude of being indifferent to them produce any other result. These methods end in self-frustration and a breakdown of relationships.

Gracious Father, Thou hast set us within Thy family, and we would not run away from others. Teach us to enter into loving relationships with one another and to help and be helped in the interplay of life on life. For Thou dost meet us in others. Help us to see Thee in them. Amen.

III John 5–8; Col. 4:11; I Cor. 3:3–9

WORKING WITH AND FOR OTHERS

The Kingdom of God is among you! The fourth attitude we can take toward others is to work with others. This sounds like a great advance over the other positions, and yet, so imperious and so demanding is the Kingdom of God that even this turns out to be inadequate. For we may work with others and yet reserve our inner life from others. So sensitive are these laws of the Kingdom that an outer conformity to brotherhood will not do. If the inner self is withheld the relationships break down.

There is only on attitude toward others that will work. Fifth: Work with and for others. You must not only work with people; you must work for them as well. There must be positive outgoing good will, a desire to help the other person as you would be helped. Labor and capital can work together, but in a suspicious, semihostile mood, fulfilling the letter of contracts. But this relationship is only suppressed war, and will break out into overt hostility at the first provocation. Out of this situation only minimum production results—each does as little as he can for the other. Only when the relationship is built on a generous and just basis—say a half-and-half division of profits between capital and labor—will there be relaxed attitudes of good will, a new spirit in the relationships, and a new increase in total output and hence in profits. Just generosity is literally the best policy. It obeys the law of the Kingdom, "Thou shalt love thy neighbor as thyself." This law is written into the constitution of our relationships, and hence it has the backing of the universe. Just generosity produces stability. Injustice and inequality produce instability, for they are working against the Kingdom; hence they break down.

When John Hay, the great statesman, declared that the only way for nations to get along with one another is for them to apply the Golden Rule to their relationships, he was expressing the fact that this law of positive good will is written in our relationships, and hence is inescapable.

God, our Father, forgive us that we have tried to live together on anti-Kingdom principles. We see the results in messed-up relationships and wars and poverty and general ruin. These results are inherent and not imposed. Forgive us that we do not see, do not *see*. Open our eyes that we may see—and live. Amen.

Mark 1:14–15; Matt. 12:28; 6:10

THE KINGDOM IS AT YOUR DOORS!

The Kingdom of God is at your doors! We have seen that the Kingdom of God is within you, also that the Kingdom of God is among you; we now pass on to the further step, the Kingdom of God is at your doors. The Kingdom is within us, among us; but it is also above us, beyond us, and is prepared to invade us from without.

This Kingdom is within history and beyond history; it is within time; it is beyond time—eternal; it is within us and yet stands at our doors awaiting our consent for an invasion in fullness from without. The school of though that insists that the Kingdom is within you and emphasizes that conception exclusively is based on a half-truth. On the other hand, the school of thought that insists that the Kingdom is to be found only by a divine invasion from without is also based on only a half-truth. The Kingdom is both. If you insist only on the-Kingdom-within emphasis, you end in a vague mysticism which often flattens out into humanistic techniques for awakening your latent powers. But if you insist only on the-from-without Kingdom, then you end in making sin natural, in rendering man helpless, in becoming pessimistic about human nature, and in accepting a transcendental God, more or less absentee, and wholly Other. This latter emphasis wipes out the fact that we are made in the image of God, that we have His laws stamped into our very constitution, that we are affinities with God, and that religion is therefore not unnatural but our very native air.

Nevertheless, we must emphasize the-Kingdom-from-without lest we run into vague, subjective Theosophy, which has no anchorage in history. How do we see the nature of this Kingdom—by looking within ourselves, by looking at the Kingdom within us? Yes, but not supremely. Only as we look at the historical Christ do we really see the full meaning of the Kingdom.

"You are the new order," was said to a certain Christian. But only in Christ do we really see the new Order.

O Christ, we now turn to Thee to see the meaning of that Kingdom, for we must not get this wrong—if we do, all life goes wrong with it. In our search for its meaning help us to look steadily at Thee—with our gaze on Thee we can never go astray. We thank Thee. Amen.

John 10:38; 14:7–11; 1:1–5

GOD RULES IN TERMS OF CHRIST

The Kingdom of God is at your doors! The Divine Invasion is near! The nature of that Divine Invasion is seen in Christ. He is the Personal Approach from the unseen. In Him the nature of Reality is uncovered. In Him we see into the nature of God and also into the nature of God's reign. God redeems in terms of Christ. He also rules in terms of Christ. Christ is the revelation of God and also the revelation of the Kingdom of God. He identifies Himself with God and also with the Kingdom of God.

In Christ the Kingdom is given content and character. If the Kingdom were only in us and only among us then we couldn't be sure of its character, for our characters would blur its character. But in Christ the character of the Kingdom is determined. If God is Christ universalized, so the Kingdom is the spirit of Christ regnant. This is important, for it means that we cannot bring in the Kingdom by any methods other than Christlike methods—when we thought we had brought it in, it wouldn't be the Kingdom; it would be something else. The ways we had used in our attempt to bring in the Kingdom would enter into and spoil the very goal toward which we had striven. In other words, the means would enter into and spoil the ends. "For the means pre-exist in and determine the ends."

In Christ the Kingdom is given not only a character content, but also a personal content. In Him the Kingdom is no longer merely an impersonal Order. When I give myself to the Kingdom I give myself to the Person who embodies that Kingdom. That makes my relationships with the Kingdom warm and tender and personal. I can be loyal to an Order, but I cannot love it. But in Christ it is possible both to be loyal to and to love the Kingdom. For in Him the Kingdom looks out at me with tender eyes, loves me with warm love, and touches me with strong, redemptive hands —it is Personal.

Christ is the Kingdom personalized.

Christ, in Thee I see into the heart and meaning of God's Kingdom. Thou hast fixed the character of that Reign. What can I ask more? How can I be satisfied with anything less? To such a Kingdom I can surrender with complete abandon. I do. In Thy name. Amen.

John 3:1–5; Rom. 5:1; 8:6; Luke 18:17

THE KINGDOM AND REPENTANCE

The Kingdom of God is at your doors! That Kingdom stands at our doors in the person of Christ.

There are two awakenings necessary. (1) We are to be awakened to the Kingdom within us—to discover the latent powers hidden away in the recesses of our beings, to become alive to our possibilities, to become aware of our divine origin and our divine destiny. (2) We are to be awakened to the Kingdom without us—the invading Kingdom. The presence of this invading Kingdom precipitates crisis. We sense a tension between this Kingdom and what we are. For if it is true that the Kingdom is written into the constitution of our beings, it is also true that we have tried to write something else there—incompatible ways, ways of sin. These incompatible ways of sin set up a conflict between themselves and the Kingdom within and the Kingdom without. Inner conflict ensues. The Kingdom without heightens that tension and brings it to crisis.

That crisis demands that we repent, that we submit, that we be changed, that we be converted, that we let this Kingdom without invade us with its healing, its reconciliation, its Life. When we fling open the doors of our being and let this Kingdom invasion possess us, we are not letting in something strange, something alien. We are letting in the very Fact for which we are made. The Kingdom within us rises up to meet the Kingdom without us, and together they cast out the unnatural kingdom of sin and evil.

The coming of this invading Kingdom has the feel of a homecoming about it. There is a sense that estrangement is over, that reconciliation has taken place, that the Homeland of the soul has been found. Why? Well, when we welcome the Kingdom, we welcome that for which we are made. The Kingdom within and the Kingdom without are counterparts, are one. So we feel a deep sense of unity and universal Being.

O Christ-Kingdom, Thou art the Love of my love, the Joy of my joy, the Peace of my peace, the Being of my being. When I welcome Thee, I welcome my long-estranged self—the prodigal come home. And now I am at rest, at peace, at adjustment, at home. I thank Thee. Amen.

John 3:16; Matt. 13:37–43; John 15:1–6

THE KINGDOM AS PERVASION AND INVASION

The Kingdom of God is at your doors! We saw yesterday that when we welcome this invading Kingdom, we welcome the Heavenly Natural—the Homeland of our soul. Jesus said, "The earth beareth fruit of herself"—the soil and the seed are made for each other. The soil of your being and the seed of the Kingdom are affinities. You have tried to grow the poisonous weeds of sin in the soil of your being, but the whole process brought, not comfort, but conflict; not rest, but rebellion.

When the child passes from the womb to the outer world, it finds a world for which it is made—air for its lungs, light for its eyes, food for its stomach, love for its affectional nature, and a world of growth for its latent possibilities. The child and the world are made for each other. So you and I are made for the Kingdom.

But Christianity is not merely the awakening of the Kingdom within; it is an invasion of the Kingdom from without. If it were only the first, we should get the interpretation of the nature of the Kingdom by looking within. But the nature of the Kingdom cannot be truly seen by looking within, for we have so overlaid that Kingdom by unnatural ways of life that the interpretation is blurred. Only in the face of Christ do we see the nature of the Kingdom. But we see more than the nature of the Kingdom in Christ—we see in Him what it costs God to get to us in spite of our sin. The Kingdom at our doors is there only because in Christ that Kingdom came down to us through an Incarnation, down to us through a Cross, down to us through a Resurrection, down to the very threshold of our being, there to await our consent for entrance.

Something crucial, something decisive had to happen in history before the Kingdom could stand at our doors. The barriers have been broken down from God's side by His offensive of suffering, redemptive love. The cross is therefore the pivot upon which history turns.

Gracious Christ, Thou hast come to me at supreme cost. Help me to respond to Thee with all the cost I can pay. For Thy Kingdom knocks with nail-pierced hands at my doors. Help me to open with hands that are willing to be pierced. Amen.

Rom. 6:23; Luke 18:18–27; 11:23

THE KINGDOM MEANS CHOICE, CRISIS, CONVERSION

The Kingdom of God is at your doors! Yesterday we saw that the coming of the Kingdom to our doors was costly. The realization of this Kingdom is no pink-tea affair. It cost God, and it will cost us. It cost God. Arnold Lunn satirizes current surface views of the Gospel in these words: "God so loved the world that he inspired a certain Jew that there was a great deal to be said for loving your neighbor." No. "God so loved the world, that he gave his only begotten Son, that whosoever believeth in him should not perish, but have everlasting life." Those who do not receive this Kingdom do "perish" literally, for their life forces break down through contradiction and strife. When you let in this Kingdom you have ever-lasting life—you align yourself with the eternal realities of Being; hence you live, now and everlastingly.

The coming in of that Kingdom means crisis, choice, conversion. The schools of thought which tell you that the-Kingdom-within means that you have only to evolve yourself are missing the deep tragic note of religion. Paul did not say, "O progressive creature that I am! who shall help me evolve myself?" But he did say, "O wretched man that I am! who shall deliver me from the body of this death?" or, literally, "this dead body." The figure is that of a live man with a dead body chained to him, carrying around a decaying corpse as punishment. That figure is accurate: a sinner is a man with the Kingdom of God written within him, carrying around a decaying corpse of sin—decaying through its own intrinsic anti-life ways and attitudes. Sin is anti-Kingdom, therefore anti-life; therefore it is doomed to decay; the one who harbors it "perishes." But that dead body of sin is not the real man—it is a false importation into life, a useless, infecting incumbrance. The real man is the man with the Kingdom of God written within him.

O Christ, Thou hast come to loose the chains of this dead body and to free me from decaying death. I gladly consent to let go this sin whose embrace is death. Forgive me if I hesitate, but I have lived with death so long that I think it is life. But I do consent, for I see, I see. Amen.

Luke 9:23–26; 24:49; Acts 1:8

THE CRISIS OF CONVERSION AND OF CLEANSING

The Kingdom of God is at your doors! The Divine Invasion precipitates crisis within and makes us either resist or surrender to this redemptive Invasion. Sometimes we resist. A brilliant doctor, whose inner life was a mass of conflicts, returned to me an inscribed New Testament with this written on the wrapper: "I hate Him, and I hate you." I had scarcely received this outburst when another letter came, saying: "Where is God, and where are you?" Here is the stark first stage of Kingdom invasion—a soul resisting God, and yet reaching out for Him; telling Him to go, and yet entreating Him to stay! Rebelling, repelling—relenting, repenting: these are the alternate heartbeats of the heart that feels the pressure of the Divine Invasion. Consent—conversion are the alternate beats in the first stage of acceptance.

When the consent is given the Divine Invasion usually takes place in two great crises: (1) the crisis of conversion; (2) the crisis of a deeper cleansing. The soul gets on by a series of crises, and usually by these two great crises. The crisis of conversion brings release from festering sins, and marks the introduction of a new life. Conversion is a glorious release, but not a full release. Festering sins are gone, but the roots of the disease are still there. The new life is introduced, but is not fully regnant. The old life is subdued, but not surrendered.

While I was in an acute stage of appendicitis, I was operated on. When I came to consciousness, the doctor was by my bed. He said, "I have drained the inflamed appendix, but I couldn't take it out, for there were too many adhesions. This will relieve you, but you'll have to have the appendix and the adhesions taken out later." After that I was better, but I wasn't well. Six months later I had the appendix and the adhesions taken out. Then I was not only better; I was well. Sin throws its adhesions around the organs of life, but neither the sin nor the adhesions are natural. Salvation, in these two great crises, drains the poison, unlooses the adhesions, and restores to the truly natural—gives health!

Tender and skillful Invader of my soul, I yield my stricken life to Thy healing. Drain every drop of poison from my being, and then root out the adhering results of that poison. "Be of sin the double cure." For I want not only to be better; I want also to be well. In Jesus' name. Amen.

John 8:31–32; Rom. 6:16–23; Gal. 5:1

THE KINGDOM OF GOD IS OUR OWN

The Kingdom of God is at your doors! If any man harbors sin within him, he is caught between two fires: the Kingdom of God within him and the Kingdom of God at his doors. He has to live out his life under a double protest: the protest of what he really is, in contrast to this false world he has built up, and the protest of what he might be. One protest is from the Kingdom within, and the other from the Kingdom without. Sin is therefore caught within a pincer movement. This intrusion, called evil, must surrender and succumb if the man is to live. When it truly surrenders, then the Kingdom within and the Kingdom without coalesce, and the man is possessed by an inner unity; he is possessed by Life! He is now truly natural, hence rhythmical and harmonious and adequate.

Jesus sums this up when He says: "If you are not faithful with what belongs to another, how can you ever be given what is your own?" (Luke 16:12, Moffatt.) What can it be that is "given" to us, and yet is our "own"? What but the Kingdom! The Kingdom is our "own"—it is written into the constitution of our very being; it is our real nature. But the Kingdom is also "given" to us—it is "given" when we "submit" to it and let it possess us. The paradox is this: When we find this Invading Kingdom, we find ourselves. I do not argue; I only testify that when I belong most to the Kingdom, I belong most to myself. When I try to live in un-Kingdom ways, I lose both the Kingdom and myself.

Here, then, in the Kingdom I find my perfect freedom. Think of the paradox of that statement: a Kingdom where you are ruled is a place where you are perfectly free! The freedom of the engine is the confining rails; the freedom of electricity is the confining wires—for engine and rails are made for each other; electricity and wire are made for each other. So it is with the Kingdom and me—when I am given it, I am "given that which is my own."

My God, I have arrived! I see everything clearly, and I see it whole. I take the yoke of the Kingdom, and I find it easy, for Thy yoke is my yearning. I take Thy burden, and I find it light, for Thy burden is my bounty; so, of course, Thy burden is light. I take Thee and find myself. I thank Thee. Amen.

Luke 15:15–16; Rom. 1:19–25; II Pet. 2:19–22

NATURALIZED IN THE UNNATURAL!

Seek first the Kingdom of God! We have seen that the Kingdom of God is written into our true nature and that to live according to it is to find ourselves. But we have been so accustomed to false ways of life that we think them our true nature. We hold to our unnaturalness, and suspect God's true nature. A woman who had lived all her life in the foul, heavy air of the slums of New York said that she got physically sick when she went into the country and breathed the pure, fresh air. Her lungs had become so accustomed to unnatural foulness that natural freshness was unnatural! In a South American city a new market was built, clean and sanitary, with tiled floors and walls. But the people holding the stalls in the dirty old market would not move into the new. One woman stall-holder explained her attitude thus: "That market is so clean it makes me sick. It is just like a hospital."

That is the tragedy of our humanity. We see that our ways won't work, and yet we hesitate to take God's way. The greathearted mayor of a city in India, who had cleaned up vast portions of the slums and in their stead had built lovely, neat cottages and apartments, said to me: "Sometimes I walk around the remaining wretched sections of the city at night and say to myself, 'If the people would only let me, I could do anything for them.' But they won't let me. They are naturalized in their filth, and cling to it, though it kills them off like flies." How Christlike that great, lonely figure, sighing over people who would not accept the life he offered! Christ must be doing that today! He sees us with our unworkable ways of life, running into roads with dead ends, ending in frustration and futility, losing our means of living, and our lives themselves, and He says again: "Seek ye first the kingdom of God, ... and all these things shall be added unto you." But we are seeking other things first, and all these things are being subtracted from us.

Gracious Father, we have your life strategy wrong, and things won't come out right. We become all tangled up, because we will not take Thy way. Help us to have sense— just plain sense. Then we will abandon our ways of futility for Thy ways of fruitfulness. Help us to seek first the Kingdom. In Jesus' name. Amen.

Matt. 6:24–33; Col. 3:1–2

WHAT SHALL WE SEEK FIRST?

Seek first the Kingdom of God! The struggle in the world
is over one question and only one question: What shall we
seek first? What shall ultimately command us? I do not
think that you can understand the world situation, with its
terrible clashes, unless you look on it primarily as a religious question. Sifted to its final issue, the question at bottom is this: What shall we finally obey? Where shall we
bend the knee?

Someone has said that mistakes in tactics, the detailed
carrying out of plans in war, may be forgiven; but no forgiveness can be granted for a mistake in strategy, the general plan of large-scale action. You may be forgiven if you
make detailed mistakes within a right plan of life, but no
right detailed actions can atone for a wrong life strategy. If
you get your life strategy wrong, all life will go wrong with
it. If you seek the wrong thing first, then all life goes wrong
with it.

What are the answers being given to that question, What
shall we seek first? The Japanese have their answer: "Seek
first the Emperor; be loyal to him in complete obedience,
and all these things shall be added unto you." The Chinese
have their answer: "Seek first the Family, and all these
things shall be added unto you." Governments might come
and governments might go, but the Family has been the
unit of allegiance in China. Hindu India has its answer:
"Seek first the Caste, and all these things shall be added
unto you." If only you obey caste *dharma,* or duty, then you
will get a better birth in the next turn of the Wheel of Re-
birth. The Moslem has his reply: "Seek first the fatalistic
will of Allah, and all these things shall be added unto you."
Islam literally means "submission"—submission to your fate
as decreed by Allah. Buddhism says: "Seek first nothing; cut
the root of desire, even desire for life, and Nirvana will be
added unto you."

Gracious Father, Thy children are in obvious confusion.
We live at cross-purposes in our central aims, and hence we
are at cross-purposes with each other. Take us by the hand
and help us to see things from Thy standpoint. And then
we shall see. Otherwise we are blind men groping for the
light. Help us to see in Thy light. In Jesus' name. Amen.

Luke 16:1–12

CALLING THE ROLL OF LIFE STRATEGIES

Seek first the Kingdom of God! We continue our calling of the roll of life strategies. The modern Communist says: "Seek first Society, as expressed in the will of its proletarian dictator, and all these things shall be added unto you." Society and its interests are supreme; the individual counts for little—Society is all.

The Fascist has his answer: "Seek first the State, and all these things shall be added unto you." The State is supreme: "Nothing above the State; nothing outside the State; nothing against the State—everything within the State." The Nazi is ready with his reply: "Seek first the Race, the superior Aryan Race, and all these things shall be added unto you."

Modern Capitalistic Society has its answer: "Seek first Money, and when you have that, all these things shall be added unto you." One man put it this way: "O Money, Money, Thou art life and health and peace. He that hath Thee can rattle his pockets at the devil." Many who inwardly hold that view would hesitate to put it in these bold terms, but they believe in money and act upon their belief. Modern Hedonism, the search for the pleasure principle, says: "Seek first the Thrill, and all these things shall be added unto you."

It may be added that a corollary to the aims of modern Capitalistic Society is the aim: "Seek first to be able to do without working; get to the place where others will work for you, and all these things shall be added unto you." Someone summed up this aim, in depicting heaven thus:

> "No strike—no speed-up—no lay-off—
> Everybody a coupon-clipper in heaven,
> Living in peace, on the eternal drudgery
> Of the damned."

The Christian turns to Christ for His reply: "Seek ye first the kingdom of God, ... and all these things shall be added unto you." Which life strategy is right?

God, we have come to life's supreme question and to life's supreme choice. Don't let us fumble at this place, for if we do, then everything tumbles to pieces. We approach this individual and collective choice with a prayer upon our lips, for our wisdom fails us—we need Thine. Amen.

Prov. 14:12; Rom. 3:4; 1 John 2:16–17

THE KINGDOM IS THE ETERNAL RIGHTNESS

Seek first the Kingdom of God! We have called the roll of the life strategies of various peoples and groups, and we have found: the Emperor, the Family, the Caste, the fatalistic Will of Allah, Nothingness, Society, the State, the Race, Money, Thrills, the Cessation of Work, and the Kingdom of God. Here are twelve answers—which is right?

Jesus was always so right in everything. He was never misled by a surbordinate issue, never once slipped to the marginal, the unworthwhile. He was always so centrally and fundamentally sound—was He wrong in this? Did He miss the way here? To ask the question is to answer it. His answer towers above all other answers, as Everest towers above foothills. When we state it, it is self-verifying. When we really look at the ends of other life strategies, there is no choice—we must take this answer of Jesus or brand ourselves as simple, plain fools. If this answer of Jesus isn't the answer, then there is no answer.

I have often been puzzled about the words Jesus added: "Seek ye first the kingdom of God *and his righteousness*" —why the "and his righteousness"? Is this not included in the Kingdom? Is it not a needless addition? Perhaps the answer would be found if we put it, "and his rightness." This answer of God—the Kingdom of God—is God's rightness. It is eternally "right," and everything out of harmony with it is wrong, is crooked, is out of gear, is doomed to break itself upon this Eternal Rightness. If that isn't the interpretation to be taken out of these words, it is a fact, nevertheless. When you seek first the Kingdom, then—you are right, the sum total in Reality is behind you, working with you; your life sums come out right. But if you seek something else first, you are setting yourself against the sum total of Reality; your life sums won't add up—you are wrong.

The reason the world situation is going from snarl to snarl is that we are centrally and fundamentally wrong—we are seeking the wrong thing first.

O living Christ, how can I cease thanking Thee for Thy answer. It is so right. Everything within me says so. Now help me to take it with the consent of all my being. In Thy name. Amen.

Phil. 4:5–6, 11–13, 19; II Cor. 8:14–15

GET THE SPIRITUAL STRAIGHT AND THE MATERIAL WILL BE GUARANTEED

Seek first the Kingdom of God! That is the proposal. Now, what is the product? Jesus replied: "And all these things shall be added unto you." Get the first thing straight, said Jesus, and all the things down the line will come out right—"all these things shall be added unto you." What did He mean by "all these things"? He mentioned the simple things: food, drink, and clothing. (Matthew 6:31.) In other words, the Kingdom of God is concerned not merely with supplying us a heavenly world after this life, but with supplying our need for bodily sustenance in this life. Get the central spiritual facts straight, says Jesus, and your material facts will be straight, too. They are one. You cannot go wrong in one without going wrong in the other.

In seeking first the Kingdom of God, Jesus says, the material basis of human life will be guaranteed to you. You will get what you *need*. "Your heavenly Father knoweth that ye have *need* of all these things." Note that you will get according to your *need*, not according to your *greed*. You have a right to as much of the material as will make you mentally, spiritually, and physically fit for the purposes of the Kingdom of God. You and I are constitutionally made in such a way that if we get less than we need, or more than we need, we harm ourselves. Therefore, anyone who is striving to get more than he needs is working for his own harm.

The facts bear that out. A friend of mine is in charge of the problem children of a certain city which is divided into three economic classes: 25 per cent below the poverty line, underprivileged; 25 per cent above the average level, the wealthy, the overprivileged; 50 per cent who haven't too little or too much. She says that the problem children come either from the 25 per cent underprivileged, or from the 25 per cent overprivileged. The 50 per cent are the normal, adjusted children of our civilization. The facts say that if you have too little or too much, you tend to produce the problem person and the problem society.

God, our Father, Thou hast written Thy laws into matter as well as into mind and spirit. Help us to discover those laws and live according to them. For if we do not, we hurt ourselves and others. Help us to discover Thy Mind in matter and live according to it. Amen.

Prov. 30:8; 11:24; II Cor. 9:5–12

TOO LITTLE AND TOO MUCH, ALIKE HARMFUL

Seek first the Kingdom of God! We must continue our examination of the material basis of the spiritual life. God has written into the constitution of things that too little and too much are alike, and equally, dangerous. I say "alike and equally," for the facts bear out the truth of that. We all see the devastating effects of poverty—they are manifest in sickly bodies, stunted minds, and problem souls. It is true that, here and there, a person can struggle against grinding poverty; make it sharpen his wits, his determination, his ability; and rise on obstruction to achievement. But where one triumphs, a dozen are broken or stunted by pvoerty. Let not our boasting about the achievement of the one, blind us to the devastation to the dozen. Poverty is wrong, for it produces wrongs to body, mind, and soul.

But if poverty is wrong, so are riches. The latter is not so easily seen, for it is covered up by refinements, by culture, by things, by the glamour of prestige and power. The rich die beautifully. But they die; and I don't mean just physically. Decay of the total person sets in—unless he arrests it by a planned giving away of his riches. The people who do that arrest the process of decay by putting back into life the adventure of dispensing to human need from what they have. Such people are saved. Those who hold on to what they have, inevitably decay—their faces grow dull, bovine, the light of adventure gone. The light has gone out on the face because the light has gone out in the heart. Jesus described this leaden-eyed existence in these words: "They . . . . are choked with . . . . riches." The man who holds on to riches as an end strangles the life forces within him—he suffocates, chokes himself. When we say, "Three generations from shirt sleeves to shirt sleeves," we do not mean physically; we mean in total manhood and womanhood. I have bitter tears for the underprivileged child; I have bitter tears for the overprivileged child. He is doomed to decay, unless some miracle of grace, or of personal effort, rescues him from the dead hand of riches, slowly closing in to strangle his life forces.

Gracious God, we have been blind. We have made our aim that which in the end turns out to be our poison. Forgive us this individual and collective suicide, slow though our dying may be. Help us to be so related to the material that it may be our minister and not our master. In Jesus' name. Amen.

Acts 4:32–35; Matt. 6:8, 11; 20:1–16

THE RESULTS OF TOO LITTLE AND TOO MUCH

Seek first the Kingdom of God! In order to have a proper physical basis for abundant living we must surrender the will to be rich, and determine to keep only enough wealth to supply our need—and no more. We must likewise surrender the will that reconciles itself to poverty, and determine to make enough to supply our needs—and no less. Two classes have to think too much about money—those who have too much and those who have too little. I want just enough of material goods so that I can forget about them and get on with the business of human living. Someone has said that "the poor have to think about their next meal, and the rich have to think about their last one." Both results are bad. Need should be supplied—no less, no more.

Now note: This law of "to each according to his need" is written into the constitution of things, and it is written in the Scripture. There is one, and only one, basis for the material life in the New Testament, and that basis is summed up in the phrase, "Distribution was made unto every man according as he had need." The word "need" is used in the New Testament seven times in relationship to the material. This constitutes positive proof of divine inspiration. How did the early Christians arrive at that basis? They knew no economics, no sociology, no science; but out of an experience of God they arrived at that basis. They reached it by inspiration.

And now society, by the method of trial and error, of experimentation to see what will fit the facts, is slowly but surely coming to the same conclusion.

Nothing else will fit the facts; life will back nothing else. Everything else breaks itself upon the facts written into the constitution of things, ends in self-frustration. The frustrations in modern society, its instabilities, its wars, are in large measure due to the breaking of this law of the Kingdom. Some have too little; some have too much. Result: war, instability, frustration. God's way is our way. And we take our way against God's way at our peril and to our frustration.

God, our gracious Father, Thou art saving Thy children by hard refusals. Thou wilt not let us rest in wrong, for wrong is ruin. So Thou art letting us hurt ourselves against Thy laws. May our bruises make us turn to Thee for healing and for sense. In Jesus' name. Amen.

II Thess. 3:8–10; Matt. 25:24–30

GETTING ACCORDING TO NEED, GIVING ACCORDING TO ABILITY

Last week we stressed that God guaranteed that our needs would be met. We must now go back and stress the condition upon which the guarantee is made: "Seek first the Kingdom of God." All God's promises are conditional, for God must not merely give—He must give in such a way that the person receiving is stimulated, not smothered. God must not merely make a gift; He must make a person.

Abundant living will not come through eternally receiving. One can dry up while eternally receiving. Abundant living depends upon abundant giving. If therefore we should stop at the thought "to each according to his need," we would create a parasitic society—each one would stretch out his hand and get according to his need. That would cause degeneration. The other side of the medal is, "from each according to his ability." If you do not give to the good of society according to your ability, then you will not get according to your need.

But someone throws up his hands and says, "But that is socialism!" You cannot scare me with a word! The two principles mentioned, namely, "to each according to his need," and "from each according to his ability," are deeply imbedded in the New Testament, and were there long before the label of socialism was thought of. The two principles imbedded in the New Testament are: "Distribution was made unto every man according as he had need," and, "If any would not work, neither should he eat." You might just as easily say that the spirit of co-operation is democracy as to say it is socialism, for Andrew Jackson had the second principle on one of his coins: "No labor, no food." I prefer to say that this way of life is neither socialism nor democracy, but Christianity, for that is where these twin principles originally came from. Christians should claim that which is their own. Wherever the idea came from, it is sound: if you do not give, you cannot get. Life is receptivity and response—both.

Father, Thou hast made Thy children for creative activity. Thou hast created us to be creators. Help us then to be channels of Thy creative energy. Help us to take hold of our tasks and make them the demonstration of Thy purposes. Help us to create through Thee. In Jesus' name. Amen.

Ps. 27:14; John 5:30; Luke 6:38; Heb. 11:6

SEEKING FIRST THE KINGDOM MEANS ACTION

It cannot be insisted too much that abundant living means abundant giving. You are made that way in the very structure of your being. Just as you would smother yourself to death if you only breathed in and refused to breathe out, so if you are not outgoing, the whole process of incoming will stop, and you will die spiritually, mentally, physically. If a cow is not milked, it will go dry. If you are not giving out to others, you, too, will go dry in spirit.

God will see to it that "all these things" will not "be added unto you" if you do not "seek first the Kingdom." If you do not give back to society according to ability, you will not get according to need. What would it mean to fulfill the first portion of the command, "Seek first the Kingdom of God"? Many would translate it in their thinking as "Ackowledge as first the Kingdom of God," mentally assenting to its primacy. But this goes deeper than that. I know a man who lives in a constant state of self-reference, but has on his letterheads, "In all things He might have the preëminence." The motto on the letterhead was mental compensation. No, seeking first the Kingdom means more than acknowledgment; it means action.

Seeking first the Kingdom means committing the whole of life to the proposition that the Kingdom is first, last, and always—and acting upon the committal. The context gives the content of the word "seek." Just as men "seek" food, clothing, you are to "seek" the Kingdom—it must master your thinking, your emotions, your will, you. That means that you discipline life to a one-pointedness. In every situation you ask, "In this situation what does the Kingdom demand I should do?"—and you *do* it.

In two passages the Kingdom and the doing of the will of God are made identical: "Thy kingdom come. Thy will be done in earth"—here the *coming* of the Kingdom was the *doing* of the will of God. "Not every one that saith unto me, Lord, Lord, shall enter into the Kingdom of heaven; but he that *doeth* the will of my Father." The Kingdom and the carrying out of the will of God are one and inseparable.

O God, let me commit my will to Thy will, not to be borne, but to be done. For Thou hast wrought me for strenuous endeavor; and unless I work, I wither. Put Thy zeal within me, and let me burn out for Thee. In the Master's name. Amen.

Isa. 26:2; 58:2; Matt. 28:19; I Pet. 2:9

THE KINGDOM AND THE STATE

The Kingdom of God is to be held and acted on as first. It is the Absolute, confronting all relativisms with an imperious demand: Surrender, submit, obey, lose your life to find it. There is one Absolute and only one—the Kingdom of God. All else is relative—is relative to something higher than itself from which it gets life and meaning. But this life and meaning come only when the relative surrenders to the Absolute and obeys.

The Kingdom of God confronts the relativisms of State, of Race, of Class, of Church, of Mammon, of Family, of Self, with a demand that all, and each, bend the knee, surrender, obey, and find the meaning of their relative life in the Absolute Life. Not one of these can be an end in itself. If it is, it will lose itself.

If the State becomes an end in itself, saves its life by centering upon itself as supreme, it will lose its life. When a relative thing becomes an absolute thing, you have idolatry. I love my country and will give everything to it except one thing—my conscience. That belongs to the Kingdom of God. And when there is a clash between my country and my conscience, then my conscience must bow to one authority, and only one authority—the Kingdom of God.

Our nation acknowledges that position when it gives the right of conscientious objection to war. In doing so it acknowledges that there is an authority beyond the State to which the individual conscience is amenable. The State will not ravage or coerce that conscience—it belongs to God and not to the State. The standing of the conscientious objector is therefore legal, and his patriotism as such is unquestionable. The danger to the State is not from those who have consciences, but from those who have none. They are the fifth columnists who undermine the morals and hence the morale of the country.

The State finds its meaning and its life in surrendering to and carrying out the purposes of something beyond itself, namely, the Kingdom of God.

O God, Thou hast a plan for our nation. Help us as a people humbly to surrender to Thy plan and work it out. For if we take our way, we shall lose our way. If we take Thy way, we shall find ours. In Jesus' name. Amen.

Acts 17:26; Col. 3:11; Rev. 5:9–10

THE KINGDOM AND RACE

We must continue our study of the Absolute Order, the Kingdom of God, as it makes an absolute demand on all relative orders to submit and to lose themselves in this higher Order that they may find themselves again. In Nazism the Kingdom of Race is supreme and absolute. But not alone in Nazism. Many of us have the religion of being white. Where there is a clash between the Kingdom of God and the Kingdom of Being White, we choose and act upon the fact of race. It is our god. We cannot live abundantly unless we offer our race on the altar of God. Then we can paraphrase Paul and say: "He, being in the form of the dominant race, counted it not a thing to be grasped at, but made himself of no reputation, and took on him the form of a servant, and was made in the likeness of men . . . . therefore God hath highly exalted him." How can the white race be supreme? Only in one way: Let white people become the servant of all; then they will become the greatest of all. No race can be great except as it greatly gives itself to the service of others. Those will rule the world in the future who serve the world. That is an inexorable law written into our universe and therefore inescapable. But note: "servant of *all*." Some are willing to be the servant of some—their friends, their families, their class, their race—but they pull back from being the servant of *all*.

Only two came out of the last war with enhanced reputations—Christ and the Quakers. Why? Well, the Quakers were the servants of *all*. A Polish woman saw the Quakers feeding the starving on both sides of the conflict and said to one of them: "You are feeding everybody, aren't you? Poles, Russians, Germans—everybody, friend and foe? Well, I knew there ought to be people like that in the world, but I didn't know that there actually were." No wonder the Quakers were held in such tender affection—the servants of all had become the greatest of all. The future belongs to those who belong to others in living service.

Gracious Master, Thou hast obeyed this law—Thou didst become the servant of *all*. And now Thou art enshrined in our hearts forever. Help me to lose my racialism in Thy passion for service, and thus I shall find myself again. In Thy name. Amen.

1 Cor. 1:10, 26; Rom. 1:14; 1 Tim. 6:8–11

THE KINGDOMS OF CLASS AND MONEY

The Kingdom of Class must bend the knee to the Kingdom of God. We think and act in class terms rather than in Christian terms. Before we act, we look around to see what our class approves. We do not act; we only react. We are not a voice; we are an echo. We are not conscious persons; we are class things. We don't think with our minds; we react with our emotions. This is bondage. No Christian can allow himself to become prisoner of his class and hope to remain Christian. Class consciousness and Christian consciousness are incompatibles. For the Kingdom of God is a classless society. The Communists are striving for a classless society. In the Kingdom of God we have it. Have it? Yes; for if anyone in that Kingdom begins to obey the behests of the class instead of the behests of the Kingdom, then he is automatically out. Nor can one enter the Kingdom of God unless he surrenders the Kingdom of Class.

When we lose our petty class consciousness, we find a human consciousness and with it a God-consciousness. The class must lose its life to find it again.

The Kingdom of Money must bend the knee to the Kingdom of God. In our acquisitive society Money is god. You succeed as you succeed in terms of accumulation. Our weal-th is measured by wealth. A man is "worth" the amount he accumulates. These values are false and must be surrendered. Following the god of Money leads into a road with a dead end. The wealthiest man in a certain city said pathetically: "Now that I've made my money, the two things I most want to do in the world I can't do, namely, smoke and play golf." A touch of heart trouble and his world that he had laboriously built up fell to pieces.

When Money is surrendered as an end and offered to be a means to the ends of the Kingdom, it is found again. Only those enjoy it who surrender it. To surrender it means to surrender it to God to be used for Kingdom purposes.

O Master of my heart, I offer Thee all that would divide that heart. Class has silently entered and set up its shrine within me. I overthrow it today. And Money would claim my allegiance and my heart. I tear out both altars and make Thee, O Christ, sole Lord and Liege. Amen.

Matt. 16:18; Eph. 5:25–27; 4:11–16

THE KINGDOM AND THE CHURCH

The Kingdom of the Church must bend the knee to the Kingdom of God. Just as we want our State, our Race, our Class to be dominant, so we want our Church to be dominant. The Church can be our religious self writ large—but it is still the self. It can be the group self asserting itself toward supremacy—albeit covered up with religious trappings. If the Kingdom of God comes in, we, as a Church, would like to bring it in, since the fact that we brought it in would leave us dominant.

That any one denomination is the exclusive or particular channel of God's grace is as dead as Queen Anne—and she is very dead! God sometimes works through the denomination, sometimes in spite of it, but never exclusively or particularly in any one of them. If that hurts your denominational pride, it may help your Christian humility! The saints are about equally distributed among all denominations. There is no denomination that has a corner on the saints. The degree to which God uses a person is determined, not by the denomination in which he is located, but by the depth of his surrender to God, regardless of where he is. If God seems too broad and too liberal and not sufficiently mindful of denominational distinctions, then quarrel with Him, not with me!

No one denomination has the truth. The truth is in Christ, who is "the Truth." What we hold are truths about the Truth. These "truths" more or less approximate the Truth, but are not the Truth. He is beyond us all, and more than us all. We need, then, to pool our truths, so that the sum total of our truths will more nearly approximate the Truth.

The Kingdom of the Church must surrender itself to the Kingdom of God. The Church is not an end in itself; it is a means to the end of the Kingdom of God. If the Church is an end in itself, it will lose itself. The Church, like the individual, must lose itself in the Kingdom of God to find itself again.

O God our Father, forgive us that we have made of Thy glorious Church an idol. We do so no more—we offer it to Thee to be the instrument of Thy redemption. Help us that this beautiful instrument shall remain an instrument and not become an end, lest it decay. In Jesus' name. Amen.

Matt. 12:46–50; 10:37–39

THE KINGDOM AND THE FAMILY AND THE SELF

The Kingdom of the Family must be surrendered to the Kingdom of God if it is to find itself. But the family often becomes an end in itself. Family interests decide the issues. Such a family is bound to deteriorate. A family that lives in a state of self-reference will live in a state of self-frustration. Unless the family is dedicated to something beyond itself from which it receives goal, inspiration, and guidance, it will deteriorate into a self-centered, self-seeking unit. The probabilities are that, being self-centered, it will be self-disruptive —the units, not being held together by lofty purposes, will fall apart. It is interesting to note that while divorces are one in six throughout our nation, among church people they are only one in fifty. That means, if it means anything, that to have something beyond the family, to which the family is devoted and loyal, will make that family hold together. The beyond-itself loyalty will be the cement which holds it together. A family that loses its life will save it.

And now we come to the final unit that must be surrendered—the Kingdom of the Self. We have stressed this so much that we need only mention it here. This losing of the individual in something beyond itself in order to find itself is no mere suppressing imposition laid upon life; it is the law of life running from the lowest to the highest. You have to die on one level to live on another. That is the law God has written into the constitution of things. The Mineral Kingdom surrenders itself to the Kingdom above—the Vegetable Kingdom—and is taken hold of by that kingdom and is transformed from dead matter into living forms. The Vegetable Kingdom surrenders to the Animal Kingdom, and is lifted into thinking, feeling forms. The Animal Kingdom surrenders to the Kingdom of Man and becomes assimilated into the higher life of man. The Kingdom of Man surrenders to the Kingdom of God and shares a higher life. The law of life is: Lose your life to find it.

We close this discussion with the words of Robert Browning: "Who keeps one end in view makes all things serve."

O God, we have found the Way! Thy Way is written in the ways of life from the Kingdom of Matter to the Kingdom of God. It is our Way, our Life. If we miss Thy way, we miss our way, and we miss our life. Help us this day to accept Thy way, surrender to it, live according to it, and thus Live! In Jesus' name. Amen.

Matt. 26:42; II Cor. 12:7–10; Ps. 143:10

PRAYER IS SURRENDER

We saw last week that everything from mineral to man has to lose itself in something higher in order to find itself. We love Washington because he lost his Mt. Vernon self in the cause of freedom—so he finds himself enshrined in our hearts as the Father of our country. We love Lincoln because he lost himself in the cause of freedom for the Negro —so he finds himself as the Great Emancipator. All life comes to one conclusion:

> "Sweetest the strain when in the song
> The singer has been lost."

We lose the "I-that-is" in order to find the "I-that-ought-to-be." This is done by a once-and-for-all surrender, but it is also done as a continual process. The continual process is prayer. Prayer is fundamentally and essentially self-surrender. I once asked Kagawa, the great Japanese Christian, what was the first thing in prayer, and he answered, "Surrender." He was right.

But the idea of surrender cuts across the usual idea of prayer as a method of obtaining from God your wishes. That idea is self-assertion. This is self-surrender. Then is prayer passive submission? A denial of the will to live? Is it the will to die? Far from it. Prayer is a will to die on the level of a defeated, empty, ineffective, short-circuited life, and a will to live on the level of a victorious, full, effective, and cosmic-connected life. It is self-renunciation in order to find self-realization. Your petty self is renounced in order that your potential self might be realized. Prayer is the wire surrendering to the dynamo, the flower surrendering to the sun, the child surrendering to education, the patient surrendering to the surgeon, the part surrendering to the whole— prayer is life surrendering to Life.

A branch not surrendered to the vine, but cut off and on its own, is not free; it is dead. A person who doesn't pray isn't free; he is futile. He is a blind man who won't surrender his blindness to the surgeon in order to see. He is free —to remain blind.

O God, my Father, forgive me that I fear to surrender my sundered will to Thy saving will. I am afraid—of life. Help me, as I begin this adventure of prayer, that it may be no side-line activity. May it become *me*, that I may become Thee. For I must have Thy life to live. In Jesus' name. Amen.

Luke 21:36; John 15:7; Phil. 4:6–7; Eph. 6:18

PRAYER IS ALERT PASSIVITY

We saw yesterday that prayer is essentially surrender, but not a passive surrender. It is an "alert passivity." It is a passivity that awakens us to an amazing activity. The musician listens in the silence to Music, surrenders to it, and then pours it forth with complete abandon. He is creative because he is receptive.

The scientist surrenders to the facts of Nature—he flings open the doors of his senses to be guided and directed by the facts. He is passive, but with an alert passivity. His facts now become factors—they are gathered up and put to work in factories, are turned out as finished products to serve the world. The surrender was really a mastery.

One day, in the train, instead of thinking I simply surrendered to Thought. My mind was perfectly passive, and yet perfectly active. It seemed that Thought awakened thought. I accomplished more actual thinking in those blissful hours than in days of thinking on my own. We must learn to live in the passive voice. Only those who do so, know what it means to live in the active voice. The fussy activity of the modern man is not life; it is the nervous twitching of his disordered and starved nerves. When animals lack certain vitamins, they will become nervous, jumpy, and hysterical. The rush of modern life is not the calm, poised sureness of mastery. Rather, it is the jumpy hysteria of starved nerves crying out for vitamins of real life. Someone has said that no one commits suicide because he is tired of life—he is tired of a lack of life.

Jesus put the alternatives this way: "Men ought always to pray, and not to faint." It is pray or faint—literally that. Those who pray do not faint, and those who faint do not pray. You can become alive to your finger tips—every cell in your body alert, active, creative—provided you pray. Otherwise you faint.

Pray or be a prey—a prey to fears, to futilities, to ineffectiveness.

Gracious Father, I thank Thee that power, power, power is open to me if I but take it. Help me to empty my hands of trifling toys that I may take, take, take the things Thou art offering me—release, power, victory. Why should I do myself and others this wrong?—weak when I might be strong, a victim when I might be victor. Amen.

John 14:13; Matt. 7:7; Ps. 55:22

IS PRAYER AUTOSUGGESTION?

But is not prayer "autosuggestion," "wishful thinking," "an echo of your own voice"? Suppose it were just auto-suggestion; even on that level it would be a healthy thing, for you are suggesting to yourself the highest instead of the lowest. Even if it were no more than autosuggestion, prayer would be worth while. It would heighten our powers to suggest the highest to them. But how is it that those who use prayer most are convinced that it is Other-suggestion rather than autosuggestion? Only those who use it least, or not at all, claim that it is autosuggestion. Are they compe-tent witnesses? Prayer would never have survived had it been only autosuggestion, with no Voice answering our voice, no Heart answering ours.

> "Whoso has felt the Spirit of the Highest
>   Cannot confound nor doubt Him nor deny:
> Yea, with one voice, O world, though thou deniest,
>   Stand thou on that side, for on this am I!"

Can the flower believe that the sun is only the projection of itself? The wire believe that the energy within it comes from itself, and not from the dynamo? The sense of Other-ness is in true prayer. Something answers—and answers in terms that are worthy: release, power, vitality, insight, heightened accomplishment.

Prayer is the perfect instrument of development and of doing—it is outgoing, it is incoming; it is faith in God, and faith in oneself; it is active, it is passive; it is strenuous, it is calm; it works as if the whole thing depended on us, and trusts as if the whole thing depended on God. Is such a faith, so sound and health-giving, itself a delusion? Like produces like. How is it that the bitter and disillusioned deride prayer, and the calm, the poised, the hopeful, the ra-diant delight in prayer? It was said of Gladstone, "He lived from a great depth of being." Is it better to live from a great depth of being, or to live from the shallow life around one?

My God and my Father, I would live in Thee, and have Thee live in me. For then, then my life will throb with en-ergy and poise, with power and with peace. Then I, too, shall live at a great depth of being. Teach me to pray, for I would live—live abundantly. Amen.

Jas. 5:16; Ps. 30:2; Luke 11:1; Ps. 27:14

PRAYER—THE GREATEST SINGLE POWER

Dr. William Sadler, the psychiatrist, says that in neglecting prayer we are "neglecting the greatest single power in the healing of disease." He refuses to take a patient who does not believe in God—says it is impossible to get patients straightened out unless they have something to tie to and love beyond themselves. We are literally coming down to this alternative: meditation or medication. And even the latter is not effective unless linked with the former.

Then the art of prayer must be learned, for reservoirs of power are at our disposal if we can learn this art. "If we learn it"—that is the rub. People expect results without any practice of the art. We would deem a person foolish who stepped up to a musical instrument only occasionally, expecting to tune into Music and become the instrument of Music without long training and practice. The little son of a missionary bought a mouth organ in India, and came home in tears: "That man cheated me. There is no 'God Save the King' in this mouth organ." We just as foolishly believe we can get ready-made results without the practice of prayer.

We live in an open universe. Anything that is right is possible if we will obey the laws of accomplishment and relate ourselves to its powers. Just as God has left open certain things contingent upon the human will, and they will never be accomplished unless that will decides; so He has left open certain things contingent upon prayer—things which will never be accomplished unless we pray. To paraphrase Kipling's words: "Anyone might have heard it, but His whisper came to her." Why? She was trained in the art of listening.

There are three steps in the art of prayer: (1) Listen; (2) Learn; (3) Obey. Without all three, prayer will be a farce instead of a force.

If we spent half the time in learning the art of prayer as we do in learning any other art we would get ten times the results.

Gracious Christ, teach me to pray. For if I fall down here I fall down everywhere—anemia spreads through my whole being. Give me the mind to pray, the love to pray, the will to pray. Let prayer be the aroma of every act, the atmosphere of every thought, my native air. In Thy name. Amen.

Matt. 6:5–15; Jas. 1:6

NINE STEPS IN PRAYER

While the three steps we mentioned in closing yesterday —Listen, Learn, Obey—are the three general steps in prayer, we must now come to specific steps in the art of prayer. There are nine.

1. *Decide what you really want.* I would stress the "you" —not a part of "you," a vagrant portion of "you" wandering into the prayer hour as a side adventure. It must be *"you,"* the whole "you." For prayer is not a luxury; it is a life. If you take things from God there will be one result: God will get you, or prayer will cease, blocked by the refusal of self-giving. The request must be backed by you, or the answer will not be backed by God. God cannot give things to you apart from Himself, and you cannot take things from God apart from yourself. Prayer involves a mutual self-giving. Decide what you really want, for if the whole you does not really want it, the prayer is blocked.

2. *Decide whether the thing you want is a Christian thing.* God is a Christlike God; His actions are Christlike actions; and He can answer prayer only if the thing desired is in accord with Christ. That is what Jesus meant when He said, "If ye shall ask any thing in my name . . . ."—in my character, according to my spirit. Don't try to get God to do something that isn't Christlike. He can't, for He can't do something against His own nature. Within that limit He gives you freedom to ask "anything."

3. *Write it down.* The expression will deepen the impression. I find that to write down a thing is almost destiny. I think I will change it; but once written, it is almost impossible to change it. With Pilate we say, "What I have written I have written." If you are willing to commit your prayer to paper, you probably really mean it. In writing it down you do two things: You write it more deeply on your own heart; you commit yourself more fully to a line of action. To write it down is one step in self-committal.

Patient Christ, my feet stumble on this pathway of prayer. I am learning to walk—help me over the hard places. For I would learn this art. This is life, and I must learn it. I begin to feel I can do anything in and with Thee. My liberties are dawning. I thank Thee. Amen.

Ps. 62:5; 55:22; 46:1–2, 10

FURTHER STEPS IN PRAYER

We come to the next step in the art of prayer:

4. *Still the mind.* Just as the moon cannot be reflected well on a restless sea, so God cannot get to an unquiet mind. "Be still, and know"; be unstill and you do not know —God cannot get to you. In the stillness the prayer itself may be corrected. For God does not only answer prayer; He also corrects prayer and makes it more answerable. One night I bowed my head in silent prayer before a sermon and whispered to God, "O God, help me." Very quickly came back the reply: "I will do something better; I will use you."

That amendment was decidedly better. I was asking God to help me—I was the center; I was calling God in for my purposes. But "I will use you" meant I was not the center; something beyond me was the center, and I was only the in- strument of that purpose beyond myself. God's answer shifted the whole center of gravity of the prayer.

5. *Talk with God about it.* The order of these steps is im- portant: Listen to God before you talk. For, as someone has said, "Instead of saying, 'Speak, Lord, for Thy servant heareth,' many say, 'Listen, Lord, for Thy servant speaketh.' " Let God have the first word and the last word —you take the middle word. Let your speaking with God be largely a turning over of the whole matter into His hands—you becoming the instrument of His purposes. Re- member, the word is, "Talk with God," and not, "Talk to God." Make prayer a two-way conversation.

6. *Promise God what you will do to make this prayer come true.* As the conversation is a two-way affair, so the accomplishment is a double affair. God answers the prayer, not for you, but with you. The answering of prayer is a co- operative endeavor. For God's interest is not to give you things, but to make you through the getting of those things. The end of the whole process of prayer is not the prayer but the person.

O Father, I begin to see—my object has been things I thought I needed, and now I see that Thy object is to make me. I asked for the little; Thou art giving the great, the per- manent, the everlasting. Help me to be responsive at the depth of Thy purposes. In Jesus' name. Amen.

Ps. 40:1; 121:7–8; 1 Pet. 5:10; 1 John 3:16–18

THE FINAL STEPS OF PRAYER

We pursue the nine steps of prayer.

7. *Do everything loving that comes to your mind about it.* That word "loving" is important. If the thing suggested to your mind is unloving, it is from below—perhaps from the depths of your subconscious mind; but if it is "loving," it is from above. A discerning friend said: "The only thing the devil cannot get into is the love of Christ, for if he did, he wouldn't be the devil any longer." That word "do" is also important, for if you are unwilling to do, you have tied God's hands—He can't do, if you won't. Prayer is the working out of what God works in.

8. *Thank God for answering in His own way.* Remember that "No" is an answer, as well as "Yes." Sometimes He has to save us, as Tagore says, "by hard refusals." But if He refuses on one level, He refuses only to make an offer on a higher level. His "No" is only in order to a higher "Yes." But the probabilities are that if the prayer has run the gauntlet of the previous steps and survived to this stage, it is a prayer that is answerable by "Yes." But that "Yes" may be delayed—delayed in order to put persistence and toughened fiber in us. He often holds us off to deepen our characters, so that we won't be spiritual crybabies if we don't get everything at once.

9. *Release the whole prayer from your conscious thinking.* If the prayer is real and has hold of you, it will be at work in the subconscious mind—there will be an undertone of prayer in all you do. But it should be released from the conscious mind lest it become an anxiety center and make you tense and wrought up. The very releasing of it from the conscious mind is an act of faith in God. You relax and trust God to do the right thing in the matter.

These nine steps are the ladder by which you climb from your emptiness to God's fullness. And prayer is just that—it is the opening of a channel from your emptiness to God's fullness.

Gracious Spirit, I cannot pray as I ought unless I become Spirit-taught. Inspire the prayers within me that I may pray according to Thy will, and hence be answered according to Thy power. For I would live a Spirit-inspired life, and hence a Spirit-empowered life. In Jesus' name. Amen.

Rom. 5:11, 17; 8:5; Gal. 3:2; Col. 2:6; Mark 11:24

RELAXED RECEPTIVITY

We have studied a ladder for prayer. But ladders are of small use if they suggest what all ladder-climbing must suggest, namely, tense strenuousness. You will not go far in prayer if you go in the spirit of tense strenuousness, as though you were going to wring out of the universe the object of your prayer. The spirit of prayer should be the opposite—alert passivity. Alert passivity means that while your spiritual, mental, and physical sensibilities are awake and alert to God, yet they are also relaxed and receptive. I say relaxed and receptive, but the two attitudes are really one, for relaxation is receptivity.

And yet there are two sides to real praying. If we are only relaxed we are weak. Dr. Alexis Carrel says: "Lowering of the blood pressure is also dangerous. Brain and other organs demand a certain tension of the blood." That is the alert side. But the brain and other organs demand a certain relaxation to be at their best. Prayer puts relaxation and tension together, and is therefore the perfect instrument of human well-being.

Since prayer has been presented so strongly by so many as strenuous alertness, the parable of the importunate widow being the special text of this strenuousness, we must stress the relaxed attitude in prayer. A stenographer who is all tense and keyed-up and anxious to be a good stenographer will probably be a very poor one, for the anxiety literally ties up the energies. "As they tense, two things happen: blood flows through their fibers less easily, and the taut muscle as a whole presses or strains upon some bone, sinew, vein or artery, thereby lowering all activities in such, at least for a moment.But each lowering of activity tends to block the free flow of the healing secretions and the blood." (Walter B. Pitkin, *Your Life*, January, 1941). Relaxation is receptivity, which in turn becomes resource. In the relaxed attitude you are allowing God to get to you; it is an invitation to come; you wait expectantly.

Gracious Father, I come to Thee to learn to receive. In Thy presence I let down all the bars of my being and let Thee into every fiber, every brain cell, every cranny of my being. As the blood courses through my body, cleansing and healing and restoring and empowering, so Thou art going through me—body, mind, and soul—cleansing, healing, restoring, empowering. I thank Thee. Amen.

Ps. 37:11; 119:165; John 14:27; 16:33

BODILY RELAXATION

In order to put ourselves into a mood of alert passivity, we will begin with the body, the outer framework of prayer.

Jesus said, "When thou prayest, enter into thy closet, and when thou hast shut the door, pray." Shut the door! All outer distractions should be reduced to a minimum. Every home should have a little corner, or room, or private chapel, and it should be understood that anyone who is there is not to be disturbed. He is in "the Trysting tent." (Exodus 27:21, Moffatt.) Who would disturb one when he is having an audience, say, with the king of England? To be in that Trysting Tent should make one inviolable.

As the surroundings are freed from disturbance, so attend to yourself and relax every muscle in your body. Say to your organs in succession something as follows: "My brain, you are now in the presence of God. Let go, and listen. He speaks, He penetrates, He heals. Receive, receive." And to the eyes: "My eyes, weary with looking at a distracting world, close, and inwardly see nothing except Him into whose presence you have now come. He touches my eyes and they are rested and calm and single and healed." And to the nerves: "O nerves, intelligence department of my being, strained and torn by living in a world of chaos, I now set you to work on the job of reporting better news— your God comes, comes, comes with the good news of calm, of poise, of resources, of redemption. Open every cell to that healing, to that calm, to that restoration. Receive, receive, receive." And to your sex life: "O creative part of me, I surrender you to the creator God. When denied your normal expression in procreation, I know that I can sublimate your power into other forms—art, poetry, music, creating new hopes, new souls, new life; I can become creative on another level. So I put you at God's disposal. He cleanses; He redirects." And to the whole body: "He is now in every part, untying knotty nerves in His gentleness, bathing every brain cell with His presence, reinforcing every weak place with His strength, healing all your diseases, co-ordinating all parts and making them into a co-operating whole. Open every door; give Him all the keys."

O God my Lord, my Life, I open every pore, every cell, every tissue, every artery, every vein, every bone to Thee. This body, in every part, is Thy temple—hallowed by Thy presence, cleansed by Thy purity, and taken hold of by Thy purposes. O body, behold thy Lord! Amen.

Rom. 15:13; Phil. 4:7; Col. 3:15; II Thess. 3:16

RELAXED IN SPIRIT

Dr. Alexis Carrel says, "No attempt has been made to create, in the midst of the agitation of the new city, islands of solitude, where meditation would be possible." Both the city and the home are impoverished without these "islands of solitude," hence a surface civilization and surface personalities are produced. As Kenneth Fearing says:

"And wow he died as wow he lived,
Going whop to the office, and blooie home to sleep and
    biff got married and bam had children and oof got
        fired.
Zowie did he live and zowie did he die."

We must have these "islands of solitude," or we shall produce just such frantic personalities! In these "islands of solitude" the body can be relaxed and restored, as we saw yesterday. But, deeper than the body, the spirit must be relaxed. As the body becomes tied up with physical tensions, so the soul becomes tied up in moral and spiritual tensions. These tensions of the soul are passed on to the body. No amount of techniques of bodily relaxation will avail if the tension is in the soul. Many modern techniques deal with the outworks and neglect the citadel. It is impossible to have a relaxed body if the mind and soul are full of conflict and tensions.

In Romans 12:2 (Moffatt) we read: "Instead of being molded to this world, have your mind renewed, and so be transformed in nature, able to make out what the will of God is." Note, "have your mind renewed, and *so* be transformed in nature." Evidently the renewed mind can renew the nature. The mind is the key. The mind decides what shall or shall not be the nature of your nature. It decides to what molding influences the inmost and the outmost nature shall be exposed. But the mind cannot be told to be calm and reassured and relaxed unless it rests in some assurance beyond itself. So its final calm is found in being "able to make out what the will of God is." It must ultimately acquire its poise and calm by linking itself to and having the backing of an eternal Purpose.

My Father, I see that I need all the techniques I can master; but in the ultimate analysis my surest technique is that which gives me alignment to Thy purposes and to Thy plans. I cannot be anything but frustrated if I am at cross-purposes with the universe. So I would be right with Thee in order to be right with myself. In Jesus' name. Amen.

Ps. 37:7, 9; 62:5; Isa. 40:31; Lam. 3:23–26

SETTLING DOWN IN GOD

Yesterday we saw that you must not try to get merely a foothold in life by techniques of relaxation, but a roothold in the nature of Reality. Only then can you be unshakably calm and poised. Unless you can trust and surrender to the nature of Reality and believe in it through thick and thin, you have no secret of victory. "How did you like the airplane ride?" was asked of a nervous man who went up for the first time. "Very well," he replied, "but I never did put my whole weight down." There can be no enjoyment of an airplane ride, or of this larger journey through life, unless you learn to put your whole weight down. Obviously there is nothing, absolutely nothing, upon which you can put your whole weight down, except *God*.

Those who refuse to do as the Quakers suggest—"settle down in God," or "center down in God"—but keep their troubles and disappointments in their own hands, are frustrated. The most frustrated, disrupted woman I know is a woman who believes that if she should let go and turn over these frustrations to God her universe would go to pieces. She has to hold it together, and is intensely and pathetically trying to do so. One of the most nervous and frustrated men I know is a man who feels that if he did not worry about the matter of his wife's business affairs they would go to pieces. His wife is poised and able and more businesslike than he is; but it satisfies his self-respect to think he is holding their world together by his worrying. The fact is that his worrying nervousness is self-defeating and is making him a problem, instead of solving any. He says that his "pet aversion is that faith is optimism." He doesn't see that faith as pessimism is producing a person who is a problem to himself—and to others. All the attention given to the nerves of these two people will be in vain unless at the center they let go and let God—unless they surrender in complete confidence to the will of God, and live and work as joyous children in line with that will.

O God, how can I be assured and relaxed unless I am sure that I am completely and utterly committed to Thy goodness and Thy power? Forgive my little antics of self-dependence—how invariably they let me down! Let me live on God-dependence, working out purposes not my own. Then shall I live, for I shall live in Thee. In Jesus' name. Amen.

Isa. 30:15; Heb. 3:6; 10:35; Ps. 27:1–3, 5, 13–14

RELAXED, EVEN IF NOT RELEASED

Yesterday we saw that there can never be complete relaxation unless that relaxation rests ultimately in the love and goodness of God. That love and goodness may deny the thing asked for, but only in order to give something better. The Hebrew young men could say: "God . . . . is able to deliver us from the burning fiery furnace, and he will deliver us out of thine hand, O king. But if not, ... we will not serve thy gods." (Daniel 3:17, 18.) "But if not"—if our confidence in this immediate deliverance is unfulfilled, nevertheless we go straight on. They did not rest their confidence on that immediate deliverance, but in the ultimate love and goodness of God. That is faith. Don't rest your faith in some particular happening, but in the goodness of God which will be the same whether that particular thing happens or not. "He will deliver . . . . but if not"—sometimes you will have to live on "but if not," and go straight on.

Rows of beautiful trees were laid low in a storm. Reason? The water was too near the surface; so the trees did not have to put their roots deep down to find water; hence the tragedy. God may deny us a surface answer in order to get us to put our roots deeper into eternal reality, so that in some future storm we shall be unmoved.

> "Nothing that happens can hurt me,
>   Whether I lose or win.
> Though life may be changed on the surface,
>   I do my main living within."

Said some Christians when the storm of war was raging over Europe and engulfing everybody: "On the surface there is storm, but twenty fathoms down it is quite calm."

Someone asked a happy Negro how he remained calm and poised and cheerful; to which he replied, "I have learned how to co-operate with the inevitable." That is the secret! You co-operate with the immediate inevitable because you know that in and through things God's will is being worked out, and that Will wills your good.

My God and Father, I shall have to center down in Thee. I cannot center down in the immediate, so I will have to center down in the ultimate. My faith looks, not at a panorama, but at a Person. "Change and decay in all around I see; O Thou, who changest not, abide with me." Amen.

Dan. 3:24-25; John 16:32; Ps. 27:10; Isa. 42:16

THE SECRET COMPANIONSHIP

We saw yesterday that "we must learn to live in time and in eternity simultaneously." If the time-side of life is all awry, then the eternity-side holds us steady and lets us relax "in spite of." If we cannot live "on account of," then we must learn to live "in spite of."

"Christianity is a secret companionship," said a Chinese missionary; "hence when I am out for months where no one of my race is found, I am not lonely. I have a secret companionship." It may be that you will have to walk down through life arm in arm with disappointment; but on your other side, holding your arm, is the Secret Companion, and "he who believes in Him will never be disappointed." (Romans 9:33, Moffatt.) You are disappointment-proof, for you always have an appointment with the Secret Companion. Since that center holds steady, you need not grow tense at the unsteady happenings around you.

An intelligent woman told me she was so wrought up and tense over what she thought was an inevitable marriage for her son that she began to have terrible pains in her head, and was soon in the hospital, unable to breathe. Pneumonia developed, and she continued tense until she became unconscious. Only then did she relax. When she came out of the unconsciousness, she surrendered the whole affair to God, and came back to poise and health. She came near to choking herself to death by her resentments, which produced inner tensions of soul which in turn produced a disrupted body. She allowed her life to go up and down with outer happenings instead of basing it on the Secret Companionship. If your happiness is based on happenings, it will be a fleeting, evanescent thing. You must have a love for God so strong, so elemental, that if everything around you were stripped away—your work, your family, your prestige, your power—then this thing within would go on, regardless.

"Your strength is quiet faith." (Isaiah 30:15, Moffatt.)

Gracious God, I rest not in the immediate; I rest in the ultimate—in Thee. I am therefore impregnable. I view the panorama of life in quiet confidence that the last word will be spoken by Thee. That last word will be for my ultimate good. So I wait as a weaned child in quiet confidence. I thank Thee. Amen.

Mark 9:33–34; Matt. 19:22; Luke 18:11–12; Matt. 6:1–4

SELF-REFERENCE OR GOD-REFERENCE

When you are tense and unrelaxed, you are still centered in yourself. You are the center of reference—you are trying to hold your world together. When you relax, you shift the center of reference from yourself to God. You are no longer a self-centered person, but a God-centered person. Relaxation means release—from yourself. When you are unrelaxed and tense, you are like a person who holds his breath in order to save his lungs. The lungs are saved only as you allow them to take in and give out. So you, too, are saved only as you take in—prayer, and give out—service to others.

When you live in a state of self-reference, you automatically shut yourself off from the guidance of God, and hence from His resources. The town of Lyons, Iowa, was situated at the narrow place in the Mississippi River where the railway bridge would be bound to be built, so the citizens thought. They held up the railway company for an exorbitant price for the land. The railway company therefore decided to cross at Clinton, which offered them land free. Clinton has prospered; Lyons has withered. If you live in a state of self-reference, you will end in self-impoverishment.

Dr. Alexis Carrel says: "Thus psychoanalysis, in directing the mind of the patient upon himself, may aggravate the state of unbalance. Instead of indulging in self-analysis, it is better to escape from oneself through an effort that does not scatter the mind." The only way to escape from yourself is to make God and His will the center of your consciousness and your life plans. You then live in a state of God-reference instead of in a state of self-reference.

We can make no impression on a tense conscious mind. Relaxation is receptivity. "These people won't let me do anything for them; neither will you," said Christ to a distracted soul bowed in a cathedral. When she did inwardly let go, then the power of God poured into her, lifting her up out of depression and defeat into release and victory. She now has a soul leisured from itself, the instrument of God's power to others.

My Gracious and Redeeming God, I have been blocking Thy power in my life by my tense fears and withholdings. Let me this day be as relaxed and as receptive as a little child. Then life shall become play, and my hardest tasks simply joy. Spontaneity will bubble in every act and thought as I go on my released and happy way. I thank Thee. Amen.

Ps. 5:3; 88:13; 119:147; Isa. 50:4

THE MORNING QUIET TIME

In order to have a continuous state of relaxed receptivity we must have periods of quiet when we gain the poise and power that will go through the whole day. Those who say that they can live in a state of prayer without stated times for prayer will probably find themselves without both. Those who try to live on the notion that they can live in a state of physical nourishment without stated times for meals will perish.

I asked a couple who were living defeated lives if they kept the Quiet Time; and the naïve reply came, "Yes, my husband and I sit and smoke in the quiet a half hour after breakfast." The modern equivalent of the Quiet Time! No wonder the husband had a nervous breakdown. Those sincere but defeated souls found release and victory when they set up a real Quiet Time in which they took in the resources of the living God, instead of the pitiable substitute of nicotine. Breathing God deep into your inner recesses gives a lift with no subsequent "let down."

Set up the Quiet Time, preferably in the morning before you go out into the day. James Russell Lowell says:

> "If the chosen soul could never be alone
> In deep mid-silence, open-doored to God,
> No greatness ever had been dreamed or
>   done; . . . .
> The nurse of full-grown souls is solitude."

It is best to have the Quiet Time "in the pure, strong hours of the morning, when the soul of the day is at its best." Wash your thinking in the Thought of Christ before you face the day.

> "Every morning lean thine arm awhile
> Upon the window sill of heaven
> And gaze upon thy God.
> Then, with the vision in thy heart,
> Turn strong to meet thy day."

O God, "late and soon, getting and spending, we lay waste our powers," and now we turn to Thee for repair and replenishment. Without Thee we are empty and distracted and out of sorts. With Thee we are calm and poised and full and adequate. Then, "Without Thee, not one step over the threshold; with Thee—anywhere." Amen.

Ps. 62:5; Jer. 15:16; Ps. 119:9–16

QUIET EXPECTANCY IN THE QUIET TIME

We saw yesterday that we should choose the morning for our Quiet Time. Of course, if you simply cannot arrange a morning hour, then take any hour you can. But the morning is best. A watch was running slow. The watchmaker asked when the owner wound it, and when told "at night," replied, "Wind it in the morning. Give it the fresh spring at the hardest part of the day, when you are moving about." Give your soul the fresh spring of the Morning Watch before you go out to face the hard part of the day—the daily tasks and problems.

In the Quiet Time what do you do? I can tell you only what I do. When in college I decided I would set aside at least an hour and a half a day to cultivate my Resources. I usually take one-half hour in the morning and an hour at eventide. In the morning hour I take my Bible, usually reading a chapter, sometimes only a few verses if they prove to be arresting. I take my pen—that pen is a sign of faith that something is going to come out worth noting on the margin. It seldom fails. If you do not write your inspiration down, it will fade out.

The Bible will be self-authenticating to you. It will find you at your deepest depths. You will know that it is inspired, for you will find it inspiring. You will know that God has gone into it, for God comes out of it. It is a revelation, for it reveals. It is an exhaustless mine. You think you have exhausted it, and then you put down the shaft of meditation and strike new veins of rich ore. Your very brain cells will be eager and alert with expectancy. You will have what Spinoza calls "an intellectual love of God."

Perhaps you will have to be primed and prodded into thought by one of these "helps," such as this book or other devotional literature. But they are secondary, and not a substitute for a first-hand contact with the Word of God. If the best Man that ever lived fed upon the Word of God, so must you.

O God, Thou hast breathed into these words, and they have become the Word. Thou hast touched these ways, and they have become the Way. Help me to saturate my inner thinking, my inner motives, with Thy Mind until I cannot tell where my mind ends and Thy Mind begins. Then I shall live fully and safely. In Jesus' name. Amen.

Isa. 40:29; Mic. 3:8; Zech. 4:6; Acts 1:8

LIFE NOT A RESERVOIR, BUT A CHANNEL

Now that you have read the Word of God, you have done what the aviator does when he tunes up his engine preparatory to the starting of the flight. The Word has started your thinking, your aspirations, going in the right direction, has prepared you to pray prayers that can be answered. It has aligned you with the will of God; and where the will of God is done, the power of God can come.

Now to the negative side of prayer—the getting rid of accumulated hindrances which have blocked the flow of power. I say "blocked the flow of power," for we are not reservoirs, but channels. Commenting on the words of J. A. Hadfield, David Seabury says: "Many people have the idea that in each of us there is a reservoir containing a certain supply of energy. This is . . . . supposed to be strictly limited in amount. If our expenditure is excessive, they say, our energy is depleted and we suffer from fatigue. So we take the attitude of economizing our little store of strength, conserving our resources, lest the stingy springs run dry. In contrast with this point of view is one akin to the teaching of Jesus. That is, our energies seem to be used up, not because the flow is checked, but because either the channel is blocked or we have not learned to use our capacities in the right way. In other words, we are tired not when we do too much but when we do too little. . . . . Our hidden springs are not of body but of spirit; we are not receptacles but conductors. . . . .

"Jesus knew the human tendency to live far too frugally, to forget the source of our strength and fail to make God a perpetually sustaining power. Even more, he recognized our habit of hoarding both our material and our spiritual possessions." (*How Jesus Heals Our Minds Today*, pp. 170-71, 172.)[1] His method was, "Give, and it shall be given unto you; good measure, pressed down, ... and running over." Let that burn within us: "We are not receptacles, but conductors!"

O God, I've been meager and afraid—afraid my resources would run dry if I used them. But I see that only as I give, will I get. Help me, then, to give, and give with complete abandon. And then I shall draw heavily upon Thy resources and live by them. I thank Thee for this assurance. Amen.

[1] Reprinted by permission of Little, Brown and Co., publishers.

Isa. 9:6; 14:3; Gal. 5:1, 7; Rom. 8:15

OPENING BLOCKED CHANNELS

If we are not reservoirs, but channels, then one of the first things to do in prayer, after reading the Word, is to become silent to God, and let Him put His finger on any blocked channel. The tendency will be to try to pray around that blocked place, to slur it over, to act as if it were not there. That is a part of our inner defense. But don't defend yourself, overtly or covertly. Face the blocked place frankly; confess where you have been wrong; turn over to God simply and frankly your problem, and tell Him you will do anything at any cost to right it, with His help. Or better still—He will do it with your help. For He is taking the initiative to make you the best that you can be.

Here is what one happy, released soul did: "I have been a Christian—in spots, and a church member since I was about nine years of age. . . . . But I lived by fears rather than by faith. . . . . I decided I'd had enough of it, and that if you knew the way out, I'd certainly try to follow it. Well, you did, so I moved out all the accumulated terrors and panics and anxieties, and asked God to come in where I'd never let Him come before. He did, and I am so happy, because I am sure life is never going to be the same again."

To be relaxed is to be released. Relax, then, toward God and be eagerly open to any suggestion for clearing up your life. But perhaps you are not relaxed toward people. You are holding resentments toward them. Surrender those resentments into the love of God. That love will dissolve them.

Perhaps you are tense toward others because you want to live out their lives for them. Surrender those loved ones to God. I wrote my daughter and her husband when they were married: "I would like my attitude to be, Never in the way, and never out of the way." If you are fussily trying to manage other people in their supposed interests, surrender that fussiness—it is pure selfishness. That attitude ties up yourself and others.

O Thou Tender Silence, speak as I go into silence. Speak the word that will release me and heal me and make me adequate. I consent without reservation to the draining of every swamp of self-centeredness and fear. Clean me to my depths. For the world is sick, and I want to be a part of the cure instead of the disease. In Jesus' name. Amen.

II Cor. 10:5; Luke 2:35; Heb. 4:12; Jer. 4:14

WHEN THE MIND WANDERS

Yesterday we saw that we tie ourselves up if we try to live other people's lives for them. A mother did not want her daughter to be married—she was self-centered, wanted the attention of her daughter. The daughter waited till she was thirty-one before she married. The mother fainted at the wedding. Through her self-pity she developed all sorts of diseases. But her husband developed cancer of the colon. In fighting for him and attending to him she forgot herself and became a well woman, and is well today. She shifted the basis of her relationships with others from self-interest to other-interest, and righted the relationships—and herself.

In prayer let God show you the places where you have tensions. You will be as touchy as a boil as He puts His fingers on them.

If God in the silence brings up nothing, then take it for granted there is nothing. Now you are ready for positive communion. But another difficulty arises. When you begin to enter into positive communion, your mind wanders. This greatly distresses some people. It shouldn't. Suppose the mind does wander; then let the thing to which it wanders be the medium through which you commune with God. For instance, as I was writing this line I looked up and saw a white pigeon through the window, and my mind began to wander, repeating to itself these lines:

"Every morning her white thought did beat to God-ward,
  Like a carrier dove, my name beneath its wing."

Suppose my mind did wander—in the end it wandered to God. Suppose, as someone has said, you are distracted by a siren. Then say: "Oh, that I might be warned by an even louder siren of the danger that besets torpid and careless souls!" Make the distraction into a direction—to God. Ride even on the wings of the storm—to God.

After a while you will be able to bring every thought into captivity to the obedience of Christ. For as you more and more obey Him, He will become more and more the center of your affection: and "where your treasure is, there will your heart be also."

Beautiful, strong Son of God, Thou art becoming more and more my treasure. More and more I cannot think apart from Thee, love apart from Thee, be apart from Thee. Thou hast me. And now, where my treasure is, there my heart is also. I am at rest, at poise, at power. Amen.

Ps. 130:1; Matt. 12:35; Isa. 26:3; Eph. 3:16–19

BUILDING UP FROM THE SUBCONSCIOUS

Perhaps the greatest difficulty in meditation is that you feel that nothing is happening. You agree that prayer is communing with God, but nothing seems to come back to you from God. Gerald Heard, an expert in meditation, spending hours at it each day, says: "Do not be disappointed when nothing happens, when no lucidity appears, no sense of significance, no great quiet. This process which is working on us works, or should work, first on the subconscious. What we are building up, or having built up in us, is a foundation from the sea floor of the subconscious to the surface. Bag after bag of cement is poured in, and then it rises above the surface." The habit of practicing the presence of God is being formed; new grooves in the channels of attention are being cut.

Prayer will then soon become an undertone, as well as an overtone, of your life. Of Phillips Brooks it was said, adapting the words of Tennyson, "His eyes were homes of silent prayer." His whole attitude began to be a prayer-attitude. Someone said of John Forman, a saintly missionary, "All his thoughts of people gradually turned to prayers." This means that you need never waste time, no matter in what circumstances you are placed. If people are making you wait, thus wasting your time, you can immediately turn on your prayer attention and begin to pray for the people who are making you wait, thus dissolving your resentments and making you use constructively an otherwise wasted period. You can pull the world and its need into that blank moment. Said someone regarding the Christians of Europe undergoing persecution: "Our people can stand solitary confinement better than others." Why? Because even in solitary confinement they could people the cell with people in need, brought there by reaching out hands of prayer and gathering them in.

So prayer can become habit, easier to do than not to do. But habits are formed by regularity. Pray by the clock, if necessary, and soon you will pray by inward urge. Then you will know the meaning of "detained in presence of the Eternal" (I Samuel 21:7, Moffatt)—you will not be able to tear yourself away.

Just now I would be "detained in presence of the Eternal." Here, in Thy presence, O Eternal, I place myself, my affairs, my worries, my frustrations, my possibilities, into Thy hands. I have narrowly held them; now I lovingly entrust them to Thee. Amen.

John 6:29; 9:4; Phil. 2:13; Col. 1:29; Gal. 5:6

RELAXED STRENUOUSNESS

We are learning that relaxation is release—release not only from cramping inhibitions and fears, but release also for otherwise impossible tasks. "Relaxation of the personality is really an evidence of faith and trust. . . . . The man who believes absolutely in God, in the divine reliability and goodness, does not hold himself mentally and spiritually rigid, fearful that any moment something is going to happen to him, but, on the contrary, rests in complete confidence that all things work together for good to them who believe in God. As a result, he has peace in his mind and quietness at the center of his life. . . . . This relaxed and peaceful state of mind gives him a clear brain, makes possible the free exercise of all his faculties, and thus he is able to attack his problems with every ounce of ability he possesses. The relaxed man is the powerful man. The rigid, tied-up personaility is defeated before the battle starts." (*Faith Is the Answer*, Blanton and Peale, pp. 84-85.)[1]

The end of periods of relaxation is relaxed strenuousness. The worship becomes work. Instead of "Now I lay me down to sleep," which too many grownups are prone to pray, we can say:

> "Now I get me up to work,
> I pray the Lord I will not shirk.
> If I should die before the night,
> I pray the Lord my work's all right."

As we arise from our morning communion:

> "Fronting my task, these things I ask:
> To be true, this whole day through;
> To be content with honest work,
> Fearing only lest I shirk;
> To see, and know, and do what's right;
> To come, unsullied, home at night."

Gracious Father, lovingly into Thy hands I place my affairs, knowing that only that which is for my highest good shall come to me. But now that I have placed them in Thy hands, Thou and I shall work them out together. We begin the Great Co-operation. Amen.

[1] Reprinted by permission of Abingdon-Cokesbury Press, publishers.

Ps. 37:1–11; 121

PHYSICAL AND MENTAL RELAXATION

We will use an exercise for relaxation given to us by an Occidental Ashram member who spends most of her time in a city school system teaching children and parents to relax.

1. Stand with arms over head, palms flat, and push hard against the ceiling, going up on tiptoe as far as you can. Then let arms go to side, limp. Repeat.

2. Sit in chair. Raise right arm, every muscle tight; the arm is very, very heavy. Let go, limp, to side. Repeat. Same with left arm.

3. Raise right leg, knee bent, every muscle tight—make it as heavy as possible. Let go, limp. Repeat. Same with left leg.

4. As you sit in chair sit loose, every muscle relaxed. Now you are like a rag doll, no stiff muscles; you're limp. Your hands are resting in lap with palms up. The palms up represent receptivity—you're now receiving into every pore of your being.

5. Your head falls on your chest, your eyes closed, your jaws relaxed and loose, mouth partly open.

6. Now turn your head over to the left and make a complete circle, as far back as possible; to the right, back on chest, limp. Repeat, making your nose like a piece of chalk inscribing a circle as large as possible.

7. Now I am seated, in imagination, on a quiet hillside, before me a calm lake and strong silent hills beyond with their cloud-veiled peaks. The trees lift their arms in silent prayer and absorb, absorb the strength of God. The grass also lifts its blades and receives, receives. Everything receives, and so do I. I breathe in God's peace and breathe out his calm: peace—calm; peace—calm; a gentle rhythm. In every portion of my being I am taking in the life of God —the life of God—so I am at rest, at rest, in God, in God.

I am relaxed and receptive and released.

My Father, gently and quietly I breathe Thy calm and Thy peace into every portion of my being. My fever is gone in the great quiet of God. I am receptive in every fiber and every tissue. The healing of God goes through me, through me. I am grateful, grateful. Amen.

Matt. 6:25–34; 1 Pet. 5:7

MEETING TODAY, TODAY

May I pause in this discussion to add a personal word.

Besides living physically relaxed, I live mentally and spiritually relaxed. I am spiritually relaxed because I believe the central hypothesis of my life is right. Life is one long verification of that central hypothesis. This fact gives an inner sense of steadiness. This attitude toward life was tested in an airplane over St. Louis when we circled above the clouds for two hours, trying to land. The ceiling was so low that we could not get under. I had time to think. So I wrote down a life conclusion: "I am up in this plane and we have been circling over these clouds for about two hours. If we do not land safely I would like to leave my last will and testament to my friends and fellow followers of Christ: There is peace, perfect peace. Apart from my unfaithfulness to the highest, there are no regrets about the general course of my life. Life with Christ is the way to live. In this hour there is assurance— there is God underneath all the uncertainties of human existence. So I rest in God. God's best to you all. Living or dying I am His—His alone. Glory! Signed, E. Stanley Jones."

I try to take that central assurance into my work. The thing that is so centrally right will not let me down in the details. I meet these details in confidence. The word "Comforter" means "brave together." With Him I can be "brave together."

I meet today, today. I do not telescope all next week into today. I clip off my engagements one by one as a person clips off coupons. As Dr. William Osler, the great surgeon, said: "The load of Tomorrow, added to that of Yesterday, carried Today, makes the strongest falter. We must learn to shut off the future as tightly as the past." A greater than Osler said: "Sufficient unto the day is the evil thereof." I sometimes have to put it, "Sufficient unto the hour is the evil thereof." I do not take any worries to bed with me. Bishop Quayle tells of lying awake, trying to hold the world together by his worrying, when God said, "Now, William, you go to sleep and I'll sit up."

My Gracious Father, how can I worry and fret when Thou dost live and care? As Thy happy child I play in Thy house, with no corroding care. Even my hardest work is play. I inwardly dance to my tasks, and amid them feel the gaiety of Thy love. Thou hast taught me to laugh—I laugh with incredulity that I, even I, have found this treasure. Amen.

Matt. 5:43–48; I Cor. 15:33; Gal. 2:11–12

ARE WE CIRCUMSTANCE-DIRECTED?

We come now to the matter of Guidance. If life is to be at its best we must have the sense of instrumentation, of carrying out purposes not our own, of fulfilling a Will that is ultimate. We must "regain the sense of being led," as one pastor urges. Without that sense of being led life hangs at loose ends, lacks goal, and dynamic to move on to that goal. "Anybody got a car going anywhere?" announced someone in a public meeting. No one laughed! But that announcement was revealing must go somewhere; the direction didn't matter. Much of our life is like that—lacks direction and goal.

If we lose the sense of being led, we become victims of our circumstances. The men of a church were having a supper, and, being unused to managing meals, they gave contradictory orders to the Negro caretaker. He became upset over these contradictory orders and objected. Whereupon one man asked, "Well, Henry, if you get upset with us, what do you do when the women are here?" To which he replied, "That's simple. I just throws my mind into neutral and goes where I'se pushed." A great many people simply throw their minds into neutral and go where circumstances push them. They have no sense of being led.

Or they allow other people's actions to determine their conduct. They are circumstance-directed instead of Christ-directed. Jesus warned us against allowing the other man to determine our conduct. "If a man smites you," don't take his weapons; keep your own. The best revenge you can have on an enemy is not to be like him. A bishop said that something I wrote cured him of what he called "a mild species of Episcopal swearing." When he went along the roads at night and dimmed his light at the approach of another car, if the approaching driver did not respond he would flash his lights into the other man's face to let him know what he thought of him. "Now," he said, "I dim my lights no matter what the other man does, and keep them dimmed. It's safer, and I feel more like a bishop! I don't let the other man determine my conduct."

O Christ, how often we've let circumstances and persons determine our conduct. Help us to be impelled from within, instead of being compelled from without. O Christ, let me submit to Thy direction lest I be the victim of my surroundings. I want to be a person, and not a thing. Amen.

Lam. 5:15–17; Matt. 15:14; Rev. 3:15–18

GUIDANCE AT SECONDHAND

We saw yesterday that if we are not God-led, we shall probably be mob-led. We shall not act; we shall only react —we shall become things, not persons. In trying to find a way out between America and Japan, I said to some high-up officials: "Don't you see what's happening? You are allowing the Japanese to determine your conduct. You say, 'If they do this, we shall do that.' You allow them to determine your conduct. That leads straight to war. Why don't you work out from your own principles to the situation and find a settlement through the application of your own principles?"

We Christians must work out from principles, not from pressures. No matter what the other person does, we should remain Christian. As Shakespeare puts it:

> "Let me not to the marriage of true minds
> Admit impediments. Love is not love
> Which alters when it alteration finds."

Without a sense of guidance life turns dull and insipid. "Some of the most active church leaders, well known for their executive efficiency, people we have always admired, are shown in the X-ray light of eternity to be agitated, half-committed, wistful, self-placating seekers, to whom power and serenity of the Everlasting have never come." They lack the sense of being led. That brings us to what Thomas Kelley described in these words: "The years have been getting on in average mediocrity. There is no special excellence, no special defeat in it. It's just it. And that is damnable. For the world is popping with novelty, with adventure in ideas. And we are not getting them here. We are safe and sane." Yes, safe and sane and secondhand!

When the Israelites disobeyed God the punishment was this: "I will not go with you . . . . I will send an angel in front of you." (Exodus 33:3, Moffatt.) Religion became a secondhand affair through angels, instead of a direct contact with God.

O God, we who are afraid to be led by Thee become led by things and surroundings. Our religion becomes secondhand and vague, instead of firsthand and vivid. We want to regain the sense of being led, the sense that we are in direct contact, and that life has firsthand meaning. In Jesus' name. Amen.

Isa. 8:19; 1 Kings 19:12; John 10:4; Isa. 30:2

LED OF GOD, OR LED OF THINGS?

The growth of astrology in America is a sign of the lack of firsthand contact with God. If we are not led by God, we will try to be led by stars. Turning to stars for guidance is a sign of decay, mentally and spiritually. It is sheer materialism to believe your life is determined by lumps of matter floating in space. It is a sign of failure of nerve—you don't face the facts of life in the courage and spirit of Christ, but you turn to dodging stars. Astrology laid its paralyzing hand on the mind of Greece and killed it. The Greek mind was a good mind, facing bravely the facts of life, until it lost its nerve and turned to the stars to find destiny written there. The mind of India was a creative mind, producing the amazing Sanskrit literature, until astrology made it sterile and noncreative by turning it toward the stars instead of toward the facts of life.

Men will be led by God into sure ways, or will be led by subterfuges into swamps and miasmas of despair.

We must regain the sense of being led. About two years ago, when ready to sail back to India, I announced that the Inner Voice had insisted that I stay in America, saying, "I want you here." This announcement aroused widespread comment, some of it unfavorable, as if it were a strange and superstitious thing to be led to God, directly and at first hand. This reaction was most revealing. It showed how much of American Christianity was at least one step removed from firsthand. There seemed to be knowledge of, but not acquaintance with, God.

If there is a God, He must have some plan, some purpose for every life. When He made each of us, He apparently broke the pattern—we are all different. Each life has peculiar significance. If we find that plan of God and work within it, we cannot fail. Outside of that plan we cannot succeed.

To be the instrument of the purposes of God is the highest thing in life.

Gracious Father, Thou hast paid attention to the minute, fashioning the lowliest cell with handiwork; hast Thou no plan for me and my life? Thou hast! Help me to find that plan, to pay the price of working out that plan, and to make it the adventure of my life. In Jesus' name. Amen.

Isa. 6:1–9; John 20:21; Acts 8:29

A SENSE OF MISSION AND SUBMISSION

Whenever I stand up to preach I ask the audience to bow their heads in prayer; and I invariably remind God of my verse—a verse given to me years ago at the very beginning of my ministry: "Ye have not chosen me, but I have chosen you, and ordained you, that ye should go and bring forth fruit, and that your fruit should remain: that whatsoever ye shall ask of the Father in my name, he may give it you." (John 15:16.)

The repeating of this verse gives me the sense of being sent, of having the backing of the Eternal, and of speaking in a Name not my own. But it does another thing: It lays on me the sense of obligation to surrender to and be obedient to the working out of this plan. It gives life a sense of mission and submission. The sense of mission gives dignity and meaning to life. An ambassador of a country weighs his words, for they are representative words—he is speaking in the name of his government. We, too, must feel that same representative capacity, that we are speaking and thinking and acting in a name not our own. The significance of a life is determined by the significance of what it is identified with and what it represents.

But that sense of mission brings a sense of submission. Instead of making you proud and cocky, it has the opposite effect. You are awed and humbled. You feel you must walk softly before God. You are on "the adventure of humility."

Guidance strikes at the citadel of personality and demands surrender of self-sufficiency. God is taken into the center of the life choices. Guidance involves surrender. It is the shifting of life from self-will to God's will. That will, not your own, becomes supreme. God's will becomes your constant frame of reference.

Instead of guidance being a spiritual luxury for rare souls, it is a minimum necessity for every Christian soul: "As many as are led by the Spirit of God, they are the sons of God." (Romans 8:14.) No leadership, no sonship. Guidance is of the very essence of Christianity.

O God, I begin to see that if I live, I must live in Thee or not at all. For Thou art my life and my way of life. When I find Thy plan, I find my person. For I am made in the very structure of my being for Thy ways. "Thy will is my peace." My will is my war. I am eager for Thy mind. Amen.

Deut. 31:12; Matt. 11:29; Acts 5:20; Jer. 42:6

LISTEN, LEARN, OBEY

Since God has a plan for every life, then we must become skilled in the art of knowing and working out that plan. We have suggested that when we come to prayer we should have three attitudes: "Listen, learn, obey." Some of us listen but won't learn, and some of learn but won't obey. The Christian is one who listens, who learns, who obeys. If he does not approach God in all three attitudes, then there will soon be nothing to listen to, or to learn, or to obey. The Voice will grow silent. To the degree that we do all three will there be something speaking.

If we do not have guidance, then it is probably withheld for one of two reasons: we are untrained, or we are unwilling. Guidance doesn't just happen. It is a result of placing oneself in the way of being guided. A radio doesn't just happen to pick up messages; it is tuned in by deliberate intention, and then it receives. Receptivity is necessary to perceptivity—you preceive only as you receive. To this psychology agrees when it explains life as "instrumentation." When the king complained to Joan of Arc that he never heard the voice of God, she replied, "You must listen, and then you will hear."

But many of us don't want to listen to God, for we are afraid that if God reveals His will to us it will be along the line of the disagreeable. The fact that we have changed "Thy will be done" into "Thy will be borne"—something hard and disagreeable to be borne—shows that we look on the will of God as something that mortals must accept with a sigh, like the death of a loved one.

That view of the will of God as something distasteful must be completely reversed, or we shall get nowhere with guidance. Jesus reverses that view when He says, "My meat is to do the will of him that sent me." My meat—my food. The will of God is food—food to every tissue, every brain cell, to everything that is good for us. My will is my poison when it conflicts with God's will. To real living the will of God is reinforcement, not restriction.

Forgive me, O God, that I hesitate to throw down every barrier to Thy guidance. Why should my eye be afraid of light? My stomach, pinched with hunger, afraid of food? No more should I be afraid of Thy will. I will not be. Every faculty sensitive and open to Thy suggestions, O my God! Amen.

Jer. 1:4–10; Isa. 30:20–21; Acts 15:28; 16:6–10

BE SILENT TO GOD

We saw last week that if we were not living God-directed lives the reason was that we were untrained or unwilling.

We must be trained to listen, to learn, to obey. First to listen. Many of us talk fast in the presence of God, afraid that if we keep quiet God will say something unpleasant to us. We must learn to listen, to live in the passive voice. A pastor arose in one of our Ashrams and said, "God is showing me that I must shift the emphasis of my life from talking to taking." He was learning receptivity.

One translator interprets the command, "Be still, and know that I am God," this way: "Be silent to God and He will mold you." Be silent to God and He will make and mold you to become the instrument of his purposes. An almighty Will will reinforce your weak will, but only when that weak will is aligned to the purposes of that almighty Will. An all-wise Mind will brood over your mind, awakening it, stimulating it, and making it creative. An all-embracing Love will quicken your love into world-sensitivity until "He will set the world into your heart."

God has three things in mind in reference to us:purpose, plan, person. He has a purpose to make you the best that you can be. He has a plan which embodies that purpose. God has a plan for every life. The next step is for you to be the person for the carrying out of that purpose and that plan. In the silence you listen for the unfolding of that purpose and that plan. You literally become the plan and purpose of God—an embodied thought of God, the word made flesh.

When someone listened to a man of God speaking, he looked up and then and there decided he "would make his life a miracle." He became a miracle. A piece of wire disconnected is one thing, but a piece of wire attached to a dynamo and an engine is quite another thing. Alone, you are one thing; attached to God's purposes, you are quite another thing.

O God, alone, I am a dead wire; but attached to Thee I am throbbing with energy and glowing with light. Make my connection with Thee sure, so that I shall not be periodically going dead and lightless. May I "maintain the spiritual glow" because I've maintained the connection. In Jesus' name. Amen.

Exod. 34:29–30; 40:33–34; Acts 26:19

THE PATTERN IN THE MOUNT

We saw that we must be trained and be willing if we are to be guided. We must be willing to be guided of God, not merely now and then, but as a life proposition. You cannot get light in a crisis unless you are willing to get light in the continuous. God must not be called in to get you out of scrapes in which you have entangled yourself by continuous self-will.

A Swedish literary woman wanted God to tell her what the next step in her career was to be; and at length, in a surge of abandon that broke through all her reserves, she seemed to hear God saying, "How could you expect me to speak when you have gagged me so long?" Don't gag God in the continuous and expect Him to speak in the crisis.

In the beginning of guidance, then, make a decision that decides all decisions down the line—the decision that the will of God is first, last, and always in your life. Nail that down. Let there be no loophole of exceptions. Make it absolute.

The plan of your life may be unfolded in a moment of sudden insight, or it may be a gradual unfoldment. The gradual unfoldment may be the highest form of guidance. "The steps of a good man are ordered by the Lord"—every two and a half feet. "Thy word is a lamp unto my feet." Note, "unto my feet"—just enough light by which the next step can be taken and then the next. That puts adventure into life and a moment-by-moment trust. There is a surprise around every corner.

But the life guidance may be a sudden insight. One day, as a young man, I placed a letter on a chair and knelt before it. The answer to that letter would determine my lifework. The Inner Voice said, "It's India." I arose and said, "Then, it's India." That clear moment was a real moment, and has held me steady amid low moments of discouragement about the details in India.

The Inner Voice brings inner unity.

O God, help me to build according to the pattern I see in the mount—in the moment when Thy voice is clear and I am receptive and responsive. For I cannot live on a surmise, but on a summons; not on a guess, but on a goal. I await Thy bidding and Thy blessing. Amen.

Ps. 25:9; 32:8; 73:24; Isa. 58:11

THE SEVEN WAYS OF GOD'S GUIDANCE

If guidance gives to life a sense of mission and the sense of accountability every moment, then how does God guide us?

I suppose the great problem to God is how to guide us and not override us. He must guide us and develop us as persons at the same time. To lead us and at the same time produce initiative in us is a task worthy of divine wisdom. That task is the problem of every thinking parent. Many parents are benevolent tyrants, snuffing out initiative and personality. Guidance must be such that each person is guided into a free, self-choosing, creative personality.

To do this God will guide in many ways, awakening the personality to aliveness and alertness of mind and spirit to His hidden leadings. God's leadings should be sufficiently obvious to be found, but not so obvious as to do away with the necessity of thought and discriminating insight. They must be "an open secret"—open, yet sufficiently secret to make us dig.

God will guide us in one or more or all of these ways: (1) He gives general guidance through the character and person of Christ. Christ lets us know what God is like, and, therefore, what we must be like. (2) He guides us through the collective experience of the Church—the corporate wisdom gathered through the ages. (3) He guides us through the counsel of good people. (4) He guides through opening providences—matching us against some opening opportunity or need. (5) He guides through natural law and its discoveries through science. (6) He guides through a heightened moral intelligence and insight—we become personalities who are capable of exercising sound moral judgments. (7) He guides us through the direct voice of the Spirit within us—He speaks to us in unmistakable terms in the depths of our being.

The probabilities are that God will guide us in more than one of these ways, lest one method narrow us.

Gracious Father, my being within me is atingle to find out Thy way and be led into it. For I know that Thy way is really my way—the way I am made in my inner structure to obey. So help me to seek Thy way with my whole being and without reservations. For I know that Thy hand is my health. In Jesus' name. Amen.

John 13:15; 14:6–9; 1 Pet. 2:21

GENERAL GUIDANCE THROUGH THE REVELATION IN CHRIST

We now look at those seven ways of guidance in a little more detail. (1) *God gives general guidance through the character and person of Christ.* Christ has revealed to us the nature of God—has shown us what He is like; He has lifted up into bold relief the laws that underlie our moral universe, and the laws that underlie our own spiritual, intellectual, and physical beings. In short, He has revealed to us the nature of Reality. Then Christ is our "general guidance." If we want to live according to the nature of Reality, then we must live according to Christ.

The Mohammedan says you cannot get guidance from Christ, for He was not married—He can give no guidance to the married. There are two ways to be an example: One is to live in every possible situation and then to show everybody how to live in that particular situation—a married man how to live as a married man, a mechanic how to live as a mechanic, and so forth. This type of guidance is obviously impossible. The other way to be an example is to live in such a way that one's life in a particular situation is lived on universal principles, so that the spirit of these principles can be applied anywhere. Jesus took the latter method. There is no situation conceivable where His spirit is not the norm for that situation. He is the universal conscience of humanity.

When you have this general guidance in Christ, there is no use to ask for specific guidance which is covered by this general guidance. Often we ask for specific guidance because we are unwilling to take the general guidance in Christ. Ask the question in any situation, "What is the Christlike thing to do?" And if you do it you will not go wrong. There is no use trying to prevail upon God to approve of any act or attitude that is other than Christlike. God cannot act or advise against His own nature, for He is Christlike.

Think of having guidance along the line of the Christlike!

O God, I see I am predestined to be conformed to the image of Thy Son, for the nature of reality is Christlike, and if I live according to it I will come out there. What a destiny awaits me! Help me to be willing to be thus predestined, for I would live. In Jesus' name. Amen.

Matt. 18:17, 20; Eph. 3:10; Acts 13:1–3

GUIDANCE THROUGH COLLECTIVE EXPERIENCE

We come to the second method through which God guides us. (2) *He guides us through the collective experience of the Church—the corporate wisdom gathered through the ages.* The importance of this method is seen when we realize that the great Roman Catholic Church makes this the sole instrument of guidance to the individual. We cannot accept it as the sole method, but certainly as one of the chief methods. The accumulated experiences of the ages are at the disposal of the individual.

The Church has been the mother of my spirit; and just as a child turns to his mother for guidance in crises, so I can turn to the Church for direction. The pastor is the mouthpiece of that collective wisdom. He should therefore not seek to be novel, but to interpret the wisdom of the ages to the people before him. A dean of girls says that problem children come from three causes: (1) proverty; (2) broken homes; (3) a lack of attending church or Sunday school.

(3) *God guides through the counsel of good people.* As we look back across the years we find that a word here, a phrase there, a conversation yonder with a friend, has lifted horizons, untangled snarled-up situations, and has sent us on our way rejoicing, with clarified minds and purposes. Counseling is no longer a hit-and-miss affair; it is becoming an art and a science. The minister who cannot combine public utterance with private counsel is "out" as a safe guide to his people. The Orientals have a saying that you don't drop eye medicine from a third-story window into a person's eye. Guidance must be intimate and personal and confidential. Counseling is a heavy responsibility. "Should I marry this man?" asked a girl after describing him. When I told her I thought not, she replied, "There, that settles it. I promised God last night that I would take your answer for His answer." I held my breath. What a responsibility!

A conversation which the young Kagawa had with a teacher started on his way a youth who has become a world asset.

Gracious Father, I thank Thee for those who have come into my life with kindly word and deep insight. Help me this day to be the agent of Thy mind to some other person. Help me to speak that word which will lift the darkness for some fumbling soul. In Jesus' name. Amen.

I Cor. 2:9; II Cor. 2:12; Rev. 3:8; I Cor. 12:8

GOD GUIDES THROUGH OPENING
PROVIDENCES AND THE NATURAL ORDER

We come to the next step in guidance: (4) *God guides through opening providences—matching us against some opening opportunity or need.* A little waif boy of the streets of London sidled up to a doctor and said, "Do youse want to see where wese live?" He took the doctor by the hand and led him into alleyways where boys slept in boxes and under steps, huddled together to keep one another warm. Before morning that doctor knew he belonged to those boys, and went out and set up Dr. Barnardo's Homes, through which thousands of boys have been blessed. God's guidance was the opening of the doctor's eyes to see a need. If God lets you see a need, the seeing of it is His invitation for you to meet that need.

(5) *God guides through natural law and its discoveries through science.* We have a primary faith in revelation and a secondary faith in science. But in a sense science is revelation—God speaking to us through the natural order. That natural order is God's order. It is dependable. It is dependable because God is dependable. He works by law and order rather than by whim and notion and fancy. There was a time when we tried to put God in the unexplained gaps in nature—we said God must be there, for these gaps are mysterious and unexplainable. But when science began to fill up these gaps, God was pushed out. To have relegated God to those gaps was a mistake, for God reveals Himself in the very law and order and the explainable facts of nature, and not merely in the unexplainable and the mysterious. The law and order express God far more than the unexplainable and mysterious. For this very law and order is of God—He is in it, is the author of it, works through it, but is not strait-jacketed by it. For this law and order is full of surprises and of freedoms. A closed system of nature is now unscientific. God guides through science. Accept that fact.

To expect to be guided by the revelations of science makes you open-minded to life around you as well as to life above you.

O God, whose will is wrought into the natural order, and who, by that very order art disciplining us to lawful, orderly living, help us to accept and rejoice in that discipline. For Thy disciplines are our freedoms. Help us to accept Thy laws, which have become our liberties. In Jesus' name. Amen.

Heb. 5:14; Luke 12:57; Eph. 1:17–18; Rom. 8:14

GUIDANCE THROUGH MORAL INTELLIGENCE AND THE INNER VOICE

Our next step in guidance is: (6) *God guides through a heightened moral intelligence and insight—we become persons who are capable of exercising sound moral judgments.* This is the usual and perhaps the most dependable form of guidance. I should think it would be the form that God most delights in. It is certainly the form discerning parents delight in, when they see their children now no longer leaning parasitically on them, but capable of exercising sound moral judgments of their own. That is the sign of a free personality. The Parent God must love that. Jesus loved it —"Why even of yourselves judge ye not what is right?" Fellowship with Christ stimulates and heightens our moral insights and judgments. He is the maker of men.

(7) *God guides through the direct voice of the Spirit within us.* I am surprised that this method of guidance is looked on by so many church leaders as something strange and occult. That it is capable of being abused is not to be denied. Thoughts may arise from our subconscious which we mistake for the voice of the Spirit. Any suggestion that speaks to us must be tested, particularly as to whether or not it fits in with the guidance we receive through the person and teaching of Christ. If the guidance is not in thorough accord with that, then suspect it and reject it. And don't depend on the Inner Voice as the usual method of guidance, for if we do we may be tempted to manufacture guidance through our own desires when no Inner Voice comes. The guidance of the Inner Voice comes, at least to me, when none of the other steps in guidance can meet my particular need. I need a special word for that special crisis. Then the Inner Voice speaks. And it is distinguishable as something self-authenticating and authoritative. When a voice rises from my subconscious it argues with me. The Voice doesn't argue; it is self-authenticating.

O God, who art guiding us through conscience, and yet guiding us beyond conscience, when choosing is not a question of right and wrong, but perhaps of good and best, help me to be sensitive to that Inner Voice. And help me to obey at any cost. For Thy leadings are Thy enablings. In Jesus' name. Amen.

John 15:1–9; Acts 4:32–35

LIFE IS CO-OPERATION, OR IT IS DEATH!

In our discussion of guidance we left out specific mention of a form of guidance which, because of its importance, needs separate treatment—group guidance. This was hinted at in the guidance through the Church, but guidance through the Church sounds too official and stilted to express what we mean by group guidance.

I am afraid of individual guidance that isn't checked up on by group guidance—the individual needs the correction or the corroboration of the group. People who say, "God told me such and such," should be willing to submit that to a disciplined group for their reaction. In the end, the individual may have to act on his own guidance, but it is not safe to do so unless one has been willing to get group judgment on it. Individualism is a half-truth, hence individual guidance is only a half-guidance, and unsafe, as such, unless corrected by corporate checkup.

Christianity began as a group movement. Jesus gathered around Him a dozen men and implanted His outlook and spirit into that group. Christianity began not as an individualism, but as a collectivism. But it was a collectivism in which the individual found his perfect freedom. For you cannot find your freedom in isolation and detachment. You find it only through a group. You are social by your very nature. Two cells came together to produce you, so you are social in your origin and constitution.

Galveston, Texas, had all the advantages of being situated on the gulf and of a wonderful harbor. But three families in Galveston began to compete with each other for the domination of the city. They canceled out each other. Galveston was stunted. Houston had almost none of the advantages of Galveston, for it was situated fifty miles up the winding river. And yet Houston has pulled away from Galveston and has become the largest city of Texas. The secret? The leaders of Houston learned to co-operate.

The law of life is: co-operate, or disintegrate and die. That law is inexorable. Christianity was right, therefore, when it began as a co-operative order—a group movement, a cell of a new world order.

O God, Thou art our Father and we are Thy family. The family has not learned how to live together, and hence we are torn into fragments. Forgive us and help us from today to learn to live with mutual aid at the very center of our beings and at the center of our purposes. Amen.

Luke 1:5–7, 13–17; Matt. 1:18–20

THE REDEMPTIONISTS

Before Jesus gathered a group movement around Him, there was another group movement out of which the group movement of Jesus grew. This existing group movement has been called "The Redemptionists"—made up of those who were "looking for the redemption of Israel."

There was decay within Israel. The voice of prophecy had ceased; religion was formal and dead: it was "dry ground" out of which the Root, Jesus, would grow. Disraeli described his religion as the "blank page between the Old and New Testaments." The page between the Old and the New was blank, except for a Remnant, the Redemptionists. They held aloft the torch of reality amid the encircling gloom. They were the seed plot of a new order, the germ of a new world.

We can trace the Redemptionists in the opening chapters of Luke's Gospel by the family likeness of ideas running through them all. The group was made up, in all probability, of Zacharias and Elisabeth, Mary and Joseph, Simeon, Anna, the shepherds. They were intensely nationalistic, and yet they were agents of a new order based on an equality of opportunity to everybody. The word "just" runs like a refrain through the account of all of them. They stood for a justice that made for equality for everybody. Zacharias and Elisabeth were "both just." The angels spoke to Zacharias of "the wisdom of the just"—a phrase which should burn itself into modern civilization; to be just is to be wise, to be unjust is to be unwise. Joseph was "a *just* man," but with a new kind of justice: "her husband was a just man and unwilling to disgrace her." (Matthew 1:19, Moffatt.) Here was a justice that was mercy, that was redemptive and not punitive. The angels said to the shepherds, "Peace on earth, good will to men"—good will to men; not to some men, but to all men, apart from race and birth and color.

O God, we see the workings of Thy purposes through those who are given to each other and to Thee. May I be a part of a nucleus in whom the future lies as an embryo in the womb—may I have within me the germs of Thy new Order. Then I shall live now and hereafter. In Jesus' name. Amen.

Job 17:9; Ps. 1; Luke 2:25–29; Prov. 10:28

A MAN FOURSQUARE

The man who summed up the spirit of the Redemptionists within himself was Simeon, probably the humble center
of this group. This man was the epitome of the new order.
"There was a man"—he was unadorned by any title of office
or rank; the emphasis was upon the fact of his being just a
man, which was the keynote of the new order. Nothing
counted except this—the man. This plain layman was the
vehicle of God's thought for the new age.

He was not only a man, but also a man foursquare: He
"was righteous"—toward man; "devout"—toward God;
"looking for the consolation of Israel"—toward his nation;
"and the Holy Spirit was upon him"—toward himself. His
faith made him sound in every relationship, a well-rounded
personality. Some are righteous toward man and not devout
toward God. Some are devout toward God and not righteous toward man. Some are patriotic lovers of their country, but are inwardly empty—the Holy Spirit is not upon
them. And some are devoutly mystical and spiritual, but
not interested in the affairs of their nation—they are narrowly personal. In Simeon God's Kingdom was working as
total wholeness and health.

Simeon was right in general, and as a result of that found
particular guidance in a particular situation. "By an inspiration of the Spirit he came to the temple." (Luke 2:27, Moffatt.) You must not expect particular guidance if you refuse to allow God to give you general guidance in the whole
of your life. God cannot be called in as a Cosmic Bellhop
to run your errands in particular situations of difficulty if
you shut Him out of the total management of your life. He
is not the Bellhop; He is the Owner and Manager of this
hotel called the world. We must come under His general
and particular guidance.

In that crisis God found a man totally prepared in his total nature to be the vehicle of a new order.

O God, just as Simeon had kept himself fit in every department of his life, so that in the crisis he was available to
Thee, help me to be fit every moment, so that I, too, may
be ready to be used in the crisis—Thy man for that job.
Help me to be disciplined and ready for Thy crises. In Jesus' name. Amen.

Luke 2:29–32; Matt. 19:26; Luke 17:12–16; I Cor. 6:11

UNVEILING HUMAN POSSIBILITIES

The whole nature of Simeon was fit and attuned, so that when the great moment of his life came, he was not caught off guard, but was ready with insight to see the meaning of the Great Event. He took the Child in his arms and saw in Him "salvation, which thou hast prepared before the face of all peoples; a light for revelation to the Gentiles, and the glory of thy people Israel." (Luke 2:30–32.)

Simeon was an intense patriot, "looking for the consolation of Israel," and yet he was not narrowed by his patriotism, for he saw this salvation was to be for "all peoples"—how prophetic his vision was; he saw the universality of Christ. But, further, he saw that Christ was not only "salvation" to the Gentiles—the Gentiles, whom the Jews called "Gentile dogs"—but was also to be the "unveiling of the Gentiles" [marginal reading]. He was to unveil the worthwhileness of the Gentiles, to uncover their possibilities. The revelation which Christ was to bring was a revelation of God, but it was also a revelation of man. Jesus uncovers our Father; He also uncovers our brother—lifts the veil from our prejudiced eyes and lets us see the infinite worthwhileness in every man, of every race, of every color, of every class. The Gentiles were to be no longer "problems"; they were to be possibilities. We speak of "the Negro problem"; we should speak of "the Negro possibility." The problem is not in the Negro; it is in us, who by our prejudices and fears have made him a problem instead of a possibility. White Christianity needs a baptism of the spirit of Simeon to make our religion into a revelation of possibilities of people instead of into something that bolsters up our prejudices. Christianity is a double revelation—of God and of man—and when it does not do that, it is not Christianity, but a religious bolstering of racialisms.

We need a religious faith that brings faith in people as well as in God.

O God, Thou art our Father and the Father of all men. Help me this day to catch Thy vision of the infinite possibitities in all people, however overlaid by strange wrappings these possibilities may be. And help me to set out on the great adventure of bringing out those possibilities in all people. Perhaps, as I do so, some of my own may be brought to light. In Jesus' name. Amen.

Luke 2:34–35; Matt. 16:21; Rom. 9:1–3

YOUR OWN SOUL PIERCED

But Simeon was no sentimentalist—he saw the depth of the issues involved in Christ: "This child is destined for the downfall as well as for the rise of many a one in Israel; destined to be a Sign for man's attack—to bring out the secret aims of many a heart. And your own soul will be pierced by a spear." (Luke 2:34–35, Moffatt.) His patriotism did not blind him to the fact that Jesus was destined for the downfall as well as for the rise of many in Israel—a nation would stumble over Him to its doom. Patriotism is prattle and piffle if it doesn't see that a nation can and often does stumble over Jesus to its doom. "Europe has lost Christ, and Europe will perish," said a Russian author; and this can be said of any nation which loses Christ.

"Destined to be a Sign for man's attack." He who came to unveil all men will make some men shrink from that unveiling, and make them attack the Light that reveals the ugly depths of their own hearts. Jesus is the world's conscience. Just as we struggle with and sometimes fight against conscience, so we struggle with and fight against this Man. Jesus is the Man we ought to be, struggling with the man that is. He brings out "the secret aims of many a heart," and many do not like their secret aims to be brought out.

"Your own soul will be pierced by a spear"—Mary suffered vicariously. The nation would suffer because of its rejection, and Mary would suffer because her nation rejected its redemption. Christ causes a twofold suffering—to those who reject, and to those who love those who reject.

But Mary would suffer because of the very message that came through her, for it was of the essence of revolution: "He hath scattered the proud by [marginal] the imagination of their heart"—self-frustration to unbending men. "He hath put down princes from their thrones"—political revolution. "He hath exalted them of low degree"—social evolution. "The hungry he hath filled with good things; and the rich he hath sent empty away"—economic revolution. With that message, no wonder she suffered.

O God, my Father, I see that the bringing in of Thy new Order is no child's play; it will cost blood and struggle—not of others, but of us who are dedicated to bringing it in. For men love dark but accustomed ways, and will fight blindly against the light. Help us to be strong, as Jesus was. Amen.

Luke 3:4–6, 11; Matt. 19:21; 20:14; Jas. 2:1–9

EQUALITY OF OPPORTUNITY—THE KEYNOTE

Anna looked for "the redemption of Jerusalem," and Simeon looked for "the consolation of Israel"—the man dealt with the large scale, Israel; and the woman dealt with the minute and the near-at-hand, Jerusalem. In this they ran true to form—man thinks of the magnificent; woman thinks of the minute. Each is needed to bring in the Kingdom.

Out of this Redemptionist Group at Jerusalem came two movements—one the movement of John the Baptist, and the other the movement of Jesus—two of the mightiest movements that ever touched our planet. The movement of John the Baptist emphasized the equalitarian attitudes of the Redemptionists: "Every valley shall be filled"—the depressed and underprivileged shall be leveled up; "every mountain and hill shall be brought low"—the overprivileged shall be brought down; "the crooked shall become straight"—men shall be judged by merit rather than by cleverness and cunning; "and all flesh shall see the salvation of God"—this equality of opportunity is open to "all flesh," rather than to racial or national groups. (Luke 3:4–6.) John continued this equalitarian emphasis in very practical application when he said, "He that hath two coats, let him impart to him that hath none; and he that hath food, let him do likewise." (Luke 3:11.)

Jesus took up the same note: "Go, sell that which thou hast, and give to the poor, ... and come, follow me." "It is my will to give unto this last, even as unto thee." Equality of opportunity before God and man and life was the keynote of the Redemptionists, and their message was caught up and fulfilled in the Kingdom which Jesus proclaimed. This small group, then, was the seed plot of a new order.

Today we must have groups which, while the old order is going to pieces, contain in themselves the germs of a new order. These small disciplined groups are the hope of the future, for the future is in them.

God, our Father, help me to become a part of those who belong not to yesterday and today only, but to tomorrow. For the yesterdays and the todays have been shocked and are shakable. Help us to be the epitome of the unshakable; help us to be ready with our answer when the half-answers break down. In Jesus' name. Amen.

Luke 12:32; Matt. 17:20; 13:31–32; Mark 9:23; Phil. 4:13

DOING THE IMPOSSIBLE

The key sentence of the Redemptionists is to be found in these words: "With God nothing is ever impossible" (Luke 1:37, Moffatt); and in Mary's response to the angel's summons to be the physical vehicle of God's redemption: "I am here to serve the Lord. Let it be as you have said" (vs. 38). The group and the individual put themselves at God's disposal. God worked through both—mightily!

The most absolutely potent thing on this planet is a small disciplined group, disciplined to great ends. A group of raindrops gathering together on a mountainside are the beginnings of a mighty river. A seed is a group of forces dedicated to growth. Jesus speaks of the seed as "the word of the kingdom" (Matthew 13:19); but He goes on and says, "The good seed, these are the sons of the kingdom" (vs. 38). Here "the word of the kingdom" becomes flesh in "the sons of the kingdom." The Sons of the Kingdom are the seeds of the new Order. They do not give the word—they are the word. They do not seek an answer—they are the answer, the Kingdom in miniature. There is nothing so absolutely potent as such a group unbreakably given to each other and unreservedly given to God. They are seed, and there is nothing more powerful than a seed.

It doesn't take many people to accomplish things. A small determined and disciplined minority can do anything. Someone has said: "Five per cent of the people think; 10 per cent of the people think they think, and the rest of the people would rather die than think." It is that 5 per cent that changes situations. A handful of people made Germany Nazi, and Italy Fascist. In 1914 someone said that to find two Communists in Paris (the home of Communism) would be a wonder, and to find four would be a miracle. And yet in five years the Communists had captured Russia and challenged the world. Less than a hundred people produced both the Renaissance and the Reformation in Europe. Ten people produced the Federal Union of America. Dr. W. H. Welch of Johns Hopkins, with a small disciplined group of young doctors around him, changed the medical life of America for decades.

Gracious Father, I see that if I am in a minority with Thee, then anything can happen. I am determined to stay in that minority with Thee—at any cost. For I see that "with Thee nothing is impossible." I am at Thy disposal: "I am here to serve the Lord." Amen.

1 Pet. 1:22–23; Matt. 25:34–40; Eph. 2:19–22

A TRACKAGE FOR FELLOWSHIP

We have been studying corporate living in the small disciplined group. We must go further and look at the laws that underlie corporate living. There is a way to get along with people, and that way is God's way. That way is written into the constitution of our relationships and is definable according to certain well-ascertained laws of association.

As you begin corporate living, let it be burned into your consciousness that life is social and that there are definite laws of association and corporate living. You can make a trackage for fellowship. Corporate living requires intelligence as well as good will.

1. *You must not try to dominate the group.* That is fatal, for it begets the same thing in others; and the stage is then set for clash and strife. At the threshold of corporate living there is self-surrender. "I cannot dominate her mind," said a bewildered man who was dealing with a strong-minded woman in his employ. I told him he had to give up the desire to dominate and begin to cultivate the will to co-operate. That changes your attitude and allows you to see the truth in the other person's position rather than to be always trying to get your position across.

2. *You must not try to use the group.* It can be sensed at once if you are trying to use the group for any ulterior purpose—self-aggrandizement, self-display, business, social climbing, a desire to stand in.

3. *Acquire and cultivate the power to put yourself in the other person's place.* That imaginative sympathy is the key to life, in fact, is life itself, for life is sensitiveness. One of the secrets of Jesus' power over us is just this quality of imaginative sympathy. But it is not just sympathy in imagination—it is sympathy in fact, or, literally, "suffering with." Our hunger becomes His; our bondages are His very own —"I was an hungred, and ye gave me meat: . . . . in prison, and ye came unto me." To the degree that we acquire and cultivate this spirit of imaginative sympathy are we Christian and can get along with other people.

O God, in this delicate, difficult, but delightful business of getting along with people, give me skill and insight and patience—infinite patience. Thou art patient with me in spite of my blunderings—help me to be patient with others, for they, too, have to put up with me. Amen.

Prov. 25:8–11; Matt. 5:25; 7:1–5; 1 John 2:8–10

FURTHER STEPS IN CORPORATE LIVING

We continue our ladder for corporate living.

4. *Determine to hold no secret criticism of one another.*
A motto in our Ashram says: "Fellowship is based on confidence; secret criticism breaks that confidence; therefore we will renounce all secret criticism." If there is no outer criticism, then we know there is no inner criticism; so the fellowship is relaxed and unrestrained. We must welcome the mutual helpfulness of constructive criticism, for "the best of us are only Christians in the making." If we are afraid of criticism we are living on the defensive, living by fear rather than by faith. Let us lower the barriers and welcome the worst, and we will probably find the best!

5. *Don't look for perfection in people.* You have to get along with yourself in spite of yourself, so make up your mind to get along with others in spite of themselves.

6. *Look on others, not as they are, but as they can be.*
That was the secret of Jesus' influence on people. He believed in them when they couldn't believe in themselves, for He saw them, not as they were, but as they could be by His help. That attitude will give you, not a querulous mood of dissatisfaction with others, but a constructive mood of expectancy of possibilities. I find myself responding to Jesus' faith in me when I have no faith in myself. I have faith in His faith!

7. *Determine to settle differences as they arise—don't let them get cold.* Most misunderstandings could be dissolved by quick action. If you let them go they fester. "Agree with thine adversary quickly, whiles thou art in the way with him."

8. *Refuse to look for slights.* Those who look for them usually find them. Have a great purpose that absorbs your attention so that you will actually not know when you are slighted. As someone says: "Having a share in shaping the world is much more important than our private happenings."

God, my Father, we begin to see that Thy way is the way, not merely of theology, but of life. For Thou has set us in relationships. "To be is to be in relationships." Help me to bring to those relationships Thy unfailing patience and good will, that I may be the dissolver of misunderstandings and the healer of hurts. In Jesus' name. Amen.

Job 22:21; Rom. 14:17; 12:10–18; I Tim. 1:4–7; II Tim. 2:24–26

KEEP THE LARGE OUTLOOK AND SPIRIT

We continue our steps for corporate living:

9. *Don't allow yourself to become petty—keep big.*
When some elements in Israel would not acknowledge Saul
as king, "he held his peace." A smaller man would have
gone into a fit of temper. Saul was never more kingly than
in that silence under provocation. "I'm not big enough, or
those things wouldn't hurt me," said a missionary with a
sigh, as he found his majestic lifework spoiled by his allowing trivialities to upset him.

10. *Look for privileges of service rather than for your
rights.* The person who goes around insisting on rights never gets them. For rights are not something that can be given
—they have to be earned. And they are earned as you give
service to others. The one who serves others gets more
rights than he knows what to do with.

11. *Don't try to do people good—love them.* Tagore
says: "He who tries to do people good stands knocking at
the door, but he who loves finds the door open." If anybody
wants to do me good, I feel like dodging around the corner;
but if anyone loves me, I'm conquered at once. A loving attitude opens all doors, anywhere in the world.

12. *Often decide with the group against yourself.* For the
group can see more objectively than you can. Keep the
power to say, "I'm sorry." Those who are always right are
always wrong. By their very attitudes they are always
wrong.

13. *If there is any basic injustice in the relationships in
the group, don't counsel patience only—right the injustice.*
It is impossible to have real fellowship over and around a
basic injustice. That basic injustice will plague your fellowship and spoil it. Right the injustice, and fellowship will
come naturally.

14. *Don't try to have fellowship—work together for
great ends and fellowship will follow.* If you try to have fellowship, you will achieve only stilted niceties. But if you
work for great Kingdom ends, the fellowship will come as a
by-product. Don't work for fellowship, but fellowship for
great causes.

O Christ, we thank Thee that in discovering the ends of
Thy Kingdom we are discovering one another. The Cause
makes us coalesce. Then fuse us together in bonds of great
endeavors. For we would not mull around on ourselves, but
be freed for Thy purposes. In Jesus' name. Amen.

Rom. 12:3–8; Eph. 4:25; John 15:11; Phil. 2:2–4

ORGANS FOR ONE ANOTHER

15. *Remember, we are "organs for one another."* This conception of Paul will keep us from jealousies. If we are "organs for one another," then the other person fills out and complements me where I am weak. If a person can sing better than I can, then that person is my organ of song —I am complemented by his strength. If another can manage things better than I can, then I must not be jealous, but recognize him as my organ of executive ability. Perhaps there is something I can do better than the other person—I am his organ in that particular thing. Such an attitude will cause us to be filled, not with jealousy, but with pride in the other person's ability.

16. *Expect the best from others.* If you expect the best, you will probably get it; if you expect the worst, you will probably get that. "According to your faith be it unto you."

17. *Help others to help themselves—don't smother them by being overanxious to help.* Be a maker of men. "Now I've really succeeded," said a great Y.M.C.A. secretary as he saw an Indian whom he had trained elected to take his place. Developing others is the only success. Don't be a benevolent tyrant. Let people around you grow.

18. *Keep your power of laughter.* When things become tense, burst out laughing on general principles. Practice laughing at yourself before the looking-glass. If you lose your power to laugh, you are sunk. Then make your voice smile when you talk. Voice cultivation is cultivating the voice to express love.

19. *Keep the thought ever before your group that the group is disciplined by something beyond itself—the Kingdom.* The group must never become an end in itself—it must remain a means to the ends of the Kingdom. If it becomes an end, it will become self-righteous and "more holy than thou" in its attitudes. It must have a constant sense of accountability to the Kingdom.

God, our Father, help me in this group to be the kind of person I want others to be. Help me to remember that people are lonesome and need love. Help me to give it unstintingly and without reserve. Help me to take the initiative and not wait for others to do so. For Thou didst not wait for me to take the initiative. I thank Thee. Amen.

Ps. 133:1; Matt. 2:1–3, 9–12; Acts 6:3; Eph. 4:13–16

GENERAL THOUGHTS ON GROUP LIVING

Some general thoughts in summing up group living:

1. God abides in and uses group life especially. "Where two or three are gathered together in my name, there am I in the midst of them." It is safer for God to use a group than to use an individual. Use of an individual may result in individualism in society, but use of a group results in corporate emphasis. The individual finds himself in that corporate living.

2. The group life must be organized around embodied objectives and not around hazy ideas, if it is to survive. The Redemptionists at Jerusalem lived on in the movement of Jesus because they were organized around the idea of equality to all. That idea is fermenting in the world, and may yet save it. The Magi, another group movement, were stargazers. They came to the Cradle, gave their homage, returned, and were never heard of again. Their movement faded out. It was organized around stargazing—it wasn't concrete or embodied. Joe Louis and Nova met for a physical encounter. They represented two ideas. Louis represented the upsurge of desire for the freedom of a people. When he struck a blow, consciously or unconsciously, that blow was for the freedom of a suppressed race. Nova, having dabbled in Hindu mysticism, believed that if you were attuned to the cosmos, you could strike a cosmic blow—the universe would strike as you struck. So a racial punch and a cosmic punch met. The racial punch knocked out the cosmic punch. Why? Well, for one thing the racial punch of Louis had a concrete cause—the freedom of a people here and now. Nova represented, in his punch, a hazy, disembodied ideal—the cosmos would strike with him. That hazy, disembodied ideal went down before the embodied cause.

Let the group take this to heart. If its driving ideas are hazy, disembodied, and out of gear with concrete reality, then the group will be pushed aside by movements which have concrete objectives in which the members have a definite task to accomplish. Let the Church also take this to heart. The future belongs to movements which are geared into concrete accomplishable tasks.

God, I would learn to submerge my will and affection in a larger will and a larger affection, that I may find my will and my affection purified, clarified, and enlarged by the group life. Help me to lose my life that I might find it again. Amen.

Eph. 5:25–33; Col. 3:18–19; Gal. 5:13–16

GUIDANCE FOR FAMILY RELATIONSHIPS

While we are discussing disciplined corporate living we will pass on some suggestions about making the marriage relationship the best it can be. The most of these suggestions are those of Dr. Paul Popenoe, as expressed in an article by Emmet Crozier in the *American Magazine* for June, 1933,[1] with added suggestions of my own here and there.

General rules for both husband and wife: (1) Don't nag. (2) Don't try to make your partner over. (3) Don't criticize. (4) Give honest appreciation. (5) Give little attentions. (6) Read a good book on the sexual side of marriage —marriage has a physical basis which should be adjusted satisfactorily to both.

For Husbands: To the following questionnaire you may answer, giving ten points to yourself if you can answer them in the affirmative.

1. Do you still "court" your wife with an occasional gift of flowers, with remembrance of her birthday and wedding anniversary, or with some unlooked-for attention and tenderness?

2. Are you careful never to criticize her before others?

3. Do you give her money, above the household expenses, to spend entirely as she chooses?

4. Do you make an effort to understand her varying feminine moods and help her through periods of fatigue, nerves, and irritability?

5. Do you share at least half of your recreation hours with your wife?

6. Do you take a definite interest in her intellectual life, her clubs and societies, the books she reads, her views on civic problems?

7. Do you keep alert for opportunities to praise her and express your admiration for her?

8. Do you thank her for the little jobs she does for you, such as sewing on a button or sending your clothes to the cleaner?

9. Do you ever pray together, go to church together?

10. Do you keep the shrine of your heart intact for her?

Our Father, who hast set us in families, and hast put us there to procreate the race, and to train us in the art of living together that we might make a Family of God out of the world chaos, help us to begin where we are. Help us to make the Kingdom operative in the little things of the home. Thus we shall be ready for the Greater Family. In His name. Amen.

[1] Reprinted by permission.

Gal. 3:28; 5:22–26; Eph. 4:1–6

GUIDANCE PARTICULARLY FOR WIVES

We continue our study of how to live together in the family unit.

For Wives: 1. Do you have an intelligent grasp of your husband's business so that you can discuss it with him helpfully?

2. Can you meet financial reverses bravely, cheerfully, without criticizing your husband for his mistakes, or comparing him unfavorably with more successful men?

3. Do you make a special effort to get along amiably with his mother or his other relatives?

4. Do you dress with an eye for your husband's likes and dislikes in color and style?

5. Do you compromise little differences of opinion in the interests of harmony?

6. Do you keep track of the day's news, the new books and new ideas so that you can hold your husband's intellectual interest?

7. Do you keep up your own prayer life so that you may meet every situation that arises in the home with the sense of poise, of divine direction and insight?

8. Have you made a little shrine in the home where your husband, you, or your children can retire and be undisturbed for quiet meditation and prayer?

9. Have you learned to say, "I am sorry," or are you always right?

10. Are you keeping up your church relationships and are you making them real, or do you just send your children to Sunday school?

11. Are you the kind of person you want your children and your husband to be?

General suggestion for both parties:

"Refrain from sharing such interests with other persons of the opposite sex as are likely to draw one into a relationship that is a threat to the marriage relation. We *can* help to keep ourselves from entangling alliances by *never starting* to share such implicating interests with the opposite sex as would lead to intimacy." (*The Family Lives Its Religion*, Regina Westcott Wieman, Harper, 1941, p. 80.)

God, these tender relationships of the home can be a shrine or they can be a snarl. Keep my inner shrine from all divided loyalties and from all querulous attitudes and from all worry and anxiety. Let me approach each day with confidence that "I can do all things through Christ which strengtheneth me." Amen.

I Cor. 9:24–27; I Tim. 6:11–12

I WILL NOT LET ANYTHING MASTER ME

The will-to-live is the urge in everything. Everything lifts up strong hands after perfection. The urge for completion is perhaps the most insistent of all urges. Religion is rooted in this life urge—religion is the life urge turned qualitative. We want to live, not merely fully, but better. The will to live may turn into the mere will to power unless ruled by qualitative factors. The will to mastery may become the will to tyranny unless controlled by the will of God.

Paul suggested this will to mastery in these words: " 'All things are lawful for me'? Yes, but I am not going to let anything master me." (I Corinthians 6:12, Moffatt.) That phrase, "I am not going to let anything master me," is one of the greatest phrases declaring a life purpose that has ever been uttered. The man who was completely mastered by the will of God said that he would not be mastered by *any-thing*. The opposite of that holds good: If you are not mastered by God you will be mastered by things, by yourself, by other persons, by circumstances, by the world, or by sorrows and disappointments.

Take the last two things that master us: the world, and sorrows and disappointments. Some are mastered by the world. It is usually a very slow and silent process. We scarcely know what is happening, but we are slowly mastered by a materialistic outlook. The story goes that a robin was offered a worm for a feather. The bird thought this a good bargain—it would save a lot of hunting for worms and he would not miss a feather. But one dreadful day the robin awoke to the fact that his feathers were gone and he could not fly. He had sold his power to fly for worms. He was earth-bound. The counterpart of that is happening all around us—the powers of soul, the ability to soar, are bartered for physical things. Soon the man is a dead soul surrounded by many things.

Then others are mastered by some bereavement or disappointment. They retreat into the kennel of life like a whipped dog. Life is too much for them. They are beaten. There they give themselves to inward self-pity. The will-to-live has become the will-to-complain-of-life.

O God, apart from Thee I am mastered by this, that, or the other. With Thee I am mastered by nothing—except Thee. Then I am free. Save me from being mastered by any sorrow or disappointment. Help me to rise, like an airplane, against resistances. In Jesus' name. Amen.

John 15:11; 16:33; Rom. 8:35–39

ABUNDANT LIVING "IN SPITE OF"

Abundant living is sometimes on account of, but more often, perhaps, in spite of. When circumstances are against us, we must be able to set the sails of our souls and use even adverse winds. The Christian faith does not offer exemption from sorrow and pain and frustration—it offers the power, not merely to bear, but to use adversities. The secret of using pain and suffering and frustration is in many ways life's greatest secret. When you have learned that, you are unbeatable and unbreakable.

A young doctor said to me: "Your way of life is different from that of the psychoanalyst, who gives the patient a knowledge of himself and then hopes to resolve his difficulties; it is also different from that of the Meyer school, which would change the environment when disturbing factors are found there. You go beyond: you give a man a knowledge of himself, try to change his environment where possible, and then get the patient to lay hold on the resources of God, so that if he can't change his environment, he can use his adverse surroundings and make them serve his purposes. Yours is a more complete and adequate way of life." He was right, except that it isn't my way! I discovered it! It is Christ's way.

The Christian "can take it," because he can take hold of adversity and use it. A teacher of slum children was drawing up a list of the qualities in Jesus which appealed to the youngsters. When the list was apparently completed, a grimy-handed newsboy put up his hand and said, "They hung him on a cross, and he could take it." The boy was right, but the reason He could take it was not because of a stoic attitude. The reason goes deeper: He could take it because He could use it. He bore the cross, for He could use the cross. You cannot bear the cross long—it will break your spirit, unless you can take that cross and make it serve higher purposes. The stoic bears the cross; the Christian makes the cross bear fruit.

Any movement that has learned the secret of making the bitterest tree—the cross—bear the sweet fruit has learned the secret of abundant living.

O Christ, we begin to see Thy secret. Thou didst lay hold of life when life was speaking its cruelest word and didst turn that very word into God's most redemptive word. Thou didst not bear the cross—Thou didst use it. Give me power to do just that. Then, in Thee, I am invincible. Amen.

Matt. 5:43–48; Rom. 12:17–21; 1 John 4:21

LET YOUR PEACE RETURN TO YOU

In connection with what Jesus was saying to His disciples, He added: "If the household is deserving, let your peace rest on it; but if the household is undeserving, let your peace return to you." (Matthew 10:13, Moffatt.) In other words, if the people will not take your peace, it returns to you—you get the peace you have, plus the peace you gave! You win in either way. It is a question of "Heads, I win; tails, you lose." Perhaps you have heard of the stone fence so broad that when it blew over it was as high as it was before! The Christian is like that! He thrives on difficulties, for he turns his very difficulties into doors, his Calvaries into Easter mornings.

Are you criticized? Then, if the criticisms are true, correct the thing criticized. Make your critics "the unpaid watchmen of your soul." All of us are "only Christians in the making"; so make your criticisms make you. If the criticisms are false, then let them make no difference in your attitude toward the critic. Let your thoughts of him turn to prayer. Out of the injustice you will wrest a moral victory. You will have no enemies, for you will have no enmity. It is an easy and bloodless way to get rid of your enemies! The only possible way to get rid of an enemy is to turn him into a friend. Even if he doesn't acknowledge that he is a friend and continues to act like an enemy, nevertheless, you have transformed him into a friend in two ways: You have only friendly feelings toward him, and you can turn his very criticisms and make them make you. Whether he wants to be or not, he is your friend. You are master.

The only way to overcome your enemy is not to be like him. Don't let him put his weapons into your hands. If he gives enmity, you give love. Keep your own weapons. Two hates never made a love affair. You be master.

Remember the phrase: "A soul breathing peace"—be that kind of a person: breathe peace upon everybody. If they don't take it, then it comes back to you.

Gracious Master, I would walk amid adversity with my head up. But I cannot do this unless I lay my head in the dust at Thy feet to learn Thy ways. For Thy ways are ways of mastery. Nothing daunted Thee; nothing stopped Thee. In Thee, too, I am invincible—humbly, gladly, joyously so. Help me to be so overflowing that I may swamp everything —enmity and all. Amen.

Jer. 5158 (Moffatt); Rom. 8:16–33; II Cor. 7:8–12

PAIN IS GOD'S PREVENTIVE GRACE

Christianity survived the worst thing that could happen to it, namely, the death of its Founder, and turned that worst thing that could happen to it into the best thing that could happen to the world. It redeemed the world through a catastrophe. A faith that can do that has survival value, and will outlast all the shallow-rooted, surface philosophies of life. Nothing less than that kind of a philosophy of life can stand up to life.

We can see why God allows pain—it is His preventive grace. Had there been no pain in the world, we should not have survived as a race. For instance, were there no pain attached to disease, we should probably allow disease to eat on—it doesn't hurt; so why bother? But pain stabs us broad awake and says: "Look out—there is something wrong here; attend to it." Pain is God's red flag run up to warn of underlying lurking danger. We can then thank God for pain.

But this we cannot do unless we can do something with pain other than bearing it stoically. Unless pain is working out to some end, it breaks us by its meaninglessness. That is why the prophet saw that "pagans waste their pains." (Jeremiah 51:58, Moffatt.) Those who live without the God-reference—the pagans—don't know what to do with pain; they waste it. Their pains end in mere dull, fruitless, meaningless suffering. It gets them nowhere. So much of the world's suffering is wasted. During 1914–18 we suffered dreadfully, and yet we wasted that world pain. The best that we could do with it was to coin it into the Versailles Treaty; and now we are back again, compelled to go through the whole miserable business once more. We may do the same thing with this present world pain unless we can transmute it into a determined purpose to make a new world out of it, so that war may never happen again. Only where we see redemption in pain can we have any release while in it—purposeless pain is paralyzing.

Christ, Thou master of the central pain, help us to master both the central and the marginal pains. Help me to take hold of life when life is hard and impossible, and thus make life not only possible, but also full of possibilities. For the struggle is on—I am to master, or to be mastered. Help me to master, through Thee, O Master. Amen.

Phil. 1:12–18; Acts 16:6–10; Gal. 4:13

DEFLECTED GRACE

If "pagans waste their pains," then we as Christians must learn to make our pains productive. Yesterday we saw that pain can be used for a purpose—redemptive pain. Paul speaks of "the pain God is allowed to guide" (II Corinthians 7:10, Moffatt)—there can be a God-guided pain. Pain can be taken up into the purposes of God and transformed into finer character, greater tenderness, and more general usefulness. It can be made into the pains of childbirth—it can bring forth new life.

Take one of the most difficult pains to bear—the frustration of one's life plans. This often throws confusion into everything, for everything had been geared into those life plans. How did Jesus meet such a situation? A small incident reveals His secret.

When Jesus healed the demoniac, the people came and saw the man, seated, "clothed, and in his right mind: and they were afraid." Afraid of sanity! They begged Jesus "to depart out of their coasts." His presence had cost them too much. He thought men were worth more than swine. Anyone who thinks that is dangerous! It is disconcerting—and to some, discouraging—to find one's best endeavors blocked by ignorance and self-centered greed.

But was Jesus blocked by this ignorance and greed? No; He was not blocked, but diverted. His grace was not dammed, but deflected. It simply turned in another direction. So He embarked—frustrated? Oh, no! The grace was deflected toward other people and situations. He did some of the greatest things of His life as a result of that blocking —that blocking turned to blessing! He healed a paralytic, called Matthew, taught regarding conservatism, healed a woman with a hemorrhage, raised the dead, and so on and on. The frustration turned to fruitfulness. If He couldn't do this, He could do that. And that "that" had in it a deeper quality of character—it had in it a victory over bitterness and resentment. So "that" was finer than "this." He gained not only victory, but victory—plus!

O Christ, I will be undeterred by petty or by decisive blocking of my plans. In neither case will I stop. I will find a way around if I cannot get through. Give me that resilience of spirit that bends, but is never broken. For upon life's resistances I will rise. Help me to be equal to anything —by Thy power. Amen.

Luke 10:25-37; 15:2-7

FRUSTRATIONS BECOMING FRUITFUL

Yesterday we saw how Jesus' life was not dammed, but deflected by opposition and frustration. That very opposition can be a spur.

Glenn Cunningham, the man who became the fastest human in a mile race, was so badly burned as a lad that the doctors thought he would always be in an invalid's chair. The boy who was destined to be an invalid turned that destiny into becoming the world's fastest human. Whistler, the painter, wanted to be a soldier; but he failed at West Point, and turned to the brush as a second choice. Walter Scott wanted to be a poet and gave up because he could not equal Byron. Ashamed of being a novelist, he wrote anonymously—but he gave the world *Ivanhoe*. A young university man had both his hands blown off in an explsion; since he could no longer use his hands he decided he would use his head the more, and became a teacher in a great university. Phillips Brooks wanted to be a teacher, failed miserably, and turned reluctantly to being a preacher, becoming one of the world's greatest.

Someone asked a man about his constitution, and he replied: "That's gone long ago—I'm now living on the by-laws." Some people live better on their by-laws than most people on their constitutions. Kagawa does—he lives radiantly and effectively on one lung, and does more with that lung than most people do with two!

Perhaps you find yourself in difficulties and frustrations because of your Christian stand. Then you will have to do as John did: "I . . . . found myself in the island called Patmos, for adhering to God's word"—isolated because of conviction. But the verse continues: "On the Lord's day I found myself rapt in the Spirit, and I heard a loud voice . . . . calling, 'Write your vision.'" (Revelation 1:9-11, Moffatt.) Isolated from men, he saw heaven opened and received the vision of the coming victory. Isolation became revelation.

Are your life plans broken up? Then you can, by God's grace, make new and better ones.

Victorious Christ, impart to me Thy secret. For life turns inevitable again and again. I am powerless to change my surroundings—then let me change my soul. And through that changed soul I shall make of unavoidable surroundings the whetstone upon which my soul shall be sharpened for Thy purposes. With Thee I cannot be beaten. Amen.

Acts 16:19–34; II Cor. 12:7–10; Matt. 10:23

ON USING ILLNESSES AND IMPEDIMENTS

We ended with the thought yesterday that frustrations can forward us. Paul was thrown aside at Galatia by an illness—frustrated? Oh, no! "It was because of an illness . . . . that I preached the gospel to you." (Galatians 4:13, Moffatt.) Thrown aside by an illness, he used that frustration and preached the gospel, through it raised up a Christian Church and wrote a letter to it—a letter which has enriched the world. That is victory.

When Paul asked God to take away the "thorn in the flesh, the messenger of Satan to buffet" him, he received the reply, "My grace is sufficient for thee: for my strength is made perfect in weakness." He was promised, not deliverance, but power to use the infirmity. He arose and said, "Most gladly therefore will I rather glory in my infirmities, ... for when I am weak, then am I strong." If the messenger of Satan was to buffet him he would determine the direction in which the blows would send him. They sent him forward! The World War left a man a cripple, confined to bed. Beaten? Oh, no! From that bed he runs a very large business and his home is the center of wholesome gaiety. He might have made his mother into an attendant on his needs. He refused; he and his mother both live out their lives in individual achievement and beautiful co-operation.

The world's greatest preacher could say, "I am no speaker, perhaps" (II Corinthians 11:6, Moffatt); but did that lack of oratorical ability stop Paul? It only spurred him on to primary successes. Had he been a good speaker, in all probability he would have depended on that, and a secondary success would have blocked a primary success. Many people are ruined by secondary successes—they become entangled in their techniques and never get to the goal. One of the most spiritually useful men in America rather glories in being his "state's worst speaker." He is, but he made that kick send him forward—he functions where his usefulness really matters.

Jesus, Thou master of every situation—even upon a cross, where Thou didst dispense forgiveness to crucifiers and gave absolution to a dying thief—give me this mastery over circumstances. For I am not beaten until beaten within. With Thee, I am not beaten there. Abide with me, and then I can abide with anything. Amen.

Matt. 14:12–21; 16:21; I Pet. 2:21–24

WORKING WITH A WOUND IN YOUR SIDE

So important is this power to turn the worst into the best, that we must tarry another week with it. For if we learn this secret, we know how to live. If we don't learn it, then we fumble this business of living. It is simply impossible, in reference to suffering, always to explain why. You cannot unravel the mystery of suffering and give a logical answer. But, while you cannot explain the Why, you can learn the How—the How of victory over it and through it and around it. There is no logical answer, but there is a life answer—you can use suffering. It is much better to give a vital answer than a verbal one. Cease worrying over the Why, and get to the How!

Look at this picture: Jesus had just heard that John the Baptist, His cousin and forerunner and beloved friend, had been beheaded, and the account continues: "When Jesus heard it, he withdrew by boat to a desert place in private" —He wanted to be alone to let the wound in His heart heal a bit—"but the crowds heard of it and followed him on foot from the towns"—they broke up His plans. "So when he disembarked, he saw a large crowd, and out of pity for them he healed their sick folk." (Matthew 14:13–15, Moffatt.) And then He fed the multitude. He worked for others with a wound in His own breast. Many of us have to go through life working with a wound. But that wound, instead of making Him bitter against the injustice of John's beheading, made Him more tender with others: *"out of pity* for them he healed their sick" and fed their hungry. If you have to work with a wound in your side, remember, that wound will be healing to others—your very hunger for consolation can feed others.

Just before he was to speak in the chapel in India, a missionary friend received a cable that his father had died. He said nothing to us before the service, but went on and preached a tenderly beautiful message—the transcript of his own beautiful soul. Only after the service did he tell us he had received the cable. He worked with a wound—and that wound was healing, to others.

Master of the inward wound, teach us Thy mastery. May I not wince, nor turn back, nor glance back, even in thought, when wounded by life. Help me to go steadily on, knowing that Thy wounds are answering my wounds. It may be that my wounds shall answer someone else's wounds. For this is a hurt world. Make my hurts healing. In Thy name. Amen.

Isa. 37:3–7; 41:10, 13; 42:16

THE BERRY IN THE MOUTH

In Africa there is a berry which, when held in the mouth, sweetens the taste of everything the African eats. The Christian has something like that—he has the power to transform every calamity into opportunity. That power to use everything is the berry that sweetens the bitterest calamity.

Someone has spoken of "getting music out of life's remainders." Somtimes life leaves nothing on our hands but remainders. But you can gather up those remainders and make music out of them? Such a person I saw yesterday—a person whose face was chiseled into strength and beauty. She was stricken with infantile paralysis at twenty-eight; her husband died when she was forty-five. She decided she would walk, even after the doctors told her the muscles were gone. She created new muscles out of her own will and the grace of God. At forty-seven she took a course in stenography, typing, and secretarial work and is now doing what everybody else is doing—and more, she is doing it in a radiant, triumphant way. She is making music out of life's remainders.

"A Christian is a man who, when he gets to the end of his rope, ties a knot and hangs on." For he knows that very extremity is God's opportunity. Someone has suggested that the "silence in heaven about the space of half an hour," spoken of in Revelation, was God shifting the scenes for the next act. The silent, suffering spaces in your life may be God getting you ready for the next great act. Hold steady; the next act will come. In the meantime, take hold of your dull drab moments and make them give forth music. Speaking of a certain person, someone suggested: "Give him a laundry list and he will set it to music."

The latent possibilities are all there in life—bring out of it what you will. The Russians say: "A hammer shatters glass but forges steel." The calamities that shatter some will forge you into character and achievement.

O God, my Father, I see I need not whine nor complain. I can make music out of misery, a song out of sorrow, and achievement out of accident. I cannot be beaten. For everything is grist for my mill. I will turn everything, good, bad, and indifferent, into something else. I thank Thee. Amen.

Gal. 4:13–15; Joel 2:25–32

BLIND AND DEAF, YET ADEQUATE

We spoke yesterday of a berry in the mouth that sweetens everything. That berry is a spirit of courage and faith. A brilliant young man, my first Sunday-school scholar, was surveying a swamp near a powder factory. He struck a piece of board on which there was a blister of nitroglycerin, and it exploded, rendering him totally blind and deaf. At twenty-six he was blind and deaf—doomed to a dungeon existence without light, without sound.

"For twenty-four hours," he said, "I was beaten. 'None of my family ever dies before eighty, and I'm twenty-six,' I said to myself, inwardly beaten." But at the end of twenty-four hours he "snapped out of it," as he puts it, and determined to meet life as a Christian—he would find grace in the dungeon. He has. He brought a family into the world and supported them through a business he set up. There is no way of communicating with him except by printing out the letters of words on the back of his hand; so all the correspondence in his business goes, not through his hands, but on the back of his hand. When I asked him how it felt to be cut off from the world, he laughed and said, "I'm not cut off from the world." He isn't—every portion of his being is vibrant with receptivity. He is informed on everything.

To my question as to what was his greatest disability, he replied, "I have a bad temper and get angry with those I love." A blind and deaf man says his greatest disability is a moral disability! When I asked him if there was anything he did not want me to say about him, he replied: "Don't put it on too thick, for people will either think you are exaggerating, or that I'm a superman. Put it just where everybody can get it: nobody need be beaten, no matter what happens."

This man illustrates the fact that the thing that matters is not what happens to you, but what you do with it after it does happen. The Christian is afraid of nothing, for he can use everything.

Jesus said: "Nothing outside a man can defile him . . . . it is what comes from him that defiles him." (Mark 7:15, Moffatt.) Your reaction to what happens to you determines the result.

Brave Christ, make me brave. Even if the worst should happen to me, we can turn it into the best. I say "we," for I cannot do it alone. With Thee I can do anything, bear anything, go through anything. Without Thee I wither. But I am with Thee; so I face the future with calm joy. Everything is under my feet. Amen.

Phil. 1:12–14; Rom. 8:28–39

MAKING ALL THINGS WORK TOGETHER
FOR GOOD

We ended yesterday on the note that nothing need beat us, provided we have the right attitude of mind. When the storm strikes the eagle, if its wings are set in a downward tilt, it will be dashed to pieces on the earth; but if its wings are tilted upward, it will rise, making the storm bear it up beyond its fury. The set of the wings decides defeat or victory.

Chistianity gives a set of the soul, so that when trouble and frustration and disaster strike one, he goes up—his soul wings are set in that direction. The same disaster strikes another, and his soul attitudes are tilted earthward; so he writhes in anguish in the dust. Death strikes a home, and in it leaves bitterness and frustration; in another, calm and quiet victory and greater usefulness.

Some students discussing Romans 8:28 said to a professor in Union Theological College, Richmond, Virginia, "But, professor, you don't believe that all things work together for good—all the pain and suffering and misery—do you?" The professor replied, "The things in themselves may not be good, but you can make them work together for good." That afternoon his wife was killed in an automobile accident, and he was left a cripple. He sent for the president of the institution and said, "Tell my students that Romans 8:28 still holds good." He died in a year. They inscribed this passage from Romans on his tomb, for it was inscribed in his convictions. One of the greatest preachers of the Southland stood again and again beside that tomb with bared head and prayed that he might have that kind of grace. The professor has gone further in his influence through his triumphant spirit, seen, as in a flash, in that tragedy, than he would have gone through long years of mediocre teaching. One can live by the hourglass, or by the heartbeat, and sometimes those who live only in the heartbeat live more fully and more influentially.

O Christ, only through three short years didst Thou live and labor. But the eternities ware packed into the hours of those years. Whether I live short or long, let my hours have eternity packed into them. Wilt Thou not be in every one of those hours? And then nothing can make me afraid. For I have the secret. I can make all things work together for good. I thank Thee. Amen.

II Cor. 2:14; John 16:32–33; Luke 23:27–28

VICTORIOUS VITALITY MASTERING CIRCUMSTANCES

Victorious vitality is a vitality capable of mastering everything because it can use everything. It can lay hold on the raw materials of human living—justice and injustice, pleasure and pain, compliment and criticism—and take them up into the purposes of our lives and transmute them into character and usefulness.

Just across the hall from where I was staying a poor fellow, beaten by life, went into a clothes closet and hung himself on a clothes bar which was only five feet from the floor, so that he had to hold up his feet until life was extinct. In deep contrast to this man, is a woman in another town whom I went that day to see. She has been forty-four years upon her bed, but is unbeaten by life. On the contrary, she has mastered life. She had three diseases, any one of which would have killed a normal person; but she is the unkillable kind. She laughingly said, "These different disease germs fell to fighting each other down on the inside of me; and as they fought, they forgot about me, and I lived on."

Lying prone upon her back, she set up a gift shop, and began to make exquisite butterfly pendants. She was soon making enough money to pay an income tax. She laughingly said, "I sent off my check to the government with my love." When you can pay your income tax with your love —well, that's a miracle! A magazine gave her one hundred dollars for the story of her gift shop and then gave her one thousand dollars for the best true story of the year. A publisher, seeking the autobiographies of great Americans, happened on her life story; and at his request she has now written a hundred thousand words of her autobiography. Her room is the confessional of the city—the bedpost upon which I leaned was literally worn down with people leaning on it and telling this invalid their troubles. Young and old go away new after opening their hearts to her gentle wisdom and sympathy. She is seventy-two, but incorrigibly gay, her face made beautiful by the beautiful spirit that lives behind it.

O Christ of the exuberant joy, give me this joy—in spite of. Save me from all self-pity, all feeling sorry for myself, and let me be outgoing and positive, taking on myself the problems of others. Don't let any corroding sorrow invade me. Help me to keep my sorrows in use as the servants of the sorrows of others. In Jesus' name. Amen.

Eph. 3:13–21; I Thess. 5:23–24; Phil. 2:12–13

GOD'S WATCH-CARE—OVER OUR SPIRIT

The gift-shop lady of whom we wrote yesterday runs "The Doctors' Exchange" of the town. Sick people call up an invalid to find out where to get a doctor! When I asked her what was the central thought of the year she replied, "God's watch-care." Think of an invalid's choosing "God's watch-care" as her central thanksgiving! If God cared, then why did He not heal her?

In the Preface we said that God heals in eight great ways: through the surgeon, the physician, climate, mental suggestion, scientific nutrition, deliverance from underlying fears, resentments, self-centeredness and guilts, the direct operation of the Spirit of God, and through the resurrection. Whatever He does not cure through the first seven ways He will cure through the eighth—the resurrection. To some He entrusts the ministry of suffering until the Day of the Final Cure—the resurrection—in the meantime giving them power, not merely to bear the suffering, but to use it. The "watch-care" of which God's noblewoman spoke was "watch-care" over her spirit, that her spirit should remain unspoiled and sound. Healed at the heart, she could say, "Let the world come on!" Sound at heart, she was ready for anything. God's watch-care may be particularly exercised in producing inner attitudes, for in our inner attitudes the battle of life is lost or won.

A lady arose in one of our meetings and said that the doctors had given her six months to live—cancer of the lungs. "At first," she said, "I was bitter and rebellious—how could I leave my children and my husband? Then I said to myself, 'If I have only six months to live, am I going to leave my children a heritage of defeat and frustration? Is that the last thing they will remember about me? Or will they have a heritage of calm poise and victory?' I decided I would leave them a Christian heritage of victory. Ever since I surrendered my rebellion and bitterness there has been calm poise, and even joy. The fact is, I've gained ten pounds." God's watch-care was over her spirit—that was intact. Nothing else really mattered!

O God, watch over my spirit and keep me sound there. For if I sag in spirit, all life sags with it. If my spirit holds up, everything holds up with it. Then help me to live within with abundance, so that it will not matter much what happens on the outside. Into Thy hands I commend my spirit this day—keep it sound and sweet and gay, in spite of! Amen.

Luke 9:12–17; Jer. 1:4–8; Exod. 4:10–16

MAKING LIFE COUNT WITH SMALL EQUIPMENT

We cannot close this week's study of how to meet calamity and frustration in any better way than by recounting the story of a missionary family. The surviving son in the family, who had to cut short a theological course because of a very serious major operation, saw me off at an airport, and said, "I'm proud of my family." "Proud of my family"— and well he might be!

The parents went to China, and there the father contracted an infection which left him blind. The mother died of cancer after a painful, lingering illness. One son died in college of Addison's disease; another son died in college from an infection following an abrasion of the skin received while in athletic activities. The daughter was stricken with infantile paralysis, and now hobbles on crutches. This is the wreckage of a family that went forth from their homeland to serve China! Is there any watch-care of God here? Does He care at all? Why was the son proud of his family? Well he might be, for though the father and daughter left at home have only a seeing-eye dog and a pair of crutches between them as their physical equipment with which to meet life, yet they are meeting it gloriously. The father is pastor of a church, and the daughter keeps house for him—on crutches. More, she organizes the games of the church, drives a specially equipped car, and is her father's right hand. Together they go on unbeaten; and not only unbeaten, but amazingly useful. The father keeps a church going, and lectures all over the country. And, better than all, he keeps a radiant soul! Yes, the young man is right—he should be proud of his family; and we are proud of the young man who can look beyond the wreckage of his family and see there the essential victory of spirit. This is the victory that overcometh the world of sorrow and frustration, even our faith. If the faith is intact, nothing else really matters—you can rise unscathed from anything.

The Christian is safe because he can use anything that happens to him.

O Jesus, hanging on the cross Thou didst say, "My God," even when the light had gone out, and everything had collapsed. With those words on Thy lips Thou didst rise gloriously from gloom to glory. Let no sorrow, no disappointment, pluck those words, "My God," from my lips and from my heart; and I, too, shall prevail over everything. I thank Thee. Amen.

Luke 2:52; Ps. 8:1–9; 90:12–17

MAKING THE TIME PROCESS BEAUTIFUL

As the years go by, they leave their deposit of suffering in our minds, in our memories, in our bodies. We have seen how to meet these deposits. But many find that the greatest deposit of difficulty and suffering left by the time process is just the fact of the process. To adjust ourselves to the time process and achieve abundant living at each stage of the process is important.

Some people remain infantile and never really pass into stages of maturity. They bring over infantilisms with them into the advancing stages. They are misfits. Some who are growing old refuse to adjust themselves to that fact, and are always sighing to be young again—fruitlessly, of course.

To be victorious at each stage one must accept the fact of change and make out of that particular period through which he is passing something very beautiful and effective. For each stage of life has something peculiar to itself in possibility and achievement. Youth is not the only age of possibility—each stage is crammed with possibility of beauty and achievement. John saw in Revelation the tree of Life bearing twelve kinds of fruit, "each month having its own fruit." (Revelation 22:2, Moffatt.) On the tree of life here and now "each month has its own fruit"—each period has something distinctive in beauty and possibility—childhood, youth, middle age, old age.

We will not pause at childhood—though it is the most important age—for the simple reason that children will not read this book. But as we go on, the message of childhood to the older stages can be summed up in a letter from a child to his parents: "Dear Mother—Father, I love you. You gave me life on earth in this body. I thank you for it. With all my heart I want to listen and learn from your experiences in life. I know that from this moment henceforth you will be just the best parents you are capable of being." Too mature? Probably; but childhood does say that, whether expressed in those words or not.

God, as we begin the adventure of living out each stage of life, give us insight and imagination that we may make each stage distinctive and beautiful. Help us not to waste our time in useless regrets, or in reaching for the moon; but help us to beautify the hours as they come and go, and to "press the signet ring of eternity upon each passing moment." Amen.

l Tim. 4:12; 5:1–2; Eccles. 12:1

A LADDER FOR YOUTH

We will begin with youth, the first stage in the life process, and give a ladder to climb upon.

1. *You are an awakening personality; let your whole being—body, mind, and spirit—awaken simultaneously.* In the stage of physical awakening some young people become acutely aware of their bodies, and especially of the fact of sex. This is normal and right. But it is possible to become so tangled up in sex thought that you become body-minded. This may degenerate into habits of self-abuse, and the culture of the mind and soul be so neglected that you become a mere physical hulk. You must awaken in your total person —in your mind and soul as well as in your body—or you will be stunted in important portions of your being.

2. *Find a Cause to which you can devote your energies and which will give life meaning, coherence, and goal.* That Cause is the Kingdom of God. "Seek ye first the kingdom of God, ... and all these things shall be added unto you." If you get the first thing first, then your life will come out right. If you get the wrong thing first, then nothing will come out right.

3. *Find a Person who embodies that Cause—a Person to whom, when you are loyal, you are loyal to that Cause.* That Person is Christ. When you are loyal to Him, then you are loyal to God's Order, embodied in Him—the Kingdom. The Kingdom meets you personalized. You are not giving yourself to an impersonal order, but to an Order that has become warm and tender and personal in Christ.

4. *Make your life decisions yourself—don't drift.* Some allow their circumstances or their companions to decide their life decisions for them. They don't act—they only react.

5. *Don't revolt against the older group and then merely echo your own group.* That is substituting one bondage for another. When your group is wrong—dare to be different. Don't act by pressures, but by principles.

O God, I am beginning this business of living in a serious way. I want a Way. I don't want to drift from wave to wave of meaningless emotion—I want a Way. If Thou, O Christ, art the Way, I will follow Thee through thick and thin, through popularity or through disfavor. I want a Cause— Thou art that Cause. I choose. Amen.

Prov. 7:7–27

THE LADDER FOR YOUTH—Continued

We continue our ladder for youth:

6. *Stand on the shoulders of the older group, but don't kick their heads; they're not wooden—at least, not all of them.* Wisdom didn't begin with you, and it won't end with you. You will soon belong to the older group; then see that the next generation has a higher vantage point when it stands on your shoulders.

7. *Challenge everything, and then challenge yourself to make things better.* The only challenge that will be listened to is a demonstration of something better. The protest must not be merely verbal; it must be vital.

8. *Don't be impatient if the world doesn't change overnight at your command.* Some youth, because they cannot do everything, do nothing. Don't be absolutist—do the next thing, and thus prepare for that greater thing.

9. *Don't try to be a leader—be the servant of all and out of that service you will gain leadership as a by-product.* Jesus said, "Nor must you be called 'leaders.'" (Matthew 23:10, Moffatt.) The attitude of the leader is: "I lead; you follow"—it is self-assertive and thus cannot be Christianized. Out of that self-assertive mentality all you produce is fussy managers of other people. Besides, given a dozen people in one situation, each of whom wants to be leader, then what? You have the stage set for clash—struggle for place. Jesus said there was one title He could trust us with—"servant"; "the servant of all becomes the greatest of all." As you lose yourself in the service of all, then you will become great by that very self-losing. But note: "servant of all"—not the servant of some, your class, your race, your color; no, the servant of *all*. Then you will become truly great.

10. *Be thorough in the small tasks and opportunities—out of these small tasks well done will grow bigger ones.* "You have been trusty in charge of a small sum: I will put you in charge of a large sum." (Matthew 25:21, Moffatt.)

God, my Father, I am trying to climb out of unworthiness to worthiness, out of barren criticism to constructive contribution, out of myself into Thee. I cannot do this alone. I need Thee. I am leaning heavily upon Thy strength, depending on Thy resources, drawing on Thy power. Alone, I cannot succeed. Walk with me down the years and I cannot fail. Amen.

Luke 14:1–14; 22:39–46; Josh. 24:14–17

TAKING GOD INTO YOUR LIFE CHOICES

We conclude the ladder for youth:

11. *Take God into your choice of a life partner.* Base your choice on something more than a physical attraction. Find a partner, if possible, in whom you will be interested and with whom you will be in love when the sex side of life has been dimmed and only the mental and spiritual remain. In other words, somebody in whose conversation you will have a lifelong interest. But don't expect perfection, since you yourself will not bring it to the partnership.

12. *Youth is the age of struggle for freedom—gain freedom through discipline.* There are two ways to try to find freedom: one is to throw off all restraint, and the other is to find freedom through disciplined obedience to high, chosen ends. You don't gain freedom from the policeman on the street corner by disobeying the law—when you disobey it you are haunted by the policeman every moment—but you gain freedom by obeying the laws for which he stands. The whole evolution of morals is to take the policeman off the street corner and put him within your heart. Then you obey from within, and hence are truly free. Those who try to gain freedom by throwing off all restraint are free—to get into trouble with themselves and others.

13. *Start the day right, and you will probably end it right. Set aside some part of the morning hour for a quiet time with God.* A doctor, after listening to the discussions of some pagan psychiatrists, said to some fellow doctors: "I don't know how you fellows feel, but I'd like to go and give my brain a bath." You will need that daily brain and soul bath, preferably in the early morning. Fix the habit so that it is not a decision to be made daily. It is something to be taken for granted and fixed with no exceptions. When you do without your quiet time with God, then do without your breakfast as a penalty. Pray whether you feel like it or not —pray by the clock, if necessary. There will be a Hand on your shoulder as you go out into the day to begin your adventure with God.

O God, as I begin this day and this new way of life, I put my hand in Thine. May I not miss step with Thee today. May I literally be "controlled by the love of Christ." May my strong urges be taken hold of by Thy love and turned toward Kingdom ends. I offer Thee my powers as well as my weaknesses. In Jesus' name. Amen.

I Cor. 13:10–11; II Cor. 10:3–5; I John 2:14–17

A LADDER FOR MIDDLE AGE

We now present a ladder for middle age:

1. *Watch for decaying enthusiasms and ideals.* Look out for a desire for softness and comfort. Remember that if "heaven lies about us in our infancy," then the world lies about our middle age. You are very liable to settle down, become safe—and decay. A middle-aged woman said in one of our Ashrams: "I'm about to jell into the kind of a woman I don't want to be."

2. *Watch the growing power of money over you.* The person may gradually become a purse—stuffed and stuffy.

3. *Watch the growing power of the crowd upon you.* In middle age we cease being different, take on protective resemblance to our environment, fit into the crowd—and die of suffocation.

4. *Watch for a flare-up of sex.* "The dangerous forties" must now be extended to "the dangerous fifties" as the span of life grows longer. Don't be afraid of this period, for it has its compensations, but watch and control this period of "flare-up." If you are as good a man at forty as you were at twenty you may take courage.

5. *Watch your middle.* There are four signs of approaching age: baldness, bifocals, bridges, and bulges! Watch those bulges—you may have God fattened out of you.

6. *Be reconverted at forty, on general principles.* If you were converted in youth, be reconverted along about middle age to take you through the days ahead with victory and a growing spiritual vitality.

7. *Remain a hero to your child.* A youth said in one of our meetings, after his father had spoken: "I want to say ditto to what my father had said, only putting in some exclamation points." Your child dittoes you, with accentuation.

8. *Keep interests outside of your immediate family, so that when the children grow up and leave, you will not feel lost.*

9. *Keep a growing mind and soul after the body stops growing.* "Education is change"—then be continually educated.

10. *Keep a living center—God—amid all the changes.*

My Father God, I am now getting to the time of life when the fires of life tend to burn low. Oh, don't let them go out within me. For if they die, then I die. As I go along I am gathering experience—help me to make that larger experience into fuller expression. Help me to grow in usefulness and power and love. I thank Thee that I can and will. Amen.

Il Tim. 4:5–8; John 21:15–19

A LADDER FOR OLD AGE

We come now to the sacred task of setting up a ladder for old age. There is only one way to remain young and that is to grow old gracefully.

1. *Accept your age.* Each age has something beautiful in it. Don't fight the fact that you are getting old—use it. You can't be twenty-eight again; then make fifty-eight or sixty-eight beautiful and useful. Each age has its own peculiar beauty and makes its own contribution. I am fifty-eight and I love it—I wouldn't be twenty-eight for anything; fifty-eight is too interesting and too full and too adventurous! I am simply tingling with interests. And in the midst of these interests there is a calm and an undisturbable poise I did not have when younger. Life begins at fifty-eight!

2. *Accept the liberties that come through advancing age.* If youth has its liberties, so has advancing age. A wonderfully useful Quaker nurse said this to a group: "Beyond fifty, after my change in life, I found a freedom and a calm, and an interest in people as people, and not merely as sex beings." Her liberty to love and help others was very real. While women find these liberties from sex after fifty, men do not as a rule gain them until after sixty. Often there is a flaring up, just before passing out. But accept the liberty to love more fully and widely when it does come.

3. *Accept the responsibilities that come through that freedom.* Your children have grown up and gone; now see what you can do for other children. I know one woman who, when her own children grew up and went away, was responsible for putting through school not less than a dozen children; and she was not wealthy either, except in spirit and in good works. But what other wealth is there? If you cannot take children, then take other responsibilities.

4. *Never retire—change your work.* The human personality is made for creation; and when it ceases to create it creaks, and cracks, and crashes. You may not create as strenuously as before; but create. Otherwise you will grow tired resting. Create, create, create!

Creative God, after my body has ceased its sexually creative function, may my mind and my soul be creative, for they never tire, they never wear out. This vehicle of body may not respond as well as before, but help me to keep it keyed up, alert and fit, for purposes of the Kingdom of God. I am at Thy service—forever! Amen.

Ps. 92:14; Acts 2:17

THE LADDER FOR OLD AGE—Continued

We continue our suggestions for old age:

5. *Don't try to tie your children to you too closely—give them rope.* The children must have sufficient room to grow on their own. Say to them: "Never in the way, never out of the way." The Bible says: "For this cause shall a man leave father and mother, ... and they twain shall be one flesh." This recognizes the necessity of young people *leaving* father and mother in order to grow on their own. Don't interfere. Remember, you wanted liberty to make mistakes when you began on your own.

6. *Surrender to God your loved ones who have died.* Do not mourn over them in useless regret. A mother monkey will often carry around with it the decaying corpse of a dead baby. Such grief is pitiful and dangerous and useless, but not more so than that of a human mother who refuses to surrender the loved ones who have passed on. One such mother, years after her baby had died, had enough milk in her breasts for twins—the doctors treating her physically could not stop the lactation. An understanding friend saw what was happening: the mother had never inwardly surrendered her child; it was still at her breast, as it were. She surrendered it into the hands of God, relaxed, and the lactation stopped. The mother was released.

Many older people spoil their lives by useless mourning over departed loved ones. I know an intelligent woman who is making her life, and the lives of those around her, miserable by her useless mourning. She thinks it is showing loyalty to her husband, but really it is a species of self-pity.

7. *Develop the mind clear up to the end and keep fit for tasks here and hereafter.* They tell us that the mind never grows old. The brain, the instrument of the mind, does grow old; but the mind can keep the brain fresh and alert if the mind doesn't let down and sag. Compel yourself to read some portion of a good book each day. Above all, fill your mind with *the* Book. Then you will never be empty or alone.

Gracious Father, help me to grow old gracefully and beautifully, to come to maturity majestically. Let me fill my mind and soul with Thee, so that when physical beauty fades, spiritual beauty may take its place. Physical beauty is an endowment; spiritual beauty an achievement—help me to achieve it by constant companionship with Thee. Amen.

Jas. 3:1–13; Luke 4:22; Acts 6:10

ADJUSTING OUR VOCABULARY TO FACT

We have been studying how to adjust ourselves to passing time if we are to live abundantly and freely. We turn now to another adjustment—the adjustment of our vocabulary to fact.

Words often lose their relation to fact. They are like institutions in this respect; for institutions, given at first for the purpose of expressing life, often end by throttling that very life, and so must be constantly readjusted and perpetually realigned to their original purposes. In like manner, our words often throttle the life they are intended to express and hence need constant reconversion and readjustment.

This is particularly true of religious words. They become sacrosanct, but all out of touch with reality. We will have to go over our vocabulary with relentless inquiry to see if we are using words out of which the content has dropped. This is important, for the younger generation has a strong sense of reality—it can sniff unreality from afar. The young people of our high schools and colleges usually give the speaker the first five minutes to prove he has reality. If they hear only words they will take out a book and read it!

We must reclothe the eternal truths of the Gospel in the language that each age can understand. But even that will not do, if the reclothing is just adopting the words of a new age. The words must have content, reality in them, or they will say nothing.

Language is a symbol, and has to be changed constantly to fit the facts. The symbols are not the facts. A map is not the territory it represents—a map has constantly to be changed to bring it nearer the facts. Maps of the air, used by aviators, have to be changed every few minutes, or they become dangerous. Vocabularies that are not being constantly changed to fit the facts of life become dangerous.

But we dislike change, especially in words. An elder in a certain denomination felt that the statement put out by the 1911 Conference was sacrosanct; and when the Church changed it, he committed suicide. But the Church would have committed suicide if it hadn't made the words fit the facts.

O God, perhaps I, too, am caught in phrases and words, and am a prisoner of my vocabulary. Then break up my speech; tear down my words, for they may be unreal and hollow. I know that nothing real will perish in the shakedown. So I surrender my words and my phrases to Thee. Make them over, and help me to co-operate in remaking them. Amen.

Ps. 15:1–3; Prov. 10:18–21; 12:18–20; Matt. 5:37

LABELS CAN BECOME LIBELS

This matter of bringing words into closer relationships with the facts they symbolize can have serious consequences. A girl had a fear of the word "mother"—whenever she saw it or heard it a fear went over her and she revolted from the word. It was found that her mother had been very cruel to her, and the content of the word came from that fact. She was released only when she was made to understand that the word "mother" could and did stand for tenderness and understanding love in the experience of thousands. The word-fact relationship was righted, and she was freed.

We mentioned a young man who was jilted as church bells were ringing, and whenever he saw or heard the word "church" or "bishop" he found himself seized by fear and revolt. Association brought this reaction. There was nothing wrong with the word "church" or "bishop," but he had carried over into the word a false meaning. His vocabulary needed to be cleaned from fear.

A theological professor rightly says: "Words in themselves mean nothing—the meanings go back to persons." We stick labels on whole people by saying, "All Japs are tricky," "All Americans are materialistic." These labels are false and unjust. Some Japanese are tricky, as some Americans are; but many Japanese are not. Some Americans are materialistic, and some are not. Such labels are libels.

A man was being introduced in a fulsome manner, so he arose and said, "The adjective is often the enemy of the noun." We must cleanse our adjectives and see that they fit the nouns. Gandhi is an example of this. He has said that he would no more use ornate language than he would use ornate clothing. He has reduced life and language to simplicity. When he speaks, his words are a revelation of fact. In Jesus this simplicity of speech came to its perfection. His words were so stripped of verbiage that they are fact. His statement was: "By thy words thou shalt be justified, and by thy words thou shalt be condemned." We must surrender our vocabulary, then, for cleansing.

O Christ, I do surrender my vocabulary to Thee, for I want my words, as Tagore says, "to come out of the heart of truth." Cleanse from my symbols of speech all unreality, all seeming, all veneer, and let me speak words that have been cleansed by the Word. In Jesus' name. Amen.

Matt. 12:36–37; Luke 20:26; Acts 26:25; 1 Cor. 14:9

STEPS TO BRIDGE THE GAP BETWEEN WORD AND FACT

Dr. Gordon Campbell, a medical psychologist and an advocate of word-fact reality, gives steps for bringing words into closer relationships with facts. I say closer relationships with facts, for word and fact can never be one—except on that single occasion when "the Word became flesh," the Word and the Fact were one. Once in human history the Symbol and the Reality coincided—but only once. Apart from that sole exception when symbol and meaning fused into one in Christ, the symbol of language must constantly be adjusted to the facts. Steps for bridging the gap between symbol and reality:

1. *Date your statement.* People change; you change. For example, if you make a statement about a person, date it; otherwise you may be talking about some other person, for in the meantime this person has changed.

2. *Index the difference.* When you make a statement about a person, then proceed to modify the statement by indexing differences between the person and the statement. The statement may be true in general, but there are other factors that modify the generalization—state those other factors. "All generalizations are false—including this one!"

3. *Put et cetera, et cetera after your statements.* You have said certain things, but you have not said everything. If you stated everything about the matter, all the facts would modify your statement. For example, in saying a thing about a person, if you don't provide for the fact that the person is changing his characteristics then the statement may be false. As Professor William James says: "If you start out to describe the universe in a sentence, then put in a comma instead of a period."

4. *Often put your statements in quotes.* When you use the word socialist, or communist, in reference to a man, put it in quotes if you desire to express the commonly accepted use of the term, which is very loose and inaccurate. Only when you are sure he is a real socialist or a real communist should you use the words without quotes.

O God, as Thou art cleansing my soul from all falsities, so cleanse my speech too from all falsities. I would be pure in speech as well as in soul. For my false speech may creep back and make false my soul. I would be a clarified person. In Jesus' name. Amen.

Matt. 7:1–5; Rom. 12:10, 16; 15:1–7

FURTHER STEPS IN WORD-FACT RELATIONSHIPS

We continue our steps in the word-fact relationship.

5. *Often hyphenate your statements.* In speaking of body and mind, it is inaccurate to put them thus apart—they should be body-mind. For the body and mind are closely intertwined.

Some further observations may be added to the above five steps. Seneca says: "A man who does not wash his hands is not a pig. He is a man who does not wash his hands." The difference in mental attitude produced by those two statements is profound. If you make one or the other of those statements, your whole attitude has to change accordingly. Again, when speaking about a person, don't say, "I don't like that person." Say, "I don't like such and such a thing about that person—I rather like the person, but I don't like this and that about him." That statement would make all the difference in the world in your attitude toward that person. Sometimes we take a particular thing about a person and chew on that one thing, and cannot see the rest of the person at all.

> "I do not love thee, Dr. Fell:
> The reason why I cannot tell;
> But this I know, and know full well:
> I do not love thee, Dr. Fell."

The probabilities are that you do not love Dr. Fell because you have isolated one thing from Dr. Fell, and you are blind to the rest of him. Turn your attitude and say, in regard to a person, "The person in general is right, but this thing isn't right." That would make you accurate, and the other person lovable. It is important that, after having segregated the thing you do not like in the person, you do not end on what you do not like, but on what you do like. Let the last impression be positive.

Loose statements about people are harmful, but sometimes amusing. A woman said, "Stanley Jones is a Communist." When asked why she said that, she replied, "Because he has written a book on Communism." She didn't pause to ask on which side I had written it!

Gracious Father, straighten me out from mind quirks which distort and disrupt. Help me to have a mind clarified of all prejudice and half-truths. May I be a person wholesome in mind and speech, for only thus can I be the person Thou dost intend me to be. In Jesus' name. Amen.

Luke 16:13–15, 19–31; Matt. 19:21–22

LOOKING OVER OUR MONEY RELATIONSHIPS

We pass on to our relationship with money, another symbol. No one can live abundantly until he has found a Christian relationship with money. The account says that "Jesus sat over against the treasury and watched." It is a solemn moment when we review our money relationships, with Him sitting beside us watching the effect of money on us.

We have seen how the life of the body depends on balance—too much or too little produces unbalance, and hence disease. Too much food is just as harmful to the body as too little. Too much or two little secretion of a gland will alike produce disease. "Balance" is the key word to bodily health—a word that we neglect only at our peril.

Yet how we have neglected that word balance in relation to possessions. We have had no brakes on accumulation—the more we possess, the more successful we are supposed to be. "I feel like a million," is our statement of the height of well-being. This unbalance in possessions is producing disease in the body of society and in the individuals concerned. Too little and too much produce a diseased society and diseased individuals. Decay sets in in the very poor and in the very rich. Where is the place of balance?

Christianity has the answer. Christianity teaches neither asceticism nor avarice—it teaches that you have the right and the duty to have your needs met. "Distribution was unto every man according as he had need." "Need" is the place of balance. Less than need produces disease and more than need produces disease. Someday we shall scientifically study the matter and we shall come to that conclusion, for that conclusion is written into the constitution of things. Said a psychiatrist: "My greatest problem is the overprivileged boy or girl who has no incentive to struggle." They, and the underprivileged, are the disrupted personalities of of our civilization. They represent unbalance. Christianity represents balance—to each according to need.

Our civilization is unbalanced because it is unchristian. Hence it topples over periodically into war.

O God, we are now in a real battle. Unnatural cravings have been created within us. We are victims of false values, of false goals. Help us to return to sanity, to equilibrium, to balance. We have hurt ourselves and others in our madness. In Jesus' name. Amen.

Mark 4:18–19; Ps. 62:10; Prov. 23:4; Jer. 9:23–24;
Luke 12:16–21; I Tim. 6:6–12, 17–19

A LADDER FOR MASTERY OVER MONEY

In order to get the mastery over money, lest it get mastery over us, we would suggest the following ladder:

1. *Hold in mind that money is a good servant, but a terrible master.* If it gets on top, and you get under it, then your life is decided by a thing; in consequence you are no longer a person, but a thing. If money is your god, then your enfeebled personality is the price you pay for the worship of that god.

2. *Reject the philosophy that you may hold vast accumulations as a trustee for the poor.* Carnegie, who was the best illustration of this philosophy, said: "The millionaire will be but the trustee of the poor, intrusted for a season with a great part of the wealth of the community, but administering it for the community far better than it would have done for itself." To which Dr. Wm. J. Tucker replied, "If the few can administer wealth for the community far better than it can do for itself, then democracy has reached the limit of intelligence and responsibility." The poor need not our charity, but our justice. When you give charity you are the brother bountiful; the poor are the recipients. When you give justice your relationships change—you become equals. It is easy to be charitable; it is difficult to be just.

3. *Nothing that you can do for your children will be more harmful than to leave so much to them that they will not have to struggle and work.* The surest way to flabby, irresponsible character is too much money.

4. *There are two ways to be wealthy—one is in the abundance of your possessions, and the other is in the fewness of your wants.* In taking the latter way to be wealthy you transfer to the inside of you the real wealth that cannot be taken away by depression or death.

5. *Put in a stop where your needs end. After that all you make belongs to other people's needs.* If you can put in that stop, you are a man of character—you master things; they do not master you.

O God, I live in an acquisitive society where worth is judged by wealth. At the same time I am a Christian, and my judgments must be different. Help me to decide the Christian way, no matter how queer I may seem to be. That queerness may be the sign that I am becoming more Christian. I want to be just that. Amen.

Acts 20:35; II Cor. 9:1–15; I Cor. 16:2;
Mal. 3:7–10; Mark 10:17–27

THE LADDER FOR MASTERY OVER
MONEY—Continued

We continue our ladder for the mastery of money:

6. *Keep your needs down to needs, not luxuries disguised as needs.* Needs contribute; luxuries choke. If you eat food beyond your needs, you simply clog the system and lay on useless fat—surplus baggage which you have to carry around. The same with money and things. If you have too much, then invest it in persons. It is the only bank that will not break. The bank of human character will pay dividends through eternity. Invest all surpluses in that bank.

7. *Settle the level of need in the full light of the needs of others, of your enlightened conscience, and of the judgment of a disciplined group.* These three things are necessary and all three should converge in the final decision. I speak of an "enlightened conscience," for a conscience trained in the half-lights of contemporary society is not an enlightened conscience. Train it at the feet of Christ. But when you come to the feet of Christ be sure that you have adequate information about the needs of others. Conscience needs wide information to be a safe guide. You train our conscience and then your conscience trains you. A disciplined group is necessary to help you to sound judgments, for the group is objective and represents the corporate conscience, which should check the individual conscience. An unchecked conscience is not safe.

8. *While you are lifting your economic level to the level of need, give a tithe of what you earn. After you have reached that level, give everything you earn.* The tithe is a token—a token that you are not owner, but ower. Just as you pay rent as a token of acknowledgment of the ownership of another, so you pay a tithe to acknowledge the ownership of God over the nine tenths. When the level of your needs has been reached, then *all* you earn belongs to the needs of others, not as charity, but as right and justice.

O God our Father, I am digging deep around the roots of my life. I am trying to tie up this root of money which is "a root of all evil." I cannot cut it entirely; but I can, and I do, tie it up so that it does not take too much nourishment from the soil of my life. I want to absorb it—I don't want it to absorb me. In Jesus' name. Amen.

Phil. 2:4; Acts 2:44–47; II Cor. 8:1–15

GOLD-SEEKERS OR GOD-SEEKERS?

Before we leave the subject of material possessions, we must spend one day in gathering up our steps in a final one:

9. *Work for a co-operative order in which each will think and work for all, and all will think and work for each.* There is no doubt that the level of need will go up, but it should go up for everybody. We would not produce less wealth in a co-operative society—we would produce more, but it would be more widely distributed—the general level of life would rise for everybody. Where there are vast inequalities, there are bound to be instability and unrest and clashes. The Scandinavian countries were on the verge of a demonstration of a wide distribution of wealth, with no very rich people and no very poor people. And they were accomplishing it quietly without revolution. We must carry on from the point where their efforts were broken off by the war.

We have had a demonstration in American history of two attitudes toward money and how they have worked out. In 1852 two sets of caravans with covered wagons started out from Omaha across the wide expanses toward the Far West. For days they went in parallel lines, and then they diverged in more ways than one. The Mormons had written on their covered wagons: "God-seekers." The other group, who represented the gold rush, put on their wagons:"Gold-seekers." The latter group was individualistic, competitive, with the attitude:"Each man for himself, and the devil take the hindmost." The former group was a society of mutual aid, seeking the good of all and of each. These two outlooks and attitudes were put under life to see which one life would approve of. The "gold-seekers" found their gold, but it went through their fingers like water. Their gold is now, for the most part, in the hands of corporations. The God-seekers settled on barren salt land, developed it, and now have a corporation for the good of the whole with assets listed at $3,500,000,000. Life approved of a society of mutual aid and doomed a ruthlessly selfish society.

O God, Thou art teaching us, through many a pain and many a frustration, that we must live as a society of mutual aid. We have been slow to learn the lesson. Our slowness is written in devastation and breakdown. Forgive us. Give us another chance, and we will learn the ways of Thy Kingdom, which are really our ways, did we but understand. In Jesus' name. Amen.

Matt. 23:8–10; Acts 13:1–3; Col. 3:11

SOME STEPS IN GETTING RID OF
RACE PREJUDICE

This co-operative order must be a co-operative order not of a class, or a color, or a creed, but the co-operation with man as man apart from these extraneous things. Cooperation of a class is snobbery; of a color, prejudice; of a creed, bigotry; of man as man, Christian. But the moment we try to start a co-operative plan of living we run into race prejudice—one of the deepest prejudices we have to encounter. How can we master it? We cannot live abundantly if we are hidebound; and color prejudice is just that—bound by hide. If we get rid of these prejudices we shall not do so by sentimental vaporings, but by facing irresistible facts. Are there such facts? Yes.

1. *We have the backing of Christianity that mankind is one.* "God . . . . hath made of one blood all nations . . . . for to dwell on all the face of the earth." "One is your Master, ... and all ye are brethren." "There is neither Jew nor Greek . . . . in Christ Jesus"—racial distinction. "The Spirit bade me go with them, making no distinction" —Peter was making a racial distinction in his mind, and the Spirit canceled this out. The early Church not only put men on a theoretical level, but actually gave them equal authority also. Paul was ordained by a Negro at Antioch— "Simeon (called Niger)"; and "Niger" is, literally, "the Black." There is no doubt whatever that these modern color prejudices were not in early Christianity. Then a man was looked on as a man—"a man for whom Christ died."

Paul gave the Christian conception of equality in these words regarding a slave: "no longer a mere slave but something more than a slave—a beloved brother; especially dear to me but how much more to you as a man and as a Christian!" (Philemon 16, Moffatt.)

Christianity was to be a revelation of both God and man —and more: it was to be a faith in both. The Christian faith is therefore creative, bringing out the best in all men. Christ is the great believer in man. He is the great believer in man—not in some men, but in all men. Hence He is the hope of the world.

Our Father, give us a faith in Thee and in one another. Doubt destroys; faith builds; help us then to look on people with the eyes of kindling faith, and not with the eyes of chilling doubt. For only thus shall we be like Thee. For Thou dost believe in us when we cannot believe in ourselves. Help us to pass on Thy faith. In Jesus' name. Amen.

1 John 4:11–12, 20–21; Acts 17:24–29; Matt. 7:12

THE BACKING OF BIOLOGY AND DEMOCRACY

2. *We have the backing of biology.* The idea of inherently superior races and inherently inferior races is being fast exploded by scientific investigation. There are undeveloped races, but no permanently inferior or superior ones. An outstanding biologist says: "There are cultural differences between races, but no biological." The four types of blood found in one race are found in every race. The I.Q.'s of the colored children in New York are as high as those of white children. The cultural background of the homes from which they come may help or retard their progress, but the raw material is the same. An English judge in Burma, who had also been a judge in England, told me he had discovered that the brain of humanity is one, for the lawyers in England and in Burma argue from the same fallacies to the same conclusions! I find as I go around the world that people of all races will laugh in exactly the same way over the same jokes. Humanity is literally one.

3. *We have the backing of democracy.* If democracy means anything, it means equal opportunity to all—and all means all, of whatever race, color, or class. If it doesn't mean that, it is not democracy, but hypocrisy—the rule of the mask, instead of the rule of the mass. The Russians said to me: "You are out-dated. We are the real inheritors of democracy. You grew afraid of your principle of democracy, tried to confine it to the political; we went on and applied it to the economic and social as well. We are therefore the inheritors of democracy." There is only one answer to that, and the answer cannot be a verbal answer—it must be a vital answer, a demonstration. When we take the pledge of allegiance to the flag and say "with liberty and justice to *all*"—"to all" must mean "all," or nothing.

Remember the words of Peter: "The Spirit bade me go with them, making no distinction." When we make racial distinction then we break with the Spirit of God and accept the spirit of arrogance. We have broken with the Christian way.

O God, help me to belng to "the community of the just." For I know that without justice there can be no community. Cleanse my heart of all that cannot be made into community—all divisiveness, all prejudice, all smallness. I want to be big—to love in spite of differences of color and race. For down underneath we are the same—and I know it. Amen.

Gal. 6:2; I Pet. 2:17; I Thess. 4:8–9

CONTINUED STEPS IN GETTING RID OF RACE PREJUDICE

Since we have the backing of Christianity, biology, and democracy that mankind is one, and that these prejudices are not innate, but artificially imposed at an early date on the mind of the child, then we can deliberately take steps to build up new attitudes toward other races.

4. *I will cease sticking labels on whole peoples.* It is not true that "Japanese are tricky," "Jews are materialistic," "Germans are Huns," "Negroes are shiftless"—some are, and some are not.

5. *I will deliberately cultivate friendships with people of another race.* I will probably find that down underneath surface differences we are fundamentally one. A German woman, after the last war, in applying for a job in which she felt there would be prejudice against her said, "Madam, we both shed the same tears." We do.

6. *I will deliberately set out to find what I can learn from people of another race.* Each race has something to teach people of other races. It takes many differing notes to make a symphony. The white and black keys on the piano are the symbol of the fact that it takes both races to bring out the full music of humanity. One year I found that the three people who had influenced me most were Gandhi, Booker T. Washington, and Kagawa—not one of them of my color or race.

7. *I will deliberately try to bring people of other races into my church fellowship.* Every white church should have at least one member of the colored race as an honored member, and every colored church at least one white member, as a symbol that the Christian Church is different from surrounding society.

8. *I will deliberately identify myself with the dispossessed and discriminated against and make their disabilities my own, until everything is thrown open to everybody on the basis of equal opportunity to all.* Their cross shall be my cross; and their resurrection, my ressurection.

Gracious Father, here I will find my cross in modern life. I will become a part of the disabilities that fall on others. Help me to choose to be identified with the forgotten and despised. And make this choice real and not mere gesture. For I am bound in the bondage of others and degraded in their degradations whether I identify myself with them or not. Help me to take it on myself. In Jesus' name. Amen.

Rom. 14:4; 1 Pet. 3:12–17

WE FACE THE QUESTION OF WAR

Those who have set out on this pilgrimage for abundant living will probably be impatient to face the vital question now facing every serious-souled person: What shall be my attitude toward war? If we do not face that question and find abundant living through, and not around it, we shall have abundant living that is unreal. It would be easier not to face this question, for equally good men are on both sides of it—easier, and more deadly. Sometimes in our discussions I have used the pronoun "I" in a representative capacity; but here I must use it in a strictly personal way, and tell you how far I have gone in my thinking and attitudes.

1. *I have determined that my attitude toward war shall not break my fellowship with those who differ from me.* I believe in liberty of conscience so much that I must give the other person liberty of conscience to differ from me without inwardly de-Christianizing him, even in thought. The fellowship must not be broken.

2. *I am completely disillusioned about the war method.* During the first world war I preached on two texts: "Herod and his soldiers set Jesus at naught"—militarism sets Jesus at naught. "But when they saw the soldiers, they stopped beating Paul"—military power can be used to protect the innocent. This last text allowed me to approve of the war. Since then I have been completely disillusioned about the ability of the military method to accomplish what its advocates believe it can.

3. *The military method cannot and does not protect the innocent.* It protects the guilty, who are behind the lines, and involves the innocent, both civilians and soldiers alike, in insensate, useless slaughter. To compare the military method to that of protecting your wife or daughter from a ravisher, is a false analogy; for war exposes wife and daughter—in fact, all innocents—to ravishment, spiritual, mental, and physical. To compare war to killing a mad dog is a false analogy. In war the mad dog—Hitler, *et al.*—is not killed, but millions of innocent youth are.

O God, my Father, I come to Thee for light and guidance in this matter of war. I am involved in it whether I choose it or not. And yet, when I inwardly repudiate it, I am not morally involved as I am when I choose and approve. Help me then inwardly to repudiate it, so that I may extricate my soul from moral involvement. In Jesus' name. Amen.

Rom. 12:17–21; I Pet. 3:8–12; Phil. 2:5

IS WAR A SURGICAL OPERATION?

We left off yesterday while discussing the inability of war to protect the innocent. "Then Abner said to Joab, 'Let the young men get up and have a fight before us.' 'Very well,' said Joab." (II Samuel 2:14, Moffatt.) It is the young men who have little or nothing to do with the precipitating of wars who have to bear the brunt of the fighting. But in modern war probably the worst suffering comes to the civil populations. War has lost any power it had to protect the innocent—it now exposes them. If it is said that there are some things worse than war, then the answer must be given in the words of another: "Yes, and war produces every one of those things."

4. *War is a means out of harmony with the ends it hopes to accomplish.* Men everywhere acknowledge that the war method is wrong, but they hope to use it to accomplish good ends. This is a fond and futile hope, for "the means pre-exist in and determine the ends." You cannot dismiss the means before they have shaped the ends. They go straight into and determine the ends. Evil means produce evil ends. If good has ever come out of war, the reason was that other constructive influences have been introduced into the process and have produced constructive ends in spite of the war method.

5. *To liken war to a surgical operation is a false analogy.* A surgical operation posits an immaculately sterilized surgeon with immaculately sterilized instruments, or else it will do more harm than good—as in my own experience, for I was infected with tetanus when operated on for appendicitis. What nation as it goes to war can claim immaculate sterility for itself and its instruments? If it did, then the first germ that would infect the body of humanity would be hypocrisy. War cannot be carried on in an immaculately sterile manner—its weapons are lies, deceits, hypocrisies. "The first casualty in war is truth"; the second is love, for it is absurd to say that you can go to war loving your enemies. If you loved your enemies you would be a very poor soldier.

Gracious Father, I come to Thee asking Thee to wash my eyes and my heart. I want to see straight and cannot unless I am straight. Then make me straight. Amid the hysterias of this hour keep my soul and my mind clean. For hate invades, and prejudices corrode, and I begin to think with my emotions. Help me to think with Thy mind. In Jesus' name. Amen.

Luke 20:25; Acts 5:29; Matt. 22:36–40

DID CHRIST APPROVE OF WAR?

6. *Nor can I draw the analogy between an army trained for war and a police force.* I can and do believe in a police force, for a police force brings the criminal to the bar of justice to be tried by a tribunal of right. An army trained in war does not bring the supposed offender to a tribunal of right, but fights it out before a tribunal of might. Moreover, the police punish the guilty; in war you punish the innocent and guilty alike—mostly the innocent. Again, a police force is trained against criminals—one police force doesn't go out and fight against another police force as does an army trained for war.

7. *Nor can I by any twisting of meanings find the approval of Christ for war.* They just don't fit in. The missionaries in Nanking, China, gave New Testaments to the Japanese soldiers. At first the officers were glad for the men to have them, but later they came to the missionaries and said, "Please don't give our men any more New Testaments, for when they read this book, it takes the fight out of them—they don't want to fight any more."

To say that Christ used force in the cleansing of the Temple is to twist the account, for He used force as follows: (1) He "overthrew the tables"—on inanimate objects He used force. (2) He took a whip of small cords and "drove out all, both the sheep and the oxen"—on animate creatures who could not understand moral force He used a whip. (3) On persons He used moral force: "Take these things hence." There is no scriptural warrant whatever that Jesus used physical violence on any person, let alone His approving of the violence of war.

When He said, "Render to Caesar the things that are Caesar's," He immediately added, "And to God the things that are God's." The first phrase is qualified by the second. In His interpretation of the Kingdom He said that all life belongs to God. Then: Render to Caesar what can be reconciled with rendering to God—if Caesar fits into the Kingdom of God—well; if not, then, "Seek ye first the kingdom." The idea that loyalty to Caesar is on a par with loyalty to God is foreign to the Christian faith.

Father, help me to get my values and my allegiances straight. I will give my loyalty to Caesar as long as it does not interfere with and contradict my loyalty to Thee. For Thou, not Caesar, art God. Help me then to fear no consequences of my loyalty to Thee, first, last, and always. Amen.

Rom. 12:21; Matt. 5:43-48

HAS GANDHI SHOWN US A WAY OUT?

Last week we were considering our Christian attitude toward war. We ended by insisting that Christ and war were incompatibles. Jesus said, "My kingdom is not of this world, else would my servants fight." Here He says definitely that His servants will not fight, for their Kingdom is different from the kingdoms of this world and their weapons are therefore different.

8. *The God I find in Christ is a God who overcomes evil with good, hate by love, and the world by a cross.* But if the objection is made that God redeems in terms of Christ, but rules in terms of a throne, my answer is that Jesus identified Himself with God and also with the Kingdom of God. He and God are one, and He and the Kingdom are one. He used "for my sake" and "for the Kingdom's sake" synonymously. He is the Kingdom personalized—the Order and the Person are one. So Jesus is both the revelation of the character of God, and the character of God's reign. God redeems in terms of Christ, and He rules in terms of Christ: the cross and the throne are one.

9. *There is a moral equivalent to war—Gandhi has shown the possibilities of putting the cross into corporate life.* Pacifism is not passivism—it is an activism from a higher level. Gandhi has shown us that a nation need not sit down under disabilities, nor need it have recourse to the barbarities of war—it can match its own capacities to suffer against the capacities of the other to give suffering—soul force against physical force. Gandhi has trained a nation to say: "We won't hate you, but we won't obey you. Do what you like." He has put the cross into public life. If our nation took the Christian way of active good will toward all, we should probably do away with nine tenths of the possibilities of invasion; if on the one tenth the Christian way should break down, we would not be lost, for one hundred and thirty million people could sit down and say to a dictator: "We won't hate you, but we won't obey you. Do what you like." We could overcome by our capacity to suffer. Twaddle? Christ tried it, and He rules the world.

O Christ, I am Thy follower. And yet, and yet I am afraid to follow Thee—all out. But I see Thy way is right. And nothing else is right. Then let me take Thy way though the heavens fall. But they will not fall, for they stand as they stand with Thee. Help me to stand with Thee. Amen.

Rom. 8:16–18; II Tim. 2:12; I Pet. 2:19–21; II Cor. 10:3–5

THE GOOD THINGS IN WAR

We left off yesterday at the possibility of a moral equivalent to war. Geo. Landsbury once objected to the use of that phrase, saying to me: "There is no moral equivalent of an evil." But while war is an evil, yet there are noble things caught up and used by war: patriotism, self-sacrifice, comradeship in a common cause. These are no necessary part of war, but they are seized hold of and used by war, and they make war bearable to troubled souls—troubled about the essential purposes of war, namely, to kill, to destroy.

The moral equivalent to war is the moral equivalent of the fine things war has gathered up and used—patriotism, comradeship, self-sacrifice. The willingness of youth to sacrifice their lives touches me deeply. We can rescue these fine qualities and use them in a higher purpose and to higher ends. Gandhi's nonviolent non-co-operation takes patriotism, self-sacrifice, and comradeship in a cause and links them to the constructive purposes of overcoming evil by good, hate by love, and the world by a cross. If our 130,000,000 people should sit down, refuse to obey, and practice nonviolent non-co-operation with a dictator, what would happen? The jails would be filled until jails would become ridiculous—an honor. They would line us up against a wall and shoot us until they would shoot themselves and their regime full of holes.

If it is said that this might work against the British in India, but not against the Germans and the Japanese, the reply is that the early Christians used this method against the most brutal empire of the day—the Roman Empire whose ordinary method of punishment was crucifixion. They used it against that empire and won. They broke the Roman Empire by their capacity to take suffering, not to give it. For the first three centuries no Christian ever went to war or stayed in the army after he became a Christian—it was incompatible. After the first three centuries, with the conversion of Constantine, no one but a Christian could get into the army. Christianity and the war method became entangled.

O God, strengthen my inner spirit with a disciplined way of life, so that I may be prepared to adopt this way of nonviolence as my way whether others take it or not. May I embrace the way of the cross even if it means the added cross of being alone. For we must find a new way—this old way is ruinous to everybody. In Jesus' name. Amen.

Acts 24:16; 1 Tim. 1:5; Rom. 13:8–10

BECOMING AN EMBODIED CONSCIENCE

As we expound this possibility of nonviolent non-co-operation there are many who say, "Well, it might work if we could convince enough disciplined people to try it. But we have disciplined our people in the other method, not in this one." True. And how do we begin? With ourselves! We cannot wait until everyone is ready; we can let this method of the cross begin in ourselves and in small groups we can gather around us.

A woman speaker was trying to whip up a frenzy of hate against our war enemies. Somehow her effort just wouldn't work. She finally turned aside and said, half-wistfully and half-disgustedly, "How can you hate with Jane Addams in the room?" Jane Addams was the new order embodied, and was the conscience of the situation.

A speaker was wired by a college president whose college he was to visit and urged to go all out for war, as Rufus Jones had been on the campus and had greatly influenced the students against war. The speaker tried his best to do as requested, but didn't get far. The president of the college said afterward, "Why didn't you really go all out?" The speaker replied, "Who can go all out for war with Rufus Jones on the platform?" Rufus Jones was the Christian conscience of the situation. The speaker had to justify himself before that conscience, and the going was hard.

This method will fail? All right, I would rather fail using this method than succeed in using the other. But will it fail? The opposite is failing to do anything for us except to get us into universal ruin. Just sheer common sense should keep us out of war. Rousseau, speaking of nations keeping out of war, said: "They do not need to be good, generous, disinterested, public-spirited, humane. They may be unjust, greedy, putting their own interests first; we ask only that they shall not be fools—and to this they will come." Kant said, "even a race of devils, provided only that they were intelligent, would be forced to find a solution other than war."

O Christ, my Lord, make me a Christian whether others become Christians or not. I feel in my heart of hearts that this way is the only way that will work. For it is Thy way. I will need courage to take this way, for so many are afraid the universe won't back it. But I am convinced that the universe is not backing the other. It is ending in futile ruin. Help me to take Thy way. Amen.

Matt. 16:18; I Cor. 10:32; Heb. 12:28

THE CHURCH IS A SOCIETY WITHIN A SOCIETY

The discussion of our attitudes toward war led to the necessity of getting small disciplined groups to be the seed plots of a new order, so that if the old order goes to pieces, the group will be the seeds of a new one. The Christian Church became just such a seed plot when the Roman Empire, founded on military might, went to pieces. The Epistle to Diognetus, written at this time of decay, says: "What the soul is to the body, so the Christians are to the world—they hold the world together." It was the Christians then who held the world together, and it is the Christians again who will now hold the world together. For we are in a similar period of decay. Sorokin, the Harvard sociologist, says that our sensate culture has exhausted itself and is dissolving, and the future must reform itself around other ideas and purposes.

The future must form around the Kingdom of God, or, in its turn, perish. For the Kingdom is the final order, and what does not fit into it shall perish. The Church is the seed plot of that Kingdom. In a mass meeting it was announced that a Japanese girl would sing. I held my breath to see the reaction of that audience. We were at war with Japan. Would they hiss her? She sang simply and beautifully: "How beautiful upon the mountains are the feet of him that bringeth good tidings, that publisheth peace." Although it was a religious service, the audience broke out into spontaneous applause. The Christian fellowship was unbroken. The Church was not at war. It was a supranational fellowship that held together in spite of the snapping of national bonds. Only in a Christian church could that have taken place in wartime—a national of a nation at war with us cheered in public! The Christian Church is different. It is a society within a society—a nation within a nation. When a nation decays, the Church need not decay—it is attached to undecaying purposes and ends. It is, or ought to be, an expression in society of that "Kingdom which cannot be shaken." To the degree that the Church is such an expression, it will stand unshaken amid a shaken world.

O God, I am so grateful that there is one island of sanity amid a raging sea of confusion and hate. Help me to be a worthy part of this glorious fellowship of those whose hearts have been touched and illuminated and changed, and who are the realized future. May I be the miniature of that future. In Jesus' name. Amen.

Col. 1:17–18; Acts 20:28; Eph. 3:14–15; 5:23–32

WHY I SHOULD GIVE MY ALLEGIANCE TO THE CHURCH

In order to give full inner consent to allegiance to the Church, perhaps you can take these steps:

1. *There is no such thing as solitary religion.* If it is solitary, it is not religion, for Jesus expressed religion as love to God and love to man. There can be no love to man unless life is lived out in relationships. "To be is to be in relations." The Christian's life can be lived only in the give-and-take of corporate relationships.

2. *The Christian Church is founded on a necessity in human nature.* The three great driving urges are self, sex, and the herd. The herd, or social drive or instinct, is frustrated if I do not work out my spiritual life in a corporate fellowship. If the Church were wiped out today it would have to be replaced tomorrow by something similar, for human nature demands it. Those who try to cultivate their spiritual lives alone, apart from the Church, are attempting to live a vertical spiritual life, without the horizontal—they are attempting the impossible. Human nature is against it.

3. *The Church, in a sense, is an extension of the life of the Incarnation.* I say "in a sense," for there was only once when "the Word became flesh"; but the Church attempts, in varying degrees, to reincarnate that Word in corporate relationships. It is the only group in human society living not for its own purposes, but for the purpose of manifesting in time an Eternal Purpose.

4. *With all its faults the Church is the best serving institution on earth.* It has many critics, but no rivals in the work of human redemption. It has filled the world with schools, hospitals, orphan, leper, and blind asylums and churches. There isn't a spot on earth where, if it is free to do so, it hasn't done so. Christians are people who care.

And they are people who care on a world scale—they care for a man as a man, apart from race, birth, and color.

O God, I thank Thee that Thou hast a Family, and that I can belong to that Family. Make me a good member of that Family. May the Family spirit be in all I do and think and say. For I want others to love this Family. Help me to bring the Family the constructive spirit of love and mutual aid. In Jesus' name. Amen.

Acts 2:46–47; 7:37–38; 16:5; 1 Cor. 16:19–20; Eph. 1:17–23

THE CHURCH—THE ONE UNBROKEN FELLOWSHIP

We continue our ladder of thought in regard to the Church:

5. *The Church with all its faults contains the best human life in the world.* Its character is higher and finer and more dependable. When a churchman goes wrong morally, it is news. Something else was expected of him. Look over the service-club groups which usually gather up the leaders in the life of a city—90 per cent or more will be churchmen. They rise to the top like cream. If, as I said before, the ratio of divorces in one in six marriages in general, but only one in fifty among church people, then evidently the Church procedures a steadier type of character—people who can get along with each other, if not on account of, then in spite of.

6. *The Church is the one unbroken fellowship around the world.* All other ties have snapped; the tie between Christians remains unbroken. The missionaries are now carrying on the work of the German missions until the war is over, but will return the work to them at the close. The Church, as we said before, is not at war. It is holding an unbroken fellowship. The Christians are therefore the bridge across all chasms.

7. *The Church is the one institution that delivers you from the present century and gives you a sense of solidarity with all the centuries.* When you are in the church, you are not a prisoner of your date—you have a sense of belonging to the ages.

8. *The Church, at its truest, breaks down all class and race barriers, and makes mankind feel it is one.* A Negro minister arose in a train in Nazi Germany, gave the German lady his seat, and stood for four hours. When the German lady was about to leave, she tried to thank him, but he couldn't understand her German, nor could she understand his English. Finally she wrote out a scripture reference from Isaiah and handed it to him: "The Lord make thee like a watered garden," etc. Isaiah, a Jew, brings together a Negro and a German in Nazi Germany! Celsus said in derision: "These Christians love each other even before they are acquainted." They do.

O God, I thank Thee that the Church has been "the mother of my spirit," the guide of my youth, the fellowship of my mature years—the home of my soul. May no class, no caste, no color lines mar the open fellowship of the Family. Help us to have a relaxed fellowship in which everyone will be at home—except those who sin against the Brotherhood. Amen.

Acts 14:22–23; I Cor. 1:2; Heb. 2:11–12

THE CHURCH—THE MOTHER OF MOVEMENTS

We gather up some concluding meditations on the Church.

9. *The Church has been and is the mother of movements.* It is a creative society. It gave birth to the arts, to education, to reform, to missionary movements, to democracy. Democracy is a child of the Christian faith. Rhode Island gave to the world democracy, and Christian thinking gave democracy to Rhode Island. The Baptists and the Quakers thought thoughts of God as Father, then of men as brothers, and then of democracy as expressing that equalitarian attitude in government. Democracy is founded on a view of God, and hence of man, and hence of government. "Democracy," says Thomas Mann, "is the political expression of Christianity." If the root of democracy decays, the fruit will die.

10. *The denomination is not the Church.* The Church is bigger than the denomination. I stood on top of a hill overlooking a valley. Here and there I could see isolated ponds of water. But they were not isolated ponds; they were portions of one winding river, only parts of which I could see at one time. The denominations are parts of a continuous river—the Church. The Church is bigger than the denominations. To think that we have roped off the grace of God and confined it within our denomination is as absurd as to say that the areas roped off for swimmers on the seabeaches are the ocean.

11. *As the denomination is not the Church, so the Church is not the Kingdom.* The Church contains the best life of the Kingdom, but is not synonymous with the Kingdom. It is a means to the ends of the Kingdom, and not an end in itself. It must lose its life for Kingdom ends and then it will find itself.

12. *The primary function of the Church is the worship of God.* Here men get in living contact with God, the Eternal, in order to meet Time, the fleeting. Here men pause and have "the signet ring of Eternity stamped on the fleeting moments of Time."

Out of that worship of God impulses and movements spring for the service of man.

Gracious Father, in Thy house I learn to live simultaneously in time and in eternity. There I know I am the child of an Eternal Purpose, and the harbinger of an Eternal Destiny. I am no longer cheap. Nor can I be given to cheap ends. Help me to hold my bosom clear for the working out of Thy Eternal Purposes. In Jesus' name. Amen.

Deut. 6:5–9; 15:12–17; Prov. 3:7–8

THE OWNER'S STAMP

We have about rounded out our study of right personal and social attitudes for abundant living. We have outlined these attitudes in our minds; now they must be stamped within them—the study must become a stamp. Paul says: "Henceforth let no man trouble me; for I bear branded on my body the marks of Jesus." (Galatians 6:17.) Or, as Moffatt puts it, "the owner's stamp of Jesus." The marks were the marks of the Owner stamped in his flesh, as a symbol that the Owner's stamp was stamped into the mental and spiritual as well.

In India you see people who have the stamp of their god branded on their foreheads—put there by a hot iron, inerasable. The bulls of Shiva are branded with the Shiva trident and are his wherever they roam. Paul was thinking of this branding when he asserted that he was free from man because bound to the Man. He asserted his freedom through a deeper bondage. Strange way to find freedom—through complete bondage! And yet he saw that Christ was the fulfillment of his being, the way he was made to live—the Way. In another passage Paul says that we are "predestined" to "share the likeness of his Son." (Romans 8:29, Moffatt.) We have argued for centuries over predestination. And yet it seems simple: If you carry out the destiny written into the constitution of your being you will be made in the likeness of Christ. You are predestined to it by the nature of your being and by the very nature of the universe. You are predestined to be a Christian, a Christlike person, if you follow the lines laid down in your being. This is your destiny, and you can escape from it only by sinning against that destiny. In other words, only by sinning against the God who wrote that destiny within you. So, "the Owner's stamp" is simply the outer sign of something that is stamped within you constitutionally. You give your consent to the constitution—the way becomes the Way. The Owner's stamp is branded upon you.

Every single organ, tissue, and nerve cell is made to work in a Christian way. That is their destiny, written into their constitutions.

O Christ, I see that Thou art the Way. If I fulfill the thing I am made for, I shall be like Thee. I dare not sin against that destiny. For I see it is not an arbitrary decree written in a book and imposed, but it is written in me and inescapable. Then help me to consent with all my being to be branded as Thine own. Amen.

Luke 19:40; Eph. 6:1–3; Prov. 17:22; Ps. 139:14–16

"IT WILL SPRING UP OUT OF THE EARTH"

We saw yesterday that we were predestined by the very laws of our being to be Christian. This is the predestination I believe in with all my heart. Dr. Bosworth once said, "If the principles of Jesus were torn out of the heavens, they would spring up out of the earth." And out of the nature of our very beings. You have Christian lungs, Christian glands, a Christian stomach, a Christian heart, a Christian liver, a Christian nervous system—the total organization is Christian; and to put these organs to unchristian uses is to throw them out of gear—and worse—to grind the gears of life against each other, to live in inner conflict.

"It will spring up out of the earth." Dr. Henry Link, in his study of psychology, gave up Christianity as an outmoded superstition. When, however, he began to try to untangle snarled-up lives, he found he had to give them something outside themselves to love. The only thing permanent he could give them was God; and soon he found he was talking himself back into being a Christian. Life wouldn't come out right in any other way. He became a Christian, and wrote two great books on the Christian way, led back to it by the very pressures of life. The Christian way, torn from the heavens, sprang up out of the earth. The study of psychology and the study of physiology will lead to the conclusion of Aunt Het, who says quaintly: "Nature tries to make us good. I used to get awful mad years ago, but I had to quit because it gave me bad digestion." Dr. Frank Crane says: "Depression, gloom, despair, pessimism—these slay ten persons to everyone murdered by typhoid, influenza, diabetes, or pneumonia. If tuberculosis is the great white plague, fear is the great black plague." But fear, depression, gloom, despair, pessimism are all unchristian. They *slay,* so the newspaper columnists say. "It will spring up out of the earth." Nature is unfolding her book, and her finger points to the central passage of the whole, and that passage reads, "Be Christian."

To be Christian is your destiny.

O Thou loving, relentless, redeeming Owner, I find Thy marks upon my being. And now I countersign Thy writing —countersign it with deep consent. Brand Thy stamp of ownership in me. For I cannot wander unowned and unclaimed. Thy will is my native air, Thy mind the climate of my being. I thank Thee. Amen.

Eph. 4:11–16; Col. 3:10; Jas. 5:15–16; Lev. 26:14–16

THE OWNER'S STAMP ALREADY THERE

We have seen that Christ is Owner whether we acknowledge that fact or not. The confession of that Ownership is
being more and more wrung from reluctant lips. A doctor
said to me: "More men get stomach ulcers from fear and
worry than from resentments and anger. I suffer from a
gastric ulcer. I used to get angry. I don't dare do that now,
for I know where anger will hit me—in the stomach! Now
when anyone is about to make me angry I simply turn on
my heels and walk off." And then he quoted Dr. Harvey
Cushing, the great surgeon who said: "Don't operate on the
stomach of a man for stomach ulcer—operate on his head."
He is worrying or harboring resentments. Dr. Taylor of
Columbia, South Carolina, says: "I've never had a case of
arthritis among Negroes, and never one among white people except among those who fear or are worried." "It will
spring up out of the earth." Faith, good will, love are not
something imposed; they are the things we are made for.

The Owner's stamp is there within you. Now take it by
consent. Where shall I be branded? Paul says, "On my
body." Perhaps you have had the Christian way painted on
you and not branded in. Therefore it has not stayed. You
are given to the wayward, instead of to the Way; you are
fickle, instead of fixed. Now this whole Way is about to be
burned in, beginning at the body. Western civilization is
body-minded, a sensate civilization, a civilization of the
senses—that which can be touched and tasted, and smelled.
Say to one of our civilization, "This will hurt your soul,"
and he will reply, "So what?" But say, "This will give you a
stomach ulcer," and he will sit up and take notice. Since we
are body-minded, we will begin at the body: "Stamp Thy
mark, O Christ, in every brain cell, in every nerve, in every
tissue, in my total physical life. I want to be branded."

This prayer upon our lips is simply the unspoken prayer
of every portion of our beings—everything within us cries
out to be Christian, for that is their destiny.

Gracious Master, I shrink from the heat of Thine iron—
the burning flesh makes me draw back. But I know that
this wandering, wobbling life must be at an end. I want
something that will brand me forever, before God and man,
that there shall be no mistaking of my identity any longer.
Let the fire of Thy Spirit brand me forever Thine. Amen.

Luke 11:4; Eph. 4:32; Col. 3:13; Mark 11:25–26

THE MARK OF JESUS—FORGIVENESS OF INJURIES

Yesterday we spoke of shrinking from the brand. But when we see what is being branded into us we shrink no longer. For we are being branded with "the marks of Jesus." Could anything be finer than that? A quaint preacher prayed and thanked God for each member of the Trinity, and when he came to Jesus he said, "O God, even you couldn't do any better than He did." He was right. Christlikeness is to be stamped into you. You cannot have too much of that. What were some of the marks of Jesus?

1. *Forgiveness of injuries.* The sublimest prayer that was ever prayed, for it embodied the sublimest spirit ever shown, was the prayer, "Father, forgive them; for they know not what they do." Sir John Seeley says that the outstanding distinguishing mark of a Christian is willingness to forgive injuries. A bandit held up a man, who gave him his wallet. "Do you need money as badly as that? I will give you some more," the man said, handing over his other wallet. "If you will take a job I'll help you to get one." The bandit dropped his gun and said, "I can't take your money; you're a Christian."

Ralph was a converted prisoner serving a sentence. A fellow prisoner said of him: "No one can hold a grudge any more when Ralph comes into the room." That was the authentic sign of being a Christian. A missionary lady in Japan was walking along the safety zone when her coat, blown by the wind, caught in the knob of a passing car and she was dragged and injured. In the hospital she begged that the driver of the taxi should not be prosecuted, or his insurance taken away, as it was an accident. The taxi driver was so moved by her attitude that he attended her funeral and became a Christian.

Now you are to be branded—branded, mind you, with the spirit of forgiveness of injuries. It is going deep, deep —never again will you retaliate or harbor resentments.

Retaliation and harboring of resentments belong to a dead past—gone forever!

O Christ, brand me deep. I surrender all hurts, all resentments, all retaliation. From henceforth I am free—free from corroding hate and cankering resentments. I shall love everyone—friend and foe—those who do me good and those who do me ill. By Thy grace I can do this, but only by Thy grace. From henceforth let no hate trouble me. I bear Thy brand. Amen.

Acts 21:10–13; Rom. 8:28; Eph. 5:20; Luke 6:20–23

THE MARK OF JESUS—NO SELF-PITY

We continue the branding with the marks of the Lord Jesus.

2. *No self-pity.* Jesus said to the daughters of Jerusalem when they wept over Him on His way to the cross: "Weep not for me." No self-pity. This is a positive negative. There can be no self-pity in the Christian's make-up. Surrender all impulses to be sorry for yourself, all feelings of inferiority, all bidding for pity from yourself and others. A pastor's father, himself a minister, lost his reputation through immorality. The disgrace left a stigma on the son—at least, so the son felt. He found himself shrinking within himself, feeling that others were holding this against him. I called his attention to the fact that in the genealogy of Jesus was this item about His chief ancestor: "David was the father of Solomon by Uriah's wife." "By Uriah's wife." That stigma. And yet Jesus never pitied Himself because of His poor ancestry, nor did He surrender to inferiorities. He took the raw materials of life—and some of them can be very raw —and turned them into a new posterity. The pastor surrendered the self-pity, held up his head once more, and was released.

Now you are to do the same. This mark of "no self-pity" is being branded into you—forever. It has no part nor lot in you henceforth. You are free. You can say: "From henceforth let no self-pity trouble me. I bear branded a freedom from it."

3. *Joy, in spite of.* Anyone can have joy on account of; but Jesus had joy *in spite of.* A Christian said in one of my Round Table conferences: "I have found that if you follow Christ three things will happen. (1) You will be delivered from all fears. (2) You will be absurdly happy. (3) You will have trouble." The absurd happiness was in spite of! A highly intelligent woman, whose life had about cracked up under inner conflict, found Christ, and her colleagues said: "It is indecent to be as happy as you are." They couldn't see the Source! Her happiness was in spite of.

And now, O Christ, I too am to have stamped within me this mark of Thine: joy, in spite of. Gloom and despair and the blues are to have no lot nor place in my life from henceforth. They are burned out in the fires of Thy joy. From henceforth, let no gloom or despairing thoughts trouble me, for I bear branded within me the marks of joy, in spite of. Amen.

Ps. 37:1–7; Heb. 10:35; Eph. 3:13–21; Isa. 40:31

THE MARK OF JESUS—CALM RECEPTIVITY

We continue the branding with the marks of the Lord Jesus.

4. *Calm receptivity.* He was constantly giving out, but only because He was constantly taking in. An organism can give out as much energy as it takes in, and no more. So you. Jesus knew how to give because He knew how to receive. His relaxed spirit kept the channels free. There were no tight knots in His life blocking the power of God. He lived in a state of alert passivity. You are to be branded with that spirit—branded—which means that alert passivity is to be a continuous state of mind, instead of an imported occasional thing in periods of relaxation. You are to live relaxed and receptive.

Mozart, when asked how he found his musical inspirations, said: "I do not know myself and can never find out. When I am in particularly good condition—perhaps riding in a carriage, or on a walk after a good meal—or during a sleepless night, then the thoughts come to me in a rush, and best of all. Whence and how—that I do not know and cannot learn." He was relaxed and receptive and attuned to Music. So Music played him all over.

You are now being branded by this mark of Jesus. You are not going to live a nervous, overwrought, fussy type of life; you are going to be relaxed, receptive and released. You are not a reservoir with a limited amount of resources; you are a channel, attached to unlimited divine Resources.

5. *Courage.* His was not the excited desperate courage of a battlefield, but the quiet courage that went on in the face of growing opposition and of certain crucifixion. Yours will be the same kind of quiet courage—courage to say "No" to enemies, also to friends; courage to be in an unpopular minority with truth and right; courage to go on undismayed when a loved companion drops beside the road and the future is all unknown—the courage of cosmic confidence.

This quiet courage is to be stamped within me; never again shall I be afraid of anything. I am free!

O Christ of the undaunted faith, give me Thy quiet confidence and courage. May I not hold my faith; may it hold me—hold me when everything else is gone. Stamp this courage into my flesh and blood and nerve tissue—into me till I shall never again be afraid of anything, because I shall want only Thee. Amen.

II Cor. 11:23–29; Gal. 1:4; Rom. 5:8; 12:1

THE MARK OF JESUS—THE POWER
TO TAKE IT

We continue listing the marks of Jesus which are to be branded within us.

6. *The power to take it.* When things happened to Him, good or bad, He could take it. A judge said to the writer: "There is an increase of the use of drugs, narcotics, and opiates because people can't stand frustration. The people that come before me have no religion, so they turn to the props of aspirin, drugs, liquor. They can't take it." Jesus could take it—yes, when popularity tried to make a king of Him, and when men blinded by hate put Him on a cross. In either extremity He could take it. And that power to take whatever comes is going to be branded within you. Never again will you whine, or complain, or retreat. You will take everything that comes and you will use it—an unbeatable way to live.

7. *He cared.* He cared little as to what happened to Him, but He cared deeply as to what happened to others. He was so deeply sensitized that every man's hunger was His own; He was bound in every man's imprisonment and lonely in every man's loneliness. To be in touch with Christ is to be sensitized. And to be fully in touch with Christ is to be sensitized on a world scale. As Von Hugel says: "Christians are people who care." They care beyond race and class and color—they care indiscriminately. Now this same spirit is to be branded into you. It will deliver you from all smug self-centered satisfaction and indifference to others. You will care—hurt in the hurts of others, and happy in their happiness.

8. *He gave Himself.* The crowning mark in Him was that He not only cared; He cared enough to give, and not only enough to give, but to give *Himself.* The ultimate test is there; we give money, interest, words, attendance—do we give *ourselves?* Now this last quality of life is being branded into you. You will give yourself to everyone of every race or class or color who needs you.

O my Christ, I await the branding, not with this or that quality of Thine—I want to be branded with Thy total spirit. Come into my blood, my nerves, my tissues, my moral consciousness—into the total me with Thy total self. For I thirst for Thee. One touch of Thee and I am set aflame for more, for more, for all. I can be satisfied only when I wake in Thy likeness. Amen.

Rom. 8:12–15; Col. 3:5–10; Phil. 3:12–14

THE DYING KICKS OF EVIL HABITS

Perhaps you are questioning the absoluteness of the deliverance depicted in the study of last week. "Branded" is a decisive word. You will be tempted to doubt if the deliverance is decisive and all at once. Don't be discouraged if the deliverance isn't all at once. It usually is. But it is sometimes gradual.

After Pentecost, which had burned out of Peter many weaknesses, there still lingered race prejudice. A special aftertouch was needed to root that out. "The Spirit bade me go with them, making no distinction." There is a lot of mopping up to be done after the citadel has been taken by Christ—little pockets of recalcitrant, fighting rebels.

When I was in college I contracted poison-ivy infection between my fingers and on my eyelids. It was so bad that even proud flesh formed between my fingers. And then I was healed. After I went to India, where there is no poison ivy, every spring at the time when I had contracted the infection the infected places would show signs of itching. The signs grew fainter and fainter each year and finally, after about twenty years, they faded out. Evil in your life will act in the same way. The roots are pulled out, and yet the dying kicks of dying habits will remind you that the evil was once there. Don't be discouraged—the kicks are dying kicks.

A lady who has helped many thousands into mental and spiritual health tells people that gradual deliverance is something like guests who have departed; good-byes are said and parting is all over, but soon the guests, having circled around the block, come back again to wave a final good-bye. So it will be with evil habits; the last good-byes are said and yet there is often a last waving of farewell. But this final one is a farewell.

The only worth-while thing that I have ever seen in newspaper comics was this from Little Orphan Annie: "Annie out of danger at last . . . . and somewhere along the dark road, in bringing Annie through, Katie shook off the clutching fear that had haunted her mind so long."

O God, perhaps that is the secret. In serving others, in losing myself in the difficulties of others, I too shall find my fears dropping away along the dark road. Their specters may haunt me even after they are buried. But they are gone —gone forever. I belong to the victorious present and the future, not to a defeated yesterday. I thank Thee. I thank Thee. Amen.

Acts 8:26–39; John 15:5, 16; Dan. 12:3; Ps. 51:12–13

A LADDER TO A CONTAGIOUS LIFE

To have the qualities of Jesus branded into our beings will not be enough unless we have the quality of contagion. For contagion makes these qualities outgoing and places them at the disposal of others. "No virtue is safe that is not enthusiastic; no heart is pure that is not passionate; no life is Christian that is not Christianizing." If there is no outflow, the inflow automatically stops.

We must deliberately set ourselves to be spiritually creative. Perhaps these seven steps will help you toward a contagious life.

1. *I am made in the inner structure of my being to be creative.* If I am not spiritually creative I shall fail to fulfill the destiny of my being. I shall live against myself.

2. *To win others to a new life is the highest form of creative activity.* I have a chance to be creative where it counts most. Physical creativity is denied many; spiritual creativity is denied none, except those who deny it to themselves.

3. *Nothing is really mine until I share it with others.* All expression deepens impression. Again, it is a law of the mind that that which is not expressed dies. I want this life to be mine, for it is life's dearest treasure.

4. *I shall have the will to evangelize.* Hitherto the desire to evangelize has been in my mind and emotion; now it gets into my will. I have decided to share with others what has been shared with me.

5. *If I am afraid of being snubbed, I shall remind myself that I have a secret ally in every heart.* There is something within the hearts of others that will take sides with me, for the heart is made for this.

6. *If I fail I shall fail in doing what I should do.* But perhaps the greatest failure is the failure to do anything.

7. *I may be unworthy, but God can use my very sins.* It may be that my past sins, and my victory over them, will inspire others to feel they also can be victorious. Far from thinking of myself as being on a pedestal, I shall consider myself a humble pedestrian asking others to try the way I am trying.

O God, I bring to Thee this noncreative life of mine for Thee to touch into creative life. If my efforts falter, perhaps that will give Thee the greater chance to work; and when I speak haltingly, perhaps Thou canst speak most clearly. But whatever happens I am committed—I am committed to getting others committed to Thee. Amen.

John 1:43–49; 4:6–42; Mark 13:11

THE FOUR STEPS IN HELPING OTHERS
TO CHRIST

Perhaps you are hesitant in attempting to win others because you are not sure how to proceed. I dislike exceedingly the idea back of "selling religion"—it smacks of commercialism, and conceives of religion as a commodity. One might as well talk of "selling friendships," or "selling art appreciations." Nevertheless, there are some things we can learn from those who sell commodities. I have watched the men who go through the trains to sell various articles. Some get a lot of customers and others get no response. The one who makes a lot of sales usually does so because of two things: First, he acts as though the merchandise he has is of real importance. But he must not overdo it, or there will be an unfavorable reaction. It must be restrained importance. Second, he doesn't walk through the train with his head in the air—he looks at each passenger as if to give each one a personal invitation to buy. Important and personal—the two watchwords.

The sales manager of the National Cash Register Company gives four steps in presenting a commodity. (1) What is it? (2) What will it do (for you)? (3) Who says so? (4) How can you get it?

In presenting the Christian way to people you will have to answer those four questions. First: *What is it?* Perhaps you will have to tell the person what it is not, in order to clear away misconceptions. It is not a mere set of beliefs to be believed, an organization to be joined, a rite or ceremony to be undergone—it may and does involve these, but it is much more than these. It is a personal relationship with God, which involves a change, gradual or sudden, from the kingdom of self to the Kingdom of God through the grace and power of Christ. The basis of life is shifted from self to God—you live in a state, not of self-reference, but of God-reference. God's will becomes supreme in your life. That will is interpreted to us in Christ. To be a Christian is to be a Christ-ian—to be committed, with all you have, to Christ in surrender and obedience.

O Christ, help me to help others to see Thee. They see so many things built up around Thee that they do not see Thee. Help me to help someone to get into personal relationships with Thee—to bend the knee to Thee and to Thee alone. They will lose themselves and then find themselves in Thee. For Thou and Thou alone art our very life. Amen.

Rom. 8:14–16; 14:17; Gal. 5:22–23; Heb. 12:1–2

THE UNIVERSAL WITNESS TO THIS WAY

We come to the second step in unfolding the Christian way to others.

Second: *What will it do* (for you)? Answer: It will give you personal relations with a Person; you will no longer be orphaned, estranged, out of gear with Reality; you will find forgiveness and cleansing from all fears, resentments, guilts, inhibitions, and complexes; you will have the sense of inner unity—no longer at war with yourself; you will find the tyranny of self-centeredness broken—you will begin to think of others—you will begin to be a person who cares; you will find yourself a part of a Kingdom which is Reality itself; you will have a Cause—the Kingdom—and that Cause will be embodied in a Person—Christ—the Order and the Person will coincide and your religion will be at once personal and social. You will begin to say, This is It! Your life will be one long verification of your central hypothesis. It will be self-authenticating and self-verifying. Moreover, it will give you power, not merely to bear trouble, suffering, and frustration, but to use them—to take them all up into the purpose of your life and transmute them into character and usefulness.

Third: *Who says so?* If only a person here and there endorsed the Christian way, its worth would be doubted. But men, women, and children in all ages, in all climes, and in all circumstances rise up and say, "I have tested and tried it. Christ is a Saviour, not merely because I hope He will save me from hell, and to heaven, but because He saves me here and now from gloom, despair, meaninglessness, purposelessness, sin, the tyranny of myself and my passions, and has made me free—free." This universal witness to a universal fact is one of the most solemn and reassuring things in life. This Way is verified on a world scale—it works to the degree that men work it. On the contrary, life lived against this Way breaks down, becomes snarled up, is self-frustrated, won't work. If all this be so, then you may add, very quietly, "I too find it works."

O Christ, help me to be Thy witness. I hear over the radio the voice of the evangelism of sensate things as it tremulously tells of what this, that, and the other gadget will do. I know this is a false emphasis on a false god. Help me then to witness all the more clearly for Thee, O Eternal Reality, and to do so with no stammering of the tongue. And help me to witness with a quenchless joy. Amen.

Josh. 24:15; John 6:67-69; Ps. 55:17; Matt. 6:22

THE FIVE STEPS IN FOLLOWING CHRIST

We come now to the last step of the four. Fourth: How *can you get it?* Jesus gives the answer in this statement: "If any man would come after me, let him deny himself, and take up his cross daily, and follow me." (Luke 9:23.) Here there are five steps:

1. *Make up your mind:* "If any man would come after me." Here is the great decision that decides all decisions. It is what they call in psychology "a major choice"—a choice which you do not have to make over again each day; a choice into which the lesser choices of life fit, and not a choice which fits into them; it is the choice which organizes everything around itself.

2. *Give up yourself:* "let him deny himself." The word literally is "fling away," or "utterly reject." "Deny" does not mean doing without things here and there; it means a denial of self as central, as a primary factor—self is subordinate to and obedient to another Will—the Will of Christ. Self abdicates and Christ mounts the throne. You decide that He shall decide.

3. *Take up your cross:* "take up his cross." This doesn't mean merely to bear patiently the troubles that come upon you—it is deeper: It means that you will deliberately take on yourself trouble, pain, sorrow, sin and make them your own, in order to free others from them. You will offer yourself as one great soul did who walked the floor the night Vanzetti was executed, put his hands to his head, and said, "O God, if there is a poor devil who does not have a voice to speak in behalf of his rights, then you can have my voice; or if there is one who cannot write his petitions, then, O God, you can have my pen to write for him."

4. *Keep up your cultivation:* "daily." There is a once-for-allness in this, and yet there is daily disciplined cultivation.

5. *Gather up your loyalties*—gather them up into a single-minded devotion: "follow me." You are not following this, that, or the other person—you are following Christ. Men may let you down—He won't. Your faith is Christ-centric.

O Christ, I know when I follow Thee I am following an unfolding Mind and an expanding Will. Thou art not static. The more I see in Thee, the more I see there is to be seen. I am on the great adventure of eternal discovery and eternal growth. My code is now a Character, my law a Life. I thank Thee. Amen.

Ps. 119:105; I Sam. 3:9; Lam. 3:25–28; II Tim. 2:15; 3:16

STEPS IN READING THE WORD

One of the steps we mentioned yesterday is connected with daily cultivation. When helping another, get that person to enroll in the School of the Word. On board ship I saw two men begin the day in different ways: One, a businessman, came down early, eagerly picked up the newssheet and turned at once to the stock-market report. His face lighted up or fell with the market. His happiness was dependent on happenings, so it went up and down. Another man leaned over the rail each morning reading the Word, and then he looked out over the open sea in meditation. His face wore calm and poise and strength. His happiness was dependent on eternal relationships, not subject to temporal happenings.

In reading the Word each morning take these steps:

1. *Relax.* You are receptive only when you are relaxed. Nothing can be inscribed on a tense conscious mind. Let every muscle, every brain cell go limp. This attitude says, "Speak, Lord, Thy servant heareth." If you go stamping through a woods in a hurry you will see little. But sit still and the squirrels will come down the trees, and the birds will draw near, and Nature will be alive in every twig and tree and flower. You are relaxed and receptive, and Nature becomes vocal. The same with the Word.

2. *Recall.* Ask these questions as you read: (a) Who is writing? (b) To whom? (c) For what purpose? (d) What is he saying? (e) How does it apply to me? (f) How shall I put it into practice? (g) When do I begin?

3. *Rehearse.* If you find something that speaks to your condition, becomes authoritative, then roll it over and over in the mind. Rolling it over in the mind, it will become an atmosphere, then an attitude, then an act. When Jesus was pressed by temptation in the wilderness He answered in the words of Scripture. These words had become a part of Him, and in the crisis they naturally passed from the stage of assimilation and atmosphere to that of attitude and act.

O Christ, let me have the Word hidden in my heart so deeply that it becomes the hidden springs of action, determining my conduct and character. The Eternal Word spoke through Thy words—let It speak through mine. Then I shall live and move and have my being in the Eternal. Amen.

Ps. 1:2; 119:9, 11, 162; Mal. 3:16

STEPS IN READING THE WORD—Continued

We continue our steps in reading the Word:

4. *Retain.* Do not merely rehearse a passage that gets you; deliberately plan to retain it. Commit it to memory. When a high-school boy, reading the Scripture before an assembly, read the passage this way: "Ye shall hate all men for my name's sake," those who heard him did not seem surprised and shocked, for they didn't know the correct reading. That generation had not been trained in memorizing Scripture and was mentally and morally the poorer as a result.

5. *Rejoice.* We must rejoice, for reading the Word is a tryst with God. As I sat reading the Word in a Pullman a bright-faced oldish lady said as she passed by: "You must love the Author, for you are reading His Word. I too love the Author." At once we were friends around the Friend. In reading the Word, remember that what you have read is all leading to His feet. The Bible is not a flat Bible from Genesis to Revelation—it is not a line like this: ———, but like this: /, leading to Christ as the final goal and the final authority. These words lead you to Him who is the Word—the Word made flesh. He made His own word final, even in Scripture: "Ye have heard that it was said . . . . of old time," "but I say unto you." Revelation is progressive, culminating in Christ. He is the test and touchstone of all. He is the Word. Rejoice in Him. Our law is a Life, our code a Character.

6. *Realign.* As you read this Word keep realigning your life with this Life. In Korea a girl did not come back for more instruction in Scripture, and when asked why the reply was: "I haven't learned yet to practice fully what I've been taught." She felt she had to keep practice abreast of teaching. Quite right. The Negro preacher prayed: "Prop us up, Lord, on our leaning side." Realign your life every day with the Word.

7. *Release.* If you find something that gets hold of you in the Word, pass it on to somebody that very day. The repetition will help the retention, and it will help to lighten the path of the other.

Thou Eternal Word, may my words be but echoes of Thee. For my words are dead unless there is a soul in them, and Thou art the Soul. Help me to be steeped in Thy Mind, fired by Thy passion, and decisive with Thy purposes. Help me to be alive, atingle with Thee. Amen.

Matt. 16:24–26; Luke 14:25–35; Gal. 2:20; Phil. 1:20–21

WE BEGIN A STUDY OF THE BEATITUDES

We ended yesterday our outlines for the study of the Word. If "the proper study of mankind is man," then the proper study of the Word is the Word. We shall pause for a moment at the opening sentences of the Sermon on the Mount, the Beatitudes. If "the Bible is distilled essence of great souls," then this Sermon is the distilled essence of the Soul of Christ. He is limning His own spirit on the canvas of these words.

The Beatitudes begin and end where Jesus began and ended in His ministry as a whole. They begin with the Kingdom (Matthew 5:3), and end with the Kingdom (vs. 9). As the Kingdom was the framework in which all His teaching was set, the Master-light in which everything was seen, so the Kingdom is supreme here. The Sermon depicts the New Order and the character of those who are citizens of that New Order. Sorokin, head of the sociology department at Harvard, after reviewing the decay and breakdown of our social order, comes to the conclusion that the new order which will replace the present order must be patterned after the Sermon on the Mount. This is the deliberate conclusion of a sociologist and not just a rhetorical gesture. The Sermon is turning out to be, not idealism, but what we have always been convinced it was—stark realism. The Kingdom is Reality—the only Reality.

Jesus is saying here what He always insisted upon: "Seek ye first the kingdom of God, ... and all these things shall be added unto you"—get this straight, and everything else will come out straight. But how do you get this supreme Value straight—by holding it as a supreme Idea? No; but by submitting to it as a supreme Loyalty. "Blessed are the renounced in spirit [lit.]: for theirs is the kingdom of heaven." The Kingdom is imperious, demanding on the very threshold a renunciation, and a renunciation at the deepest depths—in spirit.

On the very threshold of the Kingdom we meet a demand: Be renounced in spirit. If not, nothing else follows; if so, then everything follows.

O God, I know whose bonds are upon my heart. I know what I must do: I must renounce at the center—in my very spirit. With the center Thine, then all the circumference follows. Help me to let the Kingdom operate from the center of my being to the circumference of my relationships. Then I shall be a Kingdom-controlled man. In Jesus' name. Amen.

Mark 4:1–20; John 1:12; 1 Cor. 1:30

THE FIRST STEP: RECEPTIVITY

We continue our study of the Beatitudes—the study of "the happy ones." Jesus gives His recipe for happiness, and it begins with "renunciation." This reverses the ordinary recipe for happiness, which usually begins with "assert," "take," "realize." Which recipe for happiness will life back?

Now note that the first three beatitudes are all receptive instead of assertive: (1) the renounced in spirit (vs. 3); (2) those that mourn over the mistakes, sins, and failures of themselves and others, and mourn for the coming of the Kingdom (vs. 4); (3) the meek, or the disciplined (vs. 5). All three bespeak one thing: receptivity. These are all passive virtues. Then follow three positive or active virtues: (1) the merciful (vs. 7); (2) the pure in heart (vs. 8); (3) the peacemakers (vs. 9). Between these two sets of threes, passive and positive virtues, there is one (vs. 6) that is both passive and positive: "Blessed are they which do hunger and thirst after righteousness"—that is active—"for they shall be filled"—passive. This verse, made up of both, is the pivot upon which the change is made from passive to active virtues.

Now note that the Kingdom way of life begins with receptivity. Is that right? Isn't that where all life has to begin? The two cells the ovum and the sperm have to receive each other before they can begin the positive business of producing active life. The seed in the ground receives moisture and nutrition from the earth and the air before it can begin to give forth in flower and fruit. An organism can expend as much as it takes in, and no more. If it doesn't begin with receptivity, it doesn't begin. The scientist who doesn't sit down before the facts as a little child, and isn't prepared to give up every preconceived notion, and isn't willing to follow to whatever end nature will lead him, will know nothing. He has to be renounced, to mourn that he doesn't know, to be humble, or he gets nowhere. The first immutable law of all life, material and spiritual, is: receptivity. Life confronts us with the alternatives: receive or perish.

O God, I dare not perish, when I can receive. And now, renounced and receptive, I come to Thee. Take my emptiness and make it into Thy fullness; my foolishness and make it into Thy wisdom; my paralysis and make it into Thy power; myself and make it into Thee. For I hunger and thirst after Thee. I really do. Amen.

Phil. 4:13; Num. 12:3–15; II Cor. 10:1; Titus 3:1–7; Col. 3:12–17

THE ATTITUDE AND ITS OUTCOME OR REWARD

We ended yesterday by saying that the first step in abundant living is receptivity. What is received? The renounced in spirit receive the Kingdom of God; the mourners receive comfort; and the meek inherit the earth. The first attitude is general—the renounced in spirit; and the reward is general —the Kingdom of God. But note that the verse does not say that they belong to the Kingdom of God. It says that the Kingdom of God belongs to them—its powers are behind them; its resources are at their disposal; its very authority and power are at their command. They are universe-backed.

In the second the attitude is specific—those that mourn; and the reward is specific—they shall be comforted. But the comfort is *con*—"together," and *fortis*—"brave," so the meaning is "brave together." There is a sense of human-Divine togetherness; a sense of adequacy, not because of one's strength, but because of one's Resources. You and Christ are afraid of nothing, because you can use everything.

In the third the attitude is again specific—the meek; and the reward is specific—they inherit the earth. The meek are not the weak—they are the trained, the disciplined, the receptive. They inherit not heaven only, but the earth. The meek-minded scientist inherits the world of fact. Every great scientist is humble—has to be, for if he were proud, know-all in his attitudes, Nature would shut up like a clam and reveal nothing to him. When the French people voted as to the greatest Frenchman, they passed by Napoleon and fastened upon Pasteur, whose discoveries benefited so many. The meek inherited the world of affections and reverence. If the American people should vote on the greatest American, they would undoubtedly fasten upon Lincoln, the great emancipator, the humble-souled liberator of the oppressed. The earth belongs to the meek because it won't respond to the proud, the vaunting. The earth is made in its inner constitution to work in the Christian way, and hence none but the Christian meek can inherit it.

Napoleon said: "There are only two forces in the world: the spirit and the sword. And the spirit always conquers the sword."

O God, I see that the earth rots in the hands of those who try to take it by force and pride and domination. It doesn't belong to them. It belongs to Thy Son and to those who meekly follow Him. Help me to inherit Him and then I shall inherit the earth and all that is in it. Amen.

Ps. 42:1–5; 63:1–8; 107:9; John 7:37–39; II Chron. 6:41

GOODNESS IS OUR NATIVE AIR

We turn from the three receptive qualities to the pivotal quality of outgoing-incoming, positive-passive in the statement, "Blessed are those who hunger and thirst for goodness! they will be satisfied." (Matthew 5:6, Moffatt.) This group is as outreaching as hunger and as thirst, but outgoing for what? Money, fame, sex satisfaction, power? No, *goodness!* Result? They are satisfied! Those who are outreaching for money, fame, sex satisfaction, and power are forever unsatisfied—they have the doom of thirst upon them. The more they get, the more they want. Those who thirst for goodness thirst for what they are made for; hence they can be satisfied. But if the eye should thirst for darkness instead of light, the conscience thirst for error instead of truth, the aesthetic nature thirst for ugliness instead of beauty, the heart thirst for hate instead of love—the end? Dissatisfaction, frustration, conflict, breakdown.

Goodness is our native air. We live to the extent that we live in goodness; we gasp and die if we try to live in evil. These are the alternate heartbeats of healthy, abundant living: Outgoing for goodness—incoming with satisfaction; outgoing for goodness—incoming with satisfaction. A heart that beats with this rhythm lives forever.

But the heartbeat of the wrongly directed thirst is: Outgoing for evil—incoming with dissatisfaction; outgoing for evil—incoming with dissatisfaction. A heart that beats with this false rhythm dies of heart failure, eternally dies of heart failure, perishes.

Jesus said, "Whosoever drinketh of this water shall thirst again"—those who drink of the waters of lust, of money, of power, of fame, of thrills, have the doom of thirst upon them—they thirst again, inevitably and invariably. "But," continued Jesus, "whosoever drinketh of the water that I shall give him shall never thirst"—a life without exhausting thirsts! A central and fundamental satisfaction! A well of water within springing up to everlasting life!

And note that it is "springing up"—it is not a dull, bovine satisfaction, but a satisfaction that is popping with novelty and exciting adventure.

O God, my Father, Thou art giving me two satisfactions —the satisfaction of fulfillment, and the satisfaction of growth. I am deeply satisfied with Thee, and yet I am forever reaching for more. Thou dost satisfy me and stimulate me. I rest and am forever unresting till I awake in Thy likeness. I am so grateful, so grateful. Amen.

Exod. 33:13–15; Matt. 17:5–8; John 9:36–38; 12:20–21

FROM THE RECEPTIVE TO THE POSITIVE VIRTUES

We proceed in our study of the Beatitudes from the receptive side to the positive side. The first three are receptive; the fourth is partly receptive and partly outgoing; and the next three are positive and assertive: (1) the merciful who obtain mercy; (2) the pure in heart who see God; (3) the peacemakers who are called children of God.

The Kingdom-of-God life begins with receptivity and ends in positive activity—the passive becomes the positive. The positives are three: they exercise power mercifully; they have gained a central insight—they see God; they go out and are able to make men change and come to peaceful solutions.

The astonishing thing is that when Jesus turns from the passive, receptive side, the first thing He mentions is power wielded mercifully. He tells of masterful, dominating personalities who have people in their power, but who wield that power mercifully and beneficently. Does receptivity bring power over others? Yes; a receptive person becomes a vigorous person. Divine resources make the man humanly resourceful. But the vigor is constructive and redemptive—power is controlled by love, the only safe power. Jesus had all power, but He used it not for Himself, not for the destruction of enemies, not to awe His hearers, but only for purposes of mercy.

The second outgoing quality is purity of heart which has a central insight—it sees God. Those who are receptive can not only do—they can see. There are two great types of personalities—those who desire to do, to achieve, to wield power, and those who desire to have insights, to know, to gain the world of insight into the relationships of things. The first are the men of action, and the second the men of thought—the pioneers, the philosophers. Both types are produced out of receptivity, and both are needed. But the central insight that is needed is men who can see God— God at work in redemption, in science, in beauty, in the moral universe, overruling the affairs of men. The pure in heart are in the breathless adventure of seeing God everywhere!

O God, I would be pure in heart, single-minded, so that my insights may be clarified, for I want to see Thee—to see Thee in the blade of grass, in the procession of the stars, in the rough-and-tumble of human events, and in my own heart when I close the door and make tryst with Thee there. I would see Thee—Thee. Then I am satisfied. Amen.

Rom. 5:10–11; Matt. 5:23–24; Jas. 3:13–18;
Heb. 12:14; II Cor. 13:11

THE CENTER OF THE CHRISTIAN GOSPEL— RECONCILIATION

The undivided in heart see God. Where other men see dead matter, they see the Creator's delicacy of touch; where others see history as a mere matter of meaningless events, they see history as His Story; where others see the tragedy of a good man dying a martyr, they see the triumph of the God who redeems through His own death.

But they not only see; they also have the positive power to get people to see and change and come to a reconciliation on a higher level. The third positive quality is peace-making: "Blessed are the peacemakers." The receptive find power to reconcile in three directions—between man and God, between man and man, and between man and himself. They have the power to help man to be at home with God, at home with his fellow men, and at home with himself.

If I were to pick out the one verse that most nearly expresses the Christian gospel, it would be this: "God was in Christ, reconciling the world unto himself, ... and hath committed unto us the word of reconciliation." God was in the positive business of an outgoing love that reconciled man to Himself when man did not want to be reconciled. We do what God does—He commits unto us the same work of reconciling. In two outstanding passages from Moffatt we are called sons of the Father, and for the same reason: "Blessed are the peacemakers! they will be ranked sons of God" (Matthew 5:9), and "But I tell you, love your enemies and pray for those who persecute you, that you may be sons of your Father in heaven." (Matthew 5:44–45.) You are most like God when you are bringing people together in reconciliation. When I was trying to find a basis for reconciliation between Japan and America, Admiral Nomura took my hand and said, "Thank you for what you are doing. Those who are trying to reconcile others are doing the work of Heaven, for it is Heaven's work to reconcile us." A non-Christian put his finger on the central Christian quality—reconciliation.

O God, my Father, I would be like Thee. Thou art reconciling—I would be, too. Take out of me all antagonisms, all divisions, all clashes, so that those whom I meet this day will instinctively feel that I breathe "Peace." Oh, let me breathe "Peace" upon the hot hearts of men and cool them with Thy love. In Jesus' name. Amen.

1 Pet. 5:5–7; Isa. 57:15; Matt. 18:1–4;
Rom. 8:35–39; 1 Cor. 3:21–23

THE KINGDOM BELONGS TO THE RECEPTIVE—THE POSITIVE

We come to the last of the "Blesseds": "Blessed are those who have been persecuted for the sake of goodness! the Realm of heaven is theirs." (Matthew 5:10, Moffatt.) This "blessed" is the result of the other seven. Those who are so receptive that they become positive and outgoing are a judgment to others—their lives become superior; and men do not like to be silently judged, so they kick back in persecution. Society demands conformity. If you fall beneath its standards, it will punish you; if you rise above its standards, it will persecute you. It demands an average, gray conformity. But the Christian is different—he is a departure upward; his head is lifted above the multitude; hence it gets hit. If the head doesn't get hit, it is not lifted above the multitude. "Woe unto you," said Jesus, "when all men shall speak well of you," for if they do, you are like them. The Christian must therefore get used to the sight of his own blood.

But what is the result of being so positive that you are persecuted? "The Kingdom of God is theirs!" Note: they do not belong to the Kingdom of God; the Kingdom of God belongs to them—its powers are with them, behind them, at their disposal. Now note that these "Beatitudes" say that the Kingdom belongs to two: "those who are renounced in spirit"—the receptive; and "those who are persecuted for the sake of goodness"—those so positive that they are persecuted. The Kingdom of God does not belong to the receptive alone, or to the positive alone; it belongs to the receptive-positive, the incoming-outgoing type. They are the Mystic-Masters who have caught the balance between the introvert and the extrovert—they are the ambivert.

Now note: the world reverses this—it begins with positive self-assertiveness without receptivity. It soon runs through its resources and ends in receptivity by circumstances—it becomes a prey of environment, mastered by life, defeated, frustrated, empty. The Kingdom life begins with humble receptivity and ends in mastery.

O God, I thank Thee that I have hold of the right end of the handle of life—humble receptivity. Now I can wield the other end in positive achievement and output. I can never, never run through my Resources; so I shall never, never fail in result. I am but the wire along which Thy power runs. Keep me connected and insulated. Amen.

Gen. 4:14; Acts 16:25–26; Phil. 1:12–14

GRACE IN THE DUNGEON

There are many who say: "I am caught in a web of circumstances that bind me hand and foot. How can I have abundant living under those circumstances?" In answer I refer you to a passage which tells of those who "find grace in the dungeon." (Jeremiah 31:2, Moffatt.) If you find grace at all, you must find it in the dungeon. You are caught—you are not able to get out of the dungeon; then the only thing to do is to get the dungeon out of you—to find grace in that very dungeon.

The people to whom this passage was addressed did "find grace in the dungeon"—they were purified in the Exile, and became the instrument of God through that awful experience of national bondage. The dungeon became a door! You needn't accept your circumstances as from God, but you can accept them as an opportunity for God to use them to make you creative.

A girl of twenty was confined to her bed for a year with a bad heart. The first week was spent in bitter rebellion. Then she read *Christ and Human Suffering,* and it opened the possibility of not merely bearing suffering and frustration, but also of using them. It was a revelation to her. The remaining fifty-one weeks of that year were beautiful—the best year of her life. She arose out of that year awakened in soul and in mind. She determined to have a college education, and did so. She is one of the most promising and useful young people I know. She found grace in the dungeon. The frustration became fruitfulness.

Among the most beautiful of Paul's writings are these lines: "This salutation is in my own hand, from Paul. 'Remember I am in prison. Grace be with you.' " (Colossians 4:18, Moffatt.) You would have expected him to say, "I am in prison—God give me grace." But no; he puts it the other way: "I am in prison. Grace be with *you.*" I have found grace in the dungeon—enough and to spare—I pass it on to you.

Gracious God and Father, if my circumstances become a dungeon, then help me to find there grace enough for myself and to spare for others. Help me not to whine or complain, but to find resources enough to pass on. For I know that Thy grace is sufficient for me, not merely when life is free and open, but when life turns into a dungeon. I shall find grace *there.* Amen.

Rom. 8:38–39; Phil. 1:28–29; I Pet. 2:20–24

THE DUNGEON MAKES OR BREAKS US

The dungeon experience can make us or break us. Some it crushes; others it solidifies. A layman speaks of growing pains or growing conflicts. Conflicts may be of two kinds —one kind where you come out on the lower, defeat side, and the other where you come out on the higher, victory side.

It was said of Jesus that He went into the wilderness "full of the Spirit," and came out "in the power of the Spirit"—mere fullness turned to power under the stress of temptation. The dungeon of temptation resulted only in His being strengthened. The Evil One plays a losing game when he succeeds only in strengthening you through his temptations. You come out on the victory side of them. The account says: "Then Jesus told him, 'Begone, Satan! it is written, You must worship the Lord your God and serve him alone.' At this the devil left him." (Matthew 4:10–11, Moffatt.) When Jesus used the word "alone," then, "at this the devil left him." He could not stand that word "alone"— when Jesus uttered it he turned and left, because he knew that to tempt a man who stands on the word "alone" in a single-minded allegiance is only to strengthen that man. Every temptation strengthens the very fiber of such a man. He finds grace and more grace in the dungeon of temptation.

A gracious Christian lady said to another: "I know you dislike being ill. But I find the only thing to do is to get something out of every experience that comes to me. So make your illness give you something."

I find it hard to have to wait for people, but I've learned to make waiting contribute by forming the habit of immediately turning to prayer whenever I have to wait. I find that praying keeps my temper from getting ruffled and that I am also not wasting my time. It always leaves me an open door out of every dungeon. The possibility of prayer is always open, anywhere, at any time. If you lie awake at night, don't fret—pray!

Gracious Father, help me never to be nonplused. If I don't know what else to do, help me to turn naturally to prayer. Then no moment will be empty and fruitless. Every chink of every minute will be filled with the cement of prayer. So life will be held together by poise and calm and victory. I am grateful that I can always find grace in every dungeon. Amen.

Rom. 8:26, 28, 35–37; II Cor. 12:7–10

FINDING FREEDOM THROUGH LIMITATIONS

We continue our thought of "grace in the dungeon." All our limitations, our dungeons, can be places where we find grace. I have always been grateful that I went to a small, obscure college, for it left me with the sense of being uneducated. I suppose that those who go to great institutions feel secure; to mention the name of the great university which they attended brands them as educated. I have felt no such security; so I have endeavored all my life to become an educated person. I gather from every moment, every occasion, and every conversation something that will help educate me. On the tombstone of a man were these words: "He died climbing." I would like to have this inscription on mine: "He died learning." The limitation has been a liberty. I have found grace in the dungeon.

The person who has discovered and revealed to the people of Arkansas their wild flowers is shut-in, a woman crippled with arthritis. Although her hands are gnarled and twisted, she has painted exquisitely five hundred specimens. Harvard University wants to buy the collection, but there is a public movement on foot to buy them for the state of Arkansas. Miss Whitfield cheerfully held up her twisted fingers and told how, by the law of compensation, she was enabled to paint those delicate lines. Her cheer and her skill are beyond words. She has found grace in the dungeon. A shut-in knows more about the wild flowers and where they grow than anyone in the state!

I want to pay my tribute of gratitude to the single women of the world for whom life might have been a dungeon of loneliness had they not made it into something else. Around the world they have married themselves to human need; have made every waif child their own; have brightened families, while they themselves were familyless; have lifted crosses from the burdened bodies and souls of people, while they themselves have carried the cross of aloneness. They have found grace in the dungeon and have given it. Bless them!

O Christ, Thou hast shown me how to take hold of the nettle of life when it stings, and make those very stings into sensitiveness to the hurts of others. I am plunged into a dungeon. Perhaps I am in this dungeon so that I can see the stars. For I know that nothing can defeat me if I remain undefeated within. I thank Thee. Amen.

Ps. 22:1–5, 31; 23

MAKING IRRITATIONS INTO CHARACTER

Two wealthy women, whose husbands were in the lumber business, went to live in the Northern woods. Both were from great cities. The one built a mansion of a house in the woods, had her maids and butlers, imported the people of the cities for week ends, and tried to keep up the general hullabaloo of the city around her. She decayed—the dungeon got on the inside of her. The other lived in comparative simplicity, took an interest in the people in their employ, became one of them, and lifted their level. She is happy and is the salt of the situation. She found grace in what might have been a dungeon.

There is no use fighting against the inevitable. Take hold of it and use it. This motto is over the desk of a high-school principal:

> "For every evil under the sun,
>   There is a remedy, or there is none;
>   If there be one, try and find it,
>   If there be none, never mind it."

The suggestion regarding a remedyless evil, "never mind it," is good, but not quite good enough. For the remedyless evil may be so present and insistent that you cannot help but mind it. For instance, there is the dungeon of an unhappy marriage. It is impossible not to mind it—the iron of it enters into the soul every day. What is to be done?

Two things are possible: First, go over the whole matter anew. See if some of the reasons for this marital unhappiness are not in you. Be objective and relentless with yourself. Don't defend yourself. If you find places where you are at fault, confess the fault to your partner. Leave it to the other one to confess his or her fault. Don't confess the other person's sins. Try honestly to find a way of agreement. Second, if you cannot, then do what an oyster does: when it gets an irritating grain of sand in its shell it throws a pearl around the irritation. So you can throw the pearl of character around your daily irritations. You can find grace in the dungeon.

O God, my Father, I come to Thee with my dungeon life. I know that Thou canst either free me or give me grace to make the dungeon into a Trysting Place with Thee. Thou wilt make this dungeon a place where daily we shall meet and work out life together in spite of. I thank Thee. Amen.

Phil. 4:12–13; Rom. 5:3–5; Gal 4:13

MAKING CALAMITIES SERVE

Dungeons of various kinds often lead to finding grace there. Milton wrote his *Paradise Lost* when blind. Clifford W. Beers was once in an insane asylum. Later he wrote *A Mind That Found Itself*, and founded The National Commission for Mental Hygiene. The mentally upset owe much to a man who himself was mentally upset.

Darwin said: "If I had not been so great an invalid, I should not have done nearly as much as I have accomplished." Carlyle said that he wrote with "a rat continually gnawing at my stomach." A man was set aside with a broken hip; while lying in bed the wallpaper at which he had continuously to look gave him the idea of becoming a sketch artist, and he became a very successful one. He found grace in the dungeon.

A poet failed on the first night of a public reading and felt the next day that everybody was pointing the finger of scorn at him. He went home and wrote his greatest inspirational poem on the ability "to take it" when you fail. That poem fell into the hands of a man in the hospital who had lost both arms and feet, and it inspired him to become a public reader—and he became a very successful one. They both found grace in the dungeon.

A young man came to our Ashram armless. He eats and writes with his toes. At work period, refusing to be left out, he painted the side of a house by standing on one foot and painting as high up as his head with the other. He is pastor of a university church. He has found grace in the dungeon. Dr. Mary McCracken is totally crippled in her lower limbs with infantile paralysis. The medical colleges of America refused to allow her to take a medical course, saying she could never practice. She went to China, took her medical degree at Peking Medical, stood at the top of her class, came back to the very city of Philadelphia where she had been refused a medical course, and is practicing in an institution for crippled children—practicing in a wheel chair.

O God, these people have all found grace in a dungeon. Help me then to take limitations of any kind whatever and make out of them spurs to life and achievement. May I do with my limitations what the river does with its banks—the more confining they are, the swifter the stream. Oh, press my heart with pain that my life forces may flow the faster! In Jesus' name. Amen.

Exod. 3:7–10; Matt. 16:2–3; Acts 8:1, 4

GREAT MOVEMENTS BORN OUT OF TROUBLED TIMES

Great movements come out of dark periods. Men find grace in the dungeon. Dr. Kenneth S. Latourette has traced some great movements born out of dark periods. In 1789 the French Revolution broke out and was followed by the Napoleonic wars which lasted from 1792 to 1815. In the span of those distressing years the following events occurred. 1792: In the year of the Reign of Terror in Paris the Baptist Missionary Society was organized, growing out of the work of William Carey. 1799: When Napoleon was returning to France from his campaign in Egypt in an effort to break Britain's communications with India, the Church Missionary Society was formed. 1804: About the time that Napoleon was giving England the greatest threat of invasion she has had between the venture of the Spanish Armada and the Nazi attempt in 1940, the British and Foreign Bible Society was organized. 1810: At a time when New England was distraught by our attempts to maintain our neutrality in the Napoleonic wars, and when we were on the eve of our second war with Britain, the American Board of Commissioners of Foreign Missions was organized. 1812: While American ports were being blockaded by the British, *the first party of American missionaries sailed for India.*

When the world is at its worst, Christians are at their best. In Harold Church, Staunton, England, there is an inscription: "In the year 1653 when all things sacred were throughout the nation destroyed or profaned, this church was built to the glory of God by Sir Robert Shirley, whose singular praise it was to have done the best things in the worst times, and hoped for them in the most calamitous."

The Christian takes pains and makes them into pains of childbirth, bringing forth new movements when in the dungeon of calamity and limitation. Philip had "four unmarried daughters who prophesied." (Acts 21:9, Moffatt.) They took their spinsterhood, sublimated it, and made it spiritually creative. They brought forth new hope, new souls, new movements.

O my Father, Thou hast shown me the indomitable way. Even in the hell of frustration and pain Thou art there, inspiring, creating, and making victorious Thy surrendered children. How very, very grateful I am that the dungeon can do for me what the fire did for the Hebrew children—only burned off their fetters! Free me, even by fire. Amen.

I John 1:5–7; Acts 26:16–18; Jas. 4:6–10

THE FIVE STEPS OUT OF THE DUNGEON

Perhaps our world as a whole will have to find grace in the dungeon. As a world we are suffering from self-inflicted pain and self-chosen bondages. We are in dungeons of our own making. Perhaps we shall find grace in our dungeons.

As I have mentioned previously, Dr. Sorokin, head of the sociology department at Harvard, says that the world crisis is the result of the breakdown of a sensate order—an order that believed the only reality was that which comes to us through our senses. That idea has exhausted itself. It is not able to take us any further. Life must form around another idea. He says that idea is the Sermon on the Mount.

In order to make this transition, Sorokin says that society must go through five stages: (1) Crisis. (2) Ordeal. (3) Catharsis. (4) Charisma. (5) Resurrection. This is an interesting and startling conclusion, for Christianity teaches that these are the very steps through which the individual or society must go.

(1) *Crisis.* As the old order goes to pieces, the person or society is confronted with a choice of going down with the old or choosing a new way. The Chinese have a word for crisis made up of two characters: danger and opportunity. Those two things are in every crisis. (2) *Ordeal.* There is the consequent suffering of having to change. This is the ordeal of repentance and reversal. Roots have to be torn up. The suffering may be acute. (3) *Catharsis*—the cleansing from old ideas and old ways—especially old ideas that led to this bankruptcy. Repentance is metanoia—literally, "change of mind," of outlook. (4) *Charisma*—grace. Sorokin uses the New Testament Greek word, for it is God's grace we have to get—an empowering to live in new ways. (5) *Resurrection.* Life is reborn, individually and collectively. Grace has been found in the dungeon. Life had to get worse before it would get better.

Perhaps you as an individual will have to pass through these five steps to Resurrection.

O God, my Father, Thou dost make us go through dungeons to open doors. How it must wring Thy heart to have to stand aside and let us fail! But Thou dost love us too much to let us succeed on low planes. Precipitate the crisis that we may go through the catharsis to the Resurrection. For we must be new—at any price. Amen.

II Tim. 1:7–8; 2:1–5; 4:2, 5

THE AIM OF THE CHRISTIAN DISCIPLINE

In the remaining days we have left for our meditations we must gather up the strands we have been weaving. Perhaps the verse that would sum up what we have been saying is this one: "Whereas the aim of the Christian discipline is the love that springs from a pure heart, from a good conscience, and from a sincere faith." (I Timothy 1:5, Moffatt.)

The Christian discipline: The Christian way is a discipline and not merely a doctrine. The doctrine gives direction and content to the discipline. Doctrine that does not discipline is dead. Christianity is therefore not merely something that you believe, but something that you believe in enough to act upon. Your deed is your creed—the thing you believe in enough to put into practice. You do not believe in what you do not practice. Theory and practice are one. Your theory is your practice

The future of the world is in the hands of disciplined people. The undisciplined waste their energies with themselves and their own tangles. But the statement that the future of the world is in the hands of the disciplined needs to be corrected by the addition: The future of the world is in the hands of those who are disciplined to the highest. If one is disciplined to less than the highest, then the discipline will exhaust itself—it isn't backed by the ultimate. The Christian is disciplined to what? The preceding verse tells us—"the divine order which belongs to faith." The divine order is the Divine Order—the Kingdom of God. That Divine Order was embodied in the Divine Person—Jesus Christ. We are, therefore, disciplined by a Person who embodies an Order, an embodiment which makes our discipline at once personal and at once social—personal in that it is related to a Person, and social in that it is related to a new Order embodied in that Person. Disciplined to the embodied Kingdom, the Christian is bound to outthink, to outlive, to outdie, because the Kingdom out-experiences every other way of life. We can give ourselves without question to the Christian discipline!

O God, this discipline to which I have given myself is *It!* Help me now to be disciplined to this Way with no reservations and with no hesitations. May I fling every doubt and fear and hesitation to the winds. As the ancient Hebrew said: "I take the yoke of the Kingdom." I know I shall find that yoke easy, for it is my life! Amen.

John 4:14; II Cor. 2:1–4; Isa. 42:7

THE CHRISTIAN DISCIPLINE PRODUCES
SPONTANEITY

We saw yesterday that the Christian discipline is the highest discipline because it is disciplined to the highest—the Divine Order embodied in the Divine Person. This discipline is complete and totalitarian, reaching in to control and redeem the inmost thought and aspiration, and stretching out to the utmost rim of relationships. Then does it produce the robot—the marionette dancing to the invisible strings of the Divine Master back in the scenes? No! a thousand times, No! The exact opposite is true. For when you fulfill this will, you fulfill yourself. Paul expresses the spontaneity in these words: "Whereas the aim of the Christian discipline is the love that springs"—it produces spontaneity—it "springs."

Here is what the totalitarians are aiming to achieve and cannot. They cannot produce a love that springs. Their methods produce a hate that springs. They have to sit on a lid. God takes off the lid. "Love God, and do what you like." You are perfectly free, for you are free to do what you ought. Your desires and decisions fit in with the nature of Reality—hence you are living with the grain of the universe, and not against it. Let this statement soak in with its full implications: "The highest in Christ is the deepest in nature." If so, then "grace and reality came by Jesus Christ"—grace and reality are inseparable. When you are in grace, you are at the heart of reality. Now let this statement take hold of you: "Wise decisions harmonize with the fundamental truths of human nature." When you make the wise decision of being disciplined by the Christ Kingdom, you harmonize with the fundamental truths written in you by that Christ. "Without him was not any thing made that was made." The Christian discipline, therefore, produces the most truly spontaneous and natural person in the world —the real Christian. The law ends in a liberty—"love springs." The Christian is artesian.

God and Father, I surrender my lesser, uncontrolled loves of self in order to find a disciplined love to Thee. In that love I shall walk the earth a conqueror—afraid of nothing, because I want nothing but Thee. Thou art gathering up my discords into Thy harmony; my jerky, bumpy ways of life into Thy rhythm; my inner clashes into Thy great enveloping peace. I thank Thee. Amen.

II Cor. 13:8; Ps. 1:3–5; Jude 12; Matt. 13:6

"VANISHED THE RIPE FRUIT OF THY SOUL'S DESIRE!

We saw yesterday that the Christian is the natural, common-sense way to live. The opposite is true: all evil has the doom of decay upon it. There is this penetrating passage: "Vanished the ripe fruit of thy soul's desire!" (Revelation 18:14, Moffatt.) The fruit of the soul's desire is ripe, and, lo, it vanishes. Just when evil promises most, it lets us down. It "keeps the word of promise to our ear and breaks it to our hope." Lust ends in disgust—"vanished the ripe fruit of thy soul's desire." Money, after you have toiled and labored for it, ends in becoming a worry and anxiety— "vanished the ripe fruit of thy soul's desire." Recently on the train one soldier boy was telling another: "Do you know how you ended up your celebration? By spraying a lady in the opposite bunk with your vomit!" "Gosh," the other muttered in dismay, "and I promised my girl I'd quit it." That is celebration without cerebration—"vanished the ripe fruit of thy soul's desire." Just when you think you have it, it is gone! Nothing but Dead Sea fruit in your hands!

There is another passage in Revelation 17:11 (Moffatt): "As for the Beast which was and is not." That is the biography of every "Beast" with a capital "B," and every "beast" with a small "b": "The Beast which was and is not" —not "will be." Evil has no future—it was and is not. Only good was and is and will be—it has a past, a present, and a future. Evil, by its very nature, is self-destructive. It is an attempt to live against the nature of reality, and it ends only in self-destruction. The New Testament therefore says that sinners "perish"—they do here and now—the life forces break down, disintegrate. Every evil person renders himself unfit to survive. He will not obey the law of survival; so he perishes. Romans 7:5 (Moffatt) says: "The sinful cravings . . . . made us fruitful to Death." "Fruitful to Death"—just when the fruit is ripe, it rots. And the "Death" is with a capital "D"—it is a universal law.

Thou loving Ruler, Thou wilt not let us rest in self-destruction. Thou are always letting us see that Thy way is our way, but we don't see. Hence we suffer. But leave us not alone, tender Lover of our souls. Thou art saving us by hard refusals. Do not soften those refusals, for they are Thy preventive grace, holding us back from self-ruin. I thank Thee. I thank Thee. Amen.

Gen. 18·23–32

EVIL IS A PARASITE UPON THE GOOD

We must spend one more day on the self-destructiveness of evil, for many have the idea that goodness is bondage and that evil is freedom. But we know that evil is freedom only to get into trouble with ourselves.

I was urging a politician to give up an illicit affair he was having with a woman, for through it he was breaking up his own home, the home of another, and snarling up his own life. To ward off my appeal, he told of an English general who had been challenged by the Oxford Group with their four absolutes—absolute honesty, absolute purity, absolute unselfishness, and absolute love—but who was not prepared to build his life on them. So, in order to ward off this challenge, the general, half humorously and half seriously, said he was going to organize another Group movement—the Cambridge Group Movement—and its principles would be the opposite: absolute dishonesty, absolute impurity, absolute selfishness, and absolute hate. The politician expected me to laugh, but instead I replied: "Why not? Why don't you go in for evil and make it absolute? Why are you so tentative and hesitant? Why don't you sin with the stops out?" "Oh, no," replied the politician, "we couldn't make the evil absolute; for if we did, it wouldn't work." "Ah," I replied, "You have given away the case. All evil has to have enough good thrown around it to float it. It is a parasite upon some good. Pure evil would be self-destructive." You cannot build a society on absolute dishonesty, for no one would trust another; absolute impurity—the society would rot; absolute selfishness, for no one would think of another; absolute hate, for hate is centrifugal. So every dishonest man is a parasite upon the honesty of some honest man whose honesty holds society together long enough for the dishonest man to practice his dishonesty; every impure man is a parasite upon the purity of some pure man whose purity keeps the society from rotting and makes it sufficiently livable so that the impure man can practice his impurity in it. Evil could not exist were there no good thrown around it to keep it going.

O God, help me to rid myself of the parasites of evil in my life. The good within me holds together my world long enough for the evil to exist. Let me fulfill the statement of Paul: "I prove myself at all points a true minister of God." "At all points"—let there be no decaying points in my life; make all points sound and under Thy control. In Jesus' name. Amen.

I Thess. 5:23; II Cor. 5:14, 17; Col. 3:12–14

THE WHOLE NATURE DISCIPLINED BY LOVE

We turn again to the "aim of the Christian discipline, which is love that springs from a pure heart, from a good conscience, and from a sincere faith." Note that it is a love that springs from the total personality—"a pure heart," the emotional nature, "from a good conscience," the volitional nature; "from a sincere faith," the intellectual nature.

The personality expresses itself in three phases: intellect, feeling, and will. So the Christian discipline produces a love that springs, not from a portion of the being, but from the total being. This is the echo of the words of Jesus, who said the highest commandment was to "love the Lord thy God with all thy heart"—the affectional nature; "with all thy soul"—the volitional nature; "with all thy mind"—the intellectual nature; and "with all thy strength"—the physical nature. Man is to do the highest thing in the world—love —and he is to do it with every portion of his nature.

To love with every portion of one's nature is important; otherwise, one develops lopsided. The "strength" refers to the physical, but it could also refer to the rest of the personality. We are to love God with the strength of the mind, the strength of the emotion, the strength of the will. If you love Him with the strength of the mind and the weakness of the emotion, that lopsided love produces the intellectualist in religion, lacking emotional drive and appeal. To love Him with the strength of the emotion and the weakness of the mind makes the sentimentalist in religion. To love Him with the strength of the will and the weakness of the emotion makes the hard man of action, but lacking in lovableness. The only really strong Christian is the one who lets love get hold of his total nature—he loves with the strength of the mind, the strength of the emotion, the strength of the will, the strength of the body, so that the whole being is caught up by a burning passion of love. Like the rays that are gathered into our focus by a burning glass, so he kindles love and devotion in others. He is contagious. The disciplined make disciples.

My consecration shall be the burning glass that gathers everything into one focus of love. Then and then alone can I kindle others. I would kindle others. For I know that the discipline of myself is to get me beyond myself, so that I can be freed to lift and inspire others. Then let me find release from all contradictions, all cross-purposes, and let me burn—burn for Thee. In Jesus' name. Amen.

Phil. 2:3, 5; 4:7; 1 Cor. 2:16

THE MIND IS THE KEY

We said that the whole person is to be disciplined—intellect, feeling, will, body. Which is the key? Paul says, "Have your mind renewed, and so be transformed in nature, able to make out what the will of God is." (Romans 12:2, Moffatt.) The key apparently is the mind. For the verse says, "Have your mind renewed, and so be transformed in nature." Many would say that the nature transforms the mind; and there is a good deal of truth in that, for we often think with our emotions, the mind hunting for reasons to justify attitudes. Nevertheless, the mind is the master transformer. "As [a man] thinketh . . . . so is he."

The American Medical Association reports that football players raised their endurance 200 per cent in three weeks by taking sugary tablets which they believed contained gelatin, but which didn't, and which had nothing the doctors thought could raise endurance. Other football players were given sugary tablets which did contain the gelatin chemical, aminoacetic acid, which is reported to increase endurance. They too improved 200 per cent, but they did not outdo the sugar-tablet boys. "As [a man] thinketh . . . . so is he."

If you think you are beaten, you are. The mind renews the nature, and also resigns the nature to defeat. But, with the Christian, all this is not a lifting of oneself by the bootstraps. For the next portion of the verse says, "able to make out what the will of God is." Here the mind is linked with the will of God—it is not a mind seeking to play mental tricks on itself, for that soon breaks down. You can "kid" yourself so far and no farther. Only when you are linked to reality can you go all the way. The Christian mind links itself with the will of God and hence taps resources—real resources for real living. The mind thus stands between the will of God and nature and is the key to the linking of nature and the will of God. The mind throws the switch one way or the other—links you to infinite resources, or entangles you in your own futile self. "As [a man] thinketh . . . . so is he."

O God, take all defeatism, all fear, all turning in on myself, from my mind. And give me a mind that takes life by the hand and leads it to affirmation, to achievement, to victory, to the infinite resources of God. Give me a mind that minds its chief business—to find out the will of God, for the will of God is the homeland of the mind. Bring me home. Amen.

Josh. 1:5–9; Acts 4:13, 29; 5:41–42

DISCIPLINED BEYOND TIMIDITY

Before we end this week's study of the Christian discipline, we must look at another passage on discipline written to the same person, Timothy: "Hence I would remind you to rekindle the divine gift . . . . for God has not given us a timid spirit but a spirit of power and love and discipline." (II Timothy 1:6–7, Moffatt.) The first passage (I Timothy 1:5) begins with discipline, and this one ends with discipline. The Christian way begins and ends in discipline—the discipline produces a disciplined lie. The discipline may be so hidden in habit and outlook as to be almost unnoticeable, just as one can look straight through revolving blades on a plane which are spinning so fast and so rhythmically as to be unseen. The end of the Christian discipline is to hide it away into habit, into the subconscious, so that the disciplined person appears to be and is spontaneous. A musician's creative spontaneity is co-ordinated discipline which has become second nature.

Paul puts his finger on the thing that dims the spiritual life more than any other: timidity. If I had one gift to give myself and others, I would unhesitatingly give courage. For more people grow dim and need rekindling of the divine gift through lack of courage than through any other thing. First of all, the courage to take from God what He offers. That is the supreme courage: to pay the price and take the gift. That takes courage, for it shifts the whole basis of life from self-sufficiency to God-sufficiency. Then the next step: the courage to face up to the world with this appropriated gift of God and to believe that this and this alone will meet every need—and to say so, even when men are pathetically trying unworkable ways.

When I was traveling in China in 1937, amid sections that were being bombed, this verse came to me again and again: "Whatever happens, be self-possessed, flinch from no suffering, do your work as an evangelist, and discharge all your duties as a minister." (II Timothy 4:5, Moffatt.) Here in America, facing reconstruction, I have to repeat it again and again.

O God, my Father, give me the even courage of Jesus, who went quietly on, unruffled and unafraid, even though the end of the road meant disaster. I do not have to succeed. I have only to be true to the highest I know. Success and failure are in Thy hands. I must be true at any price, whether I succeed or fail. Give me the courage to fail, if necessary, doing the highest I know. Amen.

Acts 1:1–8; Gal. 1:15–24; John 15:15–19

"YOUR COMMISSION!"

We are nearing the end of the journey in our cycle of the year in quest of abundant living. I would pause with my Comrades of the Way to meditate on a verse which has spoken to me like a beating refrain down through many years: "In the presence of God who is the Life of all, and of Christ Jesus who testified to the good confession before Pontius Pilate, I charge you to keep your commission free from stain." (I Timothy 6:13–14, Moffatt.)

Your commission! You have a commission given to no one else—it is unique and different, for you are unique and different. God is opening a fresh book of revelation through your character and life. If you do not respond, if you hold back and frustrate His purposes, that book of revelation will never be revealed, and the world will be poorer—and so will you. The Laodicean church had a letter written to it from Paul (Colossians 4:16), but it was lost and never given to the Church as many of his other epistles were. Why was it lost? Perhaps because the Laodicean church was "neither cold nor hot" (Revelation 3:15). This lukewarm church did not have the insight or the loyalty to see the meaning of that letter; so it let it be lost. What might this church not have given to the world had it been spiritually keen and alert! Its name perished with that letter except as a symbol of "the-might-have-been." It lost its commission! I have just come from seeing a man who is going blind; and as the shadows close in on him and the outer life fades out, he hasn't a thing on the inside but—emptiness. When I suggestd he would have to live "within," he sighed and said there was nothing there. He had lost his commission—and himself. He has missed the purpose and the person. Had he taken the purpose, now his inner person would be rich and full and adequate and essentially undisturbed as the outer fades out. Here is the central treasure—your commission—keep that and, if all else goes, you have the one thing that matters.

Gracious Father, I have a commission from Thee. I feel that commission in my very bones. I have something at the center of life that makes life purposeful and meaningful. Help me to organize life around that one central fact, and not to organize this purpose around some triviality. For if I do, then I shall have a ceaseless whirl around a central emptiness. Quicken the sense of being commissioned! In Jesus' name. Amen.

Phil. 1:20–21; II Cor. 5:9–10; Rom. 8:11

"YOUR COMMISSION FREE FROM STAIN"

We paused to look at the commission; today we must look at the last part of the phrase: "keep your commission *free from stain.*" From stain of what? We shall begin at the periphery and work toward the center.

1. *Keep your commission free from the stain of unnecessary physical ailments.* I say "unnecessary," for many of them can be avoided by proper living and right mental and spiritual attitudes. In a mortal world the body breaks down sooner or later; so you cannot be an absolutist in regard to the body. You can be in regard to the soul, for the soul is not necessarily subject to decay—the body is. But while you may be sick, you have no right to be more sick than you need to be. Some people pass on the sickness of mind and soul to their bodies. One of the outstanding doctors of a great city said to me: "In my clinic we have decided that 75 per cent of the people who come to us would be well if they changed their attitudes. They are throwing functional disturbances into their systems by wrong moral and spiritual attitudes." A letter from a highly cultured and intelligent lady came this morning. When her husband began to pay attention to another woman, she broke out with eczema. Only when she surrendered the fear and worry to God did the eczema pass away.

Dr. W. C. Alvarez, the stomach specialist at the Mayo Clinic, says that 80 per cent of the stomach difficulties that come to them are not organic, but functional. Wrong mental and spiritual attitudes threw functional disturbance into digestion. A lady came to me and said: "You're right; I lived with my son-in-law for five years, and he developed a stomach ulcer and I developed arthritis. The tensions were responsible." A girl was taken to the hospital to be operated on for intestinal difficulty. They found she was worrying over the news of her brother who was about to lose his mind. When she brought this fear up and out, she left the hospital, well. The disturbance was the result of fear and worry.

O God, I know this body of mine is made for faith and confidence and not for worry and anxiety and fear. Then help me to help my body to be at its best for Thee. May I feed it with confidence and faith as well as with physical food. May I illustrate the words of Paul: "that the life of Jesus may come out in my body." May that be literally true. May that life bathe every brain cell and every tissue and every nerve with calm and faith. Amen.

Phil. 4:4–7; Matt. 6:24–34; 1 Pet. 5:7

YOUR COMMISSION FREE FROM STAIN OF WORRY AND FEAR

Yesterday we insisted that in order to have the best body God is capable of helping us to have, we must feed it with the best mental and spiritual food. Faith is food, and worry and fear are poison.

2. *Keep your commission free from the stain of worry and fear.* Worry is not merely weakness; it is wickedness. It is atheism. It says that God has abdicated and that we have to hold the world together by our worrying. The opposite happens. Worriers wreck their world. They have frailer bodies. The worriers are narrow-chested, say the doctors. Those who have annuities live on an average five or six years longer than those who do not. They are not killed off by worry. Just yesterday a man talked to me about his stomach ulcer. "You've been worrying, haven't you?" I said to him. He replied, "How did you know? All my life I've worried." A judge had to diet carefully while at work trying cases; but let him get out on the lake in a sailboat for several days and he could digest anything—even pork and beans! The worry upset his digestion. Worry, therefore, is sin—sin against God and ourselves. A mother told me that she became so anxious about her son's going to the front that the news of the possibility sent her to bed for three days—"sick with worry."

Fears are usually home-grown. Babies will handle snakes without fear if there are no signs of fear on the faces of those around. To impose fears on children is crime. Don't impose them on yourself or others. Live by cheer, rather than by fear. Very few worries live long unless you give them careful nursing. Dr. George Matthew Adams tells about a man who set aside an hour called "The Worry Hour." Right after dinner he went to his library and settled down to worry in earnest. But he couldn't do it on schedule! The idea was absurd. One man had "A Worry Tree" in his front yard, where he hung his worries before he came into the house. For the Christian that "Worry Tree" is the cross. Hang your worries there.

O Christ, I do hang all my worries on Thy cross. Compared to that cross, what have I ever borne? And even if I should bear such a cross, I know that out of it shall come to me what came to Thee—a resurrection! Nothing can make me afraid. I have a key in my hand—the Key of Life —Thy cross. With that I can unlock anything. I thank Thee. Amen.

Titus 3:3–8; Lev. 19:16–18; 1 John 2:9–11; 3:15; 4:20

FREE FROM HATE AND RESENTMENTS

3. *Keep your commission free from the stain of hate and resentments.* Through this war, hates are poisoning the air —and us, if we allow them. A cow ran amuck with anger and fear. They finally got her tamed down and milked her. A child fed on that milk died. Anger had turned the milk into poison. We are now feeding our people mental and spiritual and physical poison in the hate attitudes we are engendering. When a newborn baby failed to gain in weight, Doctor Luther Emmett Holt, a famous baby specialist, invariably left this prescription: "This baby is to be loved every three hours." The doctor found that babies are made for love and not for hate or indifference, and when they do not have love they do not thrive. A Swedish girl was jilted on the street—the ring returned to her there. She went to bed for six years, an invalid. The resentment made her an invalid. At the end of the six years, through a friend, she was induced to surrender the whole matter to God. She arose from her invalidism and is today radiant and useful.

A refined and cultured woman gave me her left hand, saying, "I haven't been at war with others, but with myself; hence this arthritis."

Then how can we get rid of hate and resentments? Frances Ridley Havergal, who wrote so many beautiful hymns, was so bad-tempered that she used to lie on the floor and beat her head in her tantrums. How did she gain calm and poise and good will? By doing what we all have to do, namely: bring the hate and resentments up and out; talk to the person concerned and ask forgiveness; and then simply and humbly offer these hates and resentments to Christ, asking Him to bury them miles deep at the cross. And He will! You give the consent to have them taken out and He will give the power. They will dissolve in His love.

The Christian faith shows itself completely sound when it insists on no harbored resentments. Psychology is saying the same.

"Anything God, but hate—I have known it in my day, and the best it does is to scar your soul and eat your heart away. We must know more than hate as the years go reeling on, for the stars survive and the spring survives—only man denies the dawn. God—if one prayer be mine—before the cloud-wrapped end—I am sick of hate and the waste it makes. Let me be my brother's friend." Amen.

Eph. 4:29–32; I Pet. 3:8–11; Luke 23:33–34; Philem. 10–19

FREE FROM HARSH ATTITUDES

4. *Keep your commission free from the stain of harsh attitudes.* We must not only be free from hate, but also from harshness. We try to make people good by harsh attitudes. It doesn't succeed. "Can Satan cast out Satan?" Can you, by acting like the devil, cast the devil out of people? Two hates never made a love affair, and two harshnesses never made amicable relations. "You cannot have your brother and eat him."

Paul says, "Treat one another with the same spirit as you experience in Christ Jesus." (Philippians 2:5, Moffatt.) How does He treat us? "By all the consideration of Christ." Could there be anything more lovely than just that phrase, "the consideration of Christ"? There was a spirit about Him. He and others did and said the same things, and yet there was a difference. There was an aroma of graciousness about what He did and said that made the deed and the word something different. The deed and the word had a soul. And what a soul!

Paul ends one of his epistles this way: "This is how I write. 'The grace of our Lord Jesus Christ be with you all.'" When we write do we say, "The grace of our Lord Jesus Christ be with you"? Or does our writing often leave a sting? Maude Royden says, "When in doubt about guidance, do the most loving thing."

Even a dog can tell the spirit in which you do a thing. Throw him a bone, and he'll walk off with it without a wag of his tail. But call him to you, pat him on the head, and then give him a bone, and his tail will wag its gratitude and appreciation. The relief workers were being thanked in Moscow by the Russian Government. The Quakers came last, and the toastmaster said: "Others may have fed more than these, but the Quakers wrapped every bottle of milk in a wrapper of good will." The wrappers made the gifts of the Quakers different; and people never forgot, for the flavor lingered on after the food had gone. Then go out and do something today that nobody but a Christian would do, and be sure to do it in a Christian way.

O Christ, Thy consideration breaks me down. It gets me to my depths. Then help me to give consideration to everybody. Don't permit me to let the other man's conduct and attitude determine mine. Let me be unfailingly gentle and kind, no matter what I realize in return. For I know what I shall get in return. My "peace will return to me." If they won't take it, I shall have it. I thank Thee. Amen.

Heb. 13:5–6; I Tim. 6:6–8; Jas. 2:1–4

FREE FROM STAIN OF PREJUDICE

Yesterday we were considering harsh attitudes. The most beautiful benediction, and the one most widely used in Christendom, was used by Paul to bless people who were finding fault with him, saying his "bodily presence" was "weak" and his "speech contemptible." What a temptation to pay them back in kind! Instead he says: "The grace of the Lord Jesus Christ, and the love of God, and the communion of the Holy Spirit, be with you all." (II Corinthians 13:14.) No wonder that benediction lived on in the hearts of millions, for Paul was being Christian in response to unchristian attitudes. The spirit in which you do a thing determines the very nature of that thing. Watch that spirit—do the gracious thing graciously.

5. *Keep your commission free from the stain of prejudices.* How we impoverish ourselves by our prejudices! As a child I was prejudiced against beets—I didn't like their color. If I hadn't pushed past the barriers of my prejudice, I would have inflicted on myself a life-long impoverishment. Color prejudice also cuts us off from mental and spiritual enrichment through people of another color.

God is the great artist; so He has made many colors. We are not artistic; so we insist on one color—white. We make a religion out of being white. It is a false religion—and cruel. Someone had a tulip bed in which there were all colors but one. So he invented a black tulip which set off all the other colors. Prejudice against black would have impoverished that bed of tulips. Race prejudice impoverishes us.

6. *Keep your commission free from the stain of self-pity and complaint.* We speak of sickness as "complaints"— sicknesses often come out of complaints. Feel sorry for yourself, and you will soon have a self that is worth feeling sorry for.

Paul says: "I have learned, in whatever state I am, therein to be content." The word is "therein," and not "therewith," as often quoted. He was often not content with the state, but in spite of the state. He had contentment in spite of—anywhere, under any conditions. For it was dependent on inner states of mind.

Gracious God, help me to live in a state that triumphs over all surroundings and all conditions. Then no self-pity will ever invade and corrupt my inmost soul. For how can I pity myself when Thou art within me? With that fact secure, I can survive anything. I thank Thee. Amen.

John 7:37–39; 4:13–14; Eph. 3:14–19; 5:18

FREE FROM STAIN OF EMPTINESS

7. *Keep your commission free from the stain of emptiness.* This is the most frequent stain on the Christian soul —just emptiness. We are not bad—we are just not good enough. We lack the vital contagion and the enough and to spare. In Texas, where rain is desperately needed at times, someone asked a ranger about some clouds in the sky. He looked at them, shook his head, and replied, "They're just empties drifting by." Just empties drifting by! How many of us are the moral and spiritual equivalent of just that! When people need the refreshing rain of abundant living so desperately, we are just empties drifting by. A minister said with a sigh: "When you use the word 'adequacy' it makes me shudder, for it is a word that I don't know—I'm not adequate."

In the passage quoted, Paul says that you are to keep your commission free from stain in the light of two facts: First, "In the presence of God who is the Life of all"—in the presence of God's abundant fullness, keep your commission free from the stain of what? Apparently, emptiness. With all these resources of God, why be empty when you can attach yourself to these resources? Life isn't attainment —it is obtainment. Out of that obtainment you find attainment. But try attainment without obtainment, and all you produce is fussy doing. A friend gave a lovely home to his sisters, and all was in readiness for occupancy—the ranges were in, ready for cooking, but it was discovered that the main in the street had not been tapped. The whole apparatus was useless without attaching it to the power. Life comes through attachment to power. A colored minister arose in our Ashram and quoted these lines:

> "Read yourself full;
>   Think yourself straight;
>   Pray yourself hot;
>   Let yourself go!"

Good, but the "letting yourself go" is first as well as last. You surrender to Power; then Power surrenders itself to you.

O God, save me from the central wrong of being empty in a world of human need. For many look to me for help —may they not look in vain. Like the man at midnight, I stand asking for bread for the man who in his journey is come unto me. Give me bread. I cannot return empty, to the empty. Amen.

II Cor. 11:23–31; Acts 20:16–27; 22:17–22

WITNESSING BEFORE OUR PONTIUS PILATE

You and I have come to the last week of our pilgrimage together. We must study together the last portion of the passage on keeping our commission free from stain. In the presence of two things we are to keep that commission: (1) "In the presence of God who is the Life of all"—in the presence of the abundant resources of God—keep your commission free from the stain of emptiness, of inadequacy. If you don't, then you hurt yourself and others. (2) In the presence of Jesus Christ "who before Pontius Pilate witnessed a good confession"—in the presence of this full, abundant Life, pouring itself out in face of opposition.

We have considered the first; we must now pass on to the second. It is not enough to possess abundant life; that abundant life must be witnessed to and lived out in the presence of some Pontius Pilate—something that stands athwart this new life, and to meet it unflinchingly means that this new life will crimson into a cross. This business of being Christian in a world of this kind is no easy undertaking. We have to meet the equivalent of Pilate. And that would mean?

To discover its meaning we must ask, not *who* crucified Christ, but *what?* For the who embodied a what. Seven embodied sins combined to crucify Jesus. (1) Self-interested moral cowardice—Pilate. (2) Vested class interests—the priests. (3) Envy—the priests. (4) Faithless friendships—Judas. (5) Ignorance—the multitude. (6) Indifference—the multitude. (7) Race-prejudiced militarism—the Roman soldiers.

The probabilities are that you will have to live out your abundant life in the face of evil embodied in one or more of these forms. When you do, then this abundant life meets its cross. That cross cannot be escaped. If it is escaped, then its sequel is also escaped—the resurrection. If you become a recessive personality, refusing to face up to opposition, taking the line of least resistance, then you will never be a resurrected personality. No cross, no creation.

God and Father, I see that I must stand up to life if I am to have life. Help me to have the power "to take it." Save me from all retreatism and lack of spiritual initiative. Help me to be calm and poised in the face of opposition, and help me to win by being winsome. May none of this sour me, or give me "acidosis of the soul." In Jesus' name. Amen.

Gal. 3:26–28; Matt. 9:9–13

WITNESSING BEFORE CLASS INTERESTS

We saw yesterday that we would have to live out this new life in the face of opposition. You will have to face your Pilate. You will want to get things done, say for the sake of a community, and self-interested moral cowardice, holding power, will block you. Men in public life, for private interest, will look around to see how what you are planning to do affects them, and will decide on the basis of self-interest. Your plans are crucified on the cross of self-interest. What are you to do? Meet your opponents with their own weapons—fight fire with fire? He who fights fire with fire is sure to get burnt. In a battle of beasts the biggest beast wins. Keep your Christian attitudes—they are your one real asset. There is always one thing open—you can suffer for, and if necessary die for, your Pilate, as Jesus did for His. Jesus conquered Pilate by not being like him. He broke Pilate by letting Pilate break His body while He kept an unbroken spirit. That unbroken spirit broke Pilate and his empire. It will break anything that opposes it. Jesus wasn't on trial that day—Pilate was. And when Pilate said, "What I have written, I have written," what he wrote was his own doom, and unwittingly he proclaimed the kingship of Jesus. "I am a part of that force which constantly seeks to do evil, yet none the less creates the good," says Goethe in *Faust*.

Again, you will have to witness your confession before vested class interests. You will have to meet your chief priests. Wrong attitudes can be embodied in a class as well as in a person. Men often think according to class interests instead of as persons. There is "a class war," and the laborers did not create it—they simply proclaimed what they found. Sad to say, many laborers then proceeded to embody the class interest they deplored in others. Two class interests never made a brotherhood. What is left to you? You can suffer for, and die for, if necessary, the embodied class interests in order to have a classless society, the Kingdom of God.

O Christ, give me power to face soured, selfish religion and to die for it, if necessary. For this kind goeth not out except by prayer and fasting—and a cross. Keep my soul from all interests of class, from class thinking and class attitudes, and help me to witness against them by word and deed and attitude. Let me be a brother of men, and not a brother of a class. Amen.

John 13:21–30; Matt. 10:34–36; Ps. 41:9

WITNESSING BEFORE FAITHLESS FRIENDSHIPS

We saw yesterday that as Jesus went on His way the system of exploitation of the people by the religious leaders was endangered—their class interests were involved. But they were also envious and jealous of the growing power of Jesus. People were falling away from them and crowding around Jesus. So green-eyed envy pushed up its head and slandered Him by twisting His meanings. Jesus was crucified on misquotations.

Very often we, too, will be crucified on misquotations. A religious leader told a derogatory story about another religious leader, and when the truth of it was questioned, and the falsehood pointed out, the leader laughed it off by saying: "Well, anyway, it makes a very good story." It did, even if it did leave the reputation of another lying wounded and bleeding. Envy twisted that story. Oh, no, it only twisted itself into a snake.

You will be crucified on misquotations and twisted meanings and misrepresented motives. What are you to do? Meet blister with blister? Two blisters never made a brotherhood. Two hot words never made a warm friendship. No; you are a Christian. "You must not rule your lives by theirs." (Leviticus 18:3, Moffatt.) You can do what Jesus did. He died for the men who lied about Him. Their lies perished. He lived on. The same thing will apply with you. A lie is a waning moon; the truth is a waxing moon. A lie goes into night; the truth goes into light.

Again, you must witness before faithless friendships—your Judas. Often those who dip their hand in the same dish will betray you. When money, or position, or self-interest beckons, they fall away. It is not easy to keep from being embittered toward those who were once comrades in a cause and are now indifferent, or on the other side. What shall we do? We can still do what Christ did in the story of Dostoevski: Christ came to preach in a town in Spain. The Grand Inquisitor arrested Him, and said: "Why did you come back? You left everything to the Church—go back." Christ made no answer, but came and kissed his 90-year-old, faded lips and went away.

O Christ, help me to do just that, or the equivalent of that, to those who betray me. And help me not to betray anyone else lest Thy burning kiss be on my lips. That would be punishment indeed. I could stand anything but that. Thou terrible judging lover of my soul, Thy kiss of love reminds me of my kiss of betrayal. Help me to be true. Amen.

Rom. 10:1–4; 1 Tim. 1:12–15; Acts 3:12–21; 17:22–34

WITNESSING BEFORE DULL IGNORANCE

Perhaps we will have to witness our confession before another thing that crucified Jesus—ignorance in the multitude. For three years He had spoken as no man had spoken —had poured Himself out night and day to get the people to *see*. Even His inner circle didn't understand Him, and He sighed and said, "How long shall I be with you, and bear with you?" In the end, the ignorance of the multitude crucified Him. They chose Barabbas—literally, bar-Abba, "Son of the Father"—and crucified Jesus, also bar-Abba, "Son of the Father." They chose a local, patriotic rebel, and crucified a world redeemer.

When we meet with ignorant opposition, what are we to do? At this time when there is a pressure toward a blackout of mind by otherwise intelligent people, what can we do? Well, we'll have to do what Jesus did. He prayed, "Father, forgive them; for *they know not what they do*." And He died for them. We can do the same. And someday the resurrection will come. I remember pleading for a move in a conference in India that would reconstruct the world Church of Methodism. My proposal went "on the table" with a bang. Then, twenty years later, it was taken off the table and adopted almost to the letter, for the world structure of the Church. You can wait. The years and the centuries will speak against the hours. "Whatsoever is born of God overcometh the world"—whatever is born of ignorance perishes. Be patient. Someday the stones that are thrown at you will be gathered up and made into a monument to your insight and foresight. Grasp the truth in these words: "We triumph even in our troubles, knowing that trouble produces endurance, endurance produces character, and character produces hope." (Romans 5:3–4, Moffatt.) Note the steps: trouble, endurance, character, hope. The hope is based on the solid reality of tested character; and verse 5 adds: "a hope which never disappoints us." With a hope based on that solid reality, we can wait, for that hope never, never disappoints us.

Here hope is not dope!

O God, we know that this hope cannot disappoint us, for if we obtain nothing else out of the situation, we have the character left; and character communing with Thee is Heaven here and now, no matter what is on the outside. I thank Thee that we are unbeatable. We can put up with ignorant opposition. Let it come. Amen.

Matt. 5:43–48; Rom. 12:10, 14–15; 13:8; 1 John 4:7–21

CHRISTIANS ARE PEOPLE WHO CARE

Perhaps the cruelest verse in literature is: "And . . . . they watched him there." The multitude sat in stolid indifference and watched Him go through His agonies. It is easier to meet opposition than it is to meet indifference. You will have to witness your confession before your Gallio of indifference. "And Gallio cared for none of those things." What are you to do when people do not care?

There is only one thing to do—keep on caring. Christians are people who care for people who do not care. Love does not change, no matter the changes in the other person. To allow other people and circumstances to determine your conduct and attitudes is to become a mere reflection, the sum total of the attitudes of others.

Perhaps we shall have to do what one modern saint suggested: "Be so humble that you cannot be humiliated." I am told that in the Andes Mountains when the pack goats meet each other on a narrow ledge where it is impossible to pass, one will kneel and let the other walk over him—to the safety of both. Perhaps you will have to kneel and let people walk over you. Notice I said, "kneel," not knuckle. There is a difference—in kneeling you are bending low at the feet of Christ instead of knuckling at the behest of man. Kneeling is voluntary and for His sake. A bridge is something people walk on, but it leads from something to something. If you are to be a bridge between a man's indifference and his awakening, a bridge that bridges between groups and races, you will be walked on. Never mind; people may be getting somewhere when they walk on you. Judge Wilbur's son, a highly trained, gifted young doctor, went to China as a medical missionary. While attending typhus cases, he was stricken and ravaged by the disease. When he heard there was a coolie woman who would die if a Caesarian operation could not be performed, he bade them carry him in to the operating room. They held him up, one on each side, as he operated and saved the life of the woman and her baby. But the shock was too much for him—in two days he was dead. He cared. Perhaps the coolie woman never knew and maybe did not care. He did—that is enough.

O Christ, Thou didst care even when the multitude sat in open-mouthed indifference and watched Thee there. Help me to care like that. When everything I love is trampled on by indifferent feet, help me to go quietly on to await Thy processes of resuscitation. I can wait for Thee. Amen.

Col. 3:9–11; Acts 10:34, 44–48; 11:12

WITNESSING BEFORE RACE-PREJUDICED MIGHT

We come now to the last of the seven things that crucified Jesus and may crucify us—race-prejudiced militarism, the Romans. The Romans despised the Jews. "Am I a Jew?" sneered Pilate. When the Roman soldiers got hold of Jesus—"the King of the Jews"—they made fun of the Jews in the person of their King. They were mocking a nation— in Him. So Jesus took the scorn, intended for the Jews, and bore it for the very Jews who were crying out to crucify Him.

What are we to do in the presence of race prejudice, linked with power? We can become embittered and sullen, or we can do what Jesus did—He suffered and died for the very men who mocked Him. That possibility is always open!

Yesterday, I talked to a highly intelligent Negro cook—a graduate in chemistry of a great state university. He said, "I had high hopes while a student, but after trying in vain for two years to get a job as a chemist, or a druggist, I gave up and became a cook." Race prejudice snuffed out those high hopes and doomed him to be a cook. A few days ago a Negro teacher told me that her boys saluted the flag and ended by saying: "With liberty and justice to all—but me." The "but me" was under their breaths.

What can be done? We can do what Jesus did. That is always safe. He died for the very Romans who hated Him. Result? A slave race leads the world captive! Out of a slave race has come the world's greatest freedom. Rome and her military might perished, while Judea, in the person of the Christ, lives on in the hearts of the multitudes.

In Formosa there was the custom among a tribe to kill a man each year and lift his head up to their ancestors. A Chinese interpreter asked, "Why?" When told why, he added, "Then next year you kill a man in a red cap." Next year the chief shot a man in a red cap. It was the interpreter! The custom stopped. Now the interpreter is enshrined as a god. Someday we shall set up monuments in our hearts to the "redcaps," who carried our bags in their hands and bore our racial insults in their hearts.

O Christ, I thank Thee Thou didst take all these racial insults into Thy heart and didst emerge out of that sea of hate the Son of Man, beyond race and beyond insult. Help me to do the same. Help me to identify myself with the underprivileged and the despised, and to take no privilege they cannot take. And perhaps the custom will be broken by that cross. Amen.

Isa. 25:8–9; I John 5:4–5; I Cor. 15:51–58; II Cor. 2:14

IT IS TOMORROW!

We have been talking about the cross—is that the last word? No! God's last word in human affairs is not the cross, but the Resurrection—not defeat, but victory.

A great newspaper editor pointed to two desk drawers' and said: "On one side of that desk is a Bible, and on the other side is a typewriter. I try to make the two sides of this desk speak the same thing. For I know that if what I write in my editorials coincides with what is in that Book, it will live on; but if it is out of harmony with that Book, it will perish." That is our faith. Everything right has "Resurrection" written on it—everything wrong has "Death" written on it.

Someone asked the brilliant Bashford why, when he could be an influential bishop in America, he chose to bury himself in China, and he replied: "Because I believe in the Resurrection." That Resurrection became a fact. "Most people plot and plan themselves into mediocrity, while now and again somebody forgets himself into greatness." Bashford was such a one!

Dr. Carver, the Negro saint and scientist, who has done more for the agriculture of the South than any man living or dead, white or colored, wanted to be an artist until a teacher said, "George, your people need agriculture more than art." He put those brushes away in a trunk and did not look at them again for several years. He lost himself in his people's need. And now he has unconsciously painted his image in the hearts of all of us. He forgot himself into greatness.

Yesterday, while meditating on an address, I was tempted to be put out with some ministers who disturbed my quiet. But out of the corner of my ear I heard one tell of a boy who was suddenly and unexpectedly whisked into a long dark tunnel on the train. When the train emerged from the darkness, the sun was shining, and the boy exclaimed, "Mother, it's tomorrow!" Perhaps that is our final meditation: Out of every interruption, every disturbance, every frustration, every sorrow, out of every dark tunnel we are to rescue a "Tomorrow." That is Abundant Living!

O Christ, we thank Thee that the last word is not useless regrets over the defeated yesterdays, or the difficult todays, but the last word is the dawning tomorrows. With Thee, "the best is yet to be." We salute the Dawn with a cheer! For we have the Dawn within us. "The Holy Ghost makes me put back my shoulders." Amen.

Acts 15:22–31

A LADDER FOR GROUP DECISIONS

There are two ways to try to come to a group decision—one is the competitive; the other is the co-operative. In the competitive, you push your ideas across, argue them, take a vote and the majority carries the decision. This usually leaves behind a disgruntled minority that feels that its truth is lost sight of in the decision. In the co-operative, you come with the idea of trying to gather together partial truths into a higher synthesis—to come to a group conclusion. This leaves no disgruntled minority.

In order to gain that group decision we have worked out the following technique through years of experimentation in our Ashrams: (1) *The members are disciplined to the thought of a group conclusion, rather than of someone's personal triumph.* This brings the members together in a relaxed, receptive state of mind. The will to find agreement is present. (2) *A period of corporate silence in which we let down the barriers and become receptive.* (3) *The presentation of the matter in hand.* This is done not in an argumentative spirit, but in the spirit of wanting a solution. (4) *Another period of corporate silence.* This gives the group time to think and not arrive at snap judgments. (5) *The chairman goes around the circle and asks each member his views.* The meeting is not thrown open for general discussion, for that would allow the more vocal ones to set the debate and make the subsequent discussion revolve around their opinions and not around the subject in hand. This method gives the least vocal an equal chance. (6) *If there is practical unanimity, there is another period of silence to see if a vote should be taken now.* (7) *If there is not sufficient unanimity the decision is postponed until the next day, that God may speak to us in the subconscious during sleep.* (8) *If after a day's postponement we are still not of a common mind, we take a majority vote if a decision is imperative.* (9) *The chairman expresses himself only after the others have expressed themselves.*

In the co-operative method we get through twice the amount of work we could with the competitive. The co-operative method is the way we are made to live—it is written in the constitution of things.

O God, teach us how to come to a common mind. Help us to surrender the will to dominate. May all our decisions fit the pattern: "it seemed good to the Holy Ghost, and to us." May we be set to find Thy mind in every matter. In Jesus' name. Amen.

Acts 18:3; 20:34–35; II Thess. 3:6–10

RELAXATION THROUGH MANUAL LABOR

In our society we have set up the goal of arriving at the place where one doesn't have to work. Such a person is "well fixed," can live without work—others work for him. It is a false goal. The results are now being seen in the kickback. People who won't work deteriorate. They either get the jitters and suffer from neuroses, or, after having eaten themselves all out of shape, they settle down to a bovine existence. In either case there is deterioration. Nature seems to be forcing people to manual labor. Rightly so, for there is no health of mind and soul and body without it.

Sanitariums have been compelled to put in "occupational therapy" to help bring back nervously upset people to balance and health. That is the nemesis: a civilization that made the end of endeavor to consist in getting rid of the necessity of work, now has to pay doctors to put them back to work again!

Abundant living must include some form of creative activity with the hands. Our Christian Ashrams include in them a daily period of manual labor as an integral part of our spiritual cultivation. This breaks down the barrier between those who work with their hands and those who do not. Working together with the hands makes manual labor good form, high caste. Not to do it is bad form, low caste. Big businessmen, doctors, professors, bishops, working with their hands with manual laborers, find a comradeship never known before. My job was to go around with a sharp stick and a bag and pick up paper. Now wherever I go I see paper. I am paper-conscious! At times I have an almost irresistible impulse to jump out of a taxi and clean up the filthy sidewalks and gutters of our cities. Get the habit of some manual work each day. Then organize your communities into volunteer work squads, first to clean up the community and then to work on improvement projects.

To get the people of a community working together with their hands for the good of that community lays the foundation for comradeship in everything else.

O Son of a carpenter, and a Carpenter Thyself, take away our false pride of being able to command the labor of others and help us to join Thee in making our communities places of health and beauty—veritable cities of God. Today I offer Thee my hands. Amen.

1 Cor. 6:9–10; I Tim. 4:8–12; II Tim. 2:22

A LADDER FOR DECISIONS CONCERNING RECREATION

Life must have its rhythms. There must be periods for creation and for recreation. All creation and no recreation makes "Jack" and everyone else a dull boy. For life is made, in its inner constitution, for work and play. Since this is an inherent necessity, then recreation should be carefully chosen; for recreation can wreck, or it can re-create.

(1) *No recreation should be an end in itself—it should subserve the ends for which you really live.* To make recreation an end in itself is to defeat its purposes. If you save recreation as an end in itself, you will lose it as a recreation —it will become a drain. (2) *Any recreation that takes from one part of your life to add to another is false.* For instance, if it takes from your necessary hours of sleep it is not recreation, but a strain and hence a drain. More serious still, if it takes from your moral and spiritual life to add to your physical life, then it is a snare and a delusion. The recreation must recreate the whole person. (3) *Any recreation from which you have to recover is false.* Recreation should leave you with a sense of heightened vitality in the total being. (4) *Any recreation which leaves you with a sense of moral letdown will leave you physically let down—they react.* (5) *Expensive recreation is usually expensive in more ways than one.* Cultivate the simple, inexpensive pleasures. (6) *The Sabbath is psychologically sound as a means of quiet and recuperation.* To make it into a hectic day of running around is false. This saying has arisen out of the facts: "It's a great life if you don't week-end." (7) *A movie, and anything else, must be judged according to the direction it moves you.* (8) *Any recreation that merely kills time kills you.* Under many a bridge table are buried the dead hopes of what you might have been—kill time and it will kill you. (9) *Gambling is not recreation—it is an attempt to get something for nothing, and that is not recreation—it is sin.* (10) *Any recreation into which Christ cannot be taken is not for a Christian.*

Make your recreations re-creations.

O Christ, I come to Thee for guidance, for I want my recreations to be an integral part of my life for Thee and not a moral holiday. I submit all my recreations to Thee; cull out of them what is real and vital and let the rest be burned in the fire of my love for Thee. Amen.

Gen. 1:1; Phil. 3:12–14; I Cor. 9:24–27

NEW YEAR'S MEDITATION

Get your life direction as you start the year. Peter said, "Save yourselves from this untoward generation"—a generation that wasn't going toward anything, a generation adrift. That purposeless generation ended up with the sudden purpose of crucifying Jesus. "A lost man," said Joseph Conrad, "is a man lost in the insignificance of events."

It is not enough to wipe the slate clean; you must put something on it. What? Yourself at the center, around which life will be sketched? If so, then will be fulfilled these words: "Men who bow down to nothing cannot bear the burden of themselves"—"The tedious egotism of our day" —"Men unable to get themselves off their hands." These words echo those of Jeremiah—"went after empty idols and became empty themselves." (Jeremiah 2:5, Moffatt.) If the idol is an empty self, then life turns empty with it.

Put your hand in the hand of God as you start the New Year. Then the New Year will be a fresh adventure every morning and a quiet benediction every night. You will be alive in every portion of your being. You will be aware of God and man.

"God—let me be aware.
Let me not stumble blindly down the ways,
Just getting somehow safely through the days,
Not even groping for another hand,
Not even wondering why it all was planned,
Eyes to the ground unseeking for the light,
Soul never aching for a wild-winged flight.
Please, keep me eager just to do my share.
God—let me be aware.

"God—let me be aware.
Stab my soul fiercely with others' pain,
Let me walk seeing horror and stain.
Let my hands, groping, find others hands.
Give me the heart that divines, understands.
Give me the courage, wounded, to fight.
Flood me with knowledge, drench me in light.
Please, keep me eager just to do my share.
God—let me be aware."

—MIRIAM TEICHNER

John 15:13; Rom. 5:6–11; John 19:16–18

GOOD FRIDAY MEDITATION

Why did Good Friday have to happen? Did it just happen or was it inevitable—inevitable in a world of this kind? It was inevitable.

It was not an accidental, marginal type of happening; it grew out of the nature of the facts. It had to happen. For it is a law of life that where love meets sin in the loved one, at the junction of that sin and that love a cross of pain is set up. It is the nature of love to insinuate itself into the sins and sorrows of the loved one and make them its own. If it does not do that, then it is not love. All love has the doom of bleeding upon it whenever the object of its love goes wrong. You may say that the guilty alone should bleed, and not the innocent—it is unjust. But, just or unjust, it is a fact. If you would say to a mother whose son is breaking his own heart and hers by his waywardness: "Mother, it is unjust for you to suffer in this way. You are innocent; your son is guilty," would that mother not say in reply: "Suffer for my son, unjust? It is the very thing that motherhood within me demands that I should do." In the name of a legal justice would you deny that mother the privilege of being noble, of being a mother? There is a justice higher than legal justice—a justice in which it is right for the strong, at cost to itself, to save the weak; it is right for the holy to save the unholy. This is the law of higher justice.

If God is love, then, when that love meets sin in us, the loved ones, that love is bound to wear on its heart a cross of pain. It is inevitable. Good Friday is the outer cross telling us of the inner cross on the heart of God. There is a Christ painted in Germany during the famine days after the first World War, and the Christ is famine-stricken too. That is authentic. Christ is hungry with the hunger. He is guilty in the sinful. He makes it His own. That is atonement.

In South America I was given a stone which had a cross at its center—nature formed that cross there. The cross is at the heart of our relationships—it is built into things. It is "the ground plan of the universe." Everywhere that love meets sin love suffers. That is the meaning of the cross.

O Christ, I am bowed in the dust. If my sin is Thine, then how can I sin again? I will not. O Galilean, Thou hast conquered me. I cannot stand before this invading love. I bow forever at Thy feet. Amen.

1 Cor. 15

EASTER MEDITATION

". . . . where was a garden." There are four outstanding garden incidents in the Bible.

1. *The Garden of Transgression.* In the cool of the evening when God walked in the garden of Eden, Adam and Eve were afraid and hid from God. They were afraid, for disobedience had entered that garden.

2. *The Garden of the Confronting Conscience.* When Ahab, the king, took Naboth's vineyard and went to take possession he was in high spirits. His plan had succeeded—the vineyard was his. But there arose out of the vineyard the rugged form of the prophet Elijah, the conscience of the nation. "Hast thou found me, O mine enemy?" cried the abashed Ahab. Elijah was always spoiling his well-laid plans of evil. When you take the garden of evil you must take it with an outraged conscience which rises up and confronts you. That is the fly in the ointment.

3. *The Garden of the Divine Hesitation.* This is the garden of Gethsemane, where the Divine One hesitates at the price of man's redemption. But if it is the garden of Hesitation, it is also the garden of Decision. "Arise, let us be going"—to meet the issue—the cross.

4. *The Garden of the Divine Overcoming.* This is the garden of the Empty Tomb, and the Risen Lord. You and I need walk no longer in the Garden of Transgression, nor in the Garden of the Confronting Conscience, for since our Master has gone through the Garden of the Divine Hesitation to the Garden of the Divine Overcoming, we too can walk in that garden with the Risen Lord.

When the flood of liquor came back after prohibition a blatant tourist called out to an old Nergo gatekeeper standing at the gate of an lovely park, "Is this a beer garden?" The Nergo replied, "No sir, this ain't no place for sin, for God done walk in this garden." Henceforth, we can say: "This world—and my heart—is no place for sin, for God has walked in this Garden."

Keep that garden for Him and for Him alone.

O Risen Lord, walk in the garden of my life, and then it will be forever dedicated—forever it shall be no place for sin. It is the place of life, eternal life. I am deathless, for my garden is the garden of the Lord. Life lives here. I thank Thee. Amen.

John 1:14, 18; 14:8–9; Matt. 1:18–25

OUR CHRISTMAS MEDITATION

A little boy stood before the picture of his absent father, and then turned to his mother and wistfully said, "I wish father would step out of the picture."

This little boy expressed the deepest yearning of the human heart. We who have gazed upon the picture of God in nature are grateful, but not satisfied. We want our Father to step out of the impersonal picture and meet us as a Person. "The Impersonal laid no hold on my heart," says Tulsi Das, the great poet of India. It never does, for the human heart is personal and wants a Personal response.

"Why won't principles do? Why do we need a personal God?" someone asks. Well, suppose you go to a child crying for its mother and say, "Don't cry, little child; I'm giving to you the principle of motherhood." Would the tears dry and the face light up? Hardly. The child would brush aside your principle of motherhood and cry for its mother. We all want, not a principle nor a picture, but a Person.

The Father *has* stepped out of the picture. The Word *has* become flesh. That is the meaning of Christmas. Jesus is Immanuel—God with us. He is the Personal approach from the Unseen. We almost gasp as the Picture steps out of the frame. We did not dare dream God was like Christ. But He is. Just as I analyze chemically the tiny sunbeam and discover in it the chemical make-up of the vast sun, so I look at the character and life of Jesus, and I know what God's character is like. He is Christlike.

"You have an advantage," said Dr. Hu Shih, the father of the Renaissance Movement in China, "in that all the ideas in Christianity have become embodied in a Person." Yes, and the further advantage of our faith is this: The Christmas word must become flesh in me. I too must become the word made flesh. I must be a miniature Christmas.

The Christian spirit is the Christmas spirit, extended through the whole year. It is the attitude toward every person, the atmosphere of every act.

Gracious Father, as Thou hast stepped out of the picture, help me this day to step out of the picture and let someone see in me the meaning of a Christian. May I *be* the Christmas message. Amen.

FESTIVAL BOOKS—a mass-market paperback line featuring some of the finest in inspirational and theological reading. Here are just a few titles from this outstanding line:

Abundant Living by E. Stanley Jones $1.95 0-687-00689-9

Bless This Mess and Other Prayers by Jo Carr and Imogene Sorley $1.50 0-687-03618-6

The Divine Yes by E. Stanley Jones $1.50 0-687-10989-2

How Came the Bible? by Edgar J. Goodspeed $1.75 0-687-17524-0

Letters to Karen by Charlie W. Shedd $1.25 0-687-21566-8

The Master's Men by William Barclay $1.50 0-687-23732-7

Steps to Prayer Power by Jo Kimmel $1.50 0-687-39340-X

Strange Facts About the Bible by Webb Garrison $2.25 0-687-39945-9

Twelve Baskets of Crumbs by Elisabeth Elliot $1.75 0-687-42702-9

The Will of God by Leslie D. Weatherhead $1.25 0-687-45600-2

Buy them at your local bookstore or use this coupon for ordering

Customer Service Manager * Abingdon * 201 Eighth Ave. S. * Nashville, TN 37302

Please send the Festival books I have checked above. I am enclosing $_____ (plus 65¢ to cover postage and handling). Send check or money order. NO cash or C.O.D.s please.
_____ Please send me a free brochure listing the complete line of Festival Books.

Name _____

Address _____

City _____ State _____ Zip _____

*Please allow three weeks for delivery